Anna's House

The American Colony in Jerusalem

Odd Karsten Tveit

Translated by Peter Scott-Hansen

RIMAL PUBLICATIONS

Published in Norway as *Annas Hus* by J.W. Cappelens Forlag A.S, Oslo, 2000.

First published in English 2011
Rimal Publications,
Nicosia, Cyprus

ISBN 978-9963-610-40-2

English translation ©Peter Scott-Hansen 2009

All photos from the American Colony Collection, except pages 372, 388, 398 (Lynne Butt).

For information on our publications, visit our website
www.rimalbooks.com

This translation has been published with the financial support of NORLA.

Editor: Tabitha Morgan
Printed and bound in India by Replika Press Pvt. Ltd.

Table of Contents

Foreword

Just below the Hebrew University on Mt Scopus in Jerusalem lies a small graveyard. On one of the gravestones the name Anna T Spafford is etched. Below is written simply MOTHER. Not even the woman's children knew her full baptismal name – Anne Tobine Larsdatter Øglende. Her family knew only that their mother was born in Stavanger, Norway, on March 16, 1842, and that she left for the US as a four-year-old.

Anna and her family came to Jerusalem to experience what they thought would be Jesus' return. This, of course, did not happen, but the Holy City seduced them. Through several generations, Anna and her family experienced chaos, revolution, and war; they lived through the end of the Ottoman Empire during World War I, and decades of Arab and Jewish battles over Palestine.

Throughout the turbulence and complexity of Middle East history, Jerusalem has remained a magnet, not just for warriors, politicians and the faithful – be they Jews, Christians or Muslims – but also for poets, philosophers and the curious from all parts of the world. Anna Spafford and her American Colony welcomed many of those who played a part in shaping world history. They also welcomed Jerusalem's indigenous population - Arabs and Jews - along with tired pilgrims following in Jesus' footsteps. Anna and her sect were widely written about and were the subject of Nobel Prize winner Selma Lagerlöf's novel *Jerusalem*.

The American Colony was a landmark in Jerusalem throughout the successive tides of Ottoman, British and Jordanian rule. Since 1967, when Israel occupied East Jerusalem, the American Colony Hotel has served as a neutral corner and oasis of peace in the war-torn city, a haven for pilgrims, politicians and journalists.

I have been fascinated by Anna Spafford's life ever since the 1970s, when I first glimpsed behind the walls of the colony she had founded, and as the Norwegian Broadcasting Corporation's Middle East correspondent for nearly 20 years, I have lived for weeks and months at the American Colony Hotel.

During the work on this book I have followed Anna Spafford's journey from Stavanger via Chicago and Minnesota to Palestine. But there are perils in doing research on those who have lived and worked in Jerusalem, and, in *Anna's House*, I have frequently allowed myself to follow some of the historical and personal diversions that appeared during the course of my discoveries. I hope the reader will forgive me and will enjoy as much as I have those stories within the main narrative of the Spafford family and Palestine.

I have tried my best to be loyal to my source material – hundreds of books, unpublished manuscripts, private letters and personal interviews. Since much of my material has not been published, and because propaganda and rhetoric form an important part of the Israeli-Palestinian war of opinion, I have chosen to put in many detailed footnotes. These are also here to remind the reader to be wary when delving into the history of the Holy City: "Jerusalem is a golden bowl filled with scorpions."[1]

---

1 Al-Maqdisi, 10th century traveller and geographer.

Acknowledgments

First of all, I am appreciative of the late Mrs Valentine Vester, part-owner of the American Colony Hotel. She gave me free access to the family's extensive archives, and for many years had been a rewarding conversation partner. She also read through an early draft of the English manuscript and provided me with more insight into the Jerusalem Colony's history.

But this book would not have been published in English without Norwegian-American Peter Scott-Hansen. On his own initiative he translated the Norwegian edition of *Anna's House* and came up with many ideas to improve my original manuscript. I owe him my utmost thanks.

In addition to my research at the American Colony, for the original Norwegian text, I frequently visited several of Jerusalem's libraries. I was well received by the Fahmi Khaldi Library, the Nashashibi Cultural Center, the Arab Study Society, and the Swedish Christian Study Center. I have interviewed dozens of participants in the struggle for Palestine, and met first-hand witnesses to the unfolding events up to 1948.

I owe thanks also to the US Information Center in Oslo, the Vesterheim Genealogical Center and Research Library in Madison, and the staff of the Norwegian Archives at St Olaf College in Northfield, Minnesota. All have been very forthcoming during my work. In Minnesota, this most Norwegian of American states, I received additional help from local historical societies, and individuals in Red Wing and Wanamingo. In Chicago, church historian, Barry Smith, was very helpful, and I received excellent help in several of the city's libraries.

I have been able to work in the Norwegian Broadcasting Corporation's library, in various departments of the National Library in Oslo, the Norwegian Emigrant Museum in Hamar, the Norwegian Emigrant Center in Stavanger, and the Archives of the City of Stavanger. The Scholarship Committee of the Norwegian Association of Professional Literary Authors and Translators deserves thanks for providing me with the means for the project. My appreciation goes also to friends in Jerusalem such as Albert Aghazarian. He read through and corrected an early draft with an historian's proficiency. I am also grateful to George Hintlian, who from beginning to end assisted me in my research. Further, I would like to thank other authors who have written about Anna Spafford and Jerusalem.

It has been good to stand on their shoulders to get a better insight into her life and those of her successors, and the dramatic developments from 1881 to 1948.

Chapter 1

Jerusalem and Stavanger

Not only had the power failed in Jerusalem in May 1948, but also the water supply had been cut. The first Arab-Israeli war had arrived in the Holy City and the house lay on the Arab side, near to the frontline. The closest Arab position was in a building just across the road, while Jewish snipers lay behind their sandbags, just a few hundred yards further to the west.

With the power gone and no refrigeration, what was left of the penicillin and anti-typhus serum was put in a waterproof metal box and submerged in the cistern in the wide courtyard. Planted with orange trees, palms and flowers, the courtyard was enclosed by a stone building, which concealed it from the sharpshooters. Near the entrance, a large room on the ground floor had been converted to a receiving station for the injured. But there was no permanent doctor in the house, just a few nurses and Palestinian helpers.[2]

This large building, along with three smaller ones (also built of light-coloured Jerusalem stone) belonged to a Christian sect. Its leader, Norwegian-born Anna Spafford, had long since died. But her eldest daughter, Bertha, still lived there, and managed to raise the Red Cross flag on the main building, clearly visible from the frontlines of both sides.

By 1948, only a few of the Christian sect's original members still lived in the property, which was known as the American Colony. Those who remained worked hard to help the needy in the city and Bertha Spafford Vester, now in her 70s, was at the centre of the Colony's work. She headed the infant hospital in the Old City, ran the American Colony Hostel, and had responsibility for the Red Cross station in the largest of the three houses. Throughout her adult life, Bertha had been a prominent charity

2 Inteview: Mary Karkajian Franji, Jerusalem, August 14, 1999.

organizer, but, unlike her mother, Anna, she was not a religious leader.

During the spring of 1948, as fighting continued between Jews and Arabs, it required all of Bertha's energy and ingenuity to keep the house and its gardens free of Arab gunmen. The guerrillas were allowed to bring their wounded to the Red Cross station, but no one, to Bertha's knowledge, used the property to shoot from. The American Colony was to be neutral in the Arab-Jewish conflict over Palestine. But many knew that Mrs Spafford Vester sympathized with the Arab side.

One morning when Bertha was bandaging the arm of an Arab soldier they heard a shot close by. The wounded Arab Legion soldier ran out and found a guerrilla about to open fire on the Jewish frontline. The wounded man pointed at the Red Cross flag and shouted: "Don't shoot from there. The flag represents Allah. Respect it as you would Allah." The irregular ran off and the soldier came back to have his dressing finished.[3]

As Jewish forces attacked and occupied increasingly large portions of the city, Bertha wondered what her mother would have said, had she lived to see the offensive. Anna Spafford believed that the early Jewish immigrants to Palestine had arrived with peaceful objectives and did not want to seize control of the land from its inhabitants. She herself had moved to Jerusalem from the US in 1881, and when the first wave of Jewish immigrants came from Russia the following year, it was, for Anna, the fulfilment of a biblical prophecy. The arrival of the Jews was a sign that Jesus would return to earth in the near future. The 20 or so members of her Christian sect, known as the 'Overcomers', shared this same belief. It was rumoured that they had taken the name because Anna wanted to overcome the personal tragedies that had afflicted her family. But she always denied this.[4]

Anna Spafford was born near Stavanger, on the west coast of Norway. The family background was obscure and Anna did not even know her baptismal name – Anne Tobine Larsdatter Øglende. Her parents told her only that she was born on March 16, 1842, and had been baptized in the Cathedral of Stavanger, a city with some 6,000 inhabitants.

Anna's father already had four children before Anna came into the world – a boy and three girls, who had been without their mother for a year

---

3 Bertha Spafford Vester: *Our Jerusalem*, 2nd edition, Middle East Export Press Ltd, Lebanon 1954, p.378.
4 Writing in *Appleton's Magazine*, Alexander Hume Ford maintains that Horatio Spafford believed "desire to sin could be overcome by return to the early practices of the Christian church – for this reason he and his co-workers were termed in contemptuous ridicule, 'Overcomers', a name that long stuck to them." *Appleton's Magazine*, Vol. VIII, December 1906, p.464.

when Lars made a 40-year-old woman from the south of Norway pregnant. Barely three months later, he married Gurine Tonette Andersdatter.[5]

Lars Larsen Øglende was a carpenter and a violin maker. In addition to the income this provided, his family lived off land Lars leased from Hetland Parish, just outside of the city limits of Stavanger. The craftsman and farmer was a deeply religious man with a wide circle of acquaintances in the city and his children's godparents were all respected figures in the community. Some of them were Quakers, but Lars himself was not part of the Community of Friends. To leave the State Church and join the Quakers could lead to conflict with the authorities and many Quaker sympathizers were anxious to avoid this.

'America Fever' raged throughout Stavanger, and when one of the Quaker leaders returned from New York with stories of the 'land of opportunity', Lars and his wife decided to emigrate. There was a shortage of carpenters in the New World, and on May 10, 1846, the couple and their youngest children embarked on the sailing brig, *Norden*. Lars' eldest son, Edvard, stayed behind with relatives in the district. He would make the journey later.[6]

After 66 days on the Atlantic, the Øglende family, along with 150 other Norwegian immigrants, finally arrived in New York on July 15. The Norwegian arrivals, all dressed in their finest clothes, attracted considerable attention in the busy New World city. They were better dressed than the German or Irish immigrants, who also arrived in America in great numbers.

Lars and his family did not stay long in New York. They had heard that they could make their fortune in a city known locally as the 'Queen of the Prairie'. The family followed the example of many other Scandinavians and went to Illinois, to the city of Chicago, which, at that time, had only some 10,000 inhabitants. The city expanded rapidly along the lowlands at the southern end of Lake Michigan and on both sides of the Chicago

5 Gurine Tonette Andersdatter and Lars Larsen Øglende were married in Stavanger on September 4, 1841. See: Gunnar Skadberg: *The Girl from Stavanger Who Became Leader of a Religious Colony in Jerusalem*, unpublished manuscript, Stavanger 1998. The Norwegian Emigration Centre, Stavanger (in Norwegian). According to the passenger list of the *Norden,* the family was listed as Lars Larsen Øglende, Gurine Tobine Øglende, Hans Larsen Øglende (1 year), Laurenze Larsdatter Øglende (13), Lise Larsdatter Øglende (11), Barboe Larsdatter Øglende (later called Rachel, 9), Anne Tobine Larsdatter Øglende (later called Anna, 4). See: Gerhard B. Naeseth: *Norwegian Immigrants to The United States, A Biographical Directory, 1825-1850, Volume Two 1844-1846*, Vesterheim, Decorah, Iowa 1997, p. 233. The eldest of Anna's half-sisters, Laurenze and Lise, left the family soon after arriving in the US and Anna lost contact with them.
6 Letter from Mrs H J Urdahl to Bertha Spafford Vester, January 27, 1936, American Colony Collection, Jerusalem.

River, a lazy, slow-moving waterway with a weak current.

Low log houses sprang up along these swampy river banks. Painted white, their walls soon turned dirty grey. The settlement had no drainage, paved roads or sidewalks. But there was plenty of land to choose from, and Lars was able to buy a small plot in the northern part of Chicago. First he put up a temporary cabin, and then built a house for the family.

Like most Norwegian immigrants, Lars Larsen Øglende had changed his name when he arrived in America. Old traditional family or farmstead names sounded strange to the American ear, and even evoked laughter. But no matter how Lars twisted and turned 'Øglende', it stayed Norwegian. Eventually he decided to drop the family name and called himself Lars Lawson. His wife, Gurine Tonette, took the name Tanetta, and Tobine became Anna.

Chicago was certainly not the land of Canaan, as the immigrants had been led to expect. The climate by Lake Michigan was unhealthy, and many were plagued by illness. One of the worst was malaria, or 'ague fever' as the Norwegians called it. When cholera also erupted in May 1849, conditions grew even worse. The epidemic was particularly virulent along the sandy river banks in the northern part of Chicago, where the Norwegians had settled.[7]

Although Lars and Tanetta quickly recognized the seriousness of the sickness, their younger children understood little. Anna copied in play what she saw the adults doing. She washed and cared for her friends, who pretended to be sick, even arranging funerals for them when they played at being dead. A couple of the children narrowly escaped being suffocated in their 'graves' as a result of Anna's attentions. [8]

Anna's mother and four-year-old brother, Hans, also caught cholera. The entire family became ill to some degree, except Anna, who regularly walked through the empty streets to the pharmacy to fetch medicine and brandy. As she walked, she heard groans and cries emanating from the houses of her neighbours as the sick and delirious waited for their end to come. The source of the contagion was understood to be dirty water, and, after the epidemic, those living on the banks of the Chicago River rowed far out into Lake Michigan to fill their buckets with drinking water.

But this knowledge could not help Tanetta and little Hans. They both died at the same time. Eight-year-old Anna was woken by her older sister,

---

7 Spafford Vester: *Our Jerusalem*, 2nd edition, p.12.
8 Bertha Spafford Vester: Unpublished draft of *Our Jerusalem*, Chapter II, p.36, American Colony Collection, Jerusalem.

Rachel, who told her that their mother and youngest brother were gone. Anna was asked to get up and dress in her finest clothes, including a light-coloured flowered dress and a padded petticoat. In her heart, the little girl felt a stab of shame because she was looking forward to wearing the pretty petticoat. That small portion of joy was to remain with her, even during the funeral.[9]

For the second time, Lars became a widower, with sole responsibility for his children. The eldest girls were fortunately big enough to manage for themselves, and Anna was cared for by a childless neighbour, Mrs Sarah Ely, who grew so fond of the lively Norwegian girl that she asked to be her foster mother. Her husband also had enough money to pay for Anna to attend a suitable school, and receive singing and piano instruction.

Yet, as one anxiety began to recede for Lars, along came another: latent tuberculosis. The damp river climate in Chicago was not a good medicine, and when Lars subsequently heard that Norwegian immigrants were beginning to put down roots in Minnesota, he decided to go west. It was said that the soil in the new state was the best in the United States and that the climate could cure tuberculosis. Anna did not want to accompany him, and decided to stay behind with her new foster mother and her husband.

Lars Lawson sold the house in Chicago and left, together with his eldest son, Edvard, who was then 17. The railway to the west extended as far as the town of Galata on the Mississippi; from there the Norwegian pioneers travelled on by paddle steamer. They disembarked at the little river town of Red Wing, named after an Indian chief. From here, father and son went by oxcart into the interior, following the old Indian and buffalo trails through small forests, over rolling plains and across rivers that cut through the deep black loam.

When Lars and Edvard were about 30 miles from the Mississippi, they decided to settle down. They chose a rectangular, flat rise with good soil conditions, which was watered by a winding river and surrounded by small meadows with deciduous trees and pine. The two pioneers erected name posts around a rectangular area of approximately 200 acres before putting a roof over their heads and clearing their land.

The house was barely finished by the time the winter came, but it was good enough to live in. There were also many deer in the area, and when the ground was covered in snow the farm dog managed to hunt down enough to keep them fed for several weeks. The snow was firm enough to

support the weight of the dog, but not the deer, which Edvard killed easily

9 Ibid. p.42.

with a few blows of his axe.

In Minnesota, Lars changed his name yet again – to Lars Larson. There were so many Norwegians in the area that Larson worked better than Lawson. But the dry air did not help the tuberculosis. Lars became increasingly sick and weak, until he had no option but to write to Anna and ask for her help.

When the 14-year-old Anna understood that tuberculosis was on the verge of destroying her father, she decided to go to Minnesota to help him. She also went, in part, to escape marriage to a Norwegian man twice her age, to whom her father had promised her some time earlier.

For Anna, this new long trip westward was a memorable experience. The railway from Chicago now reached the little town of Prairie du Chien, not far from where the Wisconsin River empties into the Mississippi. From there she took a riverboat.

On the deck of the paddle steamer, Anna stood for hours gazing at the riverbanks. She saw the primitive huts of mixed-blood American Indians, and patches of land where they grew potatoes and grain. She also enjoyed wandering about the boat, through the beautiful dayrooms with paintings on the walls and chandeliers of crystal. The food was as elegant as in the finest Chicago hotels, and meals were served by tall black men in white gloves. Never before had she seen at such close quarters the contrast between refined luxury and primitive living conditions.

In Red Wing, Edvard was waiting, and after a tiring day on a bumpy cart they arrived home. Anna was happy to see her father, but she was also sad. Not only was he very sick, but Anna also realized that schooling, piano playing and voice instruction, as well as playtime with her friends, were at an end. From now on, life would involve hard physical work from morning until night.

The half-finished log house was not much larger than a scant 250 square feet. Inside, a steep ladder went up to a loft where there was room for beds. Anna set to, washing clothes, milking the cows and churning butter. Nothing was wasted, and when cows or calves were butchered, their skins were sewn into indoor shoes and jackets.

For Anna, the howling of wolves and the presence of Indians quickly became commonplace and unremarkable. By and large, though, the indigenous people were peaceful, since the state had purchased the land from them in 1853. There was only a scattering of Indian villages along the banks of the Mississippi, the largest river in the area, and the few Indians, who came into contact with the new arrivals, did so mainly to beg for bread, buy ammunition, or sell small items.

Here, on the Minnesota prairie, Anna realized that she no longer felt comfortable speaking Norwegian. After her mother had died in Chicago, she had spoken only the new language, which now seemed more familiar and easy to her.

Even though Anna wished with all her heart that her father would recover, hardly a day went by when she did not think how wonderful it would be to get back to Chicago. When her longing was strongest, she would pull out her father's accordion and go to the riverbank where she would sit by a large pool formed by the river's current. She would sit there for hours and sing to herself. She also wanted to play her father's violin, but it was difficult to tune, and Edvard had already laid claim to that instrument.

Lars did not manage to beat the tuberculosis. He died early one spring day in 1858, with Anna and Edvard at his bedside. The two half-grown children sought help from their Norwegian neighbours, and together, they made a coffin from the unfinished planks that their father had obtained to complete the house. Edvard cleaned the planks on the outside, and Anna prepared the inside with dried grass and white linen. The spring flowers had still not appeared, but Anna made a wreath of sweet-smelling branches of silver fir and laurel. They buried their father on the property between two oak trees, just east of the log cabin.[10]

After the burial, Anna wanted to get back to Chicago as quickly as possible. When she heard that a Norwegian pastor was visiting the area she thought that this might be a way for her to return to the city without the need for her brother to escort her all the way back to Red Wing. The priest was holding services and baptizing children nearby, so Anna thought she could accompany him on his return journey to the river town once he was finished with his pastoral work.

The newly graduated Pastor Laurenz Larson from Kristiansand had arrived from Norway the year before and was active in the neighbouring state of Wisconsin. He had travelled by riverboat to Red Wing, but had completed the rest of the journey on foot, after which it was said his shoes were so worn he had to borrow a pair before he could begin his priestly duties. Since there was neither priest nor church in the area, the children of the new arrivals could be baptized only when visiting priests arrived in the neighbourhood.[11]

10 Interview: Garvin Friese, Wanamingo, June 17, 1999; Sadie Morkre: *The Larson Log House*, Wanamingo Historical Society; Bertha Spafford Vester: *Our Jerusalem*, 2nd edition, pp.13-14.
11 *Holden Through One Hundred Years, 1856-1956*, Saint Olaf College, Northfield, Minnesota, p.14.

Anna packed the few things she owned into a large trunk, and Edvard drove her to the farm where the pastor was staying. Edvard did not stay long (there was much to be done on the farm) and, as he left, Anna ran after the cart for several hundred yards. As her brother disappeared around a bend, she wondered if this would be the last time she would see him. [12]

Some of the families visiting Pastor Larson at the farm that day had brought food with them, and while the women cooked and set a long table, the men chatted amongst themselves. But Anna was in no mood to celebrate, particularly not in the presence of a priest. She had bad memories of Christian meetings during her childhood years in Chicago, when several preachers had been extremely hostile to their innocent congregations. The supposedly pious Christian leaders had behaved so hypocritically that Anna did not want anything to do with the church. Her hatred had been so strong she had refused to go to services and did not even pray. But she told no one about her feelings, lest her friends in the city might mistake her convictions for arrogance.

When the suppers and baptisms were finished, Anna hoped the 25-year-old pastor would leave the farm right away. No matter how she felt about preachers, Pastor Larson was the only one who could escort her to Red Wing, a day's journey away by oxcart.

When the pastor realized that many families had still been unable to have their children baptized, he decided to stay in the district some days longer. Over the course of the next six days, approximately 100 pioneer children were baptized. Anna, meanwhile, was compelled to remain on the farm until he was finished with his duties.

She was not happy with the change of plan, but it was already too late to return to Edvard, and no one else was heading in her direction. As far as she could tell, the only occupants of the farm were an elderly man and his blind wife. The two of them made food, ate and slept in a large room on the first floor of the house. The only other room was a small loft.

When the man began to look at her with lust, the 16-year-old found it repelling and, as soon as it was dark, she crept up into the loft. Anna was so exhausted after her long day travelling that she felt her way to a stack of hay and fell asleep straight away. During the night, she was woken by the sound of someone mumbling in Norwegian and felt something touch her face. Anna did not see anything because the room was completely dark. She lay still as a mouse and held her breath. Nothing more happened, and the person crept away and lay down in another corner of the loft.

12 Spafford Vester: *Our Jerusalem*, 2nd edition, pp.14-15.

Anna remained in the hay, stiff from cold and fright. After a short while she heard snoring. For the first time in a long time she prayed: "O God, deliver me, and I will never be discontented again."

With the morning light came a revelation. Another woman was lying there, sleeping in the hay. The woman resembled an animal more than a person, and, when Anna climbed down the ladder to the first floor, she learned that the woman was the couple's mentally retarded daughter. After breakfast, the daughter also came down, but ran straight out into the forest without speaking. There she remained until evening, when she returned to eat from the plate of food her mother had placed for her outside the house.

Anna did not know if she could stand another night in the loft with this woman. But after the old man again made an approach towards her, right in front of his blind wife, Anna realized that the loft was preferable, and again crept upstairs to her sleeping place. A little later, the disturbed girl also came up, but Anna quickly realized she was not dangerous and the two got along quite well together.

Anna remained with the family until the pastor returned. The two travelled together to the riverboat station, where Pastor Larson boarded a boat that would take him to Wisconsin, while Anna travelled by steamer to Prairie du Chien and the railway that would take her further east to Chicago.

Chapter 2

The Lawyer's Wife

When Anna arrived back in Chicago she was relieved to discover her Norwegian suitor had married someone else. Less welcome was the news that Sarah Ely, her foster mother, had moved to New York. Fortunately, Anna's half-sister Rachel, the only one with whom she still had contact, remained in Chicago. Rachel had married, and her new family name was Fredrickson, and she was more than willing to help Anna. Rachel's husband was a ship's carpenter and earned enough to enable Anna to continue the schooling she had interrupted.

Anna still wanted nothing to do with the church. She did not even want to go to Sunday school, even though her friends urged her to do so. "Our Sunday school teacher is different," they told her. "He doesn't talk down to us. He gives us a chance to express our own opinions, and he loves discussion." Her best friend, Jenny Simpson, told her: "It will do you good to hear Mr Spafford."[13]

Anna finally gave in, and one Sunday, went along to listen to Mr Spafford's Bible lesson. At first, the teenager was not particularly interested, but after a while she began to participate. Anna asked good questions and was unafraid to answer when she was asked something. The teacher liked the answers the blonde pupil from Norway gave, looking him straight in the eyes. And, what eyes she had! They were the bluest he had ever seen.

Over the following weeks, the 30-year-old Sunday school teacher could not put the beautiful, mature pupil out of his thoughts. Anna did not attend any further classes, but her teacher remembered her blonde hair, white teeth, mouth, cheekbones, ears, and, of course, those eyes. He remembered also her thorough and well thought out responses

13 Ibid. p.16.

Anna Spafford aged 20 in Chicago

The Sunday school teacher, Horatio Gates Spafford, was a lawyer, the son of a rich professor with English ancestry. The Spofforth family estate was in Yorkshire and the world's first property registry, the Domesday Book, confirms that Horatio Spafford's ancestors had been rich landholders. Spafford himself had moved from New York to Chicago in 1856, where he became a senior partner in one of the city's well-known law firms.

Horatio Spafford visited Rachel and her husband, Christian Fredrickson, but his conversation did not suggest initially that he was in love with Anna. It was only later, when the visits became more frequent, that Rachel understood what the preacher really had in mind.

Anna was also old enough to realize that the lawyer, with his intense brown eyes, eagle-like nose, and thick hair, was interested in her, and, one Sunday afternoon, she instinctively felt the time was right for him to visit. She put on a dress that she thought Horatio Spafford would like, and braided her hair and put it up with hairpins. Rachel teased her, but she, too, made preparations, baking cakes and putting out refreshments in the living room.

But the suitor did not show up, so, at 10 in the evening, Rachel brought the drinks and glasses back to the kitchen, said good night and went off to bed. Anna did not want to go to bed, and remained there, listening for any slight sound. She was certain that Horatio Spafford would come.

The clock continued to tick, but nothing happened, so finally she gave up. The disappointed teenager was about to take the hairpins out of her long braids when there was a soft knocking. Anna took a shawl and threw it around her shoulders, and opened the door. There he was on the steps, the man she had been waiting for the entire afternoon and evening. He said: "Can you come out with me for a short walk, Annie?"[14]

Almost before Horatio had finished speaking, she was out on the steps. She had been so certain he would come that she already had her door key in her skirt pocket. At first, the usually talkative lawyer said little. The two of them went all the way down the empty street saying almost nothing, before walking back in the direction of the Fredricksons' house. Only then did Horatio Spafford dare to say: "Would you be willing to go with me to Patagonia?"

Anna thought the Sunday school teacher wanted her to be a missionary wife in the southernmost part of South America. She hated the idea of Patagonia, but answered anyway: "I will go anywhere with you."

"So, you love and trust me, then, Annie? Will you be my wife?"

"Yes."

There was no doubt in the 16-year-old's mind. She was convinced Horatio Spafford would come to be a perfect husband.

However, when Rachel found out what had happened, she opposed the marriage. Anna was still too young to marry, despite the lawyer's social status and wealth. Horatio was disappointed and rather surprised by the rejection. He had thought that Anna was older, but he agreed to wait and to pay for Anna to attend a reputable boarding school for young ladies.

Anna was thankful to get more schooling. She quickly settled in at the Ferry Institute for Young Ladies, outside Chicago, starting a Bible reading and discussion group, and was later considered one of the

---

14 Spafford Vester: Unpublished draft of *Our Jerusalem*, pp.60-61, American Colony Collection, Jerusalem.

school's outstanding alumnae.[15] Anna had a natural talent for learning, a good sense of humour and a pleasant disposition. Her music teacher felt that she could become an excellent singer, if she had the opportunity to develop her talent. Friends and teachers, however, also discovered the happy teenager had a biting sense of humour and could be mean spirited.

On December 6, 1860, Anna wrote to her former foster mother, Sarah Ely: "I am glad that you are pleased with my engagement… I wish you were acquainted with Mr Spafford. He is a true noble man [sic]. I owe him a great deal, but still would not marry merely from gratitude. I have often wondered what he sees in me to like, for I am so simple and ignorant, while he is so strong and learned. I pray to God that I may be worthy of him. It seems strange to look back at a time when I was a little girl living with you. How little I thought then of the many changes that would take place and of the dear friend I should lose… I am back at Lake Forest, at school. It is very pleasant here. There are only 12 scholars. I am getting along nicely. I study algebra, history, rhetoric, philosophy and psychology…"[16]

Anna became ever more appreciative of Spafford, with his love of music, poetry and nature. She was also impressed by his strong social conscience, and opposition to slavery. She was not at all troubled by the fact that he was so nearsighted that he could not even see the stars in the sky without glasses. Anna eventually fell so deeply in love with him that one day, she used the diamond in her engagement ring to etch a heart containing the letters HS + AL onto the windowsill in her room.[17]

Horatio continued to teach at Sunday school and to preach, in addition to his law practice. He joined the YMCA and became chairman of one of its committees. He also gave lectures, and, after just three years, during which he was acknowledged as one of the rising stars at the University of Chicago, he was appointed to a professorship there. Anna often went along to hear her fiancé lecturing. She also accompanied him to the Presbyterian Church, but declined to become a member of the congregation.[18]

It had been decided that Anna and Horatio would marry when she reached the age of 19. The ceremony was to be simple and would take

15 Spafford Vester: *Our Jerusalem*, 2nd edition, p.17.
16 Letter from Anna Lawson to Mrs Sarah Ely, December 6, 1860, Folder: Anna Spafford, American Colony Collection, Jerusalem.
17 Spafford Vester: *Our Jerusalem*, 2nd edition, p.17.
18 Anna Spafford became a member of the Second Presbyterian Church, on January 3, 1862, according to church historian, Barry Smith, Lincoln Park Presbyterian Church, Chicago.

place on September 5, 1861, in the newest Presbyterian Church in the city. It was a long, narrow church, painted white with green shutters. Only a few close friends were invited. The civil war between the North and the South had begun, and even though Chicago was a long distance from the front, it seemed inappropriate to arrange lavish festivities during wartime.

Anna's floor-length wedding gown had been sewn at home, and was made from dark blue taffeta so that it could be worn later. The dress was tight at the waist, with ribbons and a hooped overskirt. On her head she wore a small bonnet in the same colour as her dress, decorated with small pink roses. Its turned-up brim was lined with shirred pink chiffon.

To the bridal couple's great surprise, the church had been beautifully decorated with white flowers and bracken, and was filled with smiling well-wishers. Following the ceremony, the couple went straight to their new home in Lake View, a small suburb north of Chicago, between the Chicago River and Lake Michigan. Anna's sister, Rachel, had stocked the larder with all kinds of good things to eat, and they sat down alone to their first meal in their new home.

The newlyweds did not go on honeymoon, choosing instead to involve themselves in the charitable work of the church and to help those who had been wounded in the civil war. During this time, Anna had her first exposure to a type of Christianity that functioned through good works. The suffering that resulted from the war was great and affected Anna deeply. She believed that faith, without good deeds, was hypocritical.

The Spafford family lived peacefully in the suburbs away from the hectic city. Every morning, Horatio was driven to the little train station by Peter, their handyman, in a horse and carriage. From there, the lawyer took a small train to his office in the city centre. But family life was far from dull. Horatio often brought dinner guests home with him, with little warning, and Anna learned to take these things as they came. Because there were no late trains the Spaffords' guests often spent the night at their hosts' large roomy house.

Anna created a beautiful home and, together, the couple expanded the house, adding bay windows, dormers and sills. Everyone who visited observed that they had a talent for making their surroundings beautiful. The rooms were tastefully furnished and the garden planted with flowers and decorative bushes, with a bamboo sofa beneath a tall, shady plane tree. Here, Anna and Horatio could sit in the shade and enjoy the view. The area around Lake View was so attractive that one of Chicago's popular poets, Eugene Field, wrote a ballad in praise of a garden belonging to one of the Spaffords' neighbours. Fourteen years after Anna and Horatio set up home there, their property was valued at around $35,000, a far higher price than most of their neighbours could hope to get for their properties.[19]

In June 1862, nine months after their wedding, Anna gave birth to a little girl. She was baptized Anna after her mother, but was generally known as Annie. Two years later, in May, 1864, less than a year after the famous Battle of Gettysburg, little Maggie was born. She was baptized Margareth Lee, after Horatio's favourite sister, Margareth and her husband, Colonel Arthur Lee, who had been injured at Gettysburg, where more than 51,000 men were killed or severely wounded. By June 1868, when General Ulysses S Grant was sworn in as president of the United States, the Spaffords already had a third daughter, Elizabeth, known as Bessie.

Whenever Anna had given birth, Horatio had been curious to see whether their latest child had inherited its mother's wonderful eyes, her blonde hair or, particularly, her delicate ears. Alas, no, the girls all had brown eyes, brown or dark hair, and, of course, Horatio's big ears.[20]

Horatio Spafford was a Yankee of the first order, a hard-working moneymaker who wrote psalms, believed in God and headed a growing law firm. He also had many friends. One was Dwight Lyman Moody, the most popular evangelist in Chicago. Both of them had arrived in the city in 1856, one as a prominent lawyer, the other as a poor 21-year-old shoe salesman.

While Horatio Spafford had joined the Presbyterian Church, Dwight Moody followed his own path. The young shoe salesman sought out Sunday school students in Chicago's poor districts. He would knock on doors and virtually drag youngsters from their beds, insisting they attend his Bible classes.

After a modest start, the number of pupils quickly expanded. Moody borrowed a hall, which, on Saturday nights, was used for dances. He then cleaned it up before classes each Sunday morning. After two years, the young preacher and shoe salesman had 1,500 pupils in their Sunday school class. The school began to be talked about so much that newly-elected President Abraham Lincoln visited it as he passed through Chicago on his way to the White House.

Anna Spafford was particularly intrigued by the way Dwight Moody delivered the Christian message. The preacher placed more emphasis on

19 Everett Chamerlin: *Chicago and its Suburbs*, Chicago 1874, p.351, Eugene Field: *The Delectable Ballad of the Waller Lot.*
20 Spafford Vester: Unpublished draft of *Our Jerusalem*, p.113, American Colony Collection, Jerusalem.

God's love than on sinners' eternal damnation, and even though he was happy to terrify his congregation with stories of Satan and the fires of hell, he always returned to the theme of God's love. Moody also preached that the Messiah would soon return again to earth.

This was a time when a great wave of religious revivalism was washing across America. It was a direct consequence of the process of colonisation of the west. Sickness and premature death, isolation and misery were all part of the settlers' tough and difficult lives, giving them a fear of God and a strong faith. Even in big cities, such as Chicago, many people attended prayer meetings when it was known that a famous preacher would be speaking.

Anna often went to Dwight Moody's meetings, along with her two oldest daughters, Annie and Maggie. Moody's talk about the Saviour had particularly touched the children. No one else took the teachings as literally as Anna's little girls, and one day when participants in the meeting were called to join Moody's congregation, little Annie said: "Mamma, why can't we go in, too?"[21]

Anna let the children go into the so-called confessional room, where one of Moody's assistants spoke with them. Everyone present was impressed that the two children knew as much about the way to salvation as the adults.

Horatio Spafford and Dwight Moody believed Chicago's businessmen ought to have the opportunity for meditation and reflection during their busy daily routine. They decided to arrange a small prayer period at lunchtime. At first, some of the busy money men took time out to pray, but interest soon ebbed as the drive to succeed in business took the upper hand. After a while, Spafford and Moody decided that they, too, would be better able to achieve their aims if they invested in property.

Horatio wished to find a new source of income in order to have more time with his family, and for what he called his philanthropic and Christian activity. Dwight Moody needed funds for his proselytizing mission. Together with several friends, they bought up an area north of Chicago, investing all their savings and also borrowing heavily. They both believed their investment would be secure, because the city was expanding so rapidly, especially in the north.

By now, Chicago was the largest, richest and most impressive of all the cities in the centre of America. It became synonymous with American

---

21 Dwight L. Moody with Rev C. F. Gross: *Echoes from the Pulpit and Platform*, A.D. Warthington & Co., Hartford, Conn. 1900, p.362.

well-being and its expansion seemed unstoppable. The city was buzzing with business people who bought and sold, and some new arrivals in Chicago got the impression that business was all that mattered there.

Within the Spaffords' circle of friends, the privileged, newly-prosperous Americans whom they invited into their home there were few Norwegian immigrants. Anna had no strong ties to her motherland, but Horatio, for his part, maintained close contact with Britain. His work took him on trips to England and Scotland, and it was during one of these visits that he met a Scottish professor of astronomy, who would come to change both his life and Anna's.

Following a trip to Egypt, the professor, whose name was Charles Piazzi Smyth, had developed a theory to determine the exact moment of the Second Coming of Jesus. With the help of a long tape measure and the Bible, Smyth had deduced that the largest pyramid outside Cairo must have been built with divine inspiration. Through complicated calculations, he figured that Jesus would return to earth in 1881.[22]

When Horatio arrived back in Chicago he told Anna of Smyth's theories about the Old Testament's prophecies and the message of the pyramids. He also began to preach about Jesus' imminent return to his own congregation in the new church on Fullerton Avenue, not far from the Spafford home in Lake View.

In his sermons, Horatio Spafford did not threaten eternal damnation but preached of forgiveness. If God was, indeed loving, as the Bible said, then this had to be true for everyone, regardless of how sinful they might have been. This was a highly controversial doctrine, and Horatio's teachings were not well received by the majority of his congregation. But they did not reject him outright – he was, after all, one of the founders of the church.[23]

The summer of 1871 was extremely dry. It was during the middle of this dry period that Anna gave birth to their fourth daughter. She was baptized Tanetta, after her maternal grandmother. No more rain fell in the fall either, and, by the beginning of October, some scientists began to speculate about a coming shift in the climate. The city's trees took on the appearance of a huge, artificial, dried forest, their leaves, no longer green but grey, hanging limply, while dust whirled around the streets and settled all over the city's buildings.

22 Piazzi Smyth: *Our Inheritance in the Great Pyramid*, London, 1880; Leslie Greener: *The Discovery of Egypt*, New York, 1966, p.56.
23 Interview: Barry Smith, 1999, Lincoln Park Presbyterian Church, Chicago; Spafford Vester: *Our Jerusalem*, 2nd edition, p.26.

On the evening of Saturday, October 7, George Francis Train, traveller, author and a popular lecturer on moral subjects, stood at his podium in Farwell Hall in Chicago and talked to a large audience. The topic of this address is not recorded, but everyone there would remember the speaker's closing words. "This is the last public address that will be delivered within these walls," Train cried. "A terrible calamity is impending over the city of Chicago! More I cannot say; more I dare not utter."[24]

The next morning, Sunday, October 8, 1871, Anna read a warning in the *Chicago Tribune:* "One spark will be enough to start a fire which can spread through the city from end to end." Those most at risk were the poor, who lived in the industrial areas near the city's many sawmills. Every house had its own store of sawdust from the mills, which was used in cooking stoves. Houses, barns and outbuildings lay close to each other, and everyone realized that fire could be a catastrophe.

Around nine o'clock that evening a fire broke out in a barn in a poor Irish immigrant district on the west side of the city. It spread quickly to the low wooden houses in the neighbourhood. All attempts to control it failed, as water thrown onto the flames evaporated in seconds. It took half an hour for news of the blaze to reach the city's fire station. Even when the horse-drawn fire engines finally arrived that Sunday evening, the firemen's efforts had little impact. The men had already been working all night Saturday and most of Sunday, and the whiskey, which always flowed in large quantities after a big job, was still in their systems.[25]

The little barn fire had become an unstoppable flaming monster, and from the balcony at Lake View, Anna watched as Chicago became engulfed in a terrible ocean of flames.

The fire roared through the city like a storm; street after street, block after block were attacked. The flames were helped by the wooden planks, which made up not only parts of the road, but also the sidewalks. Hoards of men, women and children ran first in one direction, and then in another, screaming and shouting as they tried to save their possessions. The streets rapidly filled with wagons loaded with books, clothing, and safes, everything their owners were able to salvage. Fantastic amounts of money were offered to those who had wagons.

But not everyone fled the flames; there were many who came to watch. Some thought the fire heralded the end of the world.

Homeless refugees began to arrive in the suburb of Lake View the

24 Robert Cromie: *The Great Chicago Fire*, Rutledge Hill Press, Nashville Tennesse, 1994, p.17.
25 David Lowe: *The Great Chicago Fire, An Eyewitness Account,* New York, 1979, pp.7-10.

following morning, and the first to reach the Spafford house was an injured woman. Anna sent the handyman, Peter, to buy more food, while Chicago continued to burn, assisted by a strong wind from the prairie.

The following Tuesday afternoon, Anna saw a wagon full of dirty men, women and children approaching her house. It was only when it finally stopped that she recognized one of the refugees, as Mary Morgan, now married and known as Mary Miller, the first friend Anna had made at her exclusive private school. It had taken the family one and a half days to get away from the city and the flames. Mary's husband's eyes were burned, and he could not see, so Mary had taken over the carriage seat herself and whipped the horses through the burning city. Their hooves were now badly burned, and Anna poured cold water over them. She also tried to ease Mr Miller's burned eyelids with wet tea leaves. Mary was still breastfeeding her four-month-old baby, but her milk had dried up during the hectic flight from the fire. So Anna found a neighbouring farmer's wife to be the baby's wet nurse.

Just as the homeless refugees began to settle down in Anna's house, a message arrived that some trees nearby had begun to burn. Many families in Lake View decided to leave and Anna did the same. She left a note for Peter, who had taken the family's horse away on an errand, and, without a horse of her own, attached her wagon to the Millers' instead.

Anna and her neighbours drove westward, with no particular objective. The road was full of people fleeing the fire. Men and boys were pulling fully-laden wagons containing the sick and the old, women, children and bundles of clothing. There were even dogs carrying baskets in their mouths, or pulling small baby carriages. Everything was quiet, the refugees from the condemned city said little.

Before long, Anna's group came alongside a wagon that was being driven by a man whom Anna knew by sight, so she asked his advice as to where they should go. "You are welcome at my home in Jefferson," he replied. Anna and the Millers followed the man over a dried-out riverbed, and, when they arrived at his farm, found that there were some 20 more refugees already there. Most were complete strangers to their host, but he and his wife did everything they could to help them. Anna and her group stayed overnight before returning to Lake View.

There, they found that the house was unscathed. Loyal Peter had kept the roof of the house wet during the entire night, and the fire had been stopped at Fullerton Avenue, sparing the Spaffords' house and that of their neighbours.

Throughout these dramatic days Horatio Spafford had been in Indiana on a business trip, and news of the Great Fire came as a shock. The front pages of the newspapers carried huge headlines: "Chicago in Ashes. The Greatest Catastrophe of Our Times." The implications for Horatio's business venture were serious; Property sales had now become impossible. Who could imagine any further expansion of the city towards the north after this? He just wanted to get home as quickly as possible.

When he eventually reached Chicago, Horatio found his law offices in ruins. Only the documents in the fireproof safe were intact. He realized that his dreams of getting richer now lay in ashes. The money he had used to buy property had been borrowed and interest and capital still had to be paid. How were he and his family to survive? But Horatio's friend, the evangelist Dwight Moody, had fared even worse: he had lost everything, he said, "but my reputation and my Bible."[26]

Of Chicago's 300,000 inhabitants, 300 were killed while 90,000 became homeless. The blame for the worst catastrophe in Chicago's history until then was put on a cow that is said to have kicked over a lighted lantern in a barn. Subsequent research has revealed that this could not have been the case. But in the absence of other, more credible, explanations, the story about the cow and the lantern in the barn remains popular.

26 Moody and Gross: *Echoes from the Pulpit and Platform*, Hartford, Conn. 1900, p.55.

Chapter 3

The Shipwreck

After the fire, Chicago was divided into zones, each run by a committee responsible for arranging food, clothing and temporary housing over the winter. Anna and Horatio were part of the relief effort, and even though they had not lost their home, it was a difficult winter for both of them. Horatio had taken on such large economic obligations that he had to mortgage the house in Lake View. The fire and the strain of this, combined with the obligations of her charity work, began to take their toll on Anna's health. In an attempt to get her strength back, in May 1872, she and two of the children went to visit her sister-in-law, Margareth Lee, in Washington. But the visit was a short one. Anna wrote to her husband: "I cannot live very long without you."[27]

The family physician, Dr Samuel Hedges, thought Anna needed more rest, but also needed to have her family around her. Perhaps they all should go somewhere? Horatio thought this was a good idea. For a long time he had wanted to show Anna the museums and art galleries of Europe. First, they could travel to France, where Anna had several friends from her time at boarding school. One of them had married a wealthy doctor, while another had become the wife of a French government minister. The trip would be expensive, but so be it. Anna's health was more important than anything else.

They started making plans and decided to leave in the autumn of 1873. It was arranged that the two older girls, Annie, 10 and Maggie, nine, would attend a boarding school in Lausanne, Switzerland. The two youngest,

27 Letter from Anna Spafford to Horatio Spafford, May 6, 1872, American Colony Collection, Jerusalem.

Bessie, five, and little Tanetta, two, would be taken care of by the family's French governess, Mademoiselle Nicolette. She came from a respectable Huguenot family and was responsible and capable. She would look after the children while Anna and Horatio went on a delayed honeymoon in Switzerland. There was even talk about a visit to Stavanger.[28]

Horatio reserved two of the largest rooms on a passenger ship that sailed between New York and Le Havre. The agent told him the *Ville du Havre* was the best and newest of the vessels operating the transatlantic run. Everyone was looking forward to the trip, except for Maggie. She did not want to leave home or the playhouse in the garden.

Just before the family was due to depart, Horatio received a good offer on a property he owned jointly with friends. Negotiations were needed to complete the sale, but if it went ahead he would be debt-free. Horatio suggested that Anna, the children and Mademoiselle Nicolette should go ahead and he would follow on the next ship. The family would be accompanied by five ministers of religion, who were returning from a conference of the Evangelical Alliance (an organization that wanted to unify all the world's Christians) in New York. Three of the theologians were French, one was Spanish and the other was Swiss.[29] Anna already knew one of them, Pastor Theophile Lorriaux, because his sister had once been a governess for her children. Anna was still reluctant to travel without her husband. It was only when she heard that a neighbour, Mrs Goodwin, was also travelling on the same ship, along with her three children, that she agreed to leave.

Horatio accompanied the family to New York, but then decided Anna and the children should not have the large rooms he had reserved for them, even though Mrs Goodwin was going to be in the adjacent cabin. He had a strange feeling his family should not be in the middle of the ship. After negotiations with the purser, the Spafford family was given two new cabins further towards the bow.

As Horatio was completing these arrangements, he received a telegram telling him that the man who was to buy his property had suffered a heart attack, and that he needed to return immediately to Chicago. Spafford put the paper in his pocket without telling Anna, for he feared she would be disappointed if he told her the deal was lost. "It will be just a few short weeks before I will come," Horatio assured her. At a little past three o'clock

28 A.N. Rygg: *En merkelig livsskjebne* (A Peculiar Fate), *Nordisk Tidende*, New York, July 9, 1942, *Nordisk Tidende*, August 1950.
29 Anna later told her daughter that there had been four French priests, but had perhaps included the French-speaking Swiss theologian from Geneva as one of them.

in the afternoon, on November 15, 1873, the ship was slowly towed away from the pier.

He waited until the luxury vessel slid out into the Hudson River toward the ocean. Anna and the children stood at the rail waving. They stayed there until they could no longer pick out one person from another on land, and then went into the dining room. They sat at the long table, which they had reserved, together with Mrs Goodwin and her children. They were joined by 11-year-old Willie Culver, the son of some friends, who was going to visit his grandmother in Germany. Anna had promised that Willie would be "in the shadow of her protective wings". The three French priests, Theophile Lorriaux, Emile Cook, and Nathaniel Weiss, also shared the table, along with an Italian, Father Cesar Pronier, and a Spaniard, Father Antonio Carrasco. Everybody seemed in good humour that first evening, including the captain of the *Ville du Havre*, Marino Surmont. He was confident that, even if there were bad weather, his ship could handle a major storm.

The French ship had been the last of the paddle steamers constructed for the transatlantic route, and had originally sailed under the name *Napoleon III*. But subsequent demands for greater speed and better comfort had led the ship's owner to exchange its side-wheels for a propeller, and it had been converted two years prior. The iron hull, built by the Thames Iron Works of London, had been lengthened and the ship was given a new, stronger engine.

The first days on the open ocean were wonderful. Pastor Cook started a Sunday school for the children, and Pastor Lorriaux tried to teach Anna French, using the ship's menu. The food was excellent, and there were fresh flowers on every table. *Ville du Havre* maintained a speed of 12-13 knots, and the children loved standing on deck, studying the seagulls as they weaved back and forth over the white foamy wash from the propeller. Anna also liked being on deck, but, without her husband, she was not able to take full advantage of the opportunity for rest that the voyage afforded. On the fourth day, Pastor Weiss noticed that the endless flat sea that had shone like gold dust was beginning to change, and gradually the ocean grew darker as clouds absorbed the rays of the sun.

The following morning fewer than usual passengers appeared at the breakfast table. Most had lost their appetite after a rough night with high seas. Both the Spanish and Italian priests said they were ill, but Anna, the children and the French clergymen met up. They were not upset by the waves and even chose to eat breakfast on deck.

Suddenly, an extra large wave hit the ship, causing such a roll that many of the chairs stacked on deck tipped over. The waves got bigger and higher, as the ocean grew even wilder. It was as if a colossal force was whipping the water up from the depths, and the *Ville du Havre*, which had previously cut through the surface with self-confidence, was now subdued. Not that the ship had any problems adjusting to the force of the waves: the 3,500-horsepower engine moved the hull along without difficulty, but many of the waves washed over the sides of the ship. They came suddenly, fringed by large, broken crests. The seagulls were more numerous than before and flew, poised and tranquil, above the ship's opal-coloured wake, which mingled with large flakes of white foam that looked like boiling milk.

Some of the passengers panicked. One young American student fell to his knees and asked God for help. But Anna was calm. She felt safe on board the ship and knew this was nothing more than a strong gale. Their position was just off Newfoundland, and she had been through a similar experience on the same spot 27 years earlier, when, as a child, she had sailed with her family from Stavanger to New York. That journey, on a double-masted, 290-ton sailing ship, had been very different. Anna and her family had sailed during the summer, when most of the passengers berthed on the centre deck. The large family bunks had been filled with straw and the women had worked shifts in an improvised galley, each responsible for providing her own family with food. During those two months, the passengers had eaten only porridge and occasionally cod, which had been fished from the Newfoundland Banks. The ocean had not scared her then, and it did not this time either.

When Anna came down into the lounge of the *Ville du Havre*, she found it looked like an infirmary. Most of the passengers were pale and weak. The children had gathered in a corner to listen to a pretty young girl, who was telling them stories in such an engaging way that most of the youngsters forgot about their nausea. Pastor Weiss called her 'The Fairy', while Lorriaux referred to her as the 'Good Samaritan'. She also raised the spirits of those who were anxious and fearful by playing the piano, which had the added effect of stimulating their appetites.

"It is certainly not easy to eat," mumbled Pastor Cook, after trying in vain to prevent a plate from tipping over when the ship made another unexpected movement. Lorriaux turned around to address the captain at his table, saying: "Well captain, the wind does not seem to change."[30] Captain Surmont muttered a "no" and left the table much sooner than usual.

The next day the weather abated and the more fearful passengers calmed down. The salon and the deck looked as if they had been the scenes of some terrible struggle. Everything was overturned. Confusion and disorder reigned. Waiters and sailors were everywhere, busily cleaning and rearranging. The young American, who had been kneeling in prayer on the deck the night before, became courageous and began to mock nine-year-old Annie. As she sat quietly reading a religious book, the student said: "Oh! You certainly are a pious little girl."[31] Anna noticed the sharp look her daughter gave in return. It said so much more than words.

During the evening of November 21, the captain of the *Ville du Havre* noted in his log that visibility was good and the weather calm. They had been at sea for seven days and were half-way across the Atlantic.

That evening, the children, who had dined before the adults, came running back to the dining room to ask one of the grown-ups to come and play with them. Pastor Weiss offered his services, and while the gentlemen went to the smoking room and the ladies onto the deck, he amused the children until it was bedtime for the youngest ones. Anna helped the governess put the four girls to bed, then went back to the lounge where Pastor Weiss invited her to join him for a walk on deck. There was no moon, but the air was clear and Weiss noted the stars were unusually bright.

"The night sky seems studded with diamonds, sparkling from a thousand points," said Weiss.[32]

"Yes, the night is beautiful," answered Anna, "and I am contented."

"You were not contented before, then?"

"No, I was sick and sad at being separated from my husband and home," Anna replied.

Pastor Weiss interrupted her. "But these feeling will pass away. You must remember that this is the first time you have been separated from your husband for any length of time."

They remained on deck for some time before Anna said good night, and went back to her own cabin, humming a hymn which her children sang in Sunday school. Weiss went to the smoking room and joined Pastor Cook in a game of chess. Around midnight, he no longer felt like playing

30 Nathaniel Weiss: *Personal Recollection of the Wreck of the Ville-du-Havre and the Loch-Earn,* Anson D.F. Randolph & Co, New York, 1875, p.61.
31 Ibid. p.143.
32 Ibid. pp.99-100.

and returned to his favourite spot on deck. There he remained, looking out over the ocean and the skies. The sea appeared even more majestic in the glittering starlight.

Finally, Weiss decided to go back down to the lounge. The lights had been put out, and the waiters on night duty nodded to him in the half-darkness. He caught sight of the piano and could not resist the temptation. He sat down at the piano stool, opened the cover, and let his fingers play over the keys while he sang his favourite Neapolitan barcarolle:

> Sul maré luccica l'astro d'argento,
> Placida è l'onda, prospero è il vento
> Venite all'agile barchetta mia…
> Santa Lucia, Santa Lucia.

Pastor Weiss stopped playing and went down to his cabin where two of his colleagues were sleeping. He listened to their even breathing. Only Lorriaux was awake. Finally, he, too, fell asleep to the soft drone of the ship's engines, and the rhythmical sound of the propeller, as it drove the ship eastward.

On the bridge, French sailor Adien Emault had taken over the night watch. He had come on at midnight, and would remain there until 4am. The helmsman noted there was a light breeze and that the ship's speed was about 11½ knots. Everything was normal. Then, suddenly, just before 2am, a huge dark shadow appeared ahead of the *Ville du Havre*. It was a British sailing ship, the *Loch Earn*. The helmsmen of both vessels tried to steer clear, but one turned to port, the other to starboard. The result was catastrophic. The two collided, with the *Ville du Havre* taking the full impact of the bow of the sailing ship.[33]

The passengers on board the *Ville du Havre* were woken by the sound of two thunderous crashes, separated by only a few seconds. Then there were screams, horrible screams. The propeller turned once, twice, and then stopped. The engines fell silent. Anna leapt out of bed, put on a long dress, and, together with Nicolette, dressed the children. They ran out into the corridor, Anna first with two-year-old Tanetta on her arm. The governess and the others were hard on her heels. Then Pastor Lorriaux appeared and they all hurried up on deck.

There, 200-300 yards away, they saw the silhouette of the large sailing

---

33 From the maritime investigation report into the collision between the *Ville du Havre* and the *Loch Earn*, Lloyds Register, London. Copy in author's collection.

vessel. They could not see the name of the ship, but in the light of the stars they could make out sails and masts. The *Ville du Havre* made no movement, but it was very difficult to discover what happened. The deck was dark like the sea, illuminated only by the stars.

At that point, more people came from their cabins, some in pyjamas, and others only half-dressed. The crew ran in all directions, and panic spread quickly among the passengers. Captain Surmont shouted out orders from the bridge. Officers and crew tried to lower lifeboats but were unable to get them free; the new paint had glued everything to the lifeboat supports.

The passengers gathered in groups. Some tried to scramble over to the lifebelts which hung along the ship's rail. But they were also stuck fast. Pastor Weiss asked one of the sailors: "Can you tell me if there has been a collision and whether the ship has been damaged?"

"Do not be anxious, sir," he answered. "Even if there has, if water did come in through an opening, it would not sink a ship like this one with so many decks. You need not be troubled."

Despite assurances from the crew and officers, the passengers ran around in shock and fought to get to the lifeboats. Curses, shouts and hysterical screams turned the deck into a madhouse. Some fell to their knees in prayer, others just looked on apathetically.

Little Tanetta was heavy to carry, so her older sister, Annie, put her shoulder up under her mother's elbow to help take some of the weight. Maggie and Bessie pressed up against their mother as tightly as possible. The governess and Pastor Lorriaux stood guard over the little group. They were soon joined by Pastor Weiss. As soon as she saw the clergyman, Maggie ran towards him, seizing him and crying out in her terror: "You will stay with us, won't you?"

Weiss promised that he would, but, noticing that the little girl was shivering with cold and fright, he added: "I will take care of you, but you are shivering with cold in this little gown. I must look for something to cover you." Turning to his fellow priest he said: "You, Lorriaux, try in the meantime to keep these little ones together and find a small boat."

Down in the cabin Weiss found a coat and some blankets for the children. In the corridor he saw Pastor Cook in his nightshirt, talking in an agitated way.

"What are you doing there? Why are you not dressed?" Weiss asked him.

"Why am I not dressed? Don't you realize what has happened? I was helping a lady look for her children under the rubble and I saw the water rising fast."

Only then did Pastor Weiss understand that the ship had been holed amidships, in line with the main mast. At that point, the ship's doctor walked passed and cried: "Cover yourself, Pastor Cook, you will freeze! Put on my overcoat!"

Back up on deck there was complete hysteria. Willie Culver, the 11-year-old whom Anna had been told to protect, tried to free a lifebelt with a pocket-knife, while Mrs Goodwin and her children ran back and forth to their cabin to fetch clothing. Hundreds of passengers fought to get to the unusable lifeboats. Some tried to cling onto the benches, while others managed to rip lifebelts from the wall and jump into the ocean. The teenage girl, who had entertained the children with stories during the storm, was now reassuring her weeping mother and sister. "Don't be afraid, it will only take a moment's struggle and then we will be in Heaven," she told them. Meanwhile, a priest, whom Anna did not know, approached a group gathered around the captain. "Are you a Catholic?" asked the priest. Without waiting for an answer he continued: "Repent, and I will give you absolution."

Shortly after Captain Surmont had left to go to the bridge, the same priest tried to push his way into a lifeboat being lowered by officers and crew. Those in the greatest state of panic attempted to get into the lifeboats before they were released. Two or three of the passengers threw themselves into the sea, trusting in their life jackets.

The ship's doctor sought to reassure Anna by explaining that women and children would be the first to leave the sinking ship. Anna, the children, the governess, Mademoiselle Nicolette, and Pastor Lorriaux had been standing very close to a lifeboat, which the crew had managed to free, but they were pushed away.

"Am I doing the right thing to allow my children to be pushed away by people who only think about saving their own lives?" Anna wondered. "Should I fight for my children's lives?" Her life passed before her as in a dream. She remembered that Horatio had often criticized her for being too meek and letting others grab for themselves what rightfully belonged to her. These were desperate people. They neither cared about the children nor showed any compassion at all. To save oneself was the first and only consideration. The fight over the lifeboats became so violent that Anna stamped on the deck and shouted loudly: "I cannot save myself and the lives of my children at the expense of others."[34]

34 Bertha Spafford Vester: Unpublished draft of *Our Jerusalem*, p.156, American Colony Collection, Jerusalem.

At that moment, the ship shook. "Do you feel it?" Lorriaux asked Weiss, as some of the children began to scream. Weiss realized that there were too many people on the starboard side of the ship, causing it to list dangerously close to the ocean.[35] "Yes," he answered "let us go over to the other side, with Madame Spafford and the children, quickly!"

Then, the mainmast, together with the mizzenmast, broke, with an awful crash. The masts took with them two of the lifeboats that so many had fought over. Anna heard the deadly screams of those who were swept overboard and it occurred to her: "If I had maintained my rights, I would have disappeared, together with those who fought so hard for their lives."[36]

The *Ville du Havre*, about to disappear beneath the waves, listed to starboard. The ocean loomed closer, and Anna noticed an ominous quiet as the deck slid down toward the sea. All hope of survival was now gone. Anna remembered a time when Maggie had told her that she was afraid to die alone. She wanted her mother to accompany her. At the time Anna had tried to change the subject, but Maggie had insisted: "You must come with me into the grave." Anna remembered that she had answered: "How can you ask something like that of me?" Now an enormous grave opened up before them both.[37]

Little Maggie held Pastor Weiss by the hand. She looked up at him and begged him to pray for her. Her sisters said the same to their mother and Lorriaux. "God pardon us, God have mercy on us," answered the pastor. Then there was another cracking sound. Another mast broke and fell to the deck.[38] Maggie, who had been struck dumb, let go suddenly of the pastor's hand and went to her mother. The little girl with the glittering eyes and the brownish hair was completely calm and said, "Oh! It is all right now."

Little Tanetta hung around Anna's neck with her small plump arms. She did not cry either. Her big sister Annie, the family tomboy, continued to help keep Tanetta up, while Bessie clung to her mother's knee. Mademoiselle Nicolette and the two pastors stood quietly beside them. "Mamma, God will take good care of us," said Maggie and looked up at her mother. She had always been the most intellectual and artistic of the children. Her mother did not reply, but her sister Annie did: "Don't be afraid. The sea is His and He made it."

35 Weiss: *Personal Recollection of the Wreck of the Ville-du-Havre,* New York, 1875, pp.114-116.
36 Spafford Vester: Unpublished draft of *Our Jerusalem,* pp.142-157 American Colony Collection, Jerusalem.
37 Ibid.
38 Weiss: *Personal Recollection of the Wreck of the Ville-du-Havre,* New York, 1875, p.115.

Then, the Atlantic Ocean came rushing in over the afterdeck to perform its final act of cruelty towards ship and passengers. Anna felt little Tanetta wrenched away. She stretched her arm out and caught hold of the child's dress – but managed to hold on for only a few seconds before the cloth was ripped away. Yet again, Anna tried feverishly to search the water. All she found was a man's leg with corduroy trousers.

Men, women, and children were swirled around and around as if in some giant funnel. Some tried to hold their breath and fought their way to the surface again. Others felt as if the sea was boiling around them. Images of friends and relatives flickered through Pastor Weiss' head, as he struggled in the water.

Anna did not remember anything more until she felt a board floating under her. The next thing she heard was the lapping of the oars of a lifeboat. Her body ached, and she vomited seawater. Her hair was full of salt, and her thick dress was torn to shreds. She was alive! But, where were the children?

Anna knew instinctively that they had not been found. "Oh, God," she cried in despair, "I cannot live without them." Then she heard a voice saying: "There is a reason why you have been saved. You have work to do." Anna believed it was the Lord who spoke.[39]

Once on board the *Loch Earn* Anna heard word of the others. Pastor Lorriaux, who could not swim, had managed to cling to some wreckage, then later to a lifebelt. Finally, he clambered onto a piece of ship's decking that had stayed afloat. He watched as a full lifeboat sailed past 10-15 survivors, who were clinging to a wooden beam. When the lifeboat returned, both the beam and the people had disappeared.

The screaming died away as the ice-cold water gradually sapped the victims' strength. One man managed to keep his wife afloat until a lifeboat came to pick them up. When she was finally safe and he was about to climb into the boat, his heart gave out. Another man reached a lifeboat at the same moment as a woman. Fear had turned the man into a wild animal, and when the British sailors forced him to let the woman board first, he tried to bite their hands.

Again and again, lifeboats from the *Loch Earn* went out to search. Anna knew in her heart that her children were gone for good, but, as did many others, she ran to the rail each time a lifeboat returned. She saw a small girl around nine years old being rescued, but none of her own. Mrs Goodwin, her three children, Willie Culver and the teenage girl they had named 'the Good Samaritan' were nowhere to be seen.

39 Spafford Vester: Unpublished manuscript, p.195, American Colony Collection, Jerusalem.

Then, Anna heard that two of her own daughters had surfaced in the sea very near a man. He had grabbed hold of them and told them to hold on to his coat while he looked for something to cling to. First, the smaller one lost strength and disappeared, and, just before he reached a rescue boat, the other one also drowned.

After two hours of searching, 28 of the passengers and 59 of the crew were picked up alive. Two-hundred-and-twenty-six people had disappeared. When Anna heard that another lifeboat had reached the side of the ship, she ran yet again to the rail, but to no avail. There were no more survivors. When the final lifeboat arrived back, Anna tried to jump into the sea to die with her children. Pastor Lorriaux had to use force to hold her back.[40]

Captain William Robertson on board the *Loch Earn* was in despair. He had seen the passenger ship in the clear night darkness a long distance away, but was comfortable in the knowledge that motor-driven ships had to yield right of way to sailing ships such as his own. Just before the collision, he had watched as the *Ville du Havre* made a vain attempt to steer clear, at the same time that his own helmsman had made a similar hopeless attempt to avoid collision. Even after the accident, he had not understood the extent of the damage inflicted on the *Ville du Havre*, or that it had been split so dramatically in the middle. Captain Robertson had initially accepted Captain Surmont's shouted assurances that nothing serious had occurred. It was only after valuable time had been lost that he was able to put rescue efforts into action. If he had been able to launch his lifeboats some minutes earlier, his crew could have saved many more lives.

Lorriaux did all he could to help Anna and Pastor Weiss. The minister had been seriously injured and now lay on deck, nearly paralyzed, with his clothes covered in blood. No one had seen the Spanish and Italian clergymen. They had been given one of the rooms that had initially been reserved for the Spafford family. Anna found out that the Italian had been seen in the lounge with a large wound in his head. The Spaniard had been killed instantly when the *Loch Earn*'s bows went through the side of the *Ville du Havre*.

Despite the fact that Pastor Weiss' ribs appeared broken and he had difficulty breathing, he was anxious to know the fate of the Spafford girls. When he heard they had all perished he was filled with remorse.

"Oh! If I had only kept little Maggie with me, when she went to her mother!"

40 Weiss: *Personal Recollection of the Wreck of Ville-du-Havre*, New York, 1875, p.126.

"I must find somewhere to put you to bed, you seem very sick," said Pastor Lorriaux anxiously, but Weiss was in such pain that he begged to be left as he was. Lorriaux made his friend as comfortable as he could, covered him with a blanket, and gave him water, but Weiss soon became delirious, crying pathetically: "A drink! A drink!"

The *Loch Earn* had been badly damaged. Her bow was destroyed and the captain feared that his ship, too, would be lost. Luckily, there had been no cargo on board, so the sailing ship rode high in the water and the hole in the prow remained above the waterline. Leaks developed, however, and the water pumps were forced to run at full capacity. Robertson gave orders for the Union flag to be raised upside down, the SOS signal of the time.

Later in the morning, the wind speed increased, the air grew colder and heavy clouds appeared, looking like executioners, ready to send the rest of the passengers and crew into the deep at any time. The *Loch Earn* was more than 1,300 miles from the coast of France, but Captain Robertson nevertheless gave orders for one more search during daylight. Once more the crew put the search boats onto the water, but they found nothing more than debris from the wreck. At that moment, the watch on the bridge saw another ship coming their way. It was also British.

The helmsman of the cargo ship the *Trimountain* had seen the flag flying upside down. The ship was on its way to Bristol in England with canned goods, but it was not fully laden. For the first time, the charter company had made an error during loading in New York, and a large portion of the upper tween deck was empty. At the time, the captain of the *Trimountain*, William Urquhart, had thought how useful this empty space would be if they should ever meet a sinking ship. Even as he did so, he wondered why such a strange thought should come to him, but several more inexplicable thoughts were to follow.

About the same time that the *Ville du Havre* and the *Loch Earn* collided, Captain Urquhart asked the helmsman of the *Trimountain* to change course. He would later say that divine intervention had made him do so. Urquhart went to sleep fully dressed, even though the weather was fine, and was not entirely surprised when he was woken by the helmsman, who told of a ship sailing with its flag inverted.

The captain of the *Trimountain* offered to take the survivors to Bristol or Cardiff, and Lorriaux went into the cabin to give the pastor the news. But Pastor Weiss was too badly injured to be moved, so Cook volunteered to remain on board the damaged sailing ship with him. Lorriaux felt he had to take care of Anna and assisted her on to the *Trimountain*. The wind increased and it took more than three hours to transfer the other survivors from the *Loch Earn* to the undamaged vessel.

On board the *Trimountain*, the rescued passengers were squeezed into two small cabins. Their clothes were dried and they borrowed underclothing and woollen socks from the crew. Everyone in turn borrowed the captain's comb and a 17-year-old girl from Boston, Miss Mixter, combed the hair of each of the survivors. She had been saved, along with her 12-year-old sister, but had lost her father, mother and grandmother.

Two French ministers said prayers while Pastor Lorriaux tried to take care of Anna. She would sit silently for hours. Then, after three days, she began to speak a little, whispering to the French pastor: "God gave me four little daughters; it is He who has taken them from me. He will make me understand and accept His will."[41]

The young American student, who had teased Anna's eldest daughter about her religious convictions, now spoke to Anna. He told her that at the moment of sinking he felt his knees bend suddenly under him and a voice from the very depths of his heart cried out: " 'O God, save me!' He heard my prayers and now I, too, believe in Him."[42]

It took nine days for the *Trimountain* to reach the coast of Wales. The survivors arrived in Cardiff early in the morning of Monday, December 1, before daylight, and Anna was able to send a telegram to her husband: "Saved alone. What shall I do? Mrs Goodwin, children, Willie Culver, lost. Go with Lorriaux until reply."[43]

41 Ibid. p.140.
42 Ibid. p.143.
43 Original telegram kept in American Colony Collection, Jerusalem, later in Library of Congress, Washington.

Chapter 4

"It is Well with my Soul"

The telegram was delivered to Horatio Spafford's law office that same Monday morning, at 8 o'clock American time. Horatio had arrived late so he did not see the message until well into the afternoon. For many days he had been expecting a telegram from Anna with news of the family's safe arrival in France, and had been reassured by the thought that 'no news is good news'. When he was finally confronted with what had happened, he thought back to the night the ship had gone down. He had been attending a wedding.

Horatio sent a telegram to Anna, suggesting she should go to the home of a friend of theirs in Paris and wait for him there. He would come on the first available ship, together with their neighbour, Daniel Goodwin, whose wife and children had drowned.

Meanwhile, Anna and the other survivors were brought to London. The French shipping company obtained rooms for them all at the Charing Cross Hotel and arranged for them to get new clothing. As Anna was being served in one of London's finest women's clothing stores, she came to the decision that mourning clothes would be unsuitable. Why should she dress herself in black? The children were with God. She could even hear their voices and the expressions they had used: "Heaven is lovely, this is a happy place." Fragments of familiar biblical quotations that the children had often used flashed through her mind. "We shall see Him face to face... pearly gates... golden streets... no sorrow... no tears... no night there." Anna repeated to herself: "I have not lost my children. We are only separated for a little while."[44]

At that moment, she made up her mind. She wanted a light-coloured

44 Spafford Vester: *Our Jerusalem*, 2nd edition, pp.43-44.

42

dress. Horatio was going to have enough to deal with, and she did not want to make it worse. "My sorrow is my own," she decided, "why should I advertise it?" The others in the group did not think that a pale dress was appropriate for a woman who had lost all her children. Anna noticed their glances. But she did not bother to explain anything to them. In fact, she felt better prepared to tackle her sorrow once she had put on the new dress.

Once Horatio's initial shock had passed, he started searching for explanations for the catastrophe. Life prior to the Great Fire in Chicago had been like a wonderful cruise on a broad river. He had enjoyed economic freedom and spiritual fulfilment, blessed with four healthy children, a devoted wife, and a beautiful home. Now his world had collapsed. Surely it could not be that God had wanted to punish them.

When Horatio was on the train from Chicago to New York he wrote to his sister-in-law, Rachel Fredrickson, and asked her to go to the house in Lake View and make sure the children's toys and clothing were put away. The first ship to Europe was to leave the following day, and when he and Daniel Goodwin boarded the *SS Abyssinian Crusader* they took with them the newspapers from December 3, 1873.

During the trip across the Atlantic, Horatio wrote again to his sister-in-law:

On Thursday last we passed over the spot where she went down, in mid-ocean, the water three miles deep. But I do not think of our dear ones there. They are safe, folded, the dear lambs, and there, before very long, shall we be too. In the meantime, we will, thanks to God, have an opportunity to serve and praise Him for His love and mercy to us and ours… Please be so kind as to take care of the children's things so that they will not be damaged or disappear.[45]

Anna had accepted Pastor Lorriaux's invitation to rest for a few days with his family in the small village of Bertry just outside Paris. Anna was looked after by the pastor's wife, a practical woman with great understanding. Although she was overjoyed to get her husband back alive, she was also able to comfort Anna.

During her stay there, Anna received a letter from her husband, written before news of the catastrophe had reached him. In it, Horatio explained that their economic situation had improved and that he missed the children. Anna, for her part, often wrote down her inner thoughts.

45 Letter to Rachel Fredrickson from Horatio Spafford, December 13, 1873, American Colony Collection, Jerusalem.

On December 6, she noted on a scrap of paper: "Oh how sad my heart is without my birds. How little I thought when I left my happy home that I should set my foot first upon foreign soil alone."[46]

After some two weeks, Anna felt strong enough to visit her school friend, Bertha Johnson, as Horatio had suggested. The following day, December 16, she received a telegram telling her that her husband had arrived in Liverpool and would travel on to Paris straight away. He would arrive in Paris on Wednesday evening, together with Major Goodwin.

Daniel Goodwin wanted to find out as much as possible about his own family's last moments, and the next day he and Horatio visited Pastor Weiss. When the pastor described what he had seen and heard just as the ship went down, Goodwin said: "I am convinced that my wife and children perished in their rooms. I am comforted to think of them thus, passing all together into Eternity. They were united in life; death did not separate them; and it will not be long before I rejoin them."[47]

The French priest turned to Horatio and said he was sorry that at the last moment he had been unable to keep hold of little Maggie. Had he stopped her going to her mother, she might perhaps have been saved. "Do not say that," answered Horatio, who continued:

> One day on our voyage here, the captain took Mr Goodwin and me into his private cabin and said: 'I believe that we are now passing the place where the *Ville du Havre* sank. The reckoning was very carefully made, and this must be the spot or very near it.' I was deeply agitated, it is true, but I could not imagine my four little girls buried there at the bottom of the ocean. Involuntarily, I lifted my eyes toward heaven. Yes, I am sure they are there – on high – and happier far than if they were still with me. So convinced am I of this that I would not, for the whole world, want that one of my children should be given back to me.[48]

It was there, when the ship was still in what he later referred to as "the valley of the shadow of death", that Horatio was inspired to write a new hymn, which later became known throughout the world. He called the hymn: *It is Well with my Soul*.

Horatio and Anna decided to remain in Paris over the Christmas

46 Spafford Vester: Unpublished draft of *Our Jerusalem, Chapter IX*, Paris, p.177.
47 Weiss: *Personal Recollection of the Wreck of the Ville du Havre*, New York 1873, p.207.
48 Ibid. p.208.

holiday, but it was a sad period. In order to find something constructive to do, they spent the days before the holiday buying gifts for their friends' children. They sent the gifts with a message, which said nothing more than, "From the Children".

On Christmas Eve, Anna wrote a letter to her friend, Mary Miller, who had taken refuge in Lake View during the Great Fire:

> Yes, Mary – all are gone home – so early. How thankful I am that their little lives were so early dedicated to their Master. Now, He has called them to Himself. I thought that I was going, too, but my work is not yet finished. May the dear Lord give me strength to do His will. The dear children were so brave. They died praying. Annie said to Maggie and me just before we were swept off the steamer: 'Don't be frightened, Maggie, God will take care of us, we can trust Him, and you know, Mama, the Sea is His and He made it.' These were her last words. Maggie and Bessie prayed very sweetly. I have much to comfort me, Mary; they are not lost, only separated for a season. I will go to them – only a few years at the longest. Dear little Tanetta sang all the day before the shipwreck 'The Sweet Bye-bye'. If I never believed in religion before, I have a strong proof of it now. We have been so sustained, so comforted. God has sent peace in our hearts. He has answered our prayers. His will be done. I would not have my children back in this wicked world. With much love, your close friend, Annie Spafford. [49]

Now Anna was conscious that she had a task to fulfil, and when Christmas was over she and Horatio went to Liverpool to take a ship back to New York. There, they met their preacher friend, Dwight Moody. He was on a lecture tour of Scotland, but had, for the first time, cancelled one of his meetings when he heard that Horatio and Anna were in England. When Moody had read about the shipwreck in the newspapers, he had been struck by the thought: "This will kill her," [50] and he wanted urgently to speak to Anna.

But when the charismatic preacher saw Anna, it was he who broke down, unable to say a comforting word. He began to weep and it was the bereft Anna who had to provide comfort. When Moody finally recovered

---

49 Letter from Anna Spafford, Paris, December 24, 1873, American Colony Collection, Jerusalem, Spafford Vester: *Our Jerusalem*, 2nd edition, p.50.
50 Moody & Goss: *Echoes from the Pulpit and Platform*, Hartford, 1900, p.362.

his self-control, they began to talk about the future. He advised Anna not to shut herself away at home when she returned to Lake View. He was afraid that, strong though she was, she might become a prisoner in her own home. "Annie, you have to go into my work. Every room in your home is going to remind you of what your life was like before. You have to become so busy helping those who are in the depths of despair, that you will overcome your own sorrow," Moody told her.

When the childless parents finally returned to Lake View, they were met by the housekeeper who was standing in the doorway, crying. Inside, they found that well-meaning friends had enlarged photographs of the children, and put each one on a stand in the living room.

Some time later, Anna found a small letter in the children's toy post office, in the elm tree, in the garden. It was written in the childish handwriting of a nine-year-old: "Goodbye, dear sweet Lake View. I will never see you again. Maggie Spafford."[51]

Soon after returning home, the Spaffords learned that although Pastor Weiss continued to recover from his injuries, his colleague, Pastor Cook, had died, on January 29, 1874. Cook had volunteered to remain with his injured friend on board the *Loch Earn*. But the strain had been too great. A few days before his death, Cook had written to a friend: "I am strongly threatened with inflammation of the lungs. I have a terrible fever – BUT ALL IS WELL."[52]

Anna and Horatio found little support from the members of their Presbyterian congregation. The puritanical Calvinist theology practised by their church was rooted in the Old Testament and its strict interpretation of the Holy Scripture had remained largely inflexible during its journey from Europe to the New World. Many believed absolutely that illness and grief arose from one's own sins or those of the forefathers. One was a result of the other. Everyone around the Spaffords asked the same question – what had they done?

Horatio and Anna, however, were convinced that God was good, and that they would see their children again in heaven. They drew support from the biblical story of Job, who, despite having lived a God-fearing life, was afflicted by a long series of misfortunes.

Anna followed Dwight Moody's advice, and threw herself into social work to ease her pain. She was determined and refused to succumb to

51 Bertha Spafford Vester: *Our Jerusalem, An American Family in the Holy City*, American Colony Jerusalem, Ariel Printing House, Jerusalem 1988, p.30.
52 Weiss: *Personal Recollection of the Wreck of the Ville-du-Havre*, New York, 1875, p.208.

self-pity. She preferred to practice a form of Christianity in which she alleviated her own anguish through helping others. She thought this form of religiousness was not so far removed from Christ's own activities. Nothing less than a robust religious faith would be able to save her, and she threw herself into her work.

Anna had not participated in charity work since the time of the civil war and the aftermath of the Great Fire. She had always felt that good work began at home, and that her principle job in life was the creation of a secure home for her husband and children. Now, she asked Moody to assign her to work directly with women who needed help. This brought her into contact with a darker side of Chicago, far removed from the protected life she had known in Lake View.

Anna worked to establish a church crisis centre for married women, where their problems and complaints could be dealt with. Time after time, Anna heard about husbands who drank away their wages, and about fighting and abuse. Many of the poor women had grotesque stories to tell and vivid bruises to prove the truth of their tales. But when Anna and her husband attempted to prosecute these abusers, they encountered the same problem again and again. The police intervened, but the abused women then changed their minds and refused to press charges against the husbands. After a while Anna came to the conclusion that it was best to leave the couples to their own devices.

She also tried to help so-called 'fallen women' and she was shocked, not about the women themselves, but about the arrogance of the Christian elite and their lack of understanding. The first time she encountered this moral hypocrisy was when one of the prostitutes wanted to move out of the brothel where she was working, but had nowhere to go. Anna appealed to several institutions, but none would take the woman in. It was a huge disappointment, both for the poor woman and also for Anna, who had assumed that a Christian institution would be willing to do what it could to help a woman in need. In the end, the former prostitute, Minnie, moved into the spacious Spafford house in Lake View. Although she was lively and amusing, she soon became a burden for Anna. The weight fell from her shoulders, however, when Minnie married a kind Norwegian, moved out, and later had a child.

In November 1876, three years after the shipwreck, the cry of a newborn baby was again heard in the Spafford home. This time a son was born. He was baptized Horatio after his father and grandfather. Sixteen months later, on March 24, 1878, little Bertha arrived. She was named after Anna's friend from the international school, Bertha Johnson, who now lived in Paris. The little girl was also given the middle name of Hedges, after the family doctor, Samuel Hedges.

Finally, there was life again in the rooms of the white house and the surrounding garden. People who came to visit often found Horatio Sr walking about with two small children in his arms. He was heard speaking to his infant son about his heavenly Father and heaven as if they were the most natural things in the world.

These happy times lasted barely two years. One cold day, in February 1880, Anna and the children travelled by train to visit some friends outside Chicago. On the way Anna realized that the children had developed a fever. Anna got off at the first station, to take the next train back to Chicago, but it was delayed and together with the two children, she had to wait for several hours in the cold waiting room.

On their way home, Anna watched helplessly as the children worsened with every mile. Horatio was on a business trip out of town, but Peter was waiting at the station with the horse and open carriage. It was snowing, and a bitterly cold wind blew the snow onto Anna and the children as they sat in the carriage. When they arrived home, even their house was ice-cold. The servants had been given time off, since the family was expected to be away, and the stoves had been put at their lowest level.

When the family doctor, Dr Hedges, arrived, he diagnosed the children as suffering from scarlet fever. Young Horatio was in the worst shape. He also had a cold. Anna sent word for her sister, Rachel, who came immediately. But she was able to do little. Some time later little Horatio lost consciousness. Anna was able to send off a telegram to her husband, who barely made it home in time to become a passive observer of the death of their first and only son.

Anna could not bear to be present at little Horatio's funeral. She had developed a fear of funerals, and, as a pretext, insisted that little Bertha was too sick to be left alone with the nurse. She could not bear to think that her son was to be put into the ground, when she knew that he was in heaven. She also did not want others' pity. "I say again and again that God is love until I believe it," said Anna, as she attempted to retain her religious conviction, in the face of this latest challenge.

No one was invited to the funeral. The few who did attend knew of the couple's sorrow and came unasked. Very quietly, the child's body was put into a little white coffin and laid to rest in the family plot in Graceland Cemetery. Horatio arranged the funeral service himself, to the admiration of many and the criticism of some. The family became the subject of much gossip, and many of the details of their lives were distorted. Anna and Horatio, it was thought, were "trying to practise what they had learnt since the shipwreck, through heart-searching… wrestling with doubts and fears".[53]

According to the orthodox Presbyterian Church, which did not practice infant baptism, un-baptized children were doomed to hell. Furthermore, divine punishment was not confined to the world to come, but would also be visited on sinners in this world. Increasingly, members of the congregation were asking themselves: "What have this Spafford couple done for God to punish them so?" Many concluded that they must have sinned. The gossip was extensive and their latest misfortune merely confirmed these beliefs about sin and blame.

One day, several of the congregation's evangelical group arrived at the house in Lake View to find out what sins the Spaffords had committed. One of them, major Whittle, even suggested that little Bertha should be put up for adoption to prevent her from also becoming a victim of God's wrath. This request wounded Anna and Horatio, as they had regarded the Major as a close friend. It was the first of many crushing blows that were to follow.

In the Presbyterian Church, opposition to Horatio's views on sin and forgiveness, and on heaven and hell, was growing. Anna stood like a rock at her husband's side and spoke of her belief in God's love and God's hand everywhere. For her, it was unthinkable that the children's deaths were God's punishment, and that the youngsters could be suffering in hell. She believed that through his death Christ had taken upon himself the sins of the world. "There is no hell," she said. "Satan was cast down."[54]

But Anna's meek and mild faith found no resonance among the majority in the Presbyterian Church. The orthodox Calvinists had a firm grasp on the congregation. For years they had heard about God's heavenly wrath toward sinners and his swift and eternal punishment. They did not accept that the Spaffords were more interested in questions to which this theology had no answers.

Opposition in the congregation eventually became so strong that Anna and Horatio felt they were no longer welcome in the church. After a while they left the Fullerton Avenue Presbyterian congregation, together with their family doctor, his wife and a few others who dared to follow them.

53 Spafford Vester: Unpublished draft of *Our Jersualem*, pp.216-17.
54 Robert S. Fogarty: *All Things New. American Communes and Utopian Movements, 1860-1914*, The University of Chcago Press, Chicago and London, 1990, p.84.

These dissenters formed a new sect, based on the belief that sin could be overcome by living as the first Christians did. They did away with all forms of ritual, including the ceremony of baptism, which was replaced by a solemn promise to become one with God's will. The focus of the sect was the Spafford villa in Lake View, and the dissenters built a chapel on the property, where they held meetings every Thursday and Sunday. Their neighbours observed that the services were lively with song and cries of ecstasy.[55]

The 'Overcomers' forbade medical help for the sick and instead believed in the power of heavenly healing. Their beliefs attracted the attention of journalists in Chicago, who were curious about the group's prohibition of medical help and wondered about their belief that it was enough simply to pray.

Rumours spread that the new congregation in Lake View used spiritualist symbols. One reporter sought Anna out and asked if this were true. She answered that the mystical symbol the rumour mongers had mentioned must be a small ivory pin that she owned, with the head of a cherub. When the journalist asked what the basis of the sect's religion was, Anna replied: "Our religion is simple. We love God with all our heart and our neighbours as ourselves."[56]

The Spafford family's economic situation was gradually deteriorating. But Horatio did not want to sell the heavily mortgaged house they were living in. In order to pay off the loan, he began to secretly defraud his clients of money. His first victim was his own niece, Mary Murphy, the daughter of his deceased sister. When Mary's father also passed away, she had asked her uncle to take care of her $8,000 inheritance. These funds, plus others put in his care by two female clients, were used by Spafford to pay the installments on his own loan.[57]

Initially, Horatio told no one of his actions, but eventually he confessed his sin to his wife. Anna stood behind her husband. She understood that he had sinned, but she was also a pragmatic woman, who trusted him to correct the wrong he had done. Later, Horatio confessed to his congregation that he had used his clients' money so as not to lose his properties, promising to pay them back with interest when the value of his assets had risen sufficiently. Horatio Spafford told the congregation of his sin many times. But he said nothing to his clients.

55 Ibid. p.59, *Chicago Daily News*, December 18, 1879.
56 Spafford Vester: Unpublished draft of *Our Jerusalem*, p.229, American Colony Collection, Jerusalem.
57 Judge Thomas Taylor, Circuit Court of Cook County, Chicago, Illinois, January 29, 1900, Anna Spafford's testimony, February 8, 1896.

On the morning of January 18, 1881, Anna gave birth to a daughter. It was quite a difficult birth. Anna lay sick and weak in bed. She pondered long about what to name the child. Time and again she thought of the first four girls and of their names, but they could never be replaced, so she could not name the baby after one of them. For a moment her eyes rested on an illuminated prayer hanging on the wall: *My Grace is sufficient for thee.* She decided the little girl would be christened Grace.

While Anna was pregnant, she had dreamt many times of going to Jerusalem on pilgrimage. Following the break with their previous congregation, Horatio, too, thought of journeying to Jerusalem, where he hoped he could find peace and ease his conscience. The Holy City and Jesus' return often came up as themes in his sermons, and Anna felt that the Holy Land was, in some strange way, the key to the essential great truths. Jerusalem could perhaps help them to meet life's challenges, just as it had helped Jesus.[58]

Besides the desire to escape from a difficult economic situation in Chicago, both Anna and Horatio felt their faith also demanded that they prepare for the Second Coming of Jesus. For a long time, Horatio had been writing hymns and poems expressing his beliefs; *Waiting for the Morning, Lord How Long? Redemption Night,* and *Next Year in Jerusalem.*

The Spaffords could not rid themselves of the thought that Jesus' return was imminent, as Professor Piazzi Smyth had explained to Horatio 11 years earlier. They did not doubt that the Great Pyramid outside Cairo had been built with the power of God and that it was part of God's plan for salvation. The Scottish professor had explained to Horatio that the measurements of the Cheops Pyramid were to be found in the Bible. Its length and breadth, the height of the entrances, burial chambers and galleries could all be tied into historical events. Everything seemed to fit the prophecies in Revelations. Anna also believed Professor Smyth was correct and that the Prophet Isaiah had referred to the Great Pyramid when he wrote, "In that day shall there be an altar to the Lord in the midst of the land of Egypt, and a pillar at the border thereof to the Lord. And it shall be for a sign and for a witness unto the Lord of Hosts."[59]

The couple were excited by the possibility of being on the Mount of Olives when Jesus came back to earth on the last day. They did not consider settling permanently in the Holy Land, but hoped to find peace

---

58 Lester I. Vogel: *To See A Promised Land, Americans in the Holy Land in the Nineteenth Century,* Pennsylvania 1993, p.154.
59 Spafford Vester: *Our Jerusalem,* 2nd edition, p.25.

and comfort for their souls, and to gain a fresh perspective on God's purpose for their lives. Horatio wanted to live and suffer in the city where Jesus himself had lived and suffered. Before the Great Fire the shelves in his law office had been well stocked with books about biblical Jerusalem, but he knew little about the 19th century city.

The most famous American author to have written about Jerusalem was Samuel Clemens. The satirical newspaper articles, in which he recorded his visit to Palestine as a 27-year-old in 1869, were published together as a book, with the title *The Innocents Abroad or the New Pilgrim's Progress*. Clemens did not write under his own name, but chose as a pseudonym a phrase he had heard the pilots of the Mississippi using. As the paddle steamers negotiated a path through the shallows of the river, the pilots called out the different depths of the water. The second mark on their measuring stick was referred to as "Mark Twain".

Naturally, Mark Twain also described Jerusalem and the church built over Jesus' grave. On arrival he had squeezed his way into the doorway of the church through a cluster of beggars. He noticed a few Turkish soldiers standing guard outside. They made sure that no fights broke out in the church, since the various Christian sects each claimed a right to be there fought viciously amongst themselves in this most holy place. Even something as simple as deciding whose job it was to sweep a staircase could lead to fights between priests and monks of different religious groups, because it was viewed as an attempt to gain possession of the staircase.

Both Anna and Horatio understood the problems of schisms in the church. They had themselves experienced the way that good Christians could become merciless towards each other when disagreements arose. But they could not imagine it would be thus in Jerusalem.

For Mark Twain, it was the Turks who were to blame for the miseries and filth that surrounded the Church of the Holy Sepulchre. The author did not hide his disgust:

Rags, wretchedness, poverty and dirt, those signs and symbols that indicate the presence of Moslem rule more surely than the crescent-flag itself, abound. Lepers, cripples, the blind, and the idiotic, assail you on every hand, and they know but one word of language apparently – the eternal "bucksheesh." To see the numbers of maimed, malformed and diseased humanity that throng the holy places and obstruct the gates, one might suppose that the ancient days had come again, and that the angel of the Lord was expected to descend at any moment to stir the water of Bethesda.[60]

So wrote the American, referring to the Gospel of John. The famous author was even less generous towards the Palestinian landscape, dismissing it as dry and boring, in strong contrast to the picture that Bible readers loved to imagine. His writings were full of contempt for those American Christians who went on pilgrimages, criticizing them for not travelling with an open mind. The Presbyterians, Twain argued, looked for a Presbyterian Palestine. The Methodists, too, were hunting for proof that they had arrived in a holy land which conformed to a strictly Methodist understanding of what it should be. Twain claimed that the Baptists were the same, and the Catholics no better. All the pilgrims were seeking their own validations – that rarely conformed to reality.

So far as Jerusalem itself was concerned, Twain found the city so mournful a place, so depressing and lifeless, that he could not consider living there. But the Spaffords were not deterred. They did not intend to stay long in Jerusalem. They wanted only to go there to receive Jesus when he came – and that, they were certain, would be before the end of 1881.

---

60 Mark Twain: *The Innocents Abroad or The New Pilgrim's Progress*, Vol I, Harper & Brothers Publishers, New York and London, 1911, p.299.

Chapter 5

The Holy Land

The headline in *The Daily Inter Ocean*, on Wednesday August 17, 1881, ran "The 'Overcomers', a new religious sect, makes its appearance in Chicago". Another read, "H G Spafford the head, while the 'sign' is revealed through Mrs Lee." This article, spread out over nearly a full page, continued: "The worshippers embrace some of the best families, not only in Lake View, but in Chicago as well." But the readers of *The Daily Inter Ocean* did not know the newspaper was about to reveal that the respected lawyer, Horatio Spafford, had defrauded his clients of considerable sums of money.[61]

When a correspondent had appeared in Lake View to interview Horatio two days earlier, he had asked about his understanding of hell. "There is no hell," answered Spafford. He explained that everyone who managed to overcome his own temptations could be saved from the fiery kingdom of death and achieve eternal life on earth, but those who did not live in harmony with God's will and who refused to receive the greater light condemned their souls to a state of darkness. "But," Spafford continued, "they will not be tortured in an endless hell." The interviewer wrote everything down word for word, then asked: "Referring again to the subject of eternal punishment, do your people believe that everybody will be saved, the bad along with the good, no matter how wicked the former may have been, or how many sins they have committed?"

"Eventually yes."

"You believe then in probation after death?"

"Yes. We believe that the wicked will be purged of their sins, and they will eventually be saved."

61 *The Daily Inter Ocean*, Chicago, August 17, 1881.

"Doesn't it occur to you, Mr Spafford, that if this belief pertained generally among the wayward, it would only be an incentive to persist in their misdemeanours?"

"Such is not the case."

"If sinners are to be eventually saved after the process of purgation has been gone through, where does the punishment come in?"

"While they are upon this earth. We believe that he who commits sins here in this world will receive his punishment at the same time. Members of various denominations believe in everlasting punishment, but they are in the wrong."

The journalist then mentioned he had heard of an upcoming trip to Jerusalem, and asked straight out: "Mr Spafford, are you going to Jerusalem?"

"I hope to, some time," was the prompt reply.

"But you are going this week?"

Horatio did not answer. He got up quickly from his chair and said: "I decline to be interviewed."

"You will not answer my question, then?"

"I tell you I decline to be interviewed."

He repeated this phrase and let the journalist understand that their meeting was over. The lawyer did not wish to be caught in a lie, but also did not want it known that he and his family were leaving Chicago in two days.

The paper's readers, however, understood that, according to another source, "Mr Spafford in company with a number of the lady disciples intends to start today for Jerusalem. It is said they go to rebuild the walls, restore the Jews, etc. There is an evident desire to keep the fact of this intended pilgrimage hidden from the public."

The paper also contained interviews with two other members of the congregation who had not planned to make the trip to Jerusalem. Although they also believed that the world was heading towards the last days, they understood that this would be the beginning of a new period, as the Old Testament and the apostles had promised, rather than the advent of the return of Christ. The two congregants explained their faith and their belief in the imminence of "the morning of the Thousand-Year Kingdom", but the journalist probed deeper.

"Do you receive direct orders [from God] or do they come through one of the members?"

"Mrs Lee is Moses in the new heavenly order," one said, referring to Horatio's sister, Margareth Lee.

"Who are the other leaders of the congregation?"

"There is Mr Spafford and Mrs Spafford and Dr Hedges. These are among the leading lights."[62]

Hedges was bald with a full beard, which made his face seem longer than it was. He had no desire to go to Jerusalem having moved into the Spaffords' spacious villa with his wife and child some months earlier. He had been so overworked and depressed that Horatio and Anna had invited him to stay. It was not unusual for members of the congregation to live with the Spafford family for short or long periods. Anna's sister, Rachel, also lived in the house for a while, but she was on summer vacation in Minnesota at the time, visiting brother Edvard and his family.

Around 10am on Wednesday, August 17, Horatio asked his friend Samuel to come into the library. There he told him: "We are leaving Chicago in two to three hours. As far as this house is concerned I suggest you continue living here. I thought that a rent of $55 per month might be reasonable. Is that in order with you?"[63]

"Yes," answered Hedges, who was actually quite pleased to be able to remain living in the beautiful surroundings. "How am I to pay the rent?" he asked.

"You should pay $30 per month to my niece, Mrs Murphy, and $25 per month to Mrs Wills," answered Horatio, adding that he owed them money, but omitting to say why.

As the reading public in Chicago was gaining new insights into the beliefs of the 'Overcomers', the Spafford family and the others were aboard the river steamer, the St Lawrence, on their way to Canada. Their route, via Quebec, instead of through New York, had been chosen in order to avoid the same course that the Ville du Havre had taken across the Atlantic.

On board the river steamer, Horatio wrote several letters. One was to Samuel Hedges, who was responsible not only for the house, but also for the library of several thousand books, paintings, silver, linen, furniture, and the accumulation of all manner of things from over 20 years of married life. Horatio Spafford, who was usually so methodical and businesslike in all his transactions, even left the title deeds and other vital papers with Dr Hedges, without taking a receipt. The Spafford family had brought with them only a single trunk of clothing and a small box with dried flowers preserved from the funeral of little Horatio.

62 *Ibid.*
63 Testimony by Samuel P Hedges, June 1, 1897, Circuit Court of Cook County, Chicago, Illinois.

"My dear Doctor," wrote Spafford, using a rather poor pen. "Our Lord, through Mrs Lee, has asked me to tell you to send $3,000 through a bank transfer to us in London, as quickly as possible." Horatio was rather formal in his letters, and referred to his sister, Margareth, as Mrs Lee:

It seems we will not be in London very long. We received a blessed message today through Mrs Lee in which it was said that we are in God's Grace and that his strength will be expressed through us. When we arrive in Jerusalem, we shall see Jehovah in full splendour. Please be so kind as to get Mrs Will's address and send $25 per month and also tell her that it is at my request. I have written to Mrs Murphy and told her that you will send her $30 per month. She is a small, thin, black-haired woman. Would you perhaps ask her out on her first visit to be sure that she is the right person. You must write out the cheques in her name because her husband, D D Murphy, is not dependable.[64]

In Quebec, the Chicago group met a Canadian family, Otis and Lizzie Page and their 10-year-old daughter, Flora. They wanted very much to come along to Jerusalem. Mr Page worked as a dispatcher at a large department store belonging to Amelia Gould, a tall elegant woman, with a fine nose and silver-white hair parted in the middle, who was also a member of the sect.

Amelia Gould was among the few members of the group who had a lot of money. She had moved to Chicago together with her husband, and for many years had worked to help women living in the rougher quarters of the city. Through this work she got to know Anna, and in 1880, when it was clear that her husband did not have long to live, she went to live in the Spaffords' spacious house.[65]

A few other members of the sect also had substantial funds. Among them were Mary and John C Whiting who had left the Presbyterian Church in Chicago because of the way Horatio and Anna had been treated. The Whitings were expecting a large inheritance, but the rest of the group had rather little to contribute to the common pot.

In addition to the adults, there was 14-year-old Annie Aiken. She was the daughter of Anna's laundry woman in Lake View and was to be nursemaid in Jerusalem for Bertha and her eight-month-old sister, Grace. Horatio's

64 Letter from Horatio Spafford to Samuel P Hedges, August 20, 1881.
65 Folder: Amelia Gould, American Colony Collection, Jerusalem.

19-year-old nephew, Robert Lawrence, also came along. He was the brother of Horatio's orphaned niece, Mary Murphy, from whom he had stolen money.

The trip from Quebec to Liverpool took nine days. When they arrived in London, the $3,000 that Samuel Hedges had sent was waiting for them. The congregation had then grown by two: Captain William Sylvester, whose face was adorned by a large moustache, and his wife, Mary. It was said that in his day Sylvester had been the youngest captain in the British Army. Now he was an invalid and could walk only with the help of crutches.

News of the group had reached England, ahead of them and the Spaffords and their followers were described by a curious British press as, "a new sect of 'Overcomers' [who had] arrived in London with a band of these peculiar believers, including several children, en route to Palestine. They will proceed to the Mount of Olives, where they expect to receive a new and direct revelation from the Lord." [66]

From London the 18 adults and their children travelled by train through France to Brindisi in Italy. From there they continued by ship toward the Orient. They felt that nothing could stop them now. They had money, which they would share with the poor, and believed absolutely in the words of the Prophet Zachariah: "And His feet will then be upon the Mount of Olives, which lies east of Jerusalem," [67] They believed they would all be richly rewarded when Jesus came.

The first stop was Alexandria, Egypt, where the Americans spent some nights in a hotel, waiting for another ship to take them to Jaffa in Palestine. Early next morning, Anna heard a terrible noise outside, which she thought must be an elephant or a rhinoceros. She looked questioningly at her husband, and together they went to the window. Beneath, was a small, grey donkey. "Do you mean to tell me that this little creature can make such a terrible noise?" Anna exclaimed in astonishment. It was the first time she had heard the braying of a donkey. [68]

A few days later they took another ship to Jaffa via Port Said, and at dawn on Sunday, September 25, five weeks after leaving Chicago, they finally saw the Holy Land rising up from the blue-grey Mediterranean. The Land of the Prophets! The Land of Christ! They could see the golden shoreline, with sand stretching north and south. The coast appeared as a low and wavy contour, and towards the southeast, where the sun had just

66 Spafford Vester: *Our Jerusalem*, 2nd edition, p.64.
67 New Testament Zachariah 14:4.
68 Spafford Vester: Unpublished draft of *Our Jerusalem*, Chapter XI, p. 239, American Colony Collection, Jerusalem.

risen, lay the hills of Judea and Jerusalem, before which they could make out the fruitful plain of Sharon.[69]

The ship anchored outside Jaffa. It was a lovely town: white stone houses, huddled close together, stretched from the water's edge up onto the hillside. The passengers could not distinguish the old Crusader constructions from the more recent buildings, but they saw palm trees everywhere.

Fortunately, the Mediterranean was quiet that September morning, and after a short wait, the captain signalled to the men in rowing boats below the rails: "Come on board!" Usually this was the cue for a scuffle over passengers and baggage. Rival boat crews fought mostly with words, but occasionally they came to blows. Most of the passengers did not understand all the shouting since they knew no Arabic.

Finally, things calmed down, and the passengers were helped into the small boats. The sunburned, bare-chested men sang as they manoeuvred their long boats towards the openings in the semicircle of rocks and reefs. On shore the travellers heard friendly voices, and were lifted onto land by strong arms. After passports and customs control the new arrivals were taken to a square, surrounded by low stone buildings with flat roofs. In the middle was a well with a wooden cover, shaded by a large mulberry tree. This was the quarantine station, but since the American group had come from Europe, it was exempt.

The Overcomers were guided through this process by a professional travel agent hired by Thomas Cook & Son, the English travel agency, with which they had arranged their visit while in London. In Jaffa, the company was represented by two American brothers, who had previously come to Palestine as young members of the Church of the Latter-Day Saints. After a relatively short time the sect had been dissolved and most of its members had returned to the United States, but brothers, Frank and Herbert Clark, along with their wives, had chosen to remain. Also in the tourist industry was Rolla Floyd, who some 14 years earlier had catered for Mark Twain. Floyd had an encyclopaedic knowledge of biblical history and geography, and, as he guided tourists around the region, he could quote chapter and verse from the Holy Book and its relationship to specific places.[70]

Just like Mark Twain, the Spafford group had arrived in Palestine on a warm September day, but, unlike the Overcomers, Twain had come on horseback from Lebanon and had ridden southward. He had noted that

---

69 Sharon means 'plain' in Hebrew and refers to the coastal plain south of Caesaria.
70 Henry M. Field: *Among the Holy Hills*, Charles Scribner Sons, New York 1893, p.74.

these people, whose ancestors had known the disciples, looked swarthy, like American Indians. Some were tall and heavyset, but the women and children appeared to be undernourished and hungry. When Rolla Floyd was able to show his client finally the venerable city of Jerusalem gleaming in the sun, Mark Twain had been disappointed. "So small!" he exclaimed.[71]

In contrast to the American writer, the Overcomers found the Holy Land intoxicating. Bertha was too young to absorb all that was happening around them in Jaffa – The Bride of the Sea – but Horatio's orphaned nephew, Robert, took in every impression, and noted what he had seen. Rob, as he was called, noticed the town was surrounded by orange groves, and that the plantations stretched far inland. The streets of the town itself were narrow and crooked. Along the walls of the houses men sat making lamps, lanterns and small tin ships. They hammered at pots and pans, just as coarse and primitive in shape as those which Simon, the biblical tanner, had used in his time. According to the scriptures, the apostle, Simon Peter, had stayed at a small house in Jaffa, near the sea, that was occupied by Simon the tanner. The Spaffords were taken to the area by their guides. There was even a tannery there.

Horatio soon learned to adjust to his new environment. For example, on the first day he wrote the town name as "Joppa", in the biblical fashion. By the next day he had learned that in English the town was known as "Jaffa", and by the third day he wrote "Yaffa", as the Arabs did.

Jaffa laid claim to being one of the oldest towns in the world. The learned Roman historian, Gaius Plinius (Pliny the elder) and the Greek geographer, Strabo, had both written about it. Even before their time, around 700 years before the founding of Rome, when the country had been divided among the 12 tribes of Israel, the town was described in the Book of Joshua as coming under the tribe of Dan.[72]

Later, Jaffa was best known as the port town which supplied Jerusalem. Cedar wood from Lebanon was brought through Jaffa, en route to the Temple of Solomon. From Jaffa, Jonah was carried out in the belly of the whale, according to the Old Testament story. Here also the good Tabitha was brought back to life through the prayers of Peter the Apostle.

Jaffa had been occupied many times – by the Canaanites and

71 Mark Twain: *The Innocent Abroad or The New Pilgrim's Progress*, Chatto & Windus, London, 1921, p.514. Although this was written as a humorous travel book, the author was both anti-semitic and vehemently opposed to the local Arab population. His depiction of a deserted Palestine has subsequently been refuted by many historians.
72 Old Testament: Joshua 19:46.

Ancient Egyptians; by Phoenicians and Hebrew rebels; by the Greeks and Byzantines; by Romans, Crusaders and Saracens; by the Mamelukes; and lastly the Ottomans, who took control of the town in 1517. The Ottoman Empire had shrunk considerably since its zenith. Over the preceding 300 years, the empire had lost full control of both the Balkans and Egypt, but Arabia and Syria, including Palestine, remained under Turkish rule.

The Overcomers wandered through the town and were met by a wall of heat, a smell of oranges mixed with black tobacco and cardamom, and by unfamiliar sounds. They watched overloaded donkeys struggling down the narrow alleys, while camels strode disdainfully past. They saw veiled women, dressed in long robes, their veils decorated with two strips of coins, each with a hole through the centre, which hung on either side of their heads, like the links of a dragoon's helmet. Bedouin traders sipped tiny cups of black coffee, and puffed on hubble-bubbles, while small boys ran to and fro with hummus and bread.

To reach Jerusalem, the Overcomers had to travel by horse and cart along a road constructed 13 years before. This was the first road the Ottoman Turks had built during their centuries of rule in Palestine. Very early on the morning of September 27, 1881, the carts set off, carrying men, women, children, travel trunks and innumerable packages toward the interior. It was going to take one and a half days to get to Jerusalem. The first day ended with an overnight stay before the uphill journey to the city, some 2,500 feet above sea level, could begin.

Three-year-old Bertha Spafford had been afraid to get up on to the high seat of the cart. Her anxiety eased somewhat when the guide took her onto his lap, and when the little caravan passed through beautiful gardens with vegetables and orange trees the child completely forgot her fear of heights. Cactus and stone fences screened the orange plantations and the trees were irrigated during the summer by water pumped up from wells by so-called Persian wheels, and then directed through narrow channels to every tree.

The party passed the citrus gardens and continued through the yellow fields of the plain of Sharon, which had been devastated by drought. Wheat and rye had already been harvested the previous May, but the prickly pears remained, temptingly red, with fruit that was juicy and cool, even on the warmest days. The wagons then drove past small groves of trees – along the route that the Apostle Peter had taken nearly 1,900 years earlier.

From the town of Ramla, southeast of Jaffa, the road continued eastward, and the caravan of horses and wagons threw up red sand from the road as it progressed. Orange trees and citrus plantations lined the route. After a while the road began to wind upwards into the rocky precipices of the Judean hills. The Overcomers could see holly trees here and there, as well as hawthorn and wild roses. Their wagons continued through valleys, where the slopes were covered with terraces, and up over cliffs and crags, before dipping down again into a highland valley with olive groves and vineyards. Here lay a grouping of houses, known in earlier times as *Qaryet al-Inab* (translated into English this means Grape Vine Village). Nearby lived the infamous Abu Ghosh clan and now the village was known simply as Abu Ghosh, as it is today.

In the Bible, it was said the village lay on the border between the lands of the tribes of Judah and Benjamin and it was here the Israelites hid the Ark of the Covenant during the 20 years when the Philistines rebuilt Jerusalem. Later, when King David took the town, the Ark was moved into the temple.[73]

There were still 10 miles to go to the Holy City. When the caravan arrived at yet another high pass the pilgrims were at last able to catch sight of Bethlehem and the Mount of Olives and, in the distance, the top of the Dome of the Rock, the sacred Islamic sanctuary. Many who took this road thought their first view of Jerusalem was disappointing. Even though white limestone cornices, towers, minarets and cupolas presented a marvellous silhouette, the view could not compare with what travellers from the east would see, coming up to the Mount of Olives.

The horses and carts stopped outside one of the several narrow gates that gave entrance to the walled city, and the exhausted Overcomers were brought to the Mediterranean Hotel, just inside the walls and across from the American Consulate and Cook's Travel Bureau. The hotel was run by a German, Moses Holstein and his wife, both Jews who had converted to Christianity. Some members of the party began to complain, however, that the hotel had a foul smell, and a British guidebook warned travellers of damp rooms, poor food and bills that sometimes carried unexpected charges. But Anna was not worried about this when she and the rest of the family, along with the nursemaid, checked into rooms 38 and 39.

73 Old Testament: Samuel 2:6.

Chapter 6

The Lovers of Zion

In 1880, Jerusalem had little more than 25,000 inhabitants, and the roof of the hotel offered a wonderful view. To the east lay the Mount of Olives, an extended mountain ridge, which stretched northwards, and ended at Mount Scopus. Anna was familiar with the Mount of Olives from the story of David, who fled there from his son, Absalom, who was fomenting revolution.[74] She had also read about the dove that returned from the mountain to Noah's Ark, with an olive leaf in its beak.

The little flock at the Mediterranean Hotel spoke a great deal about the imminent return of Jesus to the Mount of Olives, and even the children were waiting in suspense. Their parents had told them of the prophecy in the Old Testament, which said:

> Then the Lord shall go forth and fight against those nations as when he fights on a day of battle. On that day his feet shall stand on the Mount of Olives, which lies before Jerusalem on the east; and the Mount of Olives shall be split in two from east to west by a very wide valley; so that one half of the mount shall withdraw northward and the other half southward.[74]

The Overcomers were ecstatic to find themselves at last in such holy places, and carried their Bibles with them wherever they went in the city. First, they visited the Church of the Holy Sepulchre, just a few minutes from the hotel. There, just as Mark Twain had described, they saw a sea of beggars and Turkish soldiers just inside the door on the left. Close by the soldiers lay a slab of marble, which covered the Rock of Salvation, the

74 New Testament: Zachariah 14:3,4.

spot where it was said that Jesus' body had been anointed with oil before burial. The rock had been covered to protect it from pilgrims who wanted to break off little pieces to take home with them. Many Christians crawled from the door to kiss and stroke the slab.

The innumerable lamps cast a golden light over the interior, which blended with dust-laden beams of sunlight. On either side stood candelabras and from the darkness of the ceiling there hung large lamps covered in pieces of red material. They gave the impression of red bats hanging with folded wings. Further back, in the shadows, visitors could see a round stone in the floor, with a canopy above it made of ornamental iron. It was said to mark the place where the Virgin Mary had been standing when Jesus' body was taken down from the cross.

The Americans also visited the Mount of Olives. From there they had a beautiful view of the Dome of the Rock and the city behind. At sunset, Jerusalem took on a golden hue, when the gilded sanctuary shone like a jewel, and the city wall around it looked like a protective chain. In the east, the pilgrims could see the Judean desert and even glimpse a distant view of the Dead Sea some 3,000 feet further down.

One day Horatio brought the group to one of the most sacred sites in Islam, *Haram al-Sharif* (the Noble Sanctuary, the site of the Dome of the Rock and al-Aqsa Mosque.) The Overcomers knew that Muslims believed in the same God, who revealed himself to the Jews and the Christians. *Haram al-Sharif* was also a holy place for Jews but they called it the Temple Mount. It was here the Temple of Solomon had once stood. It was considered so holy that even Orthodox Jews were not considered "clean" enough to set foot there. Muslim law also forbade Jews to enter the Noble Sanctuary.

It was also unlawful for Christians to enter the sanctuary. If a Christian group had entered this square some generations earlier, fanatical Muslims might well have killed them. By the late 1880s, however, a guard merely brought the group over to the Sheikh of the Sanctuary, the person in charge. When the sheikh heard that the Americans were planning to stay in Jerusalem, he explained that he had a friend who could rent his house to them. But before any rent could be negotiated, the little Christian group was given a tour.

First, they went to the Dome of the Rock, the finest architectural masterpiece in Jerusalem. The sanctuary had been built half a century after the death of the Prophet Mohammed and remains the only intact Islamic holy structure from that time. The golden dome resembles the sun, and it glistens according to the changing light of each passing day.

Before they were allowed to enter the Dome of the Rock, the visitors had to remove their footwear. A black servant gave them slippers and escorted them inside. The building was an unusual construction with beautiful designs on the ceiling and walls. Patterns of light played on the richly decorated dome from 16 vaulted windows of blue, yellow and green glass. Between the Corinthian columns, which supported the great cupola, there was a fence protecting the Rock itself – some 20 feet in diameter. This was Moriah, the rock on which Abraham had placed his son Isaac. And this was the mount, which later became a place for threshing, which David had bought for 600 gold shekels. The Jewish king built an altar there for burnt offerings and ordered his son, Solomon, to construct a temple on the site.

The guide told the American visitors that the footprint of Mohammed was visible on the rock. The imprint had been left there when the Prophet had ascended from earth to heaven. The handprint of the Archangel Gabriel could also be seen, the guide explained. The angel had held the rock down when it had tried to follow the Prophet in his flight to heaven. Eleven steps led down to a small cave under the rock, where Mohammed had knelt in prayer and which leads, according to legend, to the gates of hell.[75]

From the Dome of the Rock the little group went on to the al-Aqsa Mosque, slightly further to the south. This had originally been a church, built by the Emperor Justinian in the 6th century, and was thereafter the residence of successive kings of Jerusalem. Again, everyone had to remove their footwear before they could wander among the pillars of marble. Two of the pillars stood close together, and it was said that the person who could fit between them would also be able to pass into heaven.

Later, Horatio and Anna went to inspect the house they had been offered by the Sheikh of the Noble Sanctuary. To reach it they had to pass through the Muslim quarter to the northeast corner of the city. And it was there at the highest spot in the city that they found their house. It had been built against the walls of the Old City, over the Damascus Gate, the most attractive of Jerusalem's entrances which was also known as the Pillar or Pearl Gate, because of the beautiful stones which decorated the wall above it. The owner, an Albanian by birth, was a colonel in the Turkish police. He had built the house in the 'Jerusalem manner'. It was as if the builder had constructed a series of small houses, piled them together around a courtyard, as if they were dice, then added a few roof terraces. There were

---

75 Rev John W. Dulles: *Ride Through Palestine*, Philadelphia 1881, p.119.

no doors between the rooms so the occupants had to go outside to get from one to another.

Horatio paid one year's rent in advance, as was the custom in Jerusalem. There was not enough room for everyone in the group, so he rented a neighbouring house as well, which had an adjacent garden. The rent was 22 gold coins. This was on top of the 40 Napoleons[76] he had to pay for the larger house.

Anna did not want to move in until a fence could be built along the edge of the flat roof and terraces. The very thought that the children might fall over sent a shiver down her spine. She also wanted windows made on the first floor, since the view from that height was majestic, encompassing the Dome of the Rock, with the Mount of Olives in the background, as well as the black cupola of the Church of the Holy Sepulchre. It was also hoped that the house's location would enable the Overcomers to breathe clear air and escape the terrible stench which pervaded the lower parts of the city. The new arrivals improved the house in other ways, to the surprise of both neighbours and tourists. One Englishman passing by noticed "two unfamiliar objects standing out above the city walls against the evening sky." On inquiry he found out they were ventilation pipes. "Maybe," he wrote in his rambling journal, the Americans "wished to have a sanitated [sic] house" while they were waiting for "the day of judgement".[77]

Constant talk of how the Lord was about to come down upon the Mount of Olives created great anticipation amongst the children. One evening, when Bertha awoke to a brilliant full moon rising up over the hilltop in the east, she ran down to the dining room of the hotel. The three-year-old had never seen such a full moon and announced in a loud voice: "The Lord is come." When the adults just laughed, she returned, crestfallen, to her bed.

For both children and adults, waking up in Jerusalem was quite different from waking in Chicago. The first rays of light were accompanied by melodious tones rising from the narrow street outside the hotel. The sounds came in a pleasant rhythm, pita pat, pita pat, pita pat – from the hooves of unshod mules leading the camel caravans. Following the mules came the far softer sounds of the camels' pillowed feet, mixed with the rhythmic creaking of the straps holding their heavy burdens in place. Only after the sun had risen over the Mount of Olives did the city begin

76 One Napoleon equalled approximately 30 French francs.
77 C. R. Ashbee: *A Palestine Notebook, 1918-1923*, Garden City and New York, 1923, p.179, citing Torr, Cecil: *Small Talk at Wreyland*.

to seriously come alive. The merchants found their spots in the narrow streets and shouted out the prices of their mulberries, figs, old clothes and sesame cakes.[78]

The Americans had grown tired of living in the hotel, so they moved into the new house while the walls were still damp from the repairs. At last, they were able to create their own home with Jerusalem at their feet. The big, happy family settled well into the two houses at the highest point of the Muslim quarter, which the Christian foreigners called Bethesda. To start with, they had no blankets or pillows, but gradually they bought inexpensive mats made locally from rags, while Anna acquired cheap, red Turkish material that she used for curtains and which looked very decorative against the white-washed walls.

Some of the more practical members of the congregation, having observed the local craftsmen at work, began making furniture for themselves. Horatio's nephew Rob was particularly quick. He acquired a tool set and put up a workbench in one of the vacant rooms. Later, he made a writing desk for Horatio.

There was no problem getting domestic help. The community hired two Palestinian men, who were responsible for shopping, setting and clearing the tables and a number of other chores, and a Christian peasant woman who prepared their food. The housekeeper, who had the bearing of a queen, brought her daughter with her to work. When the two arrived in their long dresses, with embroidery on the chest and sleeves, sewn in the traditional designs worked by the women of the Ramallah area, Anna thought they resembled some of the most beautiful women in the Bible.

One day, the Spafford family went for a picnic to *Wadi el-Joz* (in English, the Valley of the Walnuts) which stretched northward from the eastern side of the city walls. On a hill overlooking the valley lived a Muslim family, and when one of the younger boys saw the foreigners, he ran down to find out who they were. Anna and Horatio had their local Palestinian interpreter with them as usual, and through him they found out that the young boy was particularly interested when he saw little Grace get her milk from a baby bottle. "My mother has twin baby girls she cannot nurse," the boy said, adding that she was trying, without much success, to find another way to feed them.[79]

Anna visited the house to find out more, and was warmly welcomed by the mother of the sick twins. Through her interpreter, Anna explained

78 Bertha Spafford Vester to *National Geographic*, December, 1964.
79 Spafford Vester: *Our Jerusalem*, 2nd edition, p.107.

that Grace had also been unable to get enough nourishment, but was now much better because she could tolerate canned milk without vomiting. Anna promised to get Nestlé milk for the twins. The company had produced canned milk since the middle of the 1870s, and it was available in Jerusalem.

Within days other Palestinian mothers came seeking advice about their children, and eventually several of the women in the congregation were busy helping Arabic and Jewish mothers.

Initially, many of the Palestinians believed the new group of Americans were missionaries, and that information and instruction would soon give way to religious preaching. When the Muslims and Jews realized the Overcomers were not missionaries, the houses on top of the Damascus Gate became a popular meeting place. Horatio also began teaching English at a boys' school in Jerusalem, the Alliance Israélite Universelle. Several of the students, some Jews, others Muslims, would later become prominent people in Palestine.

One day Horatio met a young Jewish classical scholar named Eliezer Ben-Yehuda. The slightly built 24-year-old wanted the Jews to stop using their various mother tongues, German, French, Russian or Arabic. Instead, he argued, they should all learn Hebrew, and he gave instruction cheaply in the biblical language.

The young Jew had come to Jerusalem from Lithuania on a Russian passport in October 1881, just one month after the Overcomers. On his passport his name was written as Eliezer Perlmann. One day the scholar went to the Russian Consul in the city and reported that Perlmann was dead. The consular officials refused to accept this, but the Ottoman authorities agreed to write out a new birth certificate for him with his new Hebrew name.

Ben-Yehuda was so determined that everyone should learn Hebrew that he forbade his wife and old mother from speaking Russian. Even though the language of the scriptures was dead, Ben-Yehuda was convinced he could bring it to life again for the benefit of all Jews who returned to the land of their forefathers. One day, as he and his wife were walking together in the woods, they sat down on a log to rest, and the young woman suddenly shouted in Hebrew: "Help, Eliezer! A scorpion!" Ben-Yehuda just looked at her and said: "Deborah, how many times have I told you that the Hebrew word for 'scorpion' is *akrab not akreb!*"[80]

---

80 Robert St. John: *Tongue of the Prophets, The Life Story of Eliezer Ben-Yehuda,* Melvin Powers, Hollwood, 1952, p.173.

Anna and Horatio approved of Ben-Yehuda's idea that the Jews should speak Hebrew. It fitted into their own belief that the language of the prophets should come alive again and that Jews from all over the world would come back to their promised land. They felt the Thousand-Year Kingdom had to be close, as the pace at which Jews from Eastern Europe returned to the Holy Land began to accelerate. Eventually hundreds of thousands of Jews would flee from the lands of the tsar, the result of his increasing persecution and the introduction of discriminatory laws.

On their walks around the city, the newcomers had come across several old synagogues in the southeastern sector of Jerusalem. The Americans, who were well schooled in the Bible, knew that the foundation stone of Jewish life was to maintain the covenant, which Moses made with God. The Jews believed that the Messiah – the Saviour – would return to the land and that this would be the beginning of a new Golden Age. During the time of the legendary King David, the Jews experienced their first Golden Age, and the new Messiah had to be of David's lineage.

Anna Spafford discovered that the Jewish community in Jerusalem consisted of two distinct groups. One, the Sephardim, had historically been associated with the Iberian Peninsula. But after being expelled from Spain in the 15th century, they had settled in North Africa, the Levant and other countries of the Middle East. Their traditional language was Ladino. The other group was called the Ashkenazim. They were Jews from Central and Eastern Europe, who spoke Yiddish or the language used in whatever European country they had lived in.

The two Jewish groups were organized differently and wore different clothing. The only thing they had in common, besides their faith, was their dependence on financial support and gifts of money from Jewish communities in their respective homelands. This so-called 'halukha' – 'money', was intended to enable those Jews who lived in Palestine to study the five Books of Moses, the Torah and the laws of oral tradition, on behalf of the entire Jewish diaspora. These 'students', some of whom were middle-aged or elderly, wore their hair in the traditional manner: their heads were shaved, leaving only long corkscrew curls hanging down by their ears.

The Jews in Jerusalem had no great difficulties with the Muslims in the city, and were perfectly safe walking through the Muslim quarter on their way to their most holy place, the remains of the old temple's west wall. The relationship between Christians and Jews, however, was so bad that Jews had to keep away from the Christian areas. The Christians had been taught since birth that the Jews had crucified Jesus. "Go, thou Jew, and be crucified," Christian children would often call at an adult Jew, without evoking any reaction from their parents.[81]

But it was only antipathy towards the Jews that united the Christians of Jerusalem. Children belonging to the Greek Orthodox Church would play in the streets separately from the Catholics, and the poisonous relationships that existed between the various Christian communities led to fights at the slightest provocation.

On the south side of the city wall there were two entrances. One was called The Gate of Zion, or in Arabic, *Bab al-Nabi Daud* (the Gate of the Prophet David). The other gate was referred to locally as the Gate of the Moors (*Bab al-Magharbeh*)[82] and immigrants from North Africa lived in the quarter just inside.

There was also a marketplace in that area, and by going through a narrow passage between several dilapidated walls, it was possible to reach a small square, bordered on its eastern side by a huge wall of stone blocks, each several feet long. This had once formed the western wall of King Herod's vast Jewish temple, a fertile place for religious worship. Even though there is no historical proof that this wall had ever been a particularly sacred place, the Jews of Jerusalem went there once a week to mourn their lost glories.

Practicing Jews would stand in front of the wall, the men on the left and the women on the right. They would stand or sit close together with their faces turned toward the huge stone blocks. As the sun set behind them it would cast a mournful twilight over the irregular shadows and the golden white stones. The Jews carried with them their ancient sorrows, passed from tribe to tribe through their traditional dirges. It was said that old Jews came to Jerusalem to die, and a rabbi would lead an undisciplined chorus of old men's voices and fragile women's tones, as they repeated the words of lamentation handed down from the Prophet Jeremiah:

"Because of the Palace which is deserted," sang the rabbi.[83]
"We sit alone and weep," answered the chorus.
"Because of the temple, which is destroyed; because of the walls
  which are broken down; because of our greatness which is departed;
  because of the precious stones of the temple ground to powder;
  because of our priests who have erred and gone astray; because of

81 Mary Eliza Rogers: *Domestic Life in Palestine*, London 1862, p.189.
82 Also known as 'Dung Gate'.
83 W.D. McCrackan: *The New Palestine*, The Page Company, Boston, 1922, p.129.

our kings who have condemned God."
"We sit alone and weep," answered the people.
"We beseech Thee, have mercy on Zion!"
"And gather together the children of Jerusalem,"

came the sound from the chorus, while their members rocked from side to side as if in hopeless grief, and those in front pressed their foreheads against the stone blocks.

"Make speed, make speed, O Deliverer of Zion,"

the reader continued.

"Speak after the heart of Jerusalem," the people responded.
"Let Zion be girded with beauty and with majesty."
"Show favour unto Jerusalem."
"Let Zion find her Kings."
"Comfort those who mourn over Jerusalem."
"Let peace and joy return to Jerusalem."
"Let the branch of Jerusalem put forth and bud," answered the chorus.

Then the harsh murmurs and antiphonal cries died down little by little as the Jews bowed and shifted their weight from one foot to the other.

Further west, in the Jewish quarter, the streets became congested with small stalls selling goods. Traffic pushed its way through in both directions, despite the fact that in places the alleys were so narrow that two people could not pass each other without turning sideways. Deep inside this mire, between the stalls selling herbs and tobacco, the pale faces of the merchants were just visible in the semi-darkness. To the uninitiated, everyone looked filthy, so filthy that one did not want to touch them. "Even the children had to be held at arms length," wrote a Danish tourist.[84]

Anna wrote to her sister Rachel in Chicago describing their new life in Jerusalem, and the Jews they had met:

Last Sunday, 220 Jews came and among them were three learned rabbis. Around 20 of them surrounded Horatio and the three rabbis,

84 Edv. Blaumüller: *Hellig Jord, Rejsebilleder fra Palæstina* (Holy Ground, Travel Photos from Palestine), København, 1898, p.138.

expecting a discussion. Horatio would not enter into any argument with them. He said only love would conquer the world, and before they left they seemed melted. Their questions made us realize so clearly how Christ had to answer them. They talk in the same manner now. 'Do you keep the law?' That is their great question. They are exceedingly polite to us, which they are not to everyone. They have invited us to their synagogue and to their Feast of Tabernacles.[85]

In the big house atop the Old City, Anna and Horatio would often sit up all night and pray to God that Jesus would come, but nothing happened in the course of 1881. It was not until an afternoon in May the following year that they had an experience which made them believe the Prophet would indeed come.

One day, the Americans left the city through the Damascus Gate and travelled north, passing the Jewish colony of Mea Shearim, a name taken from a verse in the Book of Moses about Isaac's seed corn, which gave him a return of 'mea shearim', or 100-fold in return.[86] They continued further towards some open fields, which were near what the Jews believed to be the grave of the High Priest, Simon the Just.[87]

There, Anna saw a group of people sitting in the shade of some primitive looking tents made of rags, sacks and mats, all of them dark-skinned, with dark hair and eyes. Both men and women were unusually beautiful. The men sported the side curls worn by Orthodox Jews, and many had long beards, but otherwise they were dressed like Arabs. They were rather short and thin, and when they stood up their stride was very graceful, just like the Bedouin.

Anna and Horatio were, as usual, accompanied by their Arab interpreter. This time, however, he had difficulty understanding what was being said. The strangers could not understand classical Arabic, and spoke a dialect their interpreter did not know, but he understood that

85 Letter from Anna Spafford to Rachel Fredrickson, American Colony Collection, Jerusalem, cited in Spafford Vester: *Our Jerusalem*, 2nd edition, p.108.
86 *Mea Shearim* was established in 1874. It was founded by five Jews who wanted to escape the dirt and overcrowding of the Old City. The founders had originally come from England, Germany, Austria, Russia and Turkey. In all, 114 Jewish families moved to *Mea Shearim*, building their own synagogue, market and religious schools. Under the rules of the settlement anyone creating "intrigues, disturbances or quarrels," was expelled. Ruth Kark: *Jerusalem Neighborhoods, Planning and By-Laws (1855–1930)*, Jerusalem 1991, p.107.
87 The grave, which lay at the entrance to the upper part of the Kedron Valley, did not in fact belong to Simon the Just. Inscriptions showed it to be the tomb of a Roman. But this fact meant little to Jerusalem's Oriental Jews who had long traditions of praying there.

they were Jews, and that they had come to Jerusalem a week earlier from their home in Yemen, southern Arabia.

The Yemeni leader explained that the Holy Spirit had come over them quite suddenly and, without any warning, they had begun to talk about going to the Promised Land. One of their rabbis had earlier written down a revelation that Venus would appear in 1882, and that a heavenly voice would say: "Today if you listen to His voice, it will be heard throughout Yemen, and it will cause all Jews to board ship and go to the Holy Land."[88]

Altogether, 500 Jews had been convinced by this messianic prophecy and decided to leave their homes in the Yemeni city of Sana'a. They sold all their belongings and set off on the journey to Jerusalem. The Jews had left Yemen with great expectations. There had long been rumours that a rich man from Europe, Baron Rothschild, had become the king of the Jews. The Yemenis thought Baron Rothschild was giving away large tracts of land in Palestine to poor Jewish immigrants. It was also said that the Ottoman sultan had issued a declaration that all Jews in the world could come to live in Palestine.[89]

When the 500 reached the Red Sea coast they were discouraged from going further. It was not true, they learned, that land was given away free. Some returned to Sana'a, others were fooled into boarding a vessel which took them to India instead of Palestine. The rest, around 200, went to Aden, where they got a steamship through the Suez Canal to Jaffa. From there they travelled on foot all the way to Jerusalem. Now, they had run out of money, but the Jews of Jerusalem would not help their fellow believers.

"Why, you are not even Jews, but Arabs," the local Jews had told them. Neither the European nor the Oriental Jews in the city wanted anything to do with the newcomers, and so the Yemenis found themselves excluded in every respect, being forced to live outside the city walls. To make matters worse, their skills were not needed in Jerusalem. In Sana'a, many of them had been among the city's foremost craftsmen, but in Palestine no one was interested in their silver work or jewellery.

The Americans were moved to the verge of tears by this story, and promised to help. For Anna and Horatio, the rabbi's explanation that the time had come for them to return to the Promised Land fitted completely with their own conviction that all the world's Jews would return to Palestine just before Jesus came back to earth.

---

88 Reuben Ahroni: *Yemenite Jewry,* Indiana University Press, 1986, p.159.
89 Yosef Tobi: *The Authority of the Community of Sanaa in Yemen Jewry,* Jewish Societies in the Middle East: Community, Culture and Authority, Washington D.C., 1982, pp.235-250.

Anna thought the facial features of the Yemenis were so refined that there could not have been any racial mixing among them. None of them looked anything like the Jews she had met in America or in Jerusalem. Was it possible that these people belonged to that biblical tribe which had been deported to Syria and from there had gone to Yemen? If so, they belonged to the tribe of Gad, one of the 10 tribes which had disappeared, to avoid being taken prisoner and sent to Babylon. The tribe stemmed from the son of Jacob and Lea's servant woman, Zilpah, and derived its name from Lea's exclamation, "Good fortune". after Zilpah gave birth to a son. The Hebrew word for fortune was *gad*.[90]

The 200 Yemeni Jews were starving and sick, some had malaria, others typhus and dysentery. Horatio explained through the interpreter, that the rabbis were welcome to come to the Christians' house just inside the Damascus Gate, the following day, for it was written in the Scriptures: "Blessed is he who increases gad."

Not all the Yemenis came, but many did. A rabbi with a turban and a white and black prayer shawl over his shoulders led the way. Behind him came men, women and children. The rabbi was calm and serious as he looked at the friendly faces around him. He prepared to show how truly thankful he was, not just in words but also in a visible way. While the Christian congregation sat agog, the rabbi brought out a small square box with long strings from inside his shirt under the shawl. He tied the box to his forehead. "What is he doing?" asked the children. "What is in the box?" The Americans believed the rabbi felt he was in a holy place. It seemed as if he wanted to demonstrate that the atmosphere in the room was comparable to that in the synagogue he had left in Yemen. And so they all got to hear yet again how the Jews in Jerusalem had rejected them.

"Is it not remarkable that our own kind refuses to help us; they say we are not Jews, but Arabs? We have told them our story, but they will neither believe us nor help us to find the man, a Jew like them, who stole and ran off with our holy writings."

"Is that the real reason why you have come to this place?" the Americans wanted to know.

"Yes. It was the theft of our Torah, which got us to leave. We felt that God was giving us a sign through this dreadful occurrence that we should return to the Promised Land."

The poorest and weakest of the Yemenis were given room in the house. The rest stayed in tents, huts or caves, just outside the city wall.

90 Old Testament: Genesis 30:10-11.

After a while, a formal delegation of Yemeni Jews presented themselves at the American colony's house. They told Horatio that a certain Orthodox Jew, one of those who had been deaf and blind to their prayers for help, was now persecuting them, accusing them of breaking Jewish custom by eating Christian food. Some of the older ones, in fact, had even refused to accept food and now were both weak and sick. Horatio understood how serious these accusations were, even if they were false, so he agreed to provide money, instead of food, and from that point on, the Yemeni leaders would come to the colony each Friday in order to receive money.

It was not long though, before the first of the immigrants from Yemen brought news that he had obtained work and no longer needed help. Even though the residents of Jerusalem were not interested in gold or silver work, there was a need for stonemasons, bricklayers and tilers. The Yemenis could handle such work very well.

But some of the established Ashkenazim accused the American group of attempting to convert the Yemenis. Horatio's Jewish friend, the language activist, Eliezer Ben-Yehuda, was able to stop the most extreme accusations. He explained that the Americans had not come to the Holy Land to convert anyone, Jews or Muslims; they were only in Jerusalem to do good works. The most critical ones calmed down with this explanation. The friendship between Ben-Yehuda and the Spafford family continued. When Ben-Yehuda's youngest daughter caught scarlet fever some years later, she was taken care of by helpers from the American colony and it was said the little girl was the first child in Jerusalem to have survived the illness.[91]

91 Interview: Valentine Vester, April 28, 2006, American Colony Hotel, Jerusalem. The information was given to her by Ben-Yehuda's youngest daughter.

Chapter 7

Jerusalem Fever

Despite their feelings of disappointment when the calculations of the Scottish astronomer Piazzi Smyth proved to be false and there was no Second Coming in 1881, the Overcomers were determined to remain in Jerusalem and to wait. While it was not an expensive place to live, money was obviously a worry. Horatio recorded a prayer in his diary: "Lord, if Thou dost send us money, we shall receive it as a sign of Thy approval of our belief… including our coming to Jerusalem and all we have done, believing it to be for Thee. Amen and Amen."[92]

Anna was quite content in Jerusalem. She felt a burden had been lifted by being away from Chicago, and noticed that Horatio also began to have a more balanced relationship to the city that was now their home. "Let's not think of the Holy City as outside of this world," he wrote in his diary. "One has here opportunities to meet people one would never meet at home under normal circumstances."[93]

One day, the Spaffords met the 'Prophet Daniel'. He had come to Jerusalem from the United States to meet a supernatural power who would reveal Daniel's true identity to the world. But the power did not come, and Daniel, his wife and five small children came down with smallpox. The youngest child died, and one of the women in the group who had taken care of the family became so exhausted that she too collapsed. At Anna's suggestion two of the Overcomers volunteered to go into isolation

---

92 Horatio Spafford's diary entry, for November 11, 1881, began: "It will be most for Thy glory, of what will most directly contribute to the establishment and triumph and peace of the Kingdom. But Lord…" American Colony Collection, Jerusalem.
93 Spafford Vester: *Our Jerusalem*, 2nd edition, p.78.

together with Daniel and his family. The religious community provided them with food and drink and after a while the 'prophet' and his family recovered. Finally, thanks to a loan from the American consul, Daniel and his family were able to return to the United States.[94]

Another community, the American Millennial Christians, was less fortunate. In 1866, one group led by a 'preacher' from Maine, George Washington Adams, collapsed in tragedy and farce. Thirteen members died, their crops failed, their food supplies ran out, and Adams, a ne'er-do-well, who was known to impersonate clergymen fraudulently, drank away the rest of the funds.[95]

Another foreign visitor to Jerusalem was a wealthy Dutch countess. She had arrived with the intention of building a house for the 144,000 people of Israel who, according to the Bible, had received the "seal upon their foreheads". She started to build a gigantic house, just outside the city walls, but the Ottoman authorities stopped the project on the grounds that it would represent a threat to public order if so many Jews gathered together in one place. The countess had not helped her cause by financing a regiment of Serbian revolutionaries, who were fighting against the forces of the Ottoman Sultan Abdul Hamid in Europe.[96]

Jerusalem seemed to be a magnet for eccentrics, fanatics, maniacs and schizophrenics. A sort of 'Jerusalem Fever' immediately infected them. Most of those who contracted the fever, also called 'The Jerusalem Syndrome', came from the United States or Europe. Almost all were Protestants. They usually claimed to be the reincarnations of famous people, kings or saints. Several of them dressed like John the Baptist or the Virgin Mary, and some claimed to be the Messiah himself. For a few, their fanaticism proved fatal. One man jumped from a church tower after he had received assurance from the Prophet Ezekiel, in a dream, that he would fly directly to heaven.[97]

That Jerusalem attracted eccentrics was no new phenomenon. Early in Christianity many religious extremists had come to Jerusalem to scourge themselves. They were followed by the Muslim whirling dervishes – who lived a life of poverty and asceticism – and found their way to spiritual ecstasy by whirling around until they lost consciousness.

94 Old Testament: Daniel 2:14, 6:23, Quoted in: Spafford Vester, draft of *Our Jerusalem*, p.359. American Colony Collection, Jerusalem.
95 Adam LeBor: *City of Oranges, Arabs and Jews in Jaffa*, Bloomsbury, London 2006, p.29.
96 A Goodrich-Freer: *Inner Jerusalem*, London 1904, pp.35-36. Quotation from John's Revelation, 7:4.
97 Amos Elon: *Jerusalem, City of Mirrors*, London 1991, p.146.

A series of self-proclaimed Jewish saviours also came to the city where the temple containing the Ark had once been.

For some the 'Jerusalem Fever' passed quickly, as in the case of one female pilgrim, who decided to enter a convent in the city and, once there, insisted on having her hair shorn immediately. A few days later, after realising that the life of an ascetic was not for her, she was found outside the American pilgrims' hotel, searching for a wig-maker.

The American sect was also viewed by many as eccentric. Other foreigners, in particular, smiled knowingly when they were told that Anna and the other Spaffordites camped out on the Mount of Olives every Sunday to wait for the Lord and to give him a good cup of tea when he arrived. Some of the Jews also thought these Christians were odd. Most of the Christian groups in Palestine were sponsored in secret by states or institutions. But not the group by the Damascus Gate. They did not go to services in any church, and had no interaction with the other Christian sects. They were also not missionaries. In fact they despised anything that smacked of mission.[98]

Many wondered where the sect got its funds from, because they never took payment for their deeds. After a while, people found out that a number of the Overcomers had significant fortunes in the United States. Among the original and eccentric people whom the sect befriended was a Dane, who later settled with his wife in a small stone house built into a rocky ridge just outside the city walls. He had worked as a carpenter in Brazil, South Africa, Congo, Algeria and Lebanon, before his odyssey brought him to Bethlehem, where he was able to earn a meagre living by making bridal chests. After a while, he found that carpentry no longer provided enough for bread and clothing, and he and his wife moved to Jerusalem, where they occupied their stone, cave house just outside the Damascus Gate.[99] There, he made carvings to sell to tourists, and worked as a tour guide, escorting visitors around a rocky outcrop resembling a human skull, that was known – for reasons that will become clear – as the 'Skull of Gordon'. This rocky escarpment derived its name from the British general who first identified it, the hero of the British war in China, General Charles Gordon, a man who was to become a good friend of Horatio and Anna.

---

98 Yehoshuah Ben-Arieyh: *Jerusalem in the 19th Century, The Emergence of a New City*, Jerusalem 1986, p.278.
99 Edv. Blaumüller: *Hellig Jord* (Holy Ground), København 1898, pp.165-70.

In 1882, the general was on sabbatical from the British army, in order to study in Jerusalem. He hoped to find the site of the Garden of Eden. He had already attempted to locate it in Mauritius and also the Seychelles, and he had made it known that he wanted to dedicate the rest of his life to study and deeper religious contemplation.[100]

Bachelor Charles Gordon, who was shy of women, along with his companion, an English priest, were often guests at the house near Damascus Gate. The general, though, had little sympathy for his host's ideas and interpretations of the Bible. He considered the colony's members a group of extravagant Americans, and disliked the fact that his companion, the Reverend Herbert Drake, was attracted to their life and teachings.

Gordon often sat on the flat roof of the Spaffords' house, reading his Bible for hours at a time and gazing out at the view. One day he noticed that parts of the rocky ridge just some 450 yards north of the city wall resembled a human skull. Some scholars claim that the Aramaic word for 'skull', as mentioned in the gospels of Matthew, Mark and John is 'golgotha'.

"Look," Gordon shouted to Horatio Spafford, "the rocky ridge looks like a huge skull. This is the true Golgotha! Not the Golgotha in the Church of the Holy Sepulchre!"[101]

Gordon drew a map and a sketch, which showed the small hilltop resembling the figure of a man, with the skull as the cornerstone. On top of the hill were an eye, nose and an open mouth. Below, lay Jeremiah's cave, where the prophet had allegedly written his Lament. The general was so obsessed by the place that he put up a tent on the ridge top.

While he was in Palestine, Gordon was asked by the King of Belgium to take over command of the Belgian Congo. He accepted. 'China-Gordon' was beginning to miss life in the field. He resigned his commission in the British army and left Jerusalem. But Pastor Herbert Drake stayed behind, becoming a member of the Spafford sect, no longer known as the Overcomers, but simply 'the Americans'.

General Gordon never did reach the Belgian Congo. He ended up instead in Sudan, where a crisis had developed. The nationalist Sudanese leader, known as the Mahdi, had started a revolution and his force had attacked the British army there. Gordon's valiant defence of Khartoum made him a hero in Britain. Despite public demand that Gordon and his garrison in Khartoum should be rescued, Prime Minister William Gladstone hesitated. After nine months of siege and just two days before

---

100 Lord Elton: *Khartoum Journal*, London 1961, p.13.
101 Olof Fahlén: *Nåsböndene i Jerusalem* (Nås Farmers in Jerusalem), Höganäs 1988, p.20.

the British forces reached them, Gordon was forced to surrender. He was killed on the spot when the Mahdi took over Khartoum.

In Jerusalem, Anna was left with only memories of Charles Gordon. Horatio had not been convinced by the general's Golgotha theory, but he had enjoyed debating with his guest, and had also kept several of his drawings. He had also received as a gift, Gordon's prayer book, but later gave it away to an American diplomat.

Neither Horatio nor Anna gave up waiting for the Lord's return, and remained convinced that the increasing pace of Jewish immigration, together with pioneering work in agriculture, were signs of Jesus' coming. Anna acknowledged there was much she did not understand, but she believed that God had spoken to her and Horatio and that He had found willing instruments in the two of them. They were both fully aware that to follow this teaching meant they themselves might die through some misinterpretation of the word, or be accused by the Presbyterian Church of being devils, or being insane.

While waiting for Jesus' return, Horatio spent much time trying to determine the number of Jews in Palestine, as he believed a sudden influx might indicate that the Second Coming was imminent. In 1883, he estimated that there were some 45,000 Jews in the Holy Land. His study was not exact, since the Turkish authorities kept no register of citizens, and because many of the Jews refused to be counted for religious reasons. They pointed to the Holy Scripture where it was written: "Satan stood up against Israel and incited David [to] number Israel. So David said to Joab and the other commanders, 'Go, number Israel from Beersheba to Dan, and bring me a report.' But Joab said, 'May the Lord add to his people a hundred times as many as they are! Are they not, my Lord the King, all of them my Lord's servant? Why should my Lord require this? Why should He bring guilt upon Israel?'"[102]

But Horatio Spafford did not just talk about the Jews, he helped them too. He had received some seeds from a friend in Tasmania, which he donated to the Jewish agricultural school, Mikveh Israel, near Jaffa. In his diary he wrote: "May a mighty blessing come through these seeds to Palestine." He thought that the seeds would yield rubber trees, but they turned out to be eucalyptus.[103]

Several years before the Spafford group came to Jerusalem, Jews in Russia had started clubs, political parties and organizations, whose objec-

102 Old Testament: Chronicles I, 21:1-6.
103 Spafford Vester: *Our Jerusalem*, 2nd edition, p.106.

tive was to prepare for emigration to the Holy Land. The organizations had different names, but they became known as – Choveiv Zion – 'Lovers of Zion.' They had no central leadership, and meetings were arranged in secret since nationalist movements among minorities were illegal in Russia.

As conditions for Jews in tsarist Russia deteriorated, these plans for mass emigration became more concrete. Members felt the people of Israel could be saved only if they established their own community in the land of Israel itself. According to one of them, their ultimate goal was to reach Palestine and to reclaim the political independence the Jews had lost 2,000 years before.[104]

The 'Lovers of Zion' eventually gained support from other parts of Europe, and groups were also formed in England and Romania. In an attempt to establish an organizational structure to arrange for the mass emigration, a group of young Russian students and academicians from the Ukraine town of Kharkov went ahead to Palestine to establish a foothold. They formed an organization, later known as 'Bilu', a Hebrew biblical acrostic. The letters 'Bilu' were spelled out by the first letters of the command: 'House of Jacob let us go.'[105]

In the summer of 1882, 13 young men and one woman from Bilu landed in Jaffa. In the small hostel where they stayed, they met a number of undernourished ultra-Orthodox Jews who were waiting for a ship to take them back to Europe. But the young enthusiasts were not discouraged and signed up for the Jewish agricultural school, which had been established 12 years earlier. There they were put to work by hard-nosed French agronomists, who had not the slightest sympathy for the zealous newcomers. One of the youths later explained that the agronomists had been instructed to drive this "foolish spirit" out of the new arrivals and convince them to return home.

Finally, help arrived for the 14 members of Bilu, in the form of two Jews from Jerusalem, who had managed to purchase land some miles from Jaffa. Once they had erected a couple of rickety houses there, the Jews called their new colony the First in Zion (Richon le Zion).

This was where the newcomers settled. They put their remaining financial assets into a common fund, and began to clear the land and plant corn and vegetables. But the harvest time had passed, and after two months money and food were at an end. The newcomers gave up. Five of

104 J. Frankel: *Prophecy and Politics. Socialism, Nationalism, and the Russian Jews, 1862-1917*, Cambridge, 1981, p.97.
105 H. M. Sachar: *A History of Israel*, New York 1981, p.27.

the original pioneers returned to the agricultural school, Mikveh Israel, while six others went back to Russia.

Around the same time, a group of Romanian Jews had settled on the west side of Mount Carmel, near Haifa. These newcomers also had no knowledge of farming, and their inexperience was compounded by the problems of mosquitoes and Bedouin. The mosquitoes drained them of their blood; the Bedouin stole their harvest and their animals. The colonists suffered from illness, the heat and exhaustion. Some moved into the towns while others went back to Europe.

There were several other experimental farming colonies in Palestine at this time. One of them, 'The Gate of Hope', which had been abandoned several years earlier, was revived by Jewish arrivals from Europe, who formed a community called Petah Tikva. They were supported by none other than Baron Edmund de Rothschild, a member of the wealthy banking family from Frankfurt am Main, which also had branches in London, Vienna and Paris.

Rothschild had originally been against Jewish nationalism and did not want to support colonization in Palestine. But after meeting the founders of the colony 'First in Zion' in the autumn of 1882, he decided to help. Initially, the young Jewish colonists were given funds to drill for water, and, later, a French agricultural expert came to Palestine to help them. Rothschild also gave money to 12 Jewish families who wanted to study at Mikveh Israel.

Another new Jewish farming colony, Rosh Pina (the Cornerstone), established in the north of the country near Lebanon and the Golan Heights, also came under the baron's protection. But Rothschild insisted that his help should remain secret. No one was to know that the famous Jewish financier was helping to create a Jewish Palestine.

This new generation of Jewish immigrants was different from those who lived in the older urban communities – the old *Yishuv*, the Hebrew word for settlement. The established Jews in Palestine wanted to preserve tradition. The immigrants – the new *Yishuv* – wanted change. However, the newcomers themselves fell into two camps: one had respect for the rigid, conservative, established Jewish views; the other wanted to create a land where Jews themselves would govern. For them, *Yishuv* meant 'state-in-waiting'.

The landless Arab farmers were powerless against Jewish buyers from Europe, who were intent on acquiring land, at almost any price. The owners of the land often did not live in Palestine, but in Beirut or Damascus, and, of course, they had every right to sell. The Jewish immigrants knew this. The newcomers, who bought and settled, knew full well what would happen to the poor Arab families who had lived and worked there for many generations. They had to leave their homes. When the Jewish colonists arrived at The Cornerstone, one of the immigrants witnessed something which would be burned into his memory. Only many years later did he write about his experience:

> Still ringing in my ears is the wailing of Arab women from the village of Jaony (al-Jaouni), now Rosh Pina, on the day their families left to settle in the Golan, on the east of the Jordan. The men were riding donkeys, and the women followed them walking and sobbing. The valley was filled with their lamentations. From time to time they stopped and kissed the rocks and the ground.[106]

The author, Yitzhak Epstein, asked the question:

> Will these dispossessed keep silent and accept what has been done to them? They will eventually wake up to gain by force what has been robbed from them by gold! Then they will take to court the foreigners who pushed them off their land, and then they may be both prosecutors and judges... And this people... are but a small part of a great nation which holds the neighbouring countries: Syria, Mesopotamia, Arabia and Egypt... At least in Palestine there is still no Arab movement in the national and political sense, but this people does not need a movement. It is big and strong and does not need a revival, because it never died, and never stopped living for a minute...Let us not provoke the sleeping lion.[107]

The author's concern over the poor relationship between the new Jewish immigrants and the Arabs of Palestine was brushed aside by the other Jewish colonists. Yet it was Epstein who was right. The conflict between Jew and Arab would pursue the colonists and their progeny for several generations.

106 Benjamin Beit-Hallahmi: *Original Sins, Reflections on the History of Zionism and Israel*, Pluto Press, London 1992, p.70.
107 Yitzhak Epstein: *Hashiloah*, 1907, quoted in Beit-Hallahmi: *Original Sins*, London, 1992, p.70.

Chapter 8

Among the Bedouin

In November 1881, the Ottoman authorities decided to stop all Jewish immigration into Palestine. They feared the Jews would bring nationalistic ideas with them. Most of the immigrants were European citizens and it was no secret that Russia and the other great powers had ambitions to gain influence in the region. However, the prohibition of immigration was not effective. The Ottoman Empire was in decline, corruption was widespread and the Jews found they could easily bribe officials to settle in Palestine.[108]

Anna Spafford objected to the fact that the Turks wanted to prevent Jews arriving. She believed the will of God constituted a higher authority than Ottoman laws, and that the Jews would continue to settle in the Holy Land whatever the Ottoman officials might do.

Anna was learning a lot about the city she now lived in. Before coming to Jerusalem, she had known its names and stories from the Bible, but now Arabic names and language had become a part of daily life. The Damascus Gate, below the house on the hill, was called the Pillar Gate in the local language (*Bab al-Amoud*), a name derived from a huge pillar at the entrance to a church that once stood 600 yards north of the city gate. Herod's Gate, to the northwest of the Spafford group's house, went by the name of the Flower Gate (*Bab al-Zahrah*), and the Jaffa Gate, at the entrance to the Christian and Armenian quarters, was known in Arabic as, The Gate of the Friend (*Bab al-Khalil*).[109]

---

108 Neville J. Mandel: *The Arabs and Zionism before World War I*, London 1980, pp.2-3.
109 The Hebron Gate derived its name from the fact that the road towards the city began there. The Arabic name for Hebron is *Khalil*. It was in Hebron, that Abraham, known in the Old Testament as "God's friend", was allegedly buried.

One spring day in 1884, one of the community's Muslim neighbours, a merchant who supplied them with vegetables, asked if he could bring some Bedouin sheikhs from the desert east of the River Jordan to visit the Americans. The merchant bought grain from the Bedouin, who belonged to the Adwan tribe, one of several living in the fertile farm areas between Amman and Damascus. The Adwan tribe had come to the region in the first half of the 17th century from the northern part of Arabia, and ever since it had resisted attempts by the Ottoman authorities to force its members to pay taxes.[110]

Anna thought it would be exciting to meet the Bedouin, with their curved knives stuck in their waist bands and ammunition belts across their chests. Some time later, a messenger came to Jerusalem from the Adwan tribe inviting Anna, Horatio and the children to visit its famous leader, Sheikh Ali al-Dhiyab. He lived near the biblical Moab Mountains, just east of the River Jordan[111](modern day Jordan) and had been released only recently from prison, where he had been sent after refusing to recognize the administration of the governor of Nablus, to the north of Jerusalem.

Horatio accepted the invitation, and their trip began early one November morning. The nursemaid, Annie Aiken, was to look after Bertha, while three-year-old Grace was to remain in Jerusalem. Anna was thrilled. One of the sheikh's sons had come to Jerusalem to escort the family and he and his companions were armed with swords, pistols and knives. Anna wished that her friends in America could have seen her alongside these wild-looking Arabs. From the Damascus Gate the group rode around the northeastern corner of the city wall in order to head eastwards down into the Kedron Valley.

To the right of their path lay a beautiful church, built on the spot where the first Christian martyr, St Stephen, had been stoned, lending his name to both the church and the nearby city gate. As with other gates, this one had several names: In Arabic it was called the Bab al-Asbat (the gate of the Tribes). It was also sometimes known as the Lion's Gate after the four lions (actually panthers, mistaken for lions) carved in stone above the entrance.

The Spafford family and their Adwan Bedouin escort then passed Gethsemane at the foot of the Mount of Olives, where, it was said, eight ancient olive trees with crooked trunks and huge roots had been standing since the time of Christ. They rode past biblical Agonia, the cave where,

---

110 Kamal Salibi: *The Modern History of Jordan*, I.B. Tauris & Co Ltd, London and New York, 1993, pp.26, 37.
111 Ibid. p.37, Spafford Vester: *Our Jerusalem*, 2nd edition, pp.151-56.

according to legend, Jesus had agonized over his impending death, and further onwards, towards the ridge between the high walls surrounding the Jewish cemetery on the side of the valley.

At the top of the ridge, below the Mount of Olives, the travellers had their last view of Jerusalem before their horses carried them into the quiet and dusty village of *Beit Ania* (biblical Bethany). It was here in *Beit Ania* (the etymology of the name is contested, and means either home of dates, or home of the poor) that Jesus had brought Lazarus back from the dead, and it was from this little village that the Saviour began his journey to Jerusalem on Palm Sunday.

Without a Bedouin escort it would have been much too dangerous for Anna and Horatio to travel from Jerusalem to Jericho. This was not because the road itself was dangerous, but because the travellers could easily fall victim to Bedouin thieves, whose ancestors had also stalked the road for many centuries. In the ancient Norwegian *Saga of Kings*, it was said that Harald the Red-Hair had "pacified the road all the way to Jordan and had killed highwaymen and other troublemakers". The Norwegian courtly poet, Stuv, had heard the story from Harald when he returned from his pilgrimage.[112] However, Anna was not concerned about the victories of long-dead Viking kings, as she rode down the windy road that separates the hills around Jerusalem from the Well of the Apostles in the valley below. After four hours in the saddle, the group arrived at the place where the Good Samaritan of the biblical parable, was said to have performed his act of altruism, helping the traveller who had been attacked by bandits. From there the road turned left, over some hills and past a deep valley. This, it was said, was the biblical Chalk Valley, or *Wadi Kelt*, where Elias had hidden as instructed by the Lord, and was fed by ravens.[113]

Anna was disappointed when they reached Jericho (*Ariha* or 'fragrant'). She had thought that the 'fragrant place' would be beautiful, but instead she found a town which was dusty and dirty. True, there was a Russian Orthodox hospice there and also a small Greek church, but they were of little help to the inhabitants of the town. Their conditions were worse than even those of the poorest Bedouin. But Jericho at least had a mild winter climate, in contrast to cold Jerusalem. The people were also warm, and received them with open arms, taking the travellers to rest in a refreshing citrus grove, after their long and dusty journey.

---

112 Snorre Sturlason: *Norges kongesagaer* (Norway's Saga of Kings), Vol. III, Oslo 1995, p.125.
113 Old Testament: Kings I 17:4.

The following morning, the Spaffords and their guide rode for an hour and a half to reach the Jordan River, which could be crossed only by primitive ferry. After another half hour's riding, the sheikh's son galloped on ahead to warn Anna and Horatio's hosts that the group would be arriving imminently. The nomads came out of their tents to bid the guests welcome, having never seen a white person, or a European before. Anna enjoyed the opportunity to rest on the woven kilims and pillows, beneath the shade of the goat-hair tents. She, Bertha and the nursemaid remained in the women's section. Horatio and the men retired to another.

The men slaughtered a lamb in honour of their guests and the Spaffords watched as the women baked flat bread – the same bread that their ancestors had made in the time of Abraham. They ate with their fingers and the host himself picked out the best pieces of meat and offered them to his guests. They were served raisin cakes – the ingredients of which Anna recognized from the scriptures.

One of the sheikh's younger sons wanted to give six-year-old Bertha a present. He had shot a small bird and thought it would be well received by his guest. Instead of doing as the Bedouin children might do – boning, roasting and eating the bird, Bertha took it into her hands carefully, dug a hole in the earth and buried the present.

That evening, a bonfire was lit and everyone sat around it. Later, when Anna was recording the experience, she found it difficult to describe adequately "the wild scene, the dark faces of the men, some of them almost entirely covered by the 'kaffiyeh' or head-dress arrangement, with only their bright eyes showing, and all of them armed with pistols and knives. It was a strange sight and, I must confess, it was a little frightening – one I had read about but never witnessed before. I have no doubt that we were as strange to them as they were to us."[114]

The following day, the Americans were taken to the mountain of Moab, a place Anna had read about in the Bible and had seen from Jerusalem. They arrived finally at the main Bedouin camp late in the afternoon. The women were separated and taken into their own section of the long tent, which had been divided in two by a beautiful kilim. Anna was received by the wife of Ali al-Dhiyab, a woman whom she thought had the bearing of a queen as she stood at the entrance, dressed in a dark blue dress, greeting the visitors. The Bedouin woman instructed her servants to bring mattresses covered in thin red satin for her guests to

---

114 Anna Spafford in a letter quoted in Spafford Vester: *Our Jerusalem*, 2nd edition, p.154.

sit on. The visitors' shoes were taken and they were brought water for washing, followed by lemonade, sweets and coffee.

After the meal – lamb and bread – came the entertainment. The tribe's poet came forward and sang in honour of the great sheikh. He told of the innumerable battles fought and won, and of the numerous enemies he had killed. Finally, he threw sand up into the air and said the sheikh had killed far more men than the grains of sand in the air – more than could be counted.

The women sang in groups as those in the Book of Samuel had done. Anna remembered the quotation from the Bible about the women who had met King Saul with songs and dances, with drums and music and shouts of joy, after he had fought the Philistines: "Saul has slain his thousands, and David his tens of thousands."[115]

After a while, Anna learned that the Bedouin had their own special laws and rules. They had been brought up to steal with cunning, to attack from behind, to kidnap and to kill in cold blood, but only under certain circumstances. A virtually identical crime could be judged quite differently, depending on the situation in which it had occurred. In one case, a killing could be looked on as a horrible crime, and in another it could be accepted. Anna was overwhelmed. Their customs had remained unchanged over several thousand years. The Bedouin had two or three wives and each had her own servant. Yet again, Anna thought how exciting it was to see how Abraham, Isaac and Jacob had lived. But at the same time, the Bedouin were feared, especially by people who travelled around the area alone. Not even the power of the Turkish military had been able to suppress them. Few dared to travel through the land unescorted, and Anna thought it amazing that she now was sitting there, with husband and child, being entertained.

The Bedouin's unwritten laws were based on high moral principles, and they followed a rigid code of honour. There had been others besides Sheikh Ali al-Dhiyab who had achieved fame and immortality through their bravery, and the stories of the Adwan tribe's leaders were diverse. When the Bedouin gathered around their bonfires, they told nearly as many stories as they drank cups of Arab coffee.

For Anna, the visit to the Adwan tribe in 1884 also marked the beginning of a lifelong friendship. Sheikh Ali and some of his sons returned with her to Jerusalem and lived with the Americans for three days. They stayed in the dayroom, leaving their pistols, rifles, knives and swords hanging on hooks on the wall. Now it was time for the Arab guests

---

115 Old Testament: Samuel I 18: 7.

to experience exotic dishes and new sounds, but by common agreement neither party suggested discussing politics or religion.

In the three years that had passed since Anna and the others had come to Jerusalem they had learnt a great deal about their Arab neighbours. Even though the foreigners were treated with friendship and respect, Anna knew enough by now to understand that many Arabs disliked Europeans for the same reasons they disliked Turks. The Europeans were foreigners, many of them citizens of countries which had ambitions to conquer land. At the same time, the Ottoman authorities had granted them tax privileges and other trade concessions.

Some Palestinians spoke about the Jews with hatred at times. The Christian Arabs were also at times negative toward the Jews. This was partly because the two minority groups were often competing for the protection and patronage of the ruling Ottoman authorities. But the pragmatic Anna had little time for the numerous tensions that existed between the different religions in Jerusalem. She had her own close contact with God. The nightly struggles with doubt and despair that she had endured in Chicago were over. With God's help the devil had been buried. "God is working wonderful with us," she wrote, "and the day will soon declare it to the world."[116]

116 Anna Spafford to Hannah Whitehall Smith, January 25, 1883, Smith Collection, Oxford, cited in Forgarty: *All Things New, American Communes and Utopian Movements, 1860-1914*, Chicago and London, 1990, p.84.

Chapter 9

The House of Temptation

It was Horatio who first came to the decision that he and Anna were no longer going to have a physical relationship. In August 1882, he wrote in his diary: "Lord, I have always up to this day been holding onto something of the flesh. Here, by Thy Grace, I lay down the 'Lot' life and take up the 'Abraham' life, the life which is by the faith of the Son of God. I make no vow, my vows are as straw. I thank God through Jesus Christ, the Lord. I crucify the flesh with its affections and lusts. Henceforward, I live a eunuch's life for the Kingdom of Heaven's sake. I rely exclusively, on the power and grace of God in Christ, *Jehova Shekina*" (Hebrew for 'God's Divine spirit').[117]

Anna had been against the suggestion, and the agreement they made with each other had been a private one. But when she later mentioned their pact to Mary Whiting, she learned that she and her husband also had no sexual life. Then it was not long before celibacy was brought in officially as the policy of the congregation. Anna mentioned that she had received a prophecy and a vision: the unmarried should live as Adam and Eve before the fall. Those who were married should live as if they were not married.

Despite this the sect continued to attract new members. One of the newcomers was a small, thin English woman, Clara Johanna Brooke. She was a missionary and ran a small kindergarten in Jerusalem, and first visited the Americans to learn about their activities. Sister Clara had been

---

117 Horatio continued: "No atom of praise will belong to any save Him! I am a miracle of grace! Blessed God, how patient Thou hast been with me. May all this company be one in all this! Amen and Amen." Horatio Spafford's Diary, 1882. American Colony Collection, Jerusalem. Horatio quoted Matthew 19:12: "and there are eunuchs which have made themselves eunuchs for the kingdom of Heaven's sake." Anna Spafford Vester: *Our Jerusalem*, 2nd edition, p.214.

warned in advance by other missionaries, who were suspicious that the sect did not heed God's word. It was widely believed that the house on Bethesda Hill was the work of the devil. But Sister Clara was not deterred, and when she eventually moved in, she brought many interesting books and pictures with her. To the delight of young Bertha Spafford, Sister Clara painted and drew.

The make-up of the sect changed during this period. Other foreign missionaries in Jerusalem also chose to join the Spafford group, believing the Americans to be closer to God than their own organizations. Jews and Muslims also came and begged to join the congregation, and all who wished to do so were baptized. Some of these Christian newcomers were the subject of much gossip and speculation. Many had become disillusioned with whatever group had brought them to Jerusalem, and broken away from them. But Anna never let herself be influenced by the rumours which followed them.

Not all of the new arrivals at the house by Damascus Gate stayed for long. Many found it hard to accept Anna's insistence that physical life should be made subservient to the spiritual one. She used the human body as an example. The various parts were led by the soul, and they worked together with the soul's will. But everything had to be subordinate to God's will. Only in that way would they achieve complete oneness. "I in them, and You in me, everything fulfilled for one goal. For only then can the world believe and see that the Father sent the Son," said Anna.[118]

To ensure that the members of the community would be able to overcome their desires and withstand the temptations of the flesh, Anna decided that everyone in the congregation should be exposed to sexual trials. She ordered that married men should maintain close contact with young women, and married women should be involved with men. When Anna saw that certain couples had difficulties being apart from one another, she instructed another woman to attempt to seduce the husband away from his wife.

It was claimed that Anna also had her tempters. One of them is said to have been Herbert Drake, 'the fine Englishman' who had first visited with General Gordon. Anna claimed to have received a divine message instructing her to become "one with another man, and it had occurred in consideration of her and her husband's spiritual training".[119]

118 Edith Larsson: *Dalafolk i heligt land*, (Dala Folk in the Holy Land) Stockholm 1957, p.30.
119 Birgitte Rahbek and Mogens Bähnche: *Tro og skjebne i Jerusalem* (Faith and Destiny in Jerusalem), København 1997, pp.41-42, 48-49.

Anna herself never confirmed whether or not this had been a sexual relationship. It was also alleged that she had been 'tempted' by Jacob Eliahu, a young man born of Jewish parents who came from Constantinople. Jacob was born in Ramallah, where his parents had gone to avoid the cholera epidemic in Jerusalem, and where missionaries from London had christened them. Jacob later attended a Jewish Mission school in the city, where he met Robert Lawrence, Horatio's orphaned nephew. After Jacob's parents died, he chose to join the American sect.

Jacob had a good ear for languages, speaking four fluently, and a basic ability in several others. He also had a winning presence, but, as with all Jewish converts, he was looked at disapprovingly by the other Jews of Jerusalem, who believed that his parents had converted to Christianity for purely economic reasons. Their criticisms did not bother Jacob and after a while he became an important member of the sect, eventually being adopted formally by Anna and Horatio, and taking the Spafford family name.

Jacob abided loyally by all the rules and unwritten laws, even the one regarding celibacy. Otis Page and his wife, Lizzie, by contrast, would not. The Canadian couple yearned to live together as before, but Anna would not hear of it, and they were expelled without funds. Their own small savings had been put into the common pot, and in Jerusalem it was difficult for Otis to earn a living through his previous trade as a shoemaker. After his wife died of tuberculosis, Otis wanted to come back. The only thing he asked was that he should be paid for his work. But Anna said no. It was against the principles of the congregation. The community had been founded on the basis that everyone within it should work according to his ability and receive according to his need. Otis Page remained excluded.

One warm September day several years later, the American colony suffered a setback when Horatio's nephew and adopted son, Robert Lawrence Spafford, died. Rob had suffered sunstroke while planting trees for an American friend who had bought a piece of land near a Palestinian village. The strong young man had not taken account of the extreme heat. Anna knew that Rob had a heart murmur, and was not surprised. Soon after John C Whiting, Mary Whiting's husband, died. He, too, had been a member from the beginning in Chicago.

When Horatio became ill some time later, Anna decided to move him out of the Old City. It was warm, and Anna was able to erect a tent on a small hill planted with fig trees and vines, not far from the walls of the city, where there was a well with clean water nearby.

The hill was owned by an American woman, Alice Davis, who had come to Jerusalem just after the Spafford group. Her dream had been to print an English language newspaper in the city. The paper was called, *The Age to Come*. Anna stayed by her husband's side most of the time and Horatio felt more comfortable in the tent where it was cooler. He even managed to write letters to friends in the US and Europe.

By now, Anna had become the most powerful person in the congregation. She led prayers and organized much of the daily work. No one in the group objected to her style of leadership, but not everyone on the outside liked what they saw. One of the critics was Alice Davis, the woman who owned the hill where Horatio lay ill. She visited him frequently and listened with interest to the conversations between Horatio and others in the sect. While his other visitors said little, Horatio spoke a great deal. When Alice Davis later came into open conflict with Anna, she wrote a letter to the US consul stating that Horatio had complained he "was no longer in harmony with the principles of the house" in which he lived. He felt "unhappy to a degree of dejection and misery". Miss Davis had also learned, she said, that Horatio had been "condemned for unfaithfulness". The others in the sect acted as if he did not exist, and no one was allowed to talk with him for 40 days.[120]

Alice Davis claimed that the sick man suffered shameful abuse and that the worst perpetrator was Anna. She cursed at her husband openly – this woman who had been an orphan when Horatio had met her, whom he had educated and married.

Horatio had contracted malaria and spoke in delirium. He became weaker each day. But Anna could not bring herself to think about death, and told her children that their father was not going to die. Only when Horatio lost consciousness, did the teenaged Bertha understand that the end was near.

Anna decided her husband should be driven back to the house in the Old City. That night, Bertha saw that a huge red moon was hanging above the Mount of Olives. She thought that everything was so still. Her father's breathing became more laboured. Anna felt his pulse, which was weak and irregular, and a little later she left his bedside. Bertha and the children's nurse remained in the room, while Anna went out into the herb garden. Not a leaf was moving on the trees that September evening, and in the moonlight Anna stood by herself. She looked up towards the sky, opened her arms and

---

120 Helga Dudman & Ruth Kark: *The American Colony, Scenes from a Jerusalem Saga*, Carta, Jerusalem 1998, p.81.

shouted: "I will dance before the Lord," meaning she would do that which was most difficult and would not give in to overwhelming sorrow. [121]

When Anna returned to her dying husband, he opened his eyes, looked at her and said: "Annie, I have experienced a great joy, I have seen wonderful things." He tried to say more, but was too weak. Anna turned to Bertha and a nurse and said: "Bertha, stay with father until the end. I must go away." Then she left. A little later, Horatio stopped breathing and Bertha ran out to her mother who was sitting with little Grace on her lap. With her throat choking with sorrow she was able to say: "He knows it all now. He has seen Him face to face. We must not sorrow like those who have no hope." Horatio Gates Spafford was just one month short of his 60th birthday. He died on September 25, 1888. It was seven years to the day since his family had arrived in Palestine.

The new widow of 46 was unable to cry, but that was not the case with the fatherless Bertha. She hid in one of the niches in the city wall just behind the house and let the tears flow. Anna, so strong in all other respects, could not bear to be present at the burial. She felt the same as she had when her son had died, so when the funeral party walked behind Horatio's coffin on the dusty road from the Damascus Gate to the little graveyard on Mount Zion, southwest of the city walls, Anna sat at home. Horses pulled the carriage with the coffin. As when her own father was buried, Anna tried to cover the rough planks with greenery. In the American wilderness she had used silver fir and laurel. Here she found branches of pine and pepper tree.

When Bertha and Grace returned home after the burial, they found that Anna was too ill to talk to them. The little girls sat outside her door for several hours and watched the faces of the adults who came and went. The same thing happened the following day. The children looked for signs that their mother was getting better. They did not understand what depression was.

After two weeks, Anna was finally persuaded to leave the house. A bed was prepared for her in a large horse-drawn carriage and she was driven to Jaffa to be cared for by Rolla Floyd, the tour guide, and his wife. After a while there, she was invited to stay with Baron Plato von Ustinow and his wife, Baroness Magdalena.

Anna had heard that the baroness was an Ethiopian princess. In reality she was the daughter of a Swiss missionary and a member of the Ethiopian court. The missionary, who had been stationed in East

121 Spafford Vester: *Our Jerusalem*, 2nd edition, pp.164-65.

Africa, had also been an enthusiastic manufacturer of weapons. Emperor Theodore of Abyssinia, who called himself Negus Negesti – King of Kings – commissioned the missionary to design and build a cannon.[122]

When the cannon was finished, the emperor, who was afraid that the missionary would defect to the enemy, took him hostage and chained him to the cannon. This inconvenience did not, however, prevent the missionary from maintaining close contact with the women in the court, one of whom became pregnant by him and subsequently gave birth to a girl. Meanwhile, the eccentric emperor had arrested all foreigners in the country, including the British diplomatic envoy. As a result the British went to war with Abyssinia, during the course of which the poor missionary – by this time also a new father – was blown up by his own cannon. The emperor committed suicide, and the baby girl, born just after the battle of Magdala, was named Magdalena.

Some years later, Magdalena came to Palestine and at the age of 22, she married 55-year-old Baron Plato von Ustinow, who now offered to take care of the grieving Anna. The couple had a large house with a wonderful garden in Jaffa, filled with unusual plants, with monkeys and cockatoos. The baron told stories, played the piano and shared Anna's ideas.

Baron von Ustinow also lived with two seemingly irreconcilable identities. His way of life appeared to combine the self-denial of a German Pietist and religious benefactor, with the indulgence of an eccentric Russian aristocrat, who lived in luxury and bathed naked in the Mediterranean.

Anna was fascinated to hear stories of Plato von Ustinow's previous life. He had been an officer in the tsar's personal guard. In the course of manoeuvres he had fallen from his horse and been bedridden for a year, followed by nine years walking on crutches. During this time he read a lot, and thought even more, particularly after meeting a priest in a colony of German Protestants on the other side of the Volga River. The priest had a beautiful daughter, in whom the baron found both spiritual and emotional fulfilment.

The Russian aristocrat, Plato Grigorievich Ustinov who, at the time, wrote his name with a 'v' decided to attach himself to both the Lutheran Church and the priest's daughter. But at that point Ustinov encountered a problem. All Russian officers had to swear an annual oath of loyalty to the tsar. Since the tsar was the head of the Orthodox Church, the oath was, in effect, one of loyalty to the church. The newly 'saved' Russian Lutheran did not want to do this, but a refusal would mean certain exile to Siberia.

---

122 Peter Ustinov: *Kjære Meg* (Dear Me), Oslo 1978, pp.14-15.

Fortunately, Ustinov had an influential uncle, who was Russia's ambassador in Constantinople. When scandalous rumours of the family's disgrace reached the Turkish capital, the ambassador returned immediately from the Golden Horn to the tsar's palace. He ended up playing cards with the tsar while they drank vodka in large quantities. The game and the atmosphere resulted in the tsar rescinding the sentence of 40 years exile. Plato Grigorievicch Ustinov freed his serfs and sold his large properties; then he went to Stuttgart, the capital of the small cultured monarchy of Württemberg.

Equally important in determining Ustinov's fate was the tsar's daughter. She had been influenced by Western ideas and was well disposed towards those who had suffered under her father's strict judgements. As a result of her intervention Plato Griogerievich Ustinov got his title back. But he now dropped his middle name, added 'von' and exchanged the 'v' for 'w' in his last name to become Plato von Ustinow.

Anna had met the baron shortly after the Americans had arrived in Palestine in 1881, and they had been guests in each other's houses many times. In addition to his residence in Jaffa, Baron von Ustinow also had a house in the Holy City, not far from the Jaffa Gate. He had arrived in Jaffa 12 years before Anna, just after a German colony of Christian Protestants had been established there. The Germans had taken over buildings from the first American congregation in Jaffa and then built others.

Plato von Ustinow bought one of these houses and converted one floor into a hospital for Jewish immigrants, where patients were treated by a Jewish doctor from Germany. The baron shared Anna's belief that the return of the Jews to Palestine was a prerequisite for the return of the Messiah. Besides his religious interests, von Ustinow was also interested in archaeology. He became a passionate collector, buying everything from old Jewish gravestones to prehistoric ceramics and Muslim Arab calligraphy. He collected Roman, Greek and Arabic coins, Bedouin jewellery and knick-knacks – with little consideration of ethnic or topographical distinction. It was said that his goal was to create a collection for the Hermitage Museum in St Petersburg, one of the largest in the world. Unknown to the baron or the grieving Anna, a large part of his collection would end up in Norway.[123]

There was one part of the baron's earlier life that Anna learnt little about – the scandal involving his first wife, the daughter of the German

123 Laszlo Berczelly: *Ustinow-samlingens historie*, (The History of the Ustinow Collection) Nicolay, *Arkeologisk tidsskift*, No. 71, 1997, pp.30-39.

priest, who ministered to the colony on the side of the Volga River. On his wedding night, the pious von Ustinow had discovered that his wife was not a virgin. He subsequently refused all sexual contact with her. Divorce for the baron, however, was even more unacceptable than infidelity, so to the outside world he pretended that nothing was wrong, and closed his eyes to his wife's further adventures.

After a while, the baron sought new horizons and moved to Italy, together with the baroness, who on paper was still his spouse. They built a villa near Genoa and lived there under the same roof, but slept in separate beds. The baroness disliked the arrangement and began an intense relationship with the gardener. Such was their passion that the two decided to kill the baron. Part of the plot hinged on taking advantage of the former officer's hot-blooded temperament. The gardener blocked the barrel of the baron's pistol with lead, with the intention of provoking him to fire. If the baron then attempted to shoot the gardener, the bullet would rebound into him. The murder attempt did not go as planned, because von Ustinow was also a man with a keen sense of order. He soon discovered that someone had tampered with his weapon, and avoided pulling the trigger. Only then did the baron choose divorce.

In 1869, the wealthy, unattached and deeply religious baron decided to go to the Holy Land. Nineteen years later, he demonstrated that he was a truly compassionate Samaritan towards the grieving Anna Spafford. After some weeks of luxury and peace, Anna felt strong enough to meet her children and begin a new life as the leader of the sect, under the name of Mother Anna.

Chapter 10

Dressed for Trial

Anna Spafford was not the first woman to lead a religious sect in Palestine. She followed in the footsteps of Clorinda Minor, another charismatic American, whose belief in the Second Coming had taken her from a comfortable life in Philadelphia in 1851 into agriculture in Palestine. After her disappointment in a failed prophecy that the end of days would take place in October 1844, Mrs Minor concluded that the Holy Land was not yet adequately prepared for such an event. So she decided it would be her mission to teach the poverty-stricken Jews of Palestine how to work the soil. She had been obsessed by the idea that all Christians had to participate in preparations for the return of the Jews. But her colony dwindled, and when she died in 1855, only her son and an adopted daughter remained. The Minor scheme was perpetuated by its incorporation into another colony, the American Agriculture Mission.[124]

Neither was Anna the first sect leader to preach celibacy. Another American woman, Jemima Wilkinson, had done so to her congregation, before Anna was born. As a young woman, Jemima, tall and graceful, with dark hair and dark eyes, had a magnetic personality and a powerful preaching style that created fervent disciples. She was beset by a debilitating illness, which culminated in a fevered, ecstatic, trance during which she sermonized, subsequently collapsing and being declared dead. After she had already been placed in a coffin, she revived and knocked from the inside. This experience motivated her to claim she was an incarnation of Jesus. Wilkinson's sect built a permanent home in Jerusalem Township, overlooking the Valley of the Brook of Kedron, in the State of New York.

124 Lester I. Vogel: *To See a Promised Land, Americans and the Holy Land in the Nineteenth Century*, The Pennsylvania State University Press, 1993, pp.129-30.

After her death in 1819, her body was left unburied to await her rising from the dead, and the faithful maintained this expectation for decades, despite her body's visible decay.

Sixty years later, Anna Spafford led her congregation in Jerusalem, not just with the help of her faith and frequent messages from God, but also with exceptional charisma and the willpower of a despot. It was said that Anna was so certain that Jesus would descend upon the Mount of Olives in the near future that she did not even bother to find a graveyard for members of the sect.

When the Norwegian pastor, Birger Hall, came to the Holy City he was greatly upset to learn this. Pastor Hall knew well that one of the first things a European or American missionary did, on arrival in the Holy Land, was to find a suitable burial place. Palestine was infamous for its deadly fevers, and no one could be certain they would survive their mission. The tall, slender Norwegian, with his narrow-bearded face arrived at the American colony in 1889. He introduced himself as a seaman's minister from Cardiff, believing this would make a good impression, since it was there that Anna and the other survivors of the *Ville du Havre* had been brought ashore 20 years earlier.

Mother Anna was not at home, but Pastor Hall was well received and brought into the largest room, furnished in an Oriental manner, with low sofas and pillows along the walls. The Norwegian was accompanied by two Danish theologians whom he had met at the Hospice of the Order of St John in the Christian quarter of the Old City. All three were sceptical of the Overcomers' theology.[125]

While the guests were waiting for Anna to arrive, Hall told everyone that he had heard about the so-called third-day fever that was ravaging Palestine. According to rumour, the fever was supposed to make people sick every third day, week, or month. Hall had been told that several of the sect's members were no longer seen in the city, and when he asked where they were, he received the reluctant answer that they had died. Pastor Hall knew that Anna refused all medical assistance, but he did not mention it.

Even if the Norwegian pastor was critical of the sect on Bethesda Hill, he was impressed that despite years of illness and challenges, the group remained true to its "fanatical ideas". He did note, however, that Anna's flock prayed, studied God's word, sang and visited the sick; that they celebrated Saturday as the Sabbath, as the Jews did, and that local

125 Birger Hall: *Bibelske Spor, Bind I, Billeder fra Det hellige land* (Biblical Paths, Volume I, Pictures from The Holy Land), Kristiania 1982, pp.85-87.

Christians, as well as Jews and Muslims, gathered each Saturday to listen to the Americans' beautiful hymns and psalms.

Hall had little regard, however, for Anna's so-called spiritualism and her contact with the 'spirit world'. What upset the Norwegian pastor most of all was the suggestion, from reliable people in Jerusalem, that the sect had broken the bonds of family and the marital relationship. He had heard that at least one of the women in the colony had been "thrown out into the desert where she died of grief".[126]

There were many who spoke ill of Anna Spafford in Jerusalem, but the US consul in the city took first prize. Selah Merrill was educated as a priest and had also received a doctorate in archaeology, following his excavations of sites near Beirut and Damascus. The consul had written a book about the digs, mentioning dark holes and filthy underground cesspools, but also Greek and Latin inscriptions written on stones which were still being used as Arab grave stones.[127]

But Merrill's reputation was widely questioned. One sceptic was the British consul in Beirut, who wrote: "Nothing will be done east of Jordan by Americans if they continue to organize their expeditions as they do." Merrill's ability as an archaeologist was further doubted by William F Albright, Dean of Biblical Archaeology in Jerusalem. He claimed the American consul did not have sufficient background in the field for his excavations.[128]

The American consul in Jerusalem had never liked the Spafford sect. From the day Horatio Spafford called at his office on a courtesy visit, the diplomat had been disagreeable. At first, neither Horatio nor Anna understood what was wrong, but after a while they came to the conclusion that Merrill had taken against them because he believed they should be carrying out missionary and philanthropic work among the heathens. Some thought that Merrill's ill-will toward the Spaffords stemmed from his belief that the sect's members lived communally and that the male members shared their women among them.[129]

Selah Merrill was a Republican, and after his party's candidate lost the American presidential election in 1885, he was recalled to the United States. He was later reinstated and returned to Jerusalem in 1891, after a subsequent Republican victory. Even then, the consul wanted nothing to do with Anna Spafford and her group, despite the fact that most of them

126 Ibid.
127 Selah Merrill: *East of Jordan*, New York 1883, pp.97-98.
128 Ruth Kark: *American Consuls in the Holy Land, 1832-1914*, p.324.
129 Dudman & Kark: *The American Colony*, Jerusalem 1998, p.47.

were American citizens. The consul put labels on everyone. He dismissed the local Jews as "ignorant, quarrelsome, vengeful, bigoted, violent, deceitful and evil". The diplomat felt that Palestine was not ready for the Jews and the Jews were not ready for Palestine.[130]

Merrill thought Jerusalem would be a better place without Anna Spafford and hoped he would be able to force her to leave. He thought his moment had come when he received a letter signed by Professor David J Lingle of the University of Chicago. The letter, dated July 10, 1893, read:

> I have a sister living with a fanatical company in the house of Mrs Spafford... I have come here to investigate the matter and if possible to remove my sister from such dangerous surroundings. And as you are our consul and have been long in Jerusalem, I take the liberty of asking you to give me all assistance you lawfully can in this matter.[131]

The letter contained many details: "Some time ago one of their members left them and went to Chicago... because she found some of the people there were living immoral lives. This revelation (and I have it in writing) has made me anxious for my sister and her children."

The person referred to was Annie Aiken, Bertha and Grace's nursemaid, the daughter of Anna's laundry woman in Chicago, who had travelled to Jerusalem with Anna and Horatio 12 years earlier. Annie was by now 26 years old, and some months earlier she had left Jerusalem and returned to the United States because of a disappointed love affair. She had fallen in love with a handsome, charming Palestinian from the rich Husseini family. Mahmoud Husseini had said many beautiful things to the lonely woman, but the Palestinian also said that he loved her like a sister, and that nothing more could come of their relationship.

Annie did not care. She was in love and fantasized that Mahmoud would look at her differently if she was not a member of the sect. Perhaps she could still convince him to become a part of her life if she left Anna's house. Her feelings for Mahmoud Husseini were so strong that one day in May 1893 she packed her things and departed. She left behind a letter written in pencil: "My dear Mother, I must go, so say goodbye to one and all. I cannot look at you, nor speak, nor see Grace, so go now. I am going to the Karmanilj's Hotel [sic] to see if they will let me stay there for the

---

130 Frank Manuel: *The Realities of American-Palestine Relations*, Washington 1949, pp.70-73.
131 Dudman & Kark: *The American Colony*, Jerusalem 1998, p.91.

present. I cannot hear nor say more – it is between me & God. Annie."[132]

When Anna found the letter she went immediately to the hotel, which was not far away. There she found Annie, who told her of her love for Mahmoud Husseini. Anna acted swiftly. She sent for the young man to meet her at the hotel, and such was Anna's reputation that he did not dare to do otherwise.

"Annie says she loves you," said Mother Anna, and looked Mahmoud right in the eyes. "I want to know what your feelings and intentions are toward her."[133]

"Annie knows that I am of noble birth and cannot marry her. She is also aware that I am an engaged man," explained the Palestinian.

Anna did not want to know anything more, except that the relationship had been an honourable one. According to Mahmoud and Annie it had. When Mahmoud had left, Anna tried to convince the lovesick woman that it would be best for her to come back to her home in Jerusalem, until she could get some money for a ticket to Chicago. But Annie Aiken did not want to. She felt she had been wronged and that Anna had ruined things for her. She had not told anyone else that she was in love, and now Anna had intervened in a relationship that Annie had hoped might develop into something more.

When Anna left, Annie felt so humiliated that she wanted revenge. She visited Consul Merrill and told him that all the rumours about the Americans' immorality were true, thus apparently corroborating Merrill's own reports of the "wild life" that went on at the house inside the Damascus Gate. Later she regretted what she had done, and when Anna asked Rolla Floyd and his wife to visit Annie and they had the chance to speak to her alone, they heard that she had never seen anything immoral and had always been treated with the utmost friendliness. Annie told them: "I am not ashamed to say that I loved 'Mahmoud Effendi' – Mahmoud the gentleman – well enough to marry him," but he had not loved her "so she had now given up hope".[134]

A little later Annie Aiken went back to the United States, after borrowing money from Samuel Hedges, the doctor who had taken over the Spafford family's house in Lake View. In Jerusalem, the sect's cash box

132 The correct name of the hotel was "Kaminitz". Letter from Annie Aiken. File: Ex member's letters+ Law suit, American Colony Collection, Jerusalem.
133 Spafford Vester: *Our Jerusalem*, 2nd Edition, 1954, p.171. Bertha concealed Annie Aiken's identity, referring to her as "Nora".
134 Statement by Rolla Floyd, May 21, 1893. Folder: Ex member's letters, American Colony Collection, Jerusalem.

was empty, even though several of the members had considerable assets back in the States, and it survived only through loans from Palestinian friends. Initially, Anna and her followers were given credit by affluent Palestinian merchants, who understood that the Americans used whatever money they had to do good works, and were not troubled by the fact that their loans were secured only by promises.

In Chicago, Annie Aiken contacted Regina Lingle, mother of one of the sect's key members, Mary Whiting. Annie told her that Mary's children, Ruth and John David, were not doing well in Jerusalem. Ruth had been a one-year-old when her parents had left Chicago, and John David had been born in December 1882, just a year after their arrival. This was just about the time when Anna officially introduced celibacy to the colony. When the children's father, John C Whiting, died years later, Ruth and John David became the sole heirs of an estate worth $60,000. The money came from their paternal grandmother.

When Annie told Mrs Lingle about their life in Jerusalem, she changed her story once more. Annie described life in the congregation as so dark and immoral that Regina Lingle became concerned and angry. This was not a life for her grandchildren. Mrs Lingle asked her son, David, to convince Mary to come home to the United States and bring the children with her. In Jerusalem, the Chicago University professor found a welcome ally in Consul Merrill. The American diplomat agreed that the two children should be brought home, even if Mary Whiting considered their life in Jerusalem to be good for them.

Anna was sitting in the colony's sewing room, when Mary came in with a letter dated July 18, 1893. "Listen to what I have received from Dr Merrill," she said and read aloud:

Dear Mrs Whiting,
There is a gentleman from America who knows you and your friends in Chicago, and would very much like to meet you and your children. He cannot very well call upon you. This note will be given to you by one of my kavasses,[135] who will wait and return with you from the Damascus Gate.[136]

---

135 An armed Ottoman police officer.
136 Letter from Selah Merrill to Mary E Whiting, July 18, 1893. Folder: 1893, American Colony Collection, Jerusalem. Spafford Vester: *Our Jerusalem*, 2nd edition, pp.172-73.

When Mary had finished, Anna said: "This sounds just like a kidnapping." Her younger daughter Grace had never heard the word kidnapping before and wanted to have it explained, to the amusement of the others. No one believed that the letter was serious, except for Anna and Mary, who felt it had to be answered immediately. Mary wrote to the consul and explained that if anyone wanted to meet her, her home was the right place. It did not take long before a man appeared, standing outside the door with the letter in hand.

Only then did Mary discover that the man was her own brother. He was invited in and explained that a carriage was ready to drive his sister and her children directly to Jaffa. He had been in Jerusalem for seven days, he had the American consul on his side, and he wanted to take Mary and the children back to the United States immediately. "I am staying here. I will follow my conscience," said Mary.

"But this concerns your children's inheritance of a large estate. The conditions are that they must live in the United States," replied David.

Mary was unyielding, and after a while the atmosphere became so tense that she asked her friends in the room not to leave her, for fear she might be kidnapped. Events would demonstrate that she had good reason, because 18 days later a uniformed consular guard arrived with another letter. This time the United States consul demanded that Mary Whiting, her children, Ruth and John David, appear at the consulate at 3pm the same day, August 5, 1893. "Refusal on your hand renders you liable to the penalties of the law," Selah Merrill had written in pencil on a small piece of paper.[137]

Anna asked Mary to contact the Austrian consul in Jerusalem. He was a friend of the American colony. The Austrian diplomat maintained that the demand was illegal and recommended that Mary should answer with a formal written reply, explaining her refusal. While Mary was still at his office, the American consul's interpreter, accompanied by an Ottoman policeman, knocked on the door of the house near Damascus Gate. Anna told him that Mary Whiting was not there, and asked to see the warrant needed to search the house. The American consular representative had no such thing, but this did not stop the policeman from ransacking the house. But he did not find Mary or the children. Consul Merrill did not give up, and five days later the diplomat's interpreter again came to the house, together with an American teacher who was working in Beirut. This time the interpreter showed an arrest warrant for Mary Whiting, but

137 Letter from Selah Merrill to Mary E Whiting, August 5, 1893. Folder II: 1893, American Colony Collection, Jerusalem.

he refused to hand it over. At that moment five more men appeared; they were American missionaries and teachers who lived in Beirut, who had been temporarily sworn in, to deputize as consular police.

At first Anna tried to reason with them, but she was soon interrupted by someone who said: "Don't listen to her; she will be the next one to be hauled out."[138] The acting consular police officials took Mary and her two children to the Grand New Hotel just inside the Jaffa Gate. The hotel was situated across the street from the American Consulate and the consul had threatened to send his own guards out with a horsewhip if any of the congregation dared to come near.

Anna wrote a letter on behalf of Mary and her children, which was signed by everyone in her flock. It demanded that Consul Merrill submit a written summons to the court. The American consul refused to receive the letter, so the colony then sent a telegram to the American State Department, accusing the consul of the unlawful arrest of Mary Whiting and her children. Their economic situation had become so strained that Anna's adopted son, Jacob, had to pawn his watch to pay for the telegram.

Two months later, Anna learnt that Mary would, most probably, be able to remain in Jerusalem when a telegram arrived from the American State Department explaining that Consul Merrill would be replaced and that his successor had already been named. The department, therefore, considered it unnecessary to continue further investigation.[139]

But on December 11, that same year, Mary Whiting received a summons, demanding that she appear in court in Massachusetts to explain why no guardian had been appointed for the children. It was alleged that Mary herself was not a suitable person to be responsible for them. The date for her appearance was set for February 1, 1894.

Anna decided that Jacob should accompany Mary to the United States. Mary did not want the children to travel with her for fear that they would be forcibly separated. Another of the sect's earliest members, Amelia Gould, also planned to travel to the United States. Her brother-in-law, John Gould, had refused to release property and valuables, which she had inherited from her husband. Gould had taken care of the businesses when Amelia left for Jerusalem, but had tried to appropriate her assets, writing to her seven years previously that he believed "in your present condition of mind and surroundings, you are not competent to take

---

138 Spafford Vester: *Our Jerusalem*, 2nd edition, p.174.
139 Copies of telegrams and letters in Folder: 1893, American Colony Collection, Jerusalem.

charge of your own finances".[140]

The treasurer of the colony, an impeccably dressed miller named William Rudy, was also going to Chicago, primarily to assist Amelia Gould. Forty-nine-year-old William possessed a strong faith, but no one knew much about his background, and no one had ever asked. When the community had left Chicago in 1881, it was rumoured that Rudy had given up his milling business after a serious illness.

The four travellers took the new train to Jaffa. The train station in Jerusalem lay a half hour's walk from the Jaffa Gate, in a southwesterly direction. Just before departure the mayor of Jerusalem visited Jacob. He unhooked a coin purse from his belt and gave it to the traveller saying: "Take this in case you should need money."[141] The mayor knew well that the Americans had become deeply in debt as they waited for the Lord, and that they helped the poor of Jerusalem with borrowed funds. He was openly on Anna's side in the conflict, and he comforted the travellers with the fact that Consul Merrill's time in the city would soon be over.

From the large house on the hill, Anna led the sect in its work, without a thought as to whether or not the needy were Christians, Jews or Muslims. Her resistance to Christian proselytizing increased further after a visit to the mission hospital in Jaffa. There, she had been distressed to find that the nurses sitting at the bedsides of dying patients insisted on reading aloud to them from the Bible. They said that the Bible readings were the price the patients had to pay for medical treatment. Anna had watched as the sick waited for these readings to be over so they could receive treatment. She had seen a sheikh with a broken leg lying in dirty clothes, stiffened with dried blood, while his nurses did nothing more than read from the scriptures. Anna was convinced that Christ would have soothed their pain with his hands and with beautiful words, but would not have attempted this kind of brainwashing.

Although the Americans did not act like missionaries, they had much to do. Despite their financial worries, theirs was a happy group that always sang and played music when they held their gospel meetings. The women in the congregation continued to teach young mothers, but everyone realized that they could not carry on like this for long if Amelia Gould could not gain access to her money. Their debt had grown to $8,000.

140 Letters from John Gould to Mrs Amelia Gould, February 19th 1887. Folder: Amelia Gould's Papers, American Colony Collection, Jerusalem.
141 Klas Pontus Arnoldson: *Jerusalems själ* (Jerusalem's Soul), Stockholm 1913, p.68.

The American Colony and Sheikh Jarrah Mosque

One day when they hardly had any food left in the house, there was a knock on the door and a Palestinian farmer stood with a carton of eggs. "This has to be a mistake," said Anna. The Arab replied:

No, it is not a mistake. The eggs are from Allah. I was walking behind my donkey through the Damascus Gate to sell my eggs, but the donkey turned to the left and went up the hill. I tried to force him back but he would not budge, and finally I thought I would give up and let the donkey go where he wanted. And he stopped here, so I understand that it is you who are to have the eggs. They are from Allah.

Anna accepted the eggs, strengthened in her faith that God would take care of all things, and repeated the farmer's story to all who would listen. Members of the community received many signs from heaven, and God appeared to take care of them in many wonderful ways. So they were further convinced that what they were doing was right.

The little sect now consisted of six adult Americans and nine children, four adult Turks with two children, and two women from England. Eleven of the members had died, and only two of the men from the United States remained. But the Overcomers had made their mark and were so well known in the city that when the Franciscan monks printed a guide for pilgrims who came to Jerusalem from Jaffa, Anna and her flock were fittingly described. The guide stressed that the sect's members did not do normal work, for they were waiting for Jesus' return and the end of the world.[142]

---

142 *The Franciscan Guide for Jaffa, Ramleh and Jerusalem* (Arabic) Jerusalem 1890, pp.204-5.

Chapter 11

Jerusalem to Chicago

Rabah Husseini Effendi was an old man when Anna Spafford settled in Jerusalem. The Husseini family can trace their ancestry directly back to the Prophet Mohammed through his grandson, Hussein.

The Muslim patriarch lived in an impressive house half a mile north of the Damascus Gate, next to the Sheikh Jarrah Mosque. The mosque, which gave its name to the neighbourhood, had been built in honour of Sheikh Jarrah, the Muslim doctor of Salah al-Din (Saladin) the famous Sultan of Damascus, who reclaimed Jerusalem for Islam and expelled the Crusaders. Rabah Husseini Effendi's house was surrounded by a walled courtyard containing a spring. There, amongst fruit trees and flowers, were the special quarters of his three wives. The venerable gentleman's own room was opposite a whitewashed reception hall and was the largest and most beautiful in the house. Its carved wooden ceiling was painted yellow, with different shades of blue and contained a cupola. At the top of this vault, painted dark blue and decorated with stars to resemble the heavens, a gilded spear pointed down. The floor was covered in thick rectangular marble, light grey, earthen red and midnight blue, cut to form a diamond pattern. The mansion was popularly referred to as "the house that had been decorated in liquid gold".[143]

One day when this distinguished Arab gentleman had invited some of his many friends to visit, one came from the Mount of Olives with a large basket of apricots. When Rabah Effendi saw the fruit, he decided to test his guests a little.

---

143 Fannie Fern Andrews: *The Holy Land under the Mandate, Volume I*, Houghton Mifflin Company, Cambridge, 1931, p.27.

"Should I divide the apricots among you according to God's or man's law?" he asked.[144]

"According to God's," responded the guests in unison.

Rabah Effendi took the basket. He gave two apricots to one man and three to another, while a third got 20, or five, and so on. It was quite random. If one of the guests protested, the Husseini clan leader put a finger to his lips and asked for quiet, then continued until each one had received a share. Then the protests began: "We asked for God's fairness." The host answered them with dignity and a smile: "Is this not the way that God has distributed nature's rich gifts? Some have much, others nothing." The guests murmured but did not protest, and Rabah Effendi was praised for his wisdom.

Even though individual Palestinians often demonstrated their concern for those around them at a personal level, the Arabs, as a people, had not progressed far in organizing themselves collectively. Of course, some small secret groups had formed which wanted to fight for Arab independence. But the Arabs had been under Ottoman domination for hundreds of years, so had not been influenced by the social radicalism and democratic ideals which the French Revolution had brought to many countries of Northern Europe. These ideas gained ground only in the European provinces of the Ottoman Empire.

Nevertheless, the idea of freedom from the Ottomans had taken root. Most of the cities were dominated by a handful of powerful Arab families. They owned large properties and derived their income from agriculture and from renting out their lands. More important than ownership was the social position of the family. Their children were better educated than others, and the male family members made a point of cultivating influential contacts in the Ottoman capital, Constantinople. Families of the wealthy elite were also able to protect their tenants, defending them against the Turks and in local feuds with other peasant farmers.

The Husseini family was one of several influential clans in Jerusalem competing for power in the city. All of them had deep and holy roots. The Alami family, for instance, laid claim to being the descendents of Hassan, another of Mohammed's grandsons. Other important Muslim families could also point to impressive ancestors. The Nusseibeh, Nashashibi, Khalidi and Dajani dynasties all had great influence, not just among the Muslim population, but also amongst Christians.

144 Spafford Vester: Unpublished draft of *Our Jerusalem*, Chapter 13, pp.253-54. American Colony Collection, Jerusalem.

The reason for this arose from the fact that two of them had been given the keys to the Church of the Holy Sepulchre. The privilege had been granted by Saladin, after his conquest of Jerusalem in 1187. Saladin had realized that the eastern and western churches in Jerusalem were enemies. Their mutual hatred was so strong that it would be difficult to allow a Christian family to guard the keys of the church and ensure that it would be opened and closed at the proper times. The keys were therefore given to two Muslim families. The Nusseibehs kept them, while the other, the Judeh family were given the task of opening and closing the church. In that way no single Muslim family was given too much power.

Six hundred years later, the Palestinians in Jerusalem were occupied with another problem. As Jewish immigration into Palestine, then a province of Ottoman Syria, increased, some Muslim leaders began to complain. As a result, in 1887, the Ottoman authorities tried to restrict the numbers of Jews migrating to the Holy Land. It was decided that European Jews were allowed to come only as pilgrims or tourists. No Jew was allowed to settle permanently in Palestine, even though there were Jewish families who had lived in Palestine for generations.[145]

There was a growing sense of Arab national identity. Just as in the Balkans, another Ottoman province, Arab intellectuals discussed alternative solutions to the 'national question'. Their debates often mirrored one another's ideas: a Greater Serbia or a Greater Syria; a federation of Balkan states or a pan-Arab revival; an Orthodox union or a new Islamic Caliphate. One thing the Palestinian thinkers agreed on was that the land should not to be handed over to Jews.

The Ottoman authorities' ban on Jewish immigration had little impact. The Turkish bureaucracy was ineffective and many in the administration were easily bribed. The Jews continued to settle in Palestine, but when living conditions in Jerusalem worsened, the local Palestinians reacted yet again. At the end of June 1891, a number of Palestinian notables signed a telegram which was sent to Constantinople. In it they demanded that the authorities enforce a ban on the purchase of land in Palestine by Russian Jews. After this, the grand vizier issued a decree that foreign Jews could stay in Jerusalem for only three months.[146]

Two weeks later, the British consul reported home: "The influx of Jews into Palestine has, of late years, become very considerable, and the

---

145 Naomi Shepherd: *The Zealous Intruders*, San Francisco 1987, p.118, A.L. Tibawi: *Jerusalem, Its Place in Islam and Arab History*, Beirut 1969, pp.27-8.
146 Neville J. Mandel: *The Arabs and Zionism before World War I*, Berkley 1976, pp.39-40.

Jewish population in Jerusalem now comprises 35,000 to 40,000 of a total of 60,000 inhabitants. Most of the Jews come from Russia and Germany, and many are in indigent circumstances."[147] This immigration of Jews to Palestine at the end of the 19th century was later dubbed the first *Aliyah* – a Hebrew word meaning ascent, used in this context to mean a 'rising up' into the promised land.

The consul reported that the Turkish ban on Jewish migration to Palestine not only affected immigrants from Russia. After a mixed group of 150 Persian Jews, who visited the city in 1891, stayed longer than the three months allowed them by the Ottoman authorities, they were held under house arrest to await transportation to Jaffa and deportation.

When a Presbyterian minister, himself a convert from Judaism, passed the house where they were being detained, he heard the pitiful cries of the Persian women. Three days later, he submitted a written account to the British consul: "There were a large crowd of Jews and others before the new stores, or shops, on the Jaffa road in front of Feil's Hotel, and in coming near I heard piteous female cries issuing from one of those stores. Those inside were trying hard to force the doors open, while police and Moslem roughs were piling big stones against them, the police striking any who succeeded in putting their heads or hands out."[148]

The minister believed that the British consul had a duty to protect the Jews in Palestine. The day before, a group of 30 Persian Jews had been sent off in wagons. He told the consul that although they were desperately poor, they were also robust and hardy, even the women, who seemed exceptionally muscular. The minister argued that the Persian Jews would be "valuable contributors in this country of slovenly and lazy people",[149] and he volunteered to take care of some himself. But despite his attempts to help, the Jews were deported. Many were to return, together with hundreds of new arrivals from Europe.

The indigenous Palestinian farmers had at first been very curious about the clothes of the European Jews, their language and customs. They were surprised by the efforts the newcomers made, by how hard they worked and how they tilled the soil. But when the colonists tried to use camels to pull their horse carts, polite Palestinian interest degenerated into laughter.[150]

---

147 Martin Gilbert: *Jerusalem, Rebirth of a City*, New York 1985, pp.206-07.
148 Ibid. pp. 211-13.
149 Ibid.
150 Mandel: *The Arabs and Zionism before World War I*, Berkley 1976, pp.34-5.

The Jewish settlers were interested neither in the Arab language nor the local customs. For example, it was usual for everyone in a community to use the outlying fields, which the farmers regarded as a gift from God – *hadiyah min Allah* – for grazing livestock. The Jews, who knew nothing of this practice and feared for their first harvests, considered the Arab goat herders intruders, and drove them away with force. Alternatively, they confiscated the goats and sheep and demanded payment from the owners, or even beat up the goatherds.

But Anna Spafford, in the Old City of Jerusalem, was not particularly concerned by the growing conflict between the newly arriving Jewish agriculturalists and Palestinian peasant farmers. Anna had her own problems, and, in an attempt to solve them, in August 1894 she and a few others in the congregation decided to travel to Chicago.

Anna specifically wanted to visit the family's former doctor and friend, Samuel Hedges. He was still living in the Spaffords' house in Lake View, which he had been renting from them since 1881. He had, however, not paid his rent regularly, and Anna was prepared to go to court, if necessary, to obtain the money that was owed to her.

The richest woman in the sect, Amelia Gould, who could have solved all its economic problems at a stroke, had not been able to access all her wealth and was preparing for her own legal battle in the United States. Mary Whiting also had to go to court to protect her children's inheritance. Having failed in her attempt to bring her grandchildren back to America by force, Mary's mother was now attempting to gain guardianship over the children, Ruth and John. But the case was postponed until the children came to the United States.

Anna had another reason to leave Jerusalem for a while. Her 16-year-old daughter, Bertha, had fallen in love with 25-year-old Frederick Vester, the son of a German-Swiss missionary couple. Anna knew the parents well, but was not happy about the teenager's romance. Frederick had recently returned from Switzerland where he had been studying after completing his military service in Germany. "You should get to know men from your own country and from your father's family and friends before you think about marriage," Anna warned her oldest daughter. She said nothing about the rule of celibacy, which she herself had introduced.

Before Anna left Jerusalem she wrote a series of letters to friends in the US informing them about her trip to Chicago. In one of these, addressed to the Reverend Abraham Jacobson in Decorah, she enclosed photographs of Bertha. Jacobson had a son in the same class as the

American president's son, and Anna was eager for Bertha to meet the Jacobson family.[151]

In Chicago, Anna rented a house on the west side of town. It had two floors, a basement and a small garden behind the house, where the washing could be hung out to dry. From the windows, the only view was of long lines of neighbouring houses. The Spafford and Whiting children hated the house immediately and longed to be back in Jerusalem.

The lawsuit instigated by Mary Whiting's mother was due to come before Judge Kohlsaat in May 1895. Anna felt the case was just as much an attack upon her and the whole congregation in Jerusalem as it was on Mary Whiting. The main witness for the prosecution was Annie Aiken, the Spafford children's erstwhile nanny. On May 13, Annie entered the witness box and told the court there was immorality within Jerusalem's American colony. Annie related how married persons had to live separately from one another, and described the extent of Anna's power and influence within the community. She spoke of the unnatural ways she and the others had been forced to adjust. She had not been able to stand that life any longer, she told the court:

> I went to a hotel in Jerusalem and afterwards to some friends. There I was watched by people from the colony in shifts. But no one managed to convince me to move back. I was tired of listening to the daily admissions of faults which everyone had to make. It seemed so stupid.

From her seat in the witness box, Annie Aiken turned and looked straight at Anna. "I have had a horrible experience. She had a terrible influence over me, but not any longer. I do not have to stand before her now in order to be forgiven."

The lawyer for the prosecution, Mr Palmer, intervened and asked: "What is your motive for being a witness in this case?"

"Because many homes have been broken up," Annie answered. "In order to rescue the children from what may happen to them in the future, because they will have to obey those signs which are given to them, regardless of what happens between heaven and earth – they won't dare resist."

---

151 Letter from Anna Spafford to Rev Abraham Jacobson, Decorah, Iowa, August 19, 1894, St Olaf College, Northfield, Minnesota.

When the defence lawyer Mr Mills asked her about the signs and warnings she referred to, Annie answered:

Mrs Spafford tells us what we are to do; she says she has signs from God, and even if heaven and earth were to move, we would not dare to refuse. Sometimes others had signs also, but Mrs Spafford told us whether or not they were true. Sometimes these warnings were visible. They came in the form of a heavy sigh, facial expressions, and sometimes those who received these signs could be changed and become noisy or run about the house. Mrs Spafford maintained that she was a prophet and that she had received a vision that we should live as Adam and Eve before the fall – those who were married had to live as if they were not.

Under cross-examination, Annie maintained that the colony's children "were neglected. No one took care of their children because the 'Thousand-Year Kingdom' could come at any moment, and Mrs Spafford said: 'They will become educated in the blink of an eye.' But with her own children, it was different. They were taken care of and forced to learn. I did not even get a chance to learn a language."

When the lawyer for the defence asked if she could say anything positive about the colony, Annie replied that they took care of the sick and did a lot for the poor. That was all that Mr Mills wanted to hear. The case was seized upon by the press. The next day the *Chicago Daily News* carried the headline "Mrs Spafford's dubious activities in old Jerusalem".

Jerusalem's ex-consul, Selah Merrill, was also due to appear as a witness, but illness prevented him from attending. Instead, he supplied the court with a written statement, which was read aloud. Merrill insisted that Anna had a hypnotic influence on members of the colony and that she ruled them with an iron hand. No one did any manual labour, and for him that was unworthy and criminal. It was also wrong that the American colony in Jerusalem was divided into two classes: those who found favour and those who did not.

Consul Merrill wrote that the children never had enough food and that some of them had died of starvation. Members of the colony had been living only on crushed wheat for months and had a debt to the small shopkeepers in Jerusalem amounting to some $8,000. The men and the women went to bed together without being married and they lived together in several large houses in a way that raised suspicions. The statement ended with a claim that the only reason Mrs Spafford had wanted Mrs Whiting to keep the children was to gain control over her and her money.

When Anna Spafford entered the witness box, everyone in the courtroom looked with curiosity at the small woman wearing a tailored black dress and a little hat. She spoke softly and told in a very gentle voice how she had prepared the children for their pilgrimage 13 years before. She had gathered several other families, along with Annie. The lawyer for the defence stopped her and asked if it was Christian religion that had taken them to Jerusalem. Anna replied: "We were 14, everyone hungered for the truth. I had suffered great losses and we all wished to come closer to God."

Mr Mills asked, "Have you ever maintained that you were a prophet?" He apparently knew that Anna's sister-in-law, Margareth Lee, at times had referred to her as 'Prophet Hannah'.[152] The spectators in the courtroom thought the small magnetic woman paused a moment and they all leaned forward to listen, as Anna quietly said: "Only the prophet which Christ wanted me to be. That is when the Holy Spirit speaks to me, but not in any other way."

"Did you hear these voices? Did the spirit speak to you?"

"Yes," answered Anna, confidently. "The spirit has spoken to me."

Then she explained how the group had wanted to go to Jerusalem, and about the Jewish prophecies. They had chosen Jerusalem because "we wanted to be there when God brought the Jews back. The change in Jerusalem is wonderful. God is finishing His work. Ten years ago there were only 4,000 Jews in Jerusalem, now there are 40,000, and settlements are being built outside the city walls." As the court reporter from the *Chicago Daily News* subsequently wrote, Anna Spafford was sure that all the biblical prophecies would be fulfilled in time.

Anna continued: "We were all deeply depressed, and I decided we had to get beyond this case, that is, that Annie Aiken had to move beyond her decision. But alas! She did not. She swore instead that she wanted to cast a slur upon me and send me to my grave in sorrow. She wanted to kill me with misery, and get my children sent to..." But before Anna could say more, her voice was drowned out by the court administrator who banged his gavel on the table. The judge yawned, the jury awoke from a catnap and there was a recess until after lunch.

Later in the afternoon, the lawyer for the prosecution began his cross-examination. Time after time Anna was asked if she had direct contact

152 Laura Petri: *På heliga vägar* (On Holy Paths), Stockholm 1931, p.150.

with God. The question was put in different ways, but Anna held firm: "As a Christian who believes in prayer, I believe that God can lead us and show us the way, but I do not claim that I have any special power." The prosecutor went further:

"You were not with your husband when he died?"

"I was with him until just a few minutes before."

"Mrs Anna Spafford," the prosecuting attorney said triumphantly: "I believe you danced when you heard that your husband was dead."

A painful expression came over Anna's face. She looked directly at her former nanny when she responded: "Not in the way you suggest." Later, the prosecuting attorney produced a diary written by the Whiting children's deceased father. The book was full of enigmatic, mystical references such as, "the old life is to be put away, and the prophet will share her power."

Judge Kohlsaat found the case unusual. It raised new questions on law and ethics, such as whether children could be taken from their mother because of her religious faith. The court had also to decide whether Mrs Lingle could gain parental rights over her grandchildren because they were being brought up in a questionable moral atmosphere. The children themselves, Ruth and John, coped well as defence witnesses. Both said they were unhappy to be away from Jerusalem and the colony there, and since they both looked sound and healthy they gained a laugh from the courtroom, because in his statement Consul Merrill had maintained that the children were undernourished.

Then, before the prosecuting lawyer was able to sum up, the judge rejected Mrs Lingle's claim. Mary Whiting was to keep her parental rights and could take the children back with her to Jerusalem. When the papers came out the following day, the *Chicago Daily News* had the headline: "The Colony is a winner."

But the fight was not yet over for Anna. She wanted to reclaim her house in Lake View, so together with Amelia Gould she went to visit Dr Samuel Hedges, the family's former friend. According to their agreement Hedges was to look after the house and pay back the money which Horatio Spafford had swindled from his clients. The women had received only their first three months' payment. The doctor, instead, had paid $20,000 to one woman, Hetty Green, who had the largest mortgage on the Lake View property. Once he had done so, Hedges declined to pay any further rent for the house.

When the two women arrived in Lake View, Anna asked him if he remembered the letter he had sent to Horatio in Jerusalem. It had stated in black and white that Horatio had the right to buy back the property for the same $20,000 which had been paid when Hedges took over the house.

Hedges remembered the letter, but when Anna told him that Mary Murphy, Horatio's niece from whom he had previously stolen money, could provide the money to buy him out, he changed his mind. He had no intention of selling the house for the same amount he had paid for it. Furthermore, Hedges added: "Horatio Spafford cheated me. He left like a snake for Jerusalem."[153]

"That is not true," the two women responded in unison. "You well know that Mr Spafford did not leave like that, and it was well known among all of us in the congregation that we were going to Jerusalem as early as the month of June. Places had even been booked on a ship." But Hedges stood his ground. His promise to sell the house back to Horatio Spafford was a personal one, he said, and was valid only between the two men. The two women could do nothing but leave.[154]

153 Testimonies of Anna Spafford and Amelia Gould, February 8, 1895, Cook County Archive, Illinois.
154 Samuel Hedges was acquitted of any wrongdoing in connection with the ownership of the Spafford House in a case before the Ilinois High Court in October 1907.

Chapter 12

The Swedish Dream

In a communal residence on Madison Avenue, Chicago, lived 30 Swedish immigrants. They were led by a 53-year-old pastor, Olof Henrik Larsson. One May morning in 1895, one of the young Swedish women in the congregation, Sister Kerstin, mentioned that she had had a wonderful dream. "I dreamed that a few [people] that had lived in Jerusalem for 14 years came to see us," she said. "They were very much like us but had a higher light, and we were commanded to unite ourselves to them."

Some days later Sister Kerstin was visited by a friend, Mrs Mortonson. They were joined by Mathilda Larsson, the pastor's wife, 11 years his junior. In the course of their conversation the court case against the congregation in Jerusalem and its leader, Anna Spafford, was mentioned. Mathilda had read about the case in the newspapers and listened with great interest.

Mrs Mortonson, who had known Anna Spafford for many years, said she was a wonderful woman with an irresistible charisma, but that she was in difficult economic circumstances. Twice a week Anna Spafford would lead open prayer meetings in Chicago which anyone could join. "She is counting on returning to Jerusalem to continue the work God has given them," explained Mrs Mortonson. [155]

Mathilda decided to learn more about this woman. She had no idea that Anna was Norwegian. Olof Henrik Larsson had also read about the court case and he remembered Sister Kerstin's dream. The following Sunday, he joined Mathilda and went to hear Anna Spafford preach. As a result, of the couple's interest a small procession from the Swedish church threaded its way to the west side of Chicago to the house of the Jerusalem group.

155 Larsson: *Dala Folk in the Holy Land*, Stockholm 1957, pp.22–24.

Anna herself stood at the door to greet all who came. Most of the Swedes were immediately impressed by the charming grey-haired woman in her early fifties, with strong blue eyes and unusually smooth skin. Mathilda thought Anna held herself like a queen, possessing both modesty and a motherly expression.

Anna announced that the reading for the day would be taken from the Revelation of John and she asked an American, whom she called Brother Jessup, to read the first 11 verses of the story of the dragon and the two beasts. When he had finished, Anna took over and said: "This shows that we must love each other, and with love wash each others' feet. It means that we must overlook each others' weaknesses and be willing to forgive, as Christ has forgiven us."

The Swedes were even more impressed. Anna's voice was beautiful and melodious. Together they said a prayer, and the meeting ended with a hymn: "Blessed be the bonds that unite our hearts in Christian love." Over lunch there was talk about how much the two small congregations had in common. They both believed that Christ would return in the near future. They believed in the 'Thousand-Year Kingdom' and in living together in one community. Anna told the Swedes:

> Soon we will be returning to Jerusalem to partake in the fulfilment of the Lord's promise. Zachariah 14:10 is about to be fulfilled. When we came, the road between Hananeel's thorn bush and the wine press was completely unoccupied, but now we have seen one new building after the other. Jerusalem is growing and the time approaches when the curse will be lifted and Jerusalem can be at peace.[156]

When the small Swedish group was back at its own church, Mathilda commented on the success of the meeting. But another woman in the group, Sister Nathalie, urged caution: "Be careful. I do not want to be fooled; I do not think this is from God."

"Nor I," said Sister Kerstin. "We have been warned against frauds who will come in the Final Days. And what do we know about these people?"

"But have you forgotten your dream?" Mathilda reminded her.

"I simply do not want to be misled," said Sister Kerstin, holding her ground.

Pastor Larsson said nothing and the discussion ended. But later,

---

156 Petri: *On Holy Paths*, Stockholm 1931, p.131.

many wondered what would happen the following Sunday. It was then that Anna and her congregation would be coming to the service in the Swedish Evangelical Church. But Pastor Larsson was also in doubt. He felt that Anna Spafford was less assertive in her teaching than he was. She also seemed very lively whilst he was a rather ponderous man who spent much time thinking and talking about the devil and the loss of paradise. He lacked Anna's warmth and persuasiveness.

The following Sunday Mathilda showed her guests around the church, while Pastor Larsson waited inside. No one seemed to notice his uncertainty. And no one other than Anna could know that she was about to take his flock from him. Anna would be the director of the drama that was to follow. She would be the executioner and Olof Henrik Larsson the victim.

When Anna came into the church, her face lit up and she exclaimed: "This is the room!" She told the gathering about a heavenly message she had received before leaving Jerusalem: she was to meet brothers and sisters in Chicago. And when she had arrived there she had received a new message from God: "I will show you a large upper room." Her words struck the Swedish congregation like a dart. And when Anna later told the story of her own life, about the fire and the economic catastrophe, about the sinking of the ship and God's message to work in Jerusalem, and the later tragedy when little Horatio died and about the congregations in Chicago and Jerusalem, her audience sat transfixed.

The Swedes had heard about Jerusalem and Zion, about the return of the Jews and the new buildings being constructed in the Holy City. Everything seemed in accordance with the biblical prophecies. Many thought this was confirmation that God's return was near. They believed Anna was being guided by God, and that it was His will that they should follow her. Some regarded their own pastor as a John the Baptist figure, someone whose task it had been to prepare the ground for the one who would come with a higher light.

But tension was discernible after the meeting. Not all the Swedes were as impressed by this extraordinary woman. A minority did not like Mrs Spafford's visions. After a long night of thought, Pastor Larsson concluded that Anna Spafford and her congregation, whose economic position he knew was precarious, should move to his church. He told his own congregation of his decision and, after discussion, it was agreed. Anna and her flock received the invitation with joy, and a few days later on November 22, 1895, with snow on the streets, they moved to Madison Avenue, in the southern section of Chicago.

Anna's little Chicago congregation included about 30 men, women and children. Among those new to the group was a Norwegian couple, Alvilde and Axel Strand. She came from Bergen, and he from Kristiania (now Oslo). But none of the new arrivals was rich. In fact, Anna's flock was so poor that when they moved to join the Swedes not everyone could afford to take the tram. The men had to walk, carrying everything they could.

From the beginning, Anna took the lead. Pastor Larsson remained passive. He said nothing when, following their first meal together, the sect leader from Jerusalem entered the pulpit, pulled out her little book where all messages from Our Lord were noted, and started to read. Anna began with the message in which God had guided her to join with brothers in faith. She read that the brothers were preparing a large upper room; that a fire of charcoal had been lighted and that fish and bread had been put on the coals. God, she continued, had decided the two groups should become one, their joint prayers would confirm this. Afterwards they sang, 'We go to Zion, blessed heavenly Zion… God's heavenly city'.

The Swedish congregants accepted this message. But not Pastor Larsson. He felt doubt gnawing at him. He did not even have an opportunity to lead his own service. That night he lay awake for a long time. The pastor was, like Anna, in his early fifties. He had also been born by the sea, although the little fishing village of Grundsund, south of Lysekil, was smaller than Stavanger. Like Anna, Olof Henrik had lost both his parents while he was still young. At first, the orphaned Swede had gone to Liverpool, where he got a job in a shipyard. Later, as a 27-year-old seaman, he travelled to America, where he found work on board a liner operating between Boston, New York and Philadelphia.

The boy from Grundsund was ambitious. He studied navigation, learned to lead others and give orders, and soon became used to people listening when he spoke. After a while, he rose in the ranks. During his first night as captain of his own ship, when he was far out at sea, he heard a voice. It asked whether fulfilling his worldly ambitions had satisfied his soul. As the night went on he became more and more restless. Finally, Captain Larsson felt such a strong calling that he threw his pipe and tobacco into the sea, and decided to resign his position at the shipping company.

Larsson then travelled to Chicago where he joined the Methodist Church. The former fisherman, shipyard worker and captain also chose to go into real estate and met and married a woman from his homeland. They had a daughter, but at the birth of their next child, both mother and infant died. Yet again, Larsson experienced a spiritual crisis and broke with his surroundings. From this point on, Larsson believed there were only two roads for him: one to heaven, the other to hell. The one was narrow and difficult, the other wide and comfortable.

Larsson chose the narrow road, which he believed meant starting his own congregation, since he no longer felt able to accept the teaching of the Methodist Church. In anticipation of this, the pastor invested more heavily in property in Chicago. The city had not only been rebuilt in record time, following the Great Fire, but it had expanded greatly, and Larsson had earned enough to afford to build a church – the foundation for his own congregation.

The core of the congregation consisted of teenage girls from Sweden who had come to Chicago to work. During their free time some of them went to Larsson's new Swedish Evangelical Church. There, they could speak Swedish and find a home when their work was done for the day- one with peace and friendship. The Swedish women gave some of the money they earned to Pastor Larsson. This was invested in a new house, registered in the pastor's name. At that time in America, it was not unusual for the leader of a congregation to own both the church and the land it was built on.

The pastor was strict with those who hoped to follow him along the narrow road to heaven. But he was also hard on himself. The congregation honoured and respected his words as if they were from the Lord. One Sunday morning in 1877, a young woman, newly arrived in the assembly, heard the pastor's words thundering from the pulpit: "Free yourself from all that keeps you from the light." Mathilda Helgsten decided to do as she was ordered.

After the service Mathilda was invited to the house behind the church. She explained that she was deeply religious and came from Nås in the western Dalarna region. She was in Chicago to take care of her married sister's children because her sister was ill. In the evenings, however, she was able to meet others of her age. Two women in the congregation had guitars, and one young man played the mandolin, so as they embroidered and knitted they would sing psalms and old Swedish folksongs.

Mathilda thought that Pastor Larsson gave her peace of mind and the pastor, for his part, felt a special interest in the young woman. One day he proposed marriage. The young Mathilda felt overwhelmed that he had chosen her to be his wife. She did not regard him as merely a lonely man seeking a wife and a mother for his daughter. Even after they were married she still held him in some awe and continued to call him Larsson.[157]

157 Ibid. p.123.

The American Colony viewed from Nablus Road

Sometime later, Mathilda and another woman from the congregation travelled to Nås in Sweden to spread the word about Pastor Larsson's work in Chicago. Larsson decided that he, too, would visit Sweden and when he arrived in Nås people flocked to his meetings to hear his message that Jesus would return and the world would end. They attended in such large numbers that the established church community in Nås began to break up. Some opponents of the new fire-and-brimstone preacher tried to disrupt the meetings. But this only made the new pastor more committed. The regional church establishment then tried to stop Pastor Larsson by refusing him access to meeting places, but worship continued in private homes and in schools until the pastor managed to win over half of the community.

While in Sweden, Mathilda gave birth to a daughter. But the couple's joy lasted only three months, because the child became seriously ill. Larsson refused to send for a doctor. "God is our doctor," he said. "Only He can heal her if that is His will, and we must have faith in Him." His wife suffered in silence, not daring to speak against her husband. The little girl died a few days later.[158]

---

158 Eric Dinsmore Matsson: *The American Colony of Jerusalem*, Menton 1992, p.15.

After two stormy years in Nås, Pastor Larsson decided to go back to Chicago. The 'Lasarenes' now numbered some 50 men and women, but the community had become deeply divided. When he left, Larsson handed over leadership of the congregation to two of his brothers-in-faith. One, Tipers Lars Larsson, was the owner of a large farm, a sinner who had received God's and the Lasarenes' forgiveness. The other, who was to lead the congregation onward in the uneasy atmosphere of Nås, was an innkeeper called Mats Matsson.

But the majority in Nås did not want to join the Lasarenes. Pastor Larsson had not flinched from condemning those who did not wish to follow his path (over half the community) to certain hell. Those who joined his church would, he assured them, reach heaven. Among them were two teenagers, Jon Jonsson, and Karin Larsson, the daughter of farmer Tipers Lars Larsson. Jon and Karin were in love.

In Chicago, the returning pastor was greeted warmly. Despite the long distance between Nås and Chicago, Olof Henrik Larsson still managed to maintain his authority over his followers in Sweden. He did as the Apostle Paul had done – he wrote long epistles that he sent to Sweden. Each week either Tipers Lars, or Mats Matsson, read out a new letter to the assembly. While the congregation expanded and Pastor Larsson's own family also increased.

At the time when Anna Spafford entered the Larsson's life, their elder daughter Edith was aged four and the younger was nearly three. In the newly unified group, Larsson's flock provided free board and food for the visitors from Jerusalem, since most of his congregation now had jobs.[159] But Anna never relinquished her authority. Soon it was routine for Anna Spafford, rather than Pastor Larsson, to read a prayer before breakfast and take the morning service. The pastor remained passive in his own chapel silently registering the evaporation of his power. Larsson did a lot of thinking and continued to write his epistles to the congregation in Nås. But he said nothing about the questions that troubled him. What had caused him to lose his authority? Was it God's will?

Anna began to speak about how they might manage if the property in Chicago were sold and everyone moved to Jerusalem. One day she said that God had shown her that "most of those living in Madison Avenue are ready to go to wait for Jesus' Second Coming. And we must go together. Even if you all agree, everything depends on whether Olof Henrik will sell the church and the property. We have no other resources, but if he

159 Larsson: *Dala Folk in the Holy Land*, Stockholm 1957, p.34.

will do this, he will have enough money for us all to make the trip and to get a house for our community in the Holy City. We therefore believe that Olof Henrik must sell and make us ready for the trip to Jerusalem."[160] No one dared to speak against God's will. "May God be praised," Anna cried. "What do you say to the Lord, brother? You have heard what the congregation wants, what do you want?"

Larsson rose and said that perhaps it was not right to sell the church. His work in Chicago was not without value. As the congregation muttered its response, someone called out loudly: "Anna Spafford has her message directly from God. No one can ignore it." Larsson left the chapel with his head bowed. His wife followed shortly after. The pastor was a deposed king. His priesthood was over. He was unhappy and unsure about God's will. If he followed Anna Spafford to Jerusalem, she would be the leader and he the assistant. On the other hand, he also believed that Jesus' return would happen soon – perhaps as early as the following year.[161]

Mathilda tried to give her husband support and suggested he write to the congregation in Nås to tell them what was about to happen. If they were against Jerusalem, then she and her husband could return to Sweden. At least there he would be welcomed as the head of the congregation. So Larsson wrote.

When his letter arrived in Nås, Tipers Lars summoned the congregation immediately to an extraordinary prayer meeting in his own home. The letter read: "Dear brothers and sisters. God's peace. Up to now I have always believed that I and you, who have come over to my teachings, were alone in this, our faith. But, thanks be to God, we have found our match here in Chicago – brothers who think and live by the same rules."[162]

The effect of the letter was electric, since it also mentioned that Pastor Larsson and his flock in Chicago were to go to Jerusalem. For the Swedish farmers, Jerusalem had always been part of the world of the Bible and the psalms. Now, the city suddenly appeared as a reality to them. But the letter did not tell the whole truth. Nothing was said about the pastor being in a desperate situation, or that he had lost his power over his own congregation.

Larsson had no difficulty selling the church. The Methodists bid $20,000 for the property, most of it in cash. The balance would be paid

160 Dinsmore Matsson: *The American Colony of Jerusalem*, Menton 1992, p.19.
161 Another Swedish-American pastor, Fredrik Fransson, predicted the date of Christ's return as being 1897. Olaf Fahlén: *Nåsbönderna i Jerusalem* (The Nås Farmers in Jerusalem), Höganäs 1988, p.39.
162 Mia Gröndahl: *Drömmen om Jerusalem* (Dreams of Jerusalem), Swedish Television, Malmö, Prod. no.30–96/ 0180.

to a lawyer. On Thursday, March 5, 1896, a total of 72 men, women and children set off by train to Philadelphia. An American passenger ship, SS *Waesaland*, was waiting at the port, bound for Liverpool. The Swedish members of the congregation had turned all their assets over to Anna. The money would contribute to their work in Jerusalem. More money also came from new members – rich farmers from Illinois, Nebraska and Kansas who had sold their farms.

The Atlantic crossing to Britain was stormy and Mathilda's brother, 31-year-old Carl-Johan Helgsten (known as Charlie) became ill. His condition gradually worsened. While sailing through the Mediterranean, Anna visited Charlie in his cabin and said to Mathilda: "I have had a revelation that Charlie will not survive." When he subsequently died, many regarded the event as a sign that Anna was a true prophet.[163]

From Jaffa, the large group went by train to Jerusalem. At the station they were welcomed by those members of the colony who had stayed behind. Among them was Frederick Vester. Anna's older daughter, Bertha, had not met anyone else in the US to whom she felt attracted. The missionaries' son had also remained faithful in his affections to the beautiful Bertha.

The arrival of the newcomers from America meant that accommodation at the Damascus Gate became very crowded. Anna began immediately to look for bigger premises. It was not long before she discovered that a beautiful house in open country, just by the Sheikh Jarrah Mosque, north of the Old City, was available. It had scarcely been lived in since the old patriarch, Rabah Husseini Effendi, had died the year before, without a male heir. Under Turkish law his estate went in various portions to the numerous members of his extended Husseini family.

The house and walled garden, built in the best Damascus style, was known to be beautiful. For Anna and her growing congregation, the house was ideal with its numerous large rooms around an open courtyard and its extensive grounds. Husseini's bedroom and offices had been on the west side of the building, facing Nablus Road. This was the men's quarters into which no women were allowed. On the east side, opening straight into the courtyard and the women's bedrooms, was a little door for women only.

The roof tiles had been imported from Marseilles, and some of the floor tiles and marble had come from Italy. In Jerusalem, houses had previously been built with domed roofs, but the European fashion had

163 Petri: *On Holy Paths*, Stockholm 1931, p.132.

gradually gained popularity among the rich throughout the Levant, so houses with tiled roofs also began to be built in Palestine. Some of the first houses of this kind in Jerusalem were built in the Sheikh Jarrah district, by the Husseinis and other prominent families such as the Nashashibis, Nusseibehs, Jarallahs, Afifis and Dajanis.[164]

The crown jewel of the house Anna wanted to rent was the room on the first floor. Anna felt this 'large upper room' would be perfect for meetings. The decorated ceiling, the heavenly vault painted in blue and covered in golden stars, and the arched windows were all unique. Just outside, to the northeast, there was a spacious terrace with room for more than 100 people.

It was no simple matter to reach an agreement with the Husseini heirs. All property according to Ottoman law was divided into 24 parts (or *carats* in Arabic). Each heir had to sign the rental agreement and receive his portion of the rent. Once the documents were completed, the community moved in.

Anna was overjoyed. At the same time she thought a lot about Annie Aiken, whose unhappiness had helped her to this victory. One day she wrote a letter to Annie in Chicago. "I want you to know that an infinitely great blessing has come to us, and we have now understood our Father, as we never would have been able to do in any other way," wrote Anna. "The words which God gave to us have been fulfilled because we were betrayed by one of our own. I feel that I must say from the bottom of my heart that I have forgiven you. As always, your friend. Anna Spafford."[165]

Anna put a copy of the letter in a drawer. No answer ever came in return.

164 Yadin Roman: "Overhead Art" in *Eretz: The Geographic Magazine of Israel*, No 49, 1996, pp.23–35.
165 Undated letter from Anna Spafford to Annie Aiken, American Colony Collection, Jerusalem.

Chapter 13

The Dalafolk in the Holy Land

In his letter to the congregation in Nås, Pastor Olof Henrik Larsson had suggested that everyone should sell up immediately and join the Swedish party in London, en route to Jerusalem. He told his flock of new information indicating that Jesus would return to earth within the coming year.[166] The idea that it was possible for his congregants to sell their land and farms in just three weeks was, of course, unrealistic. The Lasarenes in Nås, however, were convinced that they should witness the return of the Lord on the Mount of Olives in order to get to heaven. No one understood that the feared and beloved Larsson no longer led the religious community, having met his match in the form of a woman. He could not even claim to be Anna Spafford's assistant. They certainly could not know that his letter had an ulterior motive – to get as many Swedish congregants as possible to Jerusalem to help him to reclaim his former position.

Mats Matsson and Tipers Larsson wrote back to their pastor. They were unaware that the mail to and from the congregation was screened by Mother Anna. So, when the letter from Nås arrived in Jerusalem, it was read first by the sect's leader before she passed it on to Larsson and asked him to translate it aloud into English at the evening meal.

In silence, the assembly heard that many Swedes wanted to come to Jerusalem. When Larsson had finished, they praised the Lord for his help in making the sect grow. At first Anna was happy that so many new people wanted to come to Jerusalem, but later she had other thoughts. She asked Larsson to tell his friends in Sweden that they should not take action immediately. They should wait for Larsson and another member

---

166 Birgitte Rahbek & Mogens Bähncke: *Tro og skæbne i Jerusalem* (Faith and Destiny in Jerusalem), København 1996, pp.74–80.

129

of the community, Brother Jacob, to come to Sweden so that they could select only those who would fit in with the community in Jerusalem.

When the two emissaries came to Dalarna, the farmers were already in the process of selling everything they owned. Brother Jacob, who had learned some Swedish, asked them to think carefully about what they were doing. Instead of talking about the Lord's return to the Mount of Olives, he spoke about the climate and diseases, as well as all the other difficulties in Palestine. When he had finished, only four of the larger families stood by their decision to leave Sweden.

Among those who took the momentous step to relinquish all their material goods and travel to the Holy Land was Jon Jonsson, who was in love. Leaving Nås would mean saying goodbye to his ancestral farm, and his dream of cultivating the soil and building a family there. His parents were sceptical about the idea of Jerusalem and refused to go themselves. But for Jon, membership of the Lasarene sect had become much more than a weekly prayer meeting. He knew that Karin Larsson would follow her parents to Jerusalem and that if he was to marry her he would have to give up his farm to others. Jon was not a religious fanatic, he was a pragmatic, well-grounded man. He was determined to marry Karin. For him, the dream of meeting Jesus in Jerusalem was of secondary importance.

Tipers Lars Larsson was the first to sell his properties. His brother-in-law bought his farm. Gradually, one after another, all the Lasarenes got rid of their farms and when the sales were done there was a substantial sum in the cash box. This money was handed over to Brother Jacob. The farmers packed their clothes and possessions in large blue-painted chests. They took both summer and winter clothes with them, including fur-lined coats and caps with ear muffs. The women took spinning wheels and looms with spools and shuttles. The men brought tools, iron ploughs and wagon wheels, along with seed-corn and seed-potatoes.

From Nås the emigrants travelled by horse and wagon to Vansbro, from where a train took them to Göteborg. As they left their home village, in a convoy of 12 horse-drawn wagons, the 15 adults and 22 children broke into song: "We travel to Zion, blessed heavenly Zion... God's wonderful city." It was the same hymn that the two congregations in Chicago had sung when they had joined together.

July 23, 1896, was a brilliant day with sunshine and warm temperatures, and those who remained in Nås pondered Pastor Larsson's words that fire-and-brimstone would rain down on all who refused to follow him to the Holy Land. But after the Lasarenes had left, a dramatic shift occurred in the weather, and it began to hail, with stones so large that they left marks in the ground. No one in Nås had ever experienced a storm like this. When those farmers who remained went to look at their fields, they found that hardly an ear of corn was left standing. Everything had been beaten down. Later, when the local priest and his wife were driving through the village they found that the road through the surrounding forest was covered with broken branches which lay as densely packed on the gravel road as if they had been cut for a funeral. The priest's wife knew that all who had left had been spared this tempest.[167]

Brother Jacob had gone on ahead of the emigrant party, to buy tickets for the steamship the *James D Dickinson*, which would take them as far as Antwerp. There, they transferred to the SS *Andros*. This leg of their journey was like an adventure in a new world. The ship travelled along the coasts of France, Spain and Portugal, past the Rock of Gibraltar and on into the Mediterranean. Despite the fact that most of the farmers and their families had never even seen the sea before, no one was seasick. It was the first time these hard working people, who lived off the land, had ever had free time. For the young couple in love, Jon Jonsson and Karin Larsson, the trip was wonderful. They spent a lot of time on deck, marvelling at the fact that they were able to travel together to Jerusalem. Finally, three weeks after departure, the ship anchored outside Jaffa. On the morning of August 14, the migrants set foot in the Holy Land.

The children were particularly impressed by the abundance of exotic fruits and vegetables, things they knew only by name. Brother Jacob bought for all, without considering that large quantities of fresh figs, juicy apricots and peaches might present a challenge to Swedish stomachs. That afternoon, they took the train to Jerusalem. The Dala farmers, so full of hope and expectation, were surprised to find a whole delegation waiting for them on the platform in Jerusalem. Horse-drawn cabs had been laid on to drive them to their future home. In the great hall there, they were welcomed by a sign which read 'Welcome' in both English and Swedish. Everything was festive – and much more beautiful than they had imagined. Anna's flock had now increased to 133 people, consisting of Indians, Turks, Romanians, Danes, Norwegians, British, Canadians, Poles, Serbs and Spaniards, as well as the newly arrived Swedes.

A little later, the Nås farmers were told that Anna should be addressed as 'mother', and the others as 'brother' and 'sister'. This came as no great

---

167 Hulda Granberg: *Et trettiårsminne från Nås* (A Thirtieth Year Remembrance from Nås), Svenska Jerusalemsföreningens Tidsskrift, 1927, pp.105–106.

surprise, but there were a few who were shocked when Mother Anna told them that all the colonists were expected to practice celibacy. She explained that the congregation had to prove itself by overcoming the sins of the flesh and considering its members purely platonically, as brother and sister. Through doing so, the entire Jerusalem colony would become cleansed, a worthy bride ready to receive the Lord when he descended on the Mount of Olives. His arrival would mean accounting for one's life and accepting judgement.[168]

Mother Anna also told the new arrivals that it was short-sighted to cling to their native language. All attempts to speak in Swedish would be considered nationalistic. The colonists were to break with their earthly ties, so that the former communities, the Overcomers from Jerusalem, the Lasarenes from Chicago, and the Lasarenes from Nås could melt together into one great congregation. The house they lived in was referred to as the American Colony, despite the fact that the majority was now Swedish.

Anna decided that three of the rooms, which had belonged to Rabah Husseini's wives, would be shared by seven women. For herself, she had chosen the finest room in the house – the one that had been occupied by the rich Palestinian himself. It lay opposite the reception hall and opened onto a terrace. Most of the young Swedes had to sleep on cots which were then stored beneath the larger beds every morning, and at 8am they would all gather for a meeting beneath the beautiful vaulted ceiling on the first floor. There, work would be assigned to them.

The character of the community changed with the arrival of the Swedes from Nås. The Americans were mostly urban people, lawyers, businessmen and shopkeepers. They had lived in Jerusalem for 15 years, relying on outside help and the goodness of the Lord. The Swedes, by contrast, were country people, mostly artisans and farmers. The large grounds of the new house provided a great opportunity for the type of work to which they were accustomed.

But first, the Nås farmers had to learn English in order to understand the Americans, and Arabic to communicate with the local population. Many of the older Swedes did not manage to master either language, and Brother Jacob had to translate into Swedish whenever he read from the Bible. Nearly every day, at their morning meeting, Anna would tell of her latest message from God. Afterwards, many of the women would start to weave, making napkins, tablecloths, material for clothing, and rag

---

168 A. Nordlander: *Resminnen från det Heliga landet* (Travel Notes from The Holy Land), Stockholm 1901, p.297.

rugs. Much of the work for which Anna had previously employed local Palestinians was now taken over by the farmers' wives from Nås.

Norwegian Alvilde Strand was also a seamstress, and her husband, Axel, was the Colony's best tailor and shoemaker. They cut material and sewed it so beautifully that Jerusalem's mayor and other prominent Palestinians began to buy their suits and dresses from the American Colony. The eager women from Nås produced yards and yards of cloth, for curtains and sheets, and the cold stone floors of the house were soon provided with Nordic rag rugs in addition to the oriental kilims.

A stable and a garage were erected for a new horse-drawn carriage that had been ordered from Chicago. The newcomers also built a laundry, a forge, a carpentry shed and a bakery. Jon Jonsson became the Colony's first baker, with Karin Larsson his assistant. In the early dawn, while the rest of the Colony slept, Jon and Karin got up to bake the daily bread. The rule of celibacy, however, meant that Jon's love for Karin was forbidden and considered dangerous.

A barn was also built and the community bought cows, giving them access to fresh milk – a luxury in Palestine. Josef Larsson's wife, Brita, was given responsibility for the animals, which included two horses, chickens, geese and a donkey. She spoke to the cows in her mother tongue, despite the ban on speaking Swedish and gave them the same pet names she had used for the animals back home in Nås.

The arrival of so many Swedish families with children meant that Anna had to find more accommodation. She rented two smaller properties just across the gravel road from the Husseini house, which had been built in the traditional manner, facing onto an inner courtyard. Every morning at 7.30, a whistle sounded, whereupon about 40 children came streaming out of the houses to go to school. They walked, two-by-two, in a long line up to the Damascus Gate and then up the steps to the old house on the ridge. From their rooms they could look out over the entire neighbourhood.

The children were taught by the former missionary, Clara Johanna Brooke, and by Herbert Drake, the minister of religion who had come to Jerusalem with General Gordon. Miss Brooke played the piano and was a veritable human encyclopaedia, who could talk at length about any topic. Sister Clara also had piles of 'forbidden' books and newspapers in her little room. She once lent a novel by William Makepeace Thackeray to young Lars Lind from Nås. Lars tried to read it in secret, but he was discovered by Mother Anna, who reprimanded him for wasting his time.

Later, another teacher arrived, a small thin man with a large head. His name was John Dinsmore, previously a teacher of Greek, mathematics and botany in America. John and his wife Mary had been on a one-year tour of Europe, Egypt and Palestine, when they had been smitten by the charismatic Anna. Some years later, they decided to join the congregation, despite the rule of celibacy.[169]

The farmers from the Chicago group had already rented some parcels of land north of the Colony before their counterparts from Dala had arrived. The land was in a valley sloping down toward the Old City. Despite a drought, which had lasted for a large part of that year, olives, figs and grapes grew there. The Swedish and American farmers discovered quickly that the soil was poor compared with that at home, but they fertilized the ground and worked it. The harvest seemed to be a success, and towards autumn some Orthodox Jews offered to buy all their produce, at a price higher than the market rate. A condition of sale was that the Jews should to be present when the harvest was taken in. The wheat was to be used for unleavened bread, *matzah*, eaten during the Jewish Passover.

It was not long before a number of the Swedes became sick. Mosquitoes were prevalent, and despite the fact that a bite could lead to serious illness in the form of malaria and even death, Anna forbade the use of quinine or other anti-malarial medicines. Karin Tipers Larsson's mother died just a month after the Swedes had settled in Jerusalem. With Mother Anna's help, Karin was able to turn her sadness into joy. She told Karin about Horatio's death and how she had danced in praise of the Lord.

In a letter home Karin wrote: "Mamma has gone to rest. She died the 17th at one in the morning. I want to say that it was a wonderful end, for at her death life and resurrection were recognized. Several of the sisters here in the house were awoken and we gathered in her room to send up our praises to the Lord." Karin's mother was buried in an herb garden near Gethsemane. The Colony was no longer able to bury its dead at the American cemetery, where Horatio and several of those who had died earlier had been interred. One of the Colony's friends, Abu Nassib, a tall Palestinian with shining brown-black eyes, came to their rescue. He did so in secret, however, because if it had become known that he had put his property at the disposal of Anna's dead disciples he would have had problems. According to Turkish law, any property in which a body was buried was automatically declared a charitable religious institution, a so-

169 Statement by Mary S Dinsmore, Folder: Member statements, American Colony Collection, Jerusalem.

called *waqf*. Such property could never be sold or inherited.

Other Palestinians helped the colonists secretly to solve similar problems. Two of their neighbours in the Old City had a small parcel of land in the Kedron Valley, planted with olive and fig trees. *Kadar* means black in Hebrew and in the Bible the place was known as "The Valley of the Dead". Concealed within an olive grove was a grave, of the kind that, according to the gospels, Joseph of Arimathea had carved for himself out of the cliff and which he subsequently offered as the tomb for Christ. Just like Joseph's grave, the entrance was blocked by a round, flat stone, which could be rolled to the side to open it. The Swedes were told that it was a grave of this kind that Pontius Pilate had sealed. Just as Joseph of Arimathea had taken a risk, so too did the colonists' Palestinian brothers.

The fact that the Swedes were now in the majority at the Colony was of little help to Olof Henrik Larsson. He remained a shadow of his former self, and did not even object when his family of four was allocated only one room between them. His wife, Mathilda, also remained passive, and the struggle for control of the community was finally lost when Pastor Larsson, that strong ship's captain and leader of men, lapsed into a prolonged crisis of conscience. The Swede lost his title of pastor. He was not even referred to as 'brother' but just plain Mr Larsson. Later, he became a virtual hermit within the Colony, relegated to a small house, which also served as a workshop for tin repairs.

The only project in which Mr Larsson was able to take a leading role was that of procuring fish for the Colony from the River Jordan. He initially contacted boat builders in Jaffa, but they made boats for the Mediterranean and knew nothing of the small, flat-bottomed skiffs, that were suitable for river use. Larsson then decided to give the job of building appropriate vessels to two Palestinian brothers from Jerusalem, who would work at the carpentry shop at the Colony. Mr Larsson supervised the work and busied himself by making nets. By the autumn, the boats were ready and one day Olof Henrik, together with six other fishermen from the American Colony, set about transporting them to the Dead Sea by wagon. Unfortunately the wagon had no brakes and on the journey downhill towards the Dead Sea it took the combined might of all seven fishermen to restrain the wagon and stop it running away. Thanks to the presence of so many strong Swedes on either side of the wagon, the horse managed to reach the Greek Orthodox Monastery of St John, at the place where Jesus had been baptized. The Patriarch in Jerusalem had provided the colonists with a letter of introduction requesting that the monks should take care of them. The fishermen were able to sleep there, and were safe from the wild boar and hyenas that inhabited the area. The monastery could not, however, protect the fishermen from the bloodsucking mosquitoes and, alas, they were to find that the fish in the river were few.

Olof Henrik Larsson's fishing project came to an abrupt end when the fishermen all got sick, some from malaria, and others from what they called 'black fever'. Three men never recovered. Anna's insistence on using no medicine, only prayer, was absolute and the three died soon after returning to Jerusalem. Larsson survived, but he lost the respect of the community. The two rowing boats remained on the banks of the River Jordan, and were subsequently used by the monks to carry Russian pilgrims who came to be baptized in the river.

In the year before the Swedes from Nås arrived in Jerusalem, a new American consul had arrived in the city. Edwin Wallace was a Presbyterian minister from South Dakota. The fact that the consul was a Presbyterian, and a minister, was, in itself, enough to ensure that the ongoing conflict between Anna and the consulate would continue.

Consul Wallace waited until April 19, 1897, to fire his first shot. On that day two of the Colony's American members, 60-year-old John and Amelia Adamson, of Harvey, Illinois, left Anna's sect. They had received $100 from friends in America and planned to use the money to return home. The Adamsons chose, as others before them, to tell the American consul a shocking story. When the consul interviewed them he was given a new insight into why Anna Spafford's congregation had originally called themselves Overcomers. The consul sent the following summary of their conversation to Washington:

They conquer all natural affections and desires.[170]
What is their method of conquering?
By exposing themselves to all sorts of temptations, particularly sexual. Is immorality – as the word is generally understood – openly indulged in?
Not openly... [But] married men were seen by us on various occasions suspiciously intimate with certain female members of the household. As late as one o'clock in the morning, men have been with women in dark parts of the house, and afterwards in public

170 United States National Archives, Washington, record group 59 T/367 Beirut & T/471 Jerusalem, record group 84, Jerusalem File 27. Dudman & Kark: *The American Colony*, p.135.

meetings at which children were present; these night wanderers professed that they were 'seeking the flesh not the spirit'.

Consul Wallace was so shocked that he called in another Presbyterian pastor as witness. His report to Washington contained an echo of those earlier allegations made by his predecessor, Merrill. According to Edwin Wallace, the American Colony was a commune of religious fanatics who behaved unlawfully and beyond what decent society regarded as conventional custom and practice. Mrs Spafford was an absolute autocrat whom no one dared to oppose. "By falsehood," Wallace wrote, "she induces the ignorant and unsuspecting to sell all they have in America and come here... Then they cannot leave..."[171] The Adamsons had told the consul and his witness that Mrs Spafford felt she was beyond the law. Wallace's account continued:

She says straight out to those god-fearing fools that her power is greater than any earthly authority. She tries openly to separate man from wife. This leads to men and women, even if they are married according to God's laws, being separated and having what is called a 'spiritual relationship'. Some wives suffer the worst anxieties at being left, while at the same time being forced to observe their husband's affections toward other women... this is shameless immorality, and is nothing more than a whorehouse where infidelity is practiced in the name of religion. Men and women who are not married sleep together in the same bed so that they can 'overcome' their temptations. If they do not succeed, I have been told by a credible witness, the next morning they confess. Everyone, young and old alike are present as the disgusting details are reported.

There was another point the American Consul wanted to make:

The fact that Muslims have free access to the women is in itself suspicious. Anyone who knows the character of Muslims, and that includes access to close relationships, does not need to be told what the result will be if the opportunity presents itself... the problem is Mrs Spafford's charm. It is difficult to gather proof. [Visitors are spoken to] in the most appealing manner, while the immoral side, the real life of the house, is kept hidden from the visitors. The guests,

171 Helga Dudman: *Street People*, Carta Jerusalem 1983, p.97.

almost without exception, leave later with a positive impression. Politeness and Christian conversation have won them over.

The Adamsons' statement came as an unexpected gift for Wallace. Finally, he had two people whom he could use to launch an attack on the Colony. "Anna Spafford said herself that those who left the Colony 'were so evil and given over to Satan that they no longer could be tolerated' but the truth is the opposite," maintained Wallace. His report concluded with the request that the State Department should undertake an investigation into the Colony.

When Anna got word of this, she decided to send the treasurer of the Colony, William Rudy, to Washington to tell the colonists' version of events. Rudy must prove that the allegations about free sexuality were a lie, and explain that Anna Spafford's conscience was clean and that the community had overcome an earlier challenge about 'morality'.

On September 8, 1897, Brother William Rudy was driven to the railway station and took the train to Jaffa. With him he had several letters from respected citizens of Jerusalem, and he felt well prepared to meet the bureaucrats at the American State Department.

Rudy was still in Washington when, three months later, Consul Wallace sent a bulky envelope to the State Department containing alleged proof of Anna Spafford's immoral life. Rudy asked to read Wallace's report but was refused permission to do so. The envelope contained, among other things, a comprehensive report entitled: 'Spaffordism – a conclusive exposé of the Spaffordite fraud'. The report, signed by 16 missionaries, stated among other things that "the responsibilities of married life between a man and his wife were indiscriminately being broken [...] and the community embraces the principle of free love."[172]

In addition to the missionaries, many other dignitaries from Jerusalem had signed the report. The city's Anglican bishop had also composed a letter praising the American consul and criticising the Spaffordites' unique form of Christianity and their "self-constituted prophetess", on the grounds that "one who pretends to such a commission, especially being a female, must be either under a curse or an impostor".[173]

By now, Anna Spafford's name was well known to the American newspaper reading public. The *Chicago Journal* of December 20, 1897, contained a quote from the consul's report, in which he referred to Anna as "the Devil in Jehoshaphat's valley". Anna's version of her story followed

172 Folder: 1893. American Colony Collection, Jerusalem.
173 Dudman & Kark: *The American Colony*, Jerusalem 1998, p.138.

in the Christmas edition of the newspaper. Rudy, the Colony's spokesman, pulled no punches. Each and every missionary in Jerusalem who had signed the report against them was discussed. Some were dismissed as drunkards, while all the women who had signed were condemned as being "jealous of Anna Spafford".

It was not easy for outsiders to know what actually took place within the walls of the American Colony. A few months earlier, at the beginning of August 1897, the Norwegian-American, Axel Strand, had also visited the consulate, together with a Danish missionary. Strand told Consul Edwin Wallace that his wife was being held hostage there adding: "I do not even get to visit her."

"I cannot do anything, unless you report American citizens as holding your wife hostage," answered Consul Wallace, who then dictated a report, which Axel Strand signed.

"Do you swear the truth of this report?" asked the consul. But Strand would not do so. He subsequently returned to the consulate with his wife and admitted that his accusations had been false. Consul Wallace became furious and ripped the document to pieces.[174] By this stage, the American diplomat was completely convinced that immoral activities were taking place inside the walls of the Colony. He was firmly resolved to expose Anna.

174 Testimonies of Furman Baldwin, September 8, 1908, and William Henry Rudy, August 31, 1908, cited in the case of Edwin Wallace versus D. Appleton & Co, Folder: 1908, American Colony Collection, Jerusalem.

Chapter 14

Detour to Palestine

In Europe, a complex political battle over the future of Palestine was being waged – a conflict with far broader implications than the battles over the American Colony. The lead figure in the drama was Theodor Herzl, a 35-year-old man with a high forehead, a prophetic dreamy countenance and a patriarchal beard. He was born in Budapest, but had moved to Vienna as an 18-year-old. It was there, after taking a doctorate in law, that he entered journalism, becoming the Paris correspondent of the liberal Austrian newspaper *Neue Freie Presse*.

Herzl had been profoundly influenced by the infamous espionage case involving the French Jewish military officer, Alfred Dreyfus, which came to court towards the end of 1894. Herzl recognized that the false accusations levelled against Dreyfus were based solely on hatred of the Jews. The journalist, himself a Jew, concluded that the only way to end anti-semitism in Europe was for the Jews to have their own country.

There were many Jews who thought Herzl was a fanatic, dreaming that the dead sons of biblical Israel would rise from their graves and reclaim their homeland for their scattered brethren. Throughout history there had been many others who had said that 'the Chosen' would lead the Jewish people to victory.[175] The idea of settling Jews in biblical Palestine was not exclusively Jewish. When Napoleon had occupied Jaffa in 1799, he suggested that a Jewish state should be established in the region. But Napoleon did not succeed in becoming emperor of the east, and the French Zionist ideal crumbled.

175 Phillip Mansel: *Constantinople, City of the World's Desire, 1453–1924*, New York 1996, p.141, Benjamin Beit-Hallahmi: *Original Sins, Reflections on the History of Zionism and Israel*, London 1992, p.13.

In Palestine, most people knew little about Herzl or the sensation he created in 1896 with his book *Der Judenstaat*. In it, Herzl argued that the Jews were not only a religious group, but also a nation waiting to be born. He described in detail a Jewish state, but left open the question of where it should be located. Neither did he insist that the state should be for Jews alone. In his diary, however, one year before the book was published, Herzl had written:

When we occupy the land, we shall bring immediate benefits to the state that receives us. We must expropriate gently the private property on the estates assigned to us. We shall try to spirit the penniless population across the border by procuring employment for it in the transit countries, while denying it any work in our own country. The property owners will come over to our side. Both the process of expropriation and the removal of the poor must be carried out discretely and circumspectly. Let the owners of immovable property believe that they are cheating us, by selling us things for more than they are worth. But we are not going to sell anything back.[176]

Der Judenstaat caused the author to be identified immediately with what was called political Zionism. Herzl maintained that the Jewish question was an international one and should be handled as such. Political Zionism stood in contrast to practical Zionism, a phenomenon which had begun in Russia in 1881 as a result of the persecution of Jews there. It was only four years later that the term Zionism was first used in public.

The new movement had its roots in the fact that Jews were not being assimilated in Europe due to increasing anti-semitism and growing nationalism. Where nationalism created a problem for the Jews, it also gave them a solution: the idea of self-government in their own state. Zionism would found a state for the Jews in Palestine with a Jewish majority: a new society was to be built, based on freedom, democracy and social justice. But no one talked about the Arabs who were already there.[177]

Herzl's work led to his becoming the leading Zionist spokesman, and in 1897 he organized the world's first Zionist Congress in Basel, Switzerland, renting the town's public casino for the event. Herzl hung a

176 Theodor Herzl, June 12, 1895: *The Complete Diaries of Theodor Herzl, Vol. I* (Editor: Raphael Patai), Herzl Press and Thomas Yoseloff, New York 1960, p.88.
177 Avi Shlaim: *The Iron Wall, Israel and the Arab World*, New York and London 1999, p.2.

huge white flag with two blue stripes and a six-sided star over the entrance. His businessman friend, David Wolffsohn, had chosen blue and white so the delegates would associate it with the old Jewish flag. Blue and white were the colours of the Hebrew prayer shawl.[178]

Before the congress started, Herzl, who was not religious, attended prayers at the local synagogue. It was intended as a gesture toward the religious Jews whom Herzl secretly feared. He managed to say the few words in Hebrew which were needed for a blessing, but complained later that he had perspired more than if he was giving a speech. When the congress formally opened and Herzl stepped up to speak the delegates clapped and shouted: "Long live the King" – *Yehi ha-melech*, Jews from all over Europe, from America, Palestine and North Africa applauded the modern-day successor to King David.

When Herzl returned to Vienna, he wrote in his diary for September 3rd: "Were I to sum up the congress in a word, it would be this: at Basel I founded the Jewish state. If I uttered this aloud today, I would be answered by universal laughter. Perhaps in five years, and certainly in 50, everyone will know it."[179] Herzl believed that a Jewish state in Palestine could only be realized via the kaiser. He knew that Wilhelm II had large-scale plans to infiltrate Turkey. The kaiser had big ambitions: the Ottoman Empire was to become an important sphere of German interest.

In the summer of 1898, Kaiser Wilhelm and his consort went to Constantinople. As expected, the German guests were overwhelmed by their reception, from the first 105-gun salute as they sailed into Constantinople, to the fairy-tale atmosphere at the sultan's palace. Sultan Abdul Hamid II was an excellent host. He gave a state dinner for 120 guests at which the diners ate from bejewelled gold plates and drank from cut glass decorated with precious stones. A famous French chef had cooked the sumptuous meal. The German Empress, Augusta Victoria, was presented with a large bouquet of flowers from the palace gardens. The sultan himself had picked the flowers and had placed a large diamond amongst the foliage.

Augusta Victoria's visit to the sultan's harem raised a smile from those around her: when she was met at the Imperial Gate of Pleasure by an enormous black man, the empress was told that he was the head eunuch in the harem. Knowing nothing of eunuchs, and in an effort to engage him in conversation, she could think of nothing else to say than: "Was

---

178 Pawel: *The Labyrinth of Exile,* New York 1989, p.330, and Alex Bein: *Theodor Herzl. A Biography,* Philadelphia 1945, p.229.
179 *The Complete Diaries of Theodor Herzl, Volume II,* (ed.Patai), New York and London 1960, p.581.

your father also a eunuch?" [180]

Abdul Hamid II had expansionist ideas and it suited him well that the Germans wanted to build a railway to Baghdad. The sultan also had a dream of introducing railways, roads and telegraphic communication to his empire. The Ottoman sultan and the German kaiser had something else in common. Both were suspicious to the point of neurosis. In addition, the kaiser was an anti-semite. When his father lay on his deathbed with throat cancer, Wilhelm began to believe in an Anglo-Jewish plot, led by his mother, to take over Germany.

But Herzl knew nothing of the kaiser's anti-semitic views. He had no idea that Wilhelm II had written in the margins of a report from his ambassador in Switzerland following the Zionist Congress in Basel: "Let the kikes go to Palestine, the sooner the better. I am not about to put obstacles in their way."[181]

Unaware of this, Herzl wanted to meet the kaiser before he left for Constantinople. He had been assured that the German leader was sympathetic to Zionism and he hoped he would put in a good word with Abdul Hamid. Herzl believed that the Jews could be agents for European colonialism. In *Der Judenstaat*, he had suggested: "If His Majesty, the sultan, were to give us Palestine, we could in return undertake to regulate the whole finances of Turkey. There we could form part of a wall of defence for Europe in Asia, an outpost of civilization against barbarism."[182]

During the second Zionist Congress Herzl had developed his earlier theory that Asia would become the greatest diplomatic problem of the coming decades. "We may in all modesty perhaps recall to mind that we Zionists recognized, and announced as imminent, the coming development of European rivalry (i.e. the imperialist struggle to divide the world) a few years before others did."

After learning of the imperial couple's travel plans Herzl wrote an editorial in the Zionist weekly *Die Welt*. He praised Wilhelm II's liberal views and expressed the hope that the kaiser would promote Zionism in his dealings with the Ottoman sultan. This would be consistent with Germany's long-term goals.[183] Herzl sent a copy of the newspaper to the kaiser and was told that Wilhelm had read it. At the same time, Herzl

---

180 Noel Barber: *Lords of the Golden Horn, The Splendours of Islam and the Fall of the Mighty Ottoman Empire*, London 1973, p.174.
181 Pawel: *The Labyrinth of Exile*. New York 1989, p.342.
182 Theodor Herzl: *Der Judenstaat*, Köln 1914, p.30, cited in Klaus Polkehn: *Zionism and Kaiser Wilhelm*, Journal of Palestine Studies, Vol. IV, No.2, 1975, pp. 76-7.
183 Alex Bein: *Theodor Herzl. A Biography*, Philadelphia, 1945, pp.276–309.

was encouraged to forward any future articles that he considered to be of interest to the monarch. But this was still not enough for the determined Zionist leader. He wanted to talk directly to the kaiser.

Chapter 15

The Graveyard War

When Horatio Spafford died in 1888, Anna had been granted permission to bury her husband on Mount Zion, just outside the city walls and near the grave of King David – land which belonged to the Presbyterian Church. The American consul in Jerusalem was given the key to the graveyard when the Presbyterians moved their mission to Lebanon. But when Selah Merrill returned to Jerusalem as consul in 1891, he regarded the cemetery as primarily an archaeological site. He therefore decided to inspect the area more closely. One dark night at the beginning of August he began to dig for relics of the past. He continued his excavations with a small group of labourers, and although the consul found some interesting objects, a number of graves were disturbed during the course of his investigation.

No one at the American Colony knew of the consul's clandestine activities before August 13, 1891, when the burial of Anna's sister-in-law, Margareth Lee, was about to take place. She had died suddenly the day before, during a walking tour just outside the city walls. When the sect members brought her coffin to Mount Zion, they discovered to their horror that the cemetery had been desecrated. Holes had been dug and mounds of earth piled up between the gravestones. When Bertha came to her father's grave she cried out and fainted. Horatio Spafford's coffin lay at the bottom of a gaping hole.

After Anna Spafford protested, the American consul decided to end his archaeology project on Mount Zion. His relationship with Anna, however, did not improve, and when Consul Merrill left Jerusalem two years later, everyone in the American Colony was relieved.

Some years later, however, the Colony's members heard rumours that the American cemetery was to be sold to German Catholics. Again, Anna was distressed and the news prompted her to try to find a suitable graveyard for the congregation. Under Ottoman law, graveyards could not be bought or sold at will, and any applications for purchase had to be submitted in Arabic to the Ottoman authorities, via the American consulate. With the help of one of their Palestinian members, the American Colony completed the appropriate application. They found subsequently that the consul had deleted a sentence in which they explained that they now needed to buy their own graveyard "because the old one was to be sold".[184]

Previously, the new American Consul, Edwin Wallace, had told William Rudy that the board of the Presbyterian Mission to Jerusalem was considering a sale, but that this would take time. The consul had asked whether, if this happened, the colonists would take responsibility for the dead who were buried there.[185] "Of course," answered Rudy, "but I hope to be advised sufficiently in advance, because we have no other graveyard."

Wallace subsequently assured Anna that she would be notified of any change in ownership. So, the colonists expected no problems when, four years later, 51-year-old Mats Matsson died. But Olof Henrik Larsson received a similar shock when he requested the keys to the graveyard from the American consulate. "The graveyard has been sold and all the graves have been moved," said Consul Wallace. "More I cannot say." Larsson had to return without a key, and with nowhere to bury Mats Matsson.[186]

Anna's first reaction was surprise, then rage. She believed that the sale and the removal of Horatio's grave and those of the others must be part of a conspiracy. Why had the graveyard been sold without Mother Anna being informed? Who could be responsible? She was going to find out, but first she had to get Mats Matsson buried decently. The Greek Orthodox patriarch came to the rescue and, despite the fact that the farmer from Nås was a Protestant, he was buried on land belonging to the Greek church.

Some time later, 19-year-old Bertha, along with an American member of the Colony, confronted the consul and demanded to know what had happened to the remains of her father and the others.

184 Statement made by Fareed Naseef, of the American Colony, to the Circuit Court of the United States, Southern District of New York, in the case of Wallace vs. Appleton & Co, Folder: 1908, American Colony Collection, Jerusalem.
185 Statement made by William Rudy, 31st August, 1908, to the Circuit Court of the United States, Southern District of New York, Folder: 1908, American Colony Collection, Jerusalem.
186 Mats Matsson died on September 18, 1897. Statement by Olof Henrik Larsson September 28, 1908, pp. 8–9, Folder: 1908, American Colony Collection, Jerusalem.

"Is it true that the graveyard was sold?" asked Bertha as she stood in front of Consul Wallace.

"Yes," Wallace answered.

"Where are my father and my aunt, Mrs Margareth Lee, widow of Colonel Lee from the American Army?"[187]

"What do you want with your father's remains?" asked the American diplomat.

"I care a lot for my father, Mr Wallace, and I want his remains."

"It is one of your community's principles not to care about the dead," he replied.

"Did you know this to be one of our principles?"

"Why otherwise have you not put up gravestones, if you care so much?"

Changing his tone, the consul went on: "I had nothing to do with this. Mr Eddy is the man you should go to."

"Mr Wallace, you have a lot to do with this; you are the American consul, and you are the guardian of the American cemetery, you are the protector of the rights of American citizens, you are responsible both for our dead and for our rights," answered Bertha.

"I can do nothing."

"If you will not, I will report this to Washington," said Bertha, who had inherited her mother's determination.

At this point, the consul turned and left. The conversation had taken place in the front hall of the consulate. Mr Wallace had deliberately not allowed Bertha Spafford into his office.

At the American Colony, Mother Anna decided to take control of the matter. A large group of colonists, including Mary Sylvester, Mary Whiting and Amelia Gould, went to see Pastor William Eddy, the man who had sold the graveyard on behalf of the Presbyterians.

"Why have you removed the remains of our dead without our knowledge?" asked Anna.[188]

"Because the graveyard was sold," answered Pastor Eddy, "and we had every right to sell." He produced a thick document, signed and sealed, which proved he was correct.

187 Statements made by Furman Olmstead Baldwin, September 8, 1908, and Bertha Spafford Vester, September 2, 1908, in the case of Wallace vs. Appleton & Co, p. 7. Folder:1908, American Colony Collection, Jerusalem.
188 Witness statement of Mary Sylvester, September 2, 1908, in the case of Wallace vs. Appleton & Co., Circuit Court of the United States, Southern District of New York, American Colony Collection, Jerusalem.

"That is not the point," said a member of the delegation from the Colony, "we want to know why our deceased have been moved without our knowledge."

"Oh, they were all removed properly. No one meant to offend your feelings," answered the Presbyterian pastor, and ended the conversation. But Pastor Eddy did not want to reveal where the dead had been reburied. He said only that German Jesuits had bought the graveyard and that they were going to build a church there.

Some days later, Bertha went yet again to the American consulate to appeal to him. This time, Wallace told her that she had no rights since she was "only a child". This was the last straw for Bertha and she broke down.

"Please don't be theatrical," said the consul and asked her to leave.

When Bertha regained control she went to the Turkish authorities to complain. She spoke with the chief of the office of public order and told him how she had tried in vain to find out where the Colony's dead had been buried. The head of the office was a Palestinian, Ismail Husseini, who had been taught English by Horatio Spafford, and whose family lived close to the American Colony.

Ismail Husseini first contacted the court in Jerusalem, but the Ottoman judge said that he could not intervene in the internal disputes of foreign Christians. The American consul himself had agreed to the operation, together with the Presbyterians, and he had diplomatic immunity. The sale of the graveyard to the Germans had also received formal recognition, so the only way out was to contact higher American authorities.

However, the Palestinian was so furious on Anna's behalf that he decided to compose a letter to the US President: "Sir, I am not able to accept in silence what I have been witness to by your honourable government's consuls," he began. Husseini then described how the small American Christian community in Jerusalem had been defamed by two previous American consuls. Both Selah Merrill and his successor, Edwin Wallace, had worked against the sect "simply because they refused to march up the worn path to the missionaries in the city. For 18 months there has been no end to the difficulties for the Colony's people... Everything which is normally regarded as decent and proper is abused, for even if customs in the US and Palestine are different, the authorities must never tolerate the commercial selling of a graveyard. You, Mr President, will recognize that this is true, when I remind you there was a chorus of condemnation from Europe and America when it was said that the Turks had vandalized the

Armenian graves."[189]

Anna Spafford also wrote in protest to the American State Department: "We are peaceful and law-abiding people who insult no one; nor do we force our ideas on anyone." A third assistant-secretary answered: "The department finds it impossible, at this distance, to determine the merits of the controversy between yourself and Consul Wallace, but is willing to send an agent of the department to Jerusalem to look into the case."[190]

Further protests were lodged by Mary Sylvester, the widow of Captain Sylvester, who complained to the British consul in Jerusalem. The captain had been a British citizen and Mrs Sylvester demanded that his remains be buried again in a proper manner. Only after a long exchange of letters between the British consul and the Foreign Office in London did Mary Sylvester receive permission to search for her husband in the British cemetery. It was there that all the remains were supposed to lie, "numbered and separate". [191]

Early on a Monday morning in February 1898, Mary Sylvester, along with a few others from the Colony, went to the British cemetery. As well as gravediggers, the local representative of the British consulate and the consular guard were also present. When the large common grave was opened, they all saw the remains lying, not in coffins, but in boxes, some upside down, others on their sides. It was obvious that some of the boxes were far too small to contain an entire person and that some skeletons had been broken so that they could all fit in.

One after another, the boxes were brought up. Mrs Sylvester was searching for number 13, the one that should have contained the remains of her husband. The numbers 3 & 4, written on the side of one box, indicated that it contained the contents of two graves. Another box was crushed as it was removed and the contents fell out. There, to the horror of the colonists, they saw the remains of Horatio Spafford, mixed up with those of another person. Horatio's skull was easily recognizable, because he had lost his front teeth as a young boy. But Mary Sylvester had received permission to look only for her husband, not for the nine others from the Colony, and she was prevented from examining Horatio's remains any further. Finally, when the last box was exhumed, they had to give up. There was no number 13.

189 Copy of letter in American Colony's Archive.
190 Letter from the State Department to the American Colony, dated October 26, 1897, American Colony Collection.
191 Letter from John Dickson to Mary Sylvester, September 24, 1897, Exhibit no. 47, witness statement of Mary Sylvester, September 2, 1908, Folder: 1908, American Colony Collection, Jerusalem.

Later, Anna and the two other widows were given permission to bury the remains of their husbands again. Over the common grave of Horatio Spafford, William Sylvester and John Whiting a stone was erected with their names and the text: "Their identity known to God alone."[192]

The American State Department asked the consul general in Constantinople to investigate the matter. This alarmed the Board of Presbyterian Foreign Missions which sent an envoy immediately to Jerusalem. The representative wrote a report in which he explained that the Presbyterians had needed money, and since the ground had not been consecrated, they had sold it. The representative claimed to have proof that the land had not been a 'churchyard', insisting that the Turkish authorities had agreed to the sale. According to Turkish law, however, it was strictly forbidden to sell any graveyard.

The American consul general from Constantinople chose to exclude the American Colony from his investigation entirely. The diplomat concluded his report by saying that the accusations against both Selah Merrill and Edwin Wallace could not be proved. The consul general ended with the words: "I thought it was going to be a pleasure to visit Jerusalem, but instead I found an atmosphere overloaded with blame."

The 'Graveyard War' between the consulate and the American Colony did not end here, but it would be a further 10 years before Anna Spafford was able to take the revenge which, perhaps in the back of her mind, she was hoping for. This would all be played out on a public stage, initially in the form of a long magazine article, and then, two years later, in an American court room. In the meantime, Anna had to exercise patience.

192 Lars E Lind & Tord Wallström: *Jerusalemsfararne* (Jerusalem Travelers), Stockholm 1981, p.66.

Chapter 16

Secret Audience

Jerusalem seethed with conflict. There were disagreements among Jews from the east and the west, and between Christians and Jews, Christians and Muslims, and Muslims and Jews. There were also conflicts between the Turks and the Palestinians, among the various Bedouin tribes, even between those whose job it was to bring visitors to the city, Thomas Cook, head of the largest tour operator in Palestine and his challenger Rolla Floyd.

While the British company took care of most of the tourists, the best known expert on Palestine was the American. Previously, Rolla Floyd had been one of Cook's most faithful employees. It was only when he realized how much money there was in tourism, and how little he was paid, that Floyd started up by himself. This was in 1881, the same year that Anna Spafford came to Palestine.

Just as Mother Anna had to fight the US representatives in Jerusalem, Rolla Floyd had to take on the Goliath of tourism, Thomas Cook. In her fight, however, Anna Spafford had a big advantage. She was convinced that God was protecting her. She was sustained by God's words, which she had heard after the sinking of the *Ville du Havre* in 1873 and she would repeat them often: "You have been saved for one reason. You have work to fulfil." Opposition did not, therefore, affect Anna Spafford. When others complained, she would say: "The one who is unable to go through the burning oven is not of very much worth."[193]

In the dispute between Thomas Cook and Rolla Floyd, the British company had the support of the American consul. American diplomats were so poorly paid that some of them were forced to develop commercial interests as a sideline. The vice-consul under Selah Merrill had been

193 Olof Fahlén: *Nåsbönderna i Jerusalem* (Nås Farmers in Jerusalem), Höganäs 1988, p.54.

accused of issuing false passports or documents of protection. Rolla Floyd believed the American vice-consul was "just the kind of thief our consul likes. As soon as this thief leaves, the consul is going to appoint another thief."[194] According to Floyd, Merrill had also been acting improperly. In the accounts of the American State Department the annual rent for the office in Jerusalem was listed as $300. In fact, the rent was only $170. Expenses for postage were noted as $15 per month while they were actually only $4. It was also alleged by office staff at the consulate that Merrill received bribes from Cook.

Both Thomas Cook and Selah Merrill had been preachers. Cook had belonged to a Baptist Church, but had grown tired of talking about the narrow path to heaven, and chose instead the earthly Jerusalem. His first trip to Jerusalem, along with a British group, took place in 1869. They had stayed in tents outside the city walls and were served English tea and cakes on small tables covered with linen and set with a silver service.

Travel had since become easier. Steamships made the trip from London to Port Said in five or six days, while the opening of the Suez Canal also helped to increase the stream of tourists to Palestine. Even though the road between Jaffa and Jerusalem was not considered completely safe, the Turks tried to improve security by publicly beheading bandits outside the Jaffa Gate.

Thomas Cook also arranged what he called biblical education tours. These were directed particularly toward priests and Sunday school teachers. Some received a culture shock in Palestine. The earthly Jerusalem was, as many other pious people had discovered previously, more of a Levantine bazaar than heaven on earth. Even the most devout inhabitants of Jerusalem had no qualms about selling large quantities of fake antiques to the tourists. Thousands of 'Roman' copper coins and 'Israelite' silver shekels were dug from the fields outside Jerusalem. They had been lying there for a few years to acquire the necessary patina of age.

One of the biggest swindles, that still deceives people to this day, was the 'Via Dolorosa'. The street has no historic value and was purely a commercial invention. It begins about 100 yards inside St Stephen's Gate in the lower part of the city, winding upwards towards Golgotha, and was so named around 1600 by tradesmen with foresight, who wanted to cheat pilgrims out of the maximum amount of money. The historically correct

194 Rolla Floyd, Jerusalem, to Aurilla Floyd Tabbutt, Columbia Falls, September 13, 1882, September 5, 1883 and January 23, 1884, cited in Helen Palmer Parson (editor): *Letters from Palestine: 1868–1912, Written by Rolla Floyd*, Dexter, ME: private printing, 1981. pp. 65, 76–79 cited in Ruth Kark: *American Consuls in the Holy Land*, Jerusalem 1994, pp.194-95.

Via Dolorosa went from inside the Jaffa Gate, from the Citadel, down into the city to the Church of the Holy Sepulchre.

On every road, the pilgrim would encounter pushy Arabs, Jews, Armenians and Greeks. The ability to trade and barter with foreigners was in the genes of the local salesmen. The pious pilgrims coming down the Via Dolorosa with tears in their eyes, on their way to the grave of Jesus, were virtually defenceless against them. The tradesmen were not the only artists; begging itself had become an art. *Bakhshish, bakhshish* – share your wealth – was the first Arabic expression the tourists learned.

Some of the guides warned their guests about giving money for 'Christian works'. But others took a commission from the tradesmen or beggars. When the tourists and pilgrims learned that the half-naked beggar outside the Jaffa Gate was in fact the owner of over 600 olive trees and four orchards they often became disillusioned, if not distressed.[195]

A few of the local sheikhs demanded large payments not to rob tourists, and even if travellers had been promised free passage they could still be assaulted. Cook had to ask the British consul in Jerusalem for a military escort, and the company warned its customers before they went to Palestine.

But Thomas Cook's vision of how his business should develop did not coincide with that of his son, John, a hard-nosed businessman. The younger Cook was not particularly interested in arranging visits to Palestine for priests and others of the middle class. John Cook wanted to concentrate on royalty. He made sure that when Crown Prince Rudolf of Austria came to Palestine in 1881, it was Thomas Cook & Son who were responsible for the trip. The preparations were lavish. Thirty waiters and five cooks were employed. The crown prince had 28 tents put at his disposal. Two of them were decorated in silk in the Austrian national colours – green, red, and gold. There was a sleeping tent, a reception tent and a dressing room with mirrors and pitchers of Chinese porcelain. In each tent there were Persian carpets, silk sofas and armchairs, Chinese flower vases, and three different coffee sets – one Chinese, one Turkish and one made of Sèvres porcelain. Turkish *sheeshas* and cigarettes were available, along with a music box which could play 12 melodies. The royals and their retinue were offered dozens of French oysters and buckets of Russian caviar.[196]

In addition to the royal visitors, thousands of regular tourists came to Jerusalem, 'cookies' as the locals called Cook's clients, in addition to

195 Sir Frederick Treves: *The Land That is Desolate*, London 1912, p.64.
196 Amos Elon: *Jerusalem, City of Mirrors*, Glasgow 1991, pp.23 and 144–145.

hundreds of journalists. In the second half of the 19th century, more than 1,500 books about the Holy Land were published in England alone. Some contained pictures, woodcuts and water colours of the holy places and the landscape. Others depicted poverty, filth and misery. For Herman Melville, the author of *Moby Dick*, Jerusalem was "like a cold grey eye in a cold grey man", and the road to Jericho was like going through "black and funereal hillsides until it debouched on the plain of Jericho, which looked like the gate to Hell".

One of the royal visitors to Jerusalem during this period was the German Emperor Wilhelm II. His trip, in 1898, would be of great importance to the American Colony, but Anna Spafford could not have known this at the time. Neither did she know that Zionist leader Theodor Herzl was working behind the scenes to speak to the kaiser before he came to Jerusalem.

Herzl's plan was that Wilhelm II should prepare the ground for Jewish migration to Palestine. The kaiser was to ask Sultan Abdul Hamid II to approve a plan whereby European Jews could buy large areas of land in Palestine. This would enable the Jews to establish their own state under German protection. Herzl believed this would fit in with the kaiser's own plan to restore health to an ailing Turkey and give Germany greater influence in the Ottoman Empire.

Initially, Herzl got the impression that Kaiser Wilhelm II was inclined to take the expatriate Jews in Palestine under his protection. The German Ambassador, Count Phillip von Eulenburg, had suggested this might be the case, but he did not explain to Herzl why the kaiser might be so positively disposed towards Zionism.

The truth was that Wilhelm II believed that rich and ambitious Jews could bring prosperity to the Holy Land, and lead to an economic upswing throughout the whole Near East. The kaiser believed further that when Jewish efforts were focused on the development of Palestine, German Jews would have more worthy goals to pursue than "to suck the Christians dry in Europe". Wilhelm II also hoped that Jewish members of the opposition Social Democrats in Germany would be attracted by the idea of moving to the Near East.

Herzl did not know that the kaiser was a racist, who seldom let an opportunity pass without emphasizing how important it was to have a pure and exclusively Germanic race. The kaiser thought, for example, that his Germanic roots had been tarnished by his father's marriage to his mother, Princess Victoria, the daughter of Queen Victoria and Prince Albert, who was partly English. He believed that the North Sea was a "purely German sea", not to be shared with the British or the Slavs (as he called the Russians).[197]

Herzl believed that Count von Eulenburg was the only person capable of influencing the unstable kaiser. But the ambassador's advice to Herzl was not entirely impartial. Von Eulenburg, who wrote poetry and composed music, had been immediately drawn to the Jewish author. Herzl did not know that the 51-year-old count was a homosexual and part of a secret network within the kaiser's ruling circle.[198]

Von Eulenburg had previously shown little enthusiasm for Herzl's visions of a Jewish state in Palestine, but he changed his view when the latter spoke of a Jewish state under German protection. The count was also attracted by the "unusually talented" Jewish author with "a head like King David" and without a trace of being a "Jewish tradesman".[199]

When Herzl met the ambassador for the second time, von Eulenburg told him that the kaiser was excited about the idea of sending Jews to buy land in Palestine, adding the caution that the emperor had to be "greatly interested in a matter, otherwise he soon loses sight of it". Nevertheless, von Eulenburg assured Herzl that he had been "able to return to the subject repeatedly... fortunately for your cause I have also been able to win over Bülow, [the Foreign Minister], my best friend and a most outstanding statesman."[200]

The German ambassador and Herzl agreed that the Zionist leader would be granted an unofficial audience with the kaiser in Constantinople during the latter's visit there. At the meeting, Herzl would deliver the draft of a speech that he would make to the kaiser at a subsequent, official audience, in Jerusalem.[201]

Following the meeting, Herzl rapidly gathered together a delegation. They had to leave immediately in order to reach Constantinople before the kaiser. None of the four delegates was told where they were going or what their mission was about. Herzl did not dare tell anyone of his plan. He was afraid of leaks, which might ruin his chances of an audience, and it was only

197 John C. G. Röhl: *The Kaiser and His Court, Wilhelm II and the Government of Germany*, Cambridge University Press, 1994, pp.202–203.
198 In 1908 Eulenburg was the subject of a court case, concerning his homosexuality.
199 Nachlass Eulenburg, Bundesarchiv, Koblenz Nr. 52, cited in Isaiah Friedman: *Germany, Turkey and Zionism, 1897–1918*, Oxford 1977, p.62.
200 Theodor Herzl, October 7, 1898: *The Complete Diaries of Theodor Herzl* Volume II (ed. Patai) Hertz Press, New York 1960, p.689.
201 The meeting with the German Foreign Minister was arranged just before the kaiser set out on his trip to Constantinople, Jerusalem, and Damascus. Alex Bein: *Theodor Herzl*, pp.287–289.

on Sunday, October 16, when the Orient Express rolled into the station in Constantinople, that others in the party were told details of their mission.

The Zionist delegation was not in the city for very long before pessimism began to spread. The German ambassador in Constantinople did not want to receive Herzl. The ambassador's secretary had said that he did not even know of Dr Herzl, and refused to see him. It became clear to members of the delegation that they lacked allies. The German ambassador in Constantinople was not particularly in favour of Zionism, while the German Foreign Minister, Prince Bernard von Bülow, did not believe a Jewish influx to Palestine would help Turkey. He did not even believe the Ottoman Empire was sustainable. Turkey was not just 'the sick man of Europe', he thought, but a fatally ill old man.

The day after his arrival in Constantinople, Herzl was in such an agitated state that he wrote a letter directly to the kaiser, arguing in favour of German support for extensive purchases of land in Palestine by the Jews. Herzl assured Wilhelm II that a weakening France was in no position to resist and that "to Russia the Zionist solution of the Jewish question means an enormous relief… the English Church is known to be on our side. Everything depends on the form of the *fait accompli* which is to be created."[202]

Herzl thought that even if the sultan failed to understand what the Zionists could do for his deteriorating empire, he would not overlook the advice of the kaiser. Once a personal relationship between the two rulers was established they could ignore the intrigues of the other great powers. Herzl's request involved solely "permission for a 'Jewish Land Company for Syria and Palestine' under German protection, which would suffice for the moment".

Herzl's closest colleague, the wealthy businessman David Wolffsohn, delivered this letter to the imperial chamberlain. Three hours later, Herzl was on his way to see Wilhelm II. This was the moment the leader of the Zionist movement had dreamt about for years. The kaiser – dressed in a black Hussar's uniform – came towards him and bowed deeply. Herzl was disconcerted to find that the German foreign minister also was there, seated, like Herzl, in the customary manner, with his silk hat held between his knees. The kaiser listened politely to all that was said, before explaining his own interest in Zionism.

---

202 Theodor Herzl, October 17, 1898. Theodor Herzl: *The Complete Diaries II*, New York & London, 1960, p.716.

"There are some of your people whom it would be beneficial to let settle in Palestine. I am thinking about those from the province of Hesse. They are practicing usury among the farming community there. If they were to take their capital and settle in the colonies, then these Jews would be useful."[203]

Herzl was angered by the implication that all Jews were moneylenders, but he kept a cool head and later made a short speech about anti-semitism, maintaining that it was the best of Jews who were affected most. The foreign minister cited the example of the Imperial House of Hohenzollern which had always been appreciative of German Jews, while many Jews, for their part, had disloyally supported a revolutionary party. Herzl then used his favourite argument to press home his point: Zionism would eliminate domestic revolutionary movements.

When the kaiser looked at his watch for the second time, Herzl understood that the audience was nearing its end. But before he got up Wilhelm said: "Write down your address and give it to von Bülow... just tell me in a word what you want me to ask the sultan for."

"A chartered company under German protection," answered Herzl. He spoke in English to make the point clearer.[204]

"Good, a company," the kaiser said, shaking hands and departed. The secret audience had lasted an hour without the kaiser mentioning the real reason for his interest in a Jewish state in Palestine. But subsequent correspondence between the kaiser and one of his nephews revealed his true thoughts: "Nine out of ten Germans would be shocked if they thought that I sympathized with the Zionists or would become their protector. Yet, when you consider the extremely dangerous power which international Jewish capital represents, it would be in the German interest if the Hebrew world were to regard us with gratitude."[205]

En route to Palestine, by way of Athens and Alexandria, Herzl had redrafted his speech to the kaiser. He argued that the Jews should be allowed to colonize the land between the Nile and the Euphrates. During a transition period, the land could be divided into districts, coming under Jewish administration as soon as there was a Jewish majority.[206] For tactical

203 Alex Bein: *Theodor Herzl. A Biography*, New York 1945, pp.294–295.
204 Desmond Steward: *Theodor Herzl, Artist and Politician, A Biography of the Father of Modern Israel*, Doubleday & Company, Inc. New York, 1974, p.268.
205 Letter of Sept. 29, 1898 cited in Hermann and Bessi Ellern: *Herzl, Hechler, Storhertugen av Baden og den tyske keiseren 1898–1904* (Herzl, Hechler, The Grandduke of Baden and the German Kaiser 1898-1904), (Hebrew), Tel Aviv 1961, p.48.
206 Dr. M. I. Bodenheimer: *So Wurde Israel* (And Thus Became Israel), Frankfurt am Main 1958, p.100.

reasons Herzl did not want to discuss such demands openly. He told the others in the delegation that "the time was not ripe" for such thoughts and that it would be more appropriate to create a microbe, which could grow, organically, into a state.

When the ship arrived in Jaffa, Herzl had half expected to be arrested. He had received a letter from Eliezer Ben-Yehuda, the teacher who was attempting to revive Hebrew and who had befriended the Spafford family, warning him against coming to Palestine. Ben-Yehuda feared that Herzl would be killed by the Turks, who were against Zionism. For that reason, Herzl had composed a letter to the kaiser, which was to be used only in case of emergency. In the meantime, though, passport control had been temporarily taken over by the German police. Wearing their white helmets, they just waved Herzl and his group past the Turkish functionaries.

Herzl's fear of arrest was not without reason. Waiting for him on the pier in Jaffa was Mendel Kramer, a Jewish informant in the service of the Turkish police. Kramer had been given the task of shadowing Herzl, and in his pocket he had an arrest warrant. It was signed and sealed, but was to be used only if the Zionist leader created a disturbance in Palestine.

In Jerusalem, Anna Spafford remained busy leading her flock, reading the Bible and making notes of her spiritual conversations with God. "Christ has power over devils, Christ has power over disease, Christ has power over death," she wrote in the margins of her Bible. The pages of the Book of Revelations – which told of ancient prophecies – were particularly full of Anna's comments.[207]

Mother Anna had a special love of the word 'bride'. Her notes in the margins refer to the 'victorious bride', the 'bride's image' and 'the bride's intercession'. The Colony was the chosen bride of Jesus waiting for the bridegroom's arrival and its task was to bring the whole world back to God through its example of love, purity and harmony. But the bride first had to be dead to the material world, and one of the questions that Anna kept returning to at the morning meetings was: "Have we died this death?"

Anna Spafford was also busy with the visit of the kaiser because all of Jerusalem was to be cleaned up and the Colony's members were involved in the preparations in several ways. All the houses and open areas were to be washed and swept clean. The Turks had made a new road up to the Mount of Olives. Palestinian labourers had crushed tons of rock for the road and farm women, almost as strong, had carried the gravel and dumped it onto the surface. The gravel was then covered with white sand

207 Petri: *On Holy Paths*, Stockholm 1931, p.150.

and rolled flat. The road builders broke Roman columns into suitable lengths, inserted iron bolts into either end, to make rollers, which were pulled by horses back and forth until the roadway was smooth.

At the Jaffa Gate, the Turks made a 15-yard wide opening in the city wall so that the imperial pilgrim could ride into the Old City wearing his spiked helmet. New trees were planted and just outside the city wall the Jews planned to erect a wooden sign which would bear the text: "Blessed be, he who comes in the name of the Lord". All the houses in Jerusalem were to be lighted every evening during the kaiser's stay. A large tented encampment was put up in fields just outside the Damascus Gate. In addition to the 26 colourful oriental tents, the Germans had arranged for prefabricated houses to be built from asbestos. These were to be the sleeping quarters for the imperial couple.

Bertha Spafford became involved in two aspects of these preparations. She had been asked to choose furniture and carpets for the kaiser's tents. Bertha managed this by emptying a Turkish town house of its most beautiful objects. Her second task was to find a gift for the Empress Augusta Victoria. Twenty-year-old Bertha, who, together with one of the older women in the community, had been head teachers of the only Muslim girls' school in Jerusalem, was to let the students make and present a gift. This, however, would not have a happy outcome.

Chapter 17

The Imperial Visit

The imperial yacht anchored outside Haifa harbour, and Wilhelm II and Augusta Victoria were put ashore at the foot of Mount Carmel. It was warm, so warm that the kaiser had to sit down and rest on a bench. Flies swarmed around him. The leader of Haifa's German Protestant Church declared proudly that the Apostle Paul had lived nearby. The kaiser said: "That is all well and good, but I'd prefer a glass of soda water to a sermon. I want to wash the dust out of my mouth."[208]

From Haifa, the imperial couple travelled to Jaffa with an entourage of 150 officials, 42 musicians, 200 cooks and waiting staff, 500 cavalrymen and two regiments of infantry. There had been a drought, and on the way many of the horses died of thirst. But the couple suffered no inconvenience and in Jaffa they stayed overnight at the Hotel du Parc, which belonged to Baron von Ustinow.

The American Colony also had two representatives in Jaffa – Elijah Meyers, who had with him a large camera, and Frederick Vester. Vester, who had joined the Colony in 1894, wanted to start a photography business and had obtained a camera "that was discarded by a passing tourist".[209]

It was Elijah, though, who took the pictures. He had arrived in Jerusalem in 1889 after 15 adventurous years of travelling. It was rumoured he was the son of an Indian rabbi, that the Meyers family was rich, but that the father had disinherited the son. Meyers had worked as a Christian

208 *Memoirs of Prince von Bülow, Vol. 1, From Secretary of State to Imperial Chancellor*, Little, Brown, and Company, Boston 1931, p.295.
209 Memorandum re: Origins and Developments of Disputes within The American Colony, Early Years, p.3, Folder: General memoranda, American Colony Collection, Jerusalem.

missionary, studied at Oxford, and courted an English aristocratic lady. When he came to Jerusalem, he presented himself as a reincarnation of the Prophet Elijah. He walked about the Old City wearing a flowing cape of the finest Indian silk, with a brilliant green turban. He sought out Anna Spafford and asked to live and work at the American Colony, believing it would have an essential role to play at the time of the Second Coming. Elijah was a jack-of-all-trades who, in addition to taking photographs, could mend clocks, make batteries, spin thread, weave, and plate silver.[210]

The Colony had received its first order for photos before the kaiser came to Palestine. Herzl had requested a series of photographs of the Jewish colonies in Palestine to present to the German emperor.

When Herzl arrived in Palestine, some of the 4,000 Jewish settlers there thought he was planning to cover the royal visit for his newspaper. No one knew his real intentions, but they might have become suspicious from the fact that he wanted to see Jewish agricultural settlements. Herzl and his entourage toured what he called a "neglected landscape established by the Arabs" before visiting the settlement known as 'The First in Zion'. The colony's leader was friendly, but remained a little cool because he knew that Herzl did not particularly like the colony's mentor, Baron Rothschild.

Herzl was unimpressed by 'The First in Zion' where 400 Jewish farmers lived in poverty under Rothschild's authoritarian administration, growing grapes and producing wine. He wrote in his diary: "I have always believed that with enough money one can establish industry anywhere. With the millions of stolen money here, squandered and poured into the sand, one could have achieved something quite different. Palestine needs the Zionists, not Barons without vision."[211]

The following morning Herzl's driver took him to see the three other Jewish settlements. Everywhere Jews came out to greet the famous man. The greatest enthusiasm was shown by a colony of immigrants from Warsaw. They had managed without Rothschild's help, and had become self-sufficient by growing vegetables and fruit. Herzl and his group drove through a string of Palestinian villages, but it was as if Palestine's Arabs did not exist for them. Herzl's diaries make no mention of the many others who were already living in the country.

210 Lind & Wallström: *Jerusalem Travelers*, Stockholm 1981, p.42.
211 *Theodor Herzl: Diary notation, October 27, 1898, cited in The Complete Diaries of Theodor Herzl* (ed. Raphael Patai), New York 1960, Vol II, pp.737–741.

Before the kaiser and his entourage were to ride from Jaffa to Jerusalem, Herzl returned to visit the Jewish agricultural school. He wanted to make his presence visible, to remind the kaiser of what he had said at their first meeting. The school principal had refused Herzl's request to speak with the kaiser, reminding him that he was an uninvited guest, and asking him to remain silent. Any attempt to draw attention to himself could be interpreted as Zionist provocation. When the kaiser passed, Herzl removed his helmet and the students standing in a line began to sing the national anthem. Seated on his white stallion, Wilhelm II must have seen Herzl at a distance. He stopped in front of the Zionist leader and, extending his right hand, said: "How are you?"[212]

"Thank you, Your Majesty, I am touring the country. How has the journey agreed with you so far?"

"Very hot. But Palestine has a future."

"At the moment it is still sick," Herzl replied, wishing to emphasize that the Jews could cure Palestine, if only they were given a chance.

"Water is what is needed, a lot of water!"

Rothschild's protegés at the agricultural school looked on in silence. The kaiser's sudden stop came as a complete surprise to them and people crowded around him. The photographer from the American Colony was not there, but Herzl's colleague, David Wolffsohn, raised his camera and took two quick photos. Unfortunately, his hands were shaking, and only the kaiser's profile and Herzl's left foot showed up on the picture. The official picture of the meeting between Kaiser Wilhelm II and Theodor Herzl, released later, was a fake, a montage made in a photo laboratory.[213]

The Zionist representatives were in an ecstatic mood when they drove back to Jaffa to take the train to Jerusalem, but it was delayed, with the result that the Sabbath would have begun before they arrived. Herzl had to decide whether to ignore the Jewish religious prohibition on travel on the Sabbath in order to reach Jerusalem before the imperial couple. The strongly religious Wolffsohn suffered great doubts. Finally, he agreed to go along with Herzl's decision to travel, but Herzl compromised by agreeing that on arrival they should walk to the hotel. They had to drag their baggage for 20 minutes to the Kaminitz Hotel just outside the Jaffa Gate.

When the kaiser later rode into Jerusalem through the specially made opening in the wall, Herzl, exhausted by his return journey, chose to stay

212 Ibid. p.743.
213 Shown at the exhibition at the Central Zionist Archive, Jerusalem, Autumn 1999, Dudman & Kark: *The American Colony*, Jerusalem 1998, p.155.

indoors and update his diary. But from the window of the hotel he could see the imperial pilgrims' triumphal entry into the Old City. The kaiser was dressed in a white lancer's uniform, over which he wore a white silk cape, glittering in the sun. Over his helmet he wore a *kaffiyeh* – the Arabs' traditional head covering – in white and gold.

Local Zionists wanted Herzl to welcome the kaiser to Jerusalem but the city's Jewish anti-Zionists, who knew nothing of Herzl's audience with the German emperor in Constantinople, did not. For his part, Herzl did not know that Kaiser Wilhelm had by now lost interest in Zionism. The Turkish ambassador to Berlin, who had accompanied the kaiser to the Near East, made it clear to Wilhelm that the sultan "would have nothing to do with Zionism and an independent Jewish Kingdom". The Turks were fearful that a German-Jewish Palestine would become a variation of the Francophile Lebanon. The Turkish Foreign Minister, Ahmed Tewfik, worded his objection in another way. He said the Turks had "taken care of" the Armenians in the course of three days, but to manage the Zionists would take just three hours. On the German side, Foreign Minister Bülow considered it his duty to water down the kaiser's previous enthusiasm for Herzl's dream.[214] Nevertheless, speculation about Sultan Abdul Hamid's actual views on the Jewish question continued.

The day after the kaiser's arrival in Jerusalem, Herzl walked through the Old City to the Wailing Wall. He remained unmoved by the holy place, but was troubled by the presence of many beggars in the area. He wrote in his diary: "If I ever get Jerusalem, the first thing I would do is clean it up and clear out everything that does not qualify as sacred. I would build workers' homes outside the city, clear out the filthy hovels, raze them, burn all non-sacred ruins, and transfer the bazaars elsewhere. Then, while retaining the old architectural style as much as possible, I would erect a comfortable, airy city with proper sewerage around the holy places."[215]

Near the Church of the Holy Sepulchre a magnificent new German building had been erected, called the Church of the Redeemer. The Lutherans had no foothold in the Church of the Holy Sepulchre, not even a small chapel, and had, therefore, built themselves an entirely new structure. Kaiser Wilhelm was to officiate at the opening on Monday, October 31. The day was not chosen by chance. It was the date when Martin Luther had nailed his theses on the door of the church in Wittenberg in 1517.

214 Prince Bernhard von Bülow: *Memoirs of Prince von Bülow, From Secretary of State to Imperial Chancellor 1897-1903*, Vol. I, Boston 1931, p.296.
215 Extract from Theodor Herzl's diary October 31, 1898, Pawel: *The Labyrinth of Exile*, p.385.

The procession of churchmen and other dignitaries that left the Jaffa Gate included the Bishop of Kristiania, Anton Christian Bang. King Oscar II had asked him and the Bishop of Visby to represent Norway and Sweden on the kaiser's trip. Turkish soldiers stood guard along the route and kept the masses well away. The procession included the Knights of St John in their plush hats and black capes with white crosses. People crowded at windows and on balconies and roofs, and even if most of them did not know who the two Scandinavians were, the bishops were satisfied, having been given prominent places in the procession.[216]

When Wilhelm and Augusta Victoria arrived finally, the church doors were opened and the Turkish military orchestra started to play. The church bells rang out and after the service the kaiser went up to the altar. He dropped to his knees in prayer, and then gave a speech, declaring that he would be the protector of German Christians in the Ottoman Empire. Through his friend, Sultan Abdul Hamid, the kaiser had secured permission for German Catholics to buy part of Mount Zion where, according to tradition, the Virgin Mary had been buried.[217] But his speech mentioned nothing about the Jews or the Zionists.

The imperial couple had been up to the Mount of Olives the previous day. As they rode past the American Colony in an open carriage, all the residents assembled to watch. The children had been practicing for this moment for weeks. When a signal was given they all shouted three times: "Hip-hip hurrah for the German kaiser."

The American Colony's photographer followed hot on the kaiser's heels. His photo wagon, pulled by two horses, followed the kaiser's carriage, and after each photo session one of the young assistants hurried back to the Colony with the glass plates in boxes. The studio team took over in the darkroom, making prints en masse to send to London and Berlin via the Austrian postal service.[218]

But if things were going well for Elijah Meyers, Bertha suddenly found she had an unexpected problem. As one of the heads of the Muslim girls' school, she had, for several weeks, been supervising the students as they worked on a gift for Empress Augusta Victoria. The girls had woven a small tapestry containing the coat of arms of the Turkish army. It was

216 K.H.G. Von Schéele: *På helig mark* (On Holy Ground), Stockholm 1899, p.94.
217 Percy Evans Lewin: *The German Road to the East*, London 1916, p. 105, Isaiah Friedman: *Germany, Turkey and Zionism 1897–1918*, Oxford 1977, p.81.
218 Mia Gröndahl: *The Dream of Jerusalem, Lewis Larsson and the American Colony Photographers*, Journal, Stockholm, 2005, p. 82.

the only gift they had been able to finish in the time available. The picture was framed and put in a box made of olive wood.

But none of the pupils' parents would allow their daughter to have the honour of presenting the gift. They were afraid of the 'evil eye' – the eye of envy, which would expose the child selected to bad luck. The problem was solved only when the Colony's neighbour, the director of the office of public affairs, intervened. Ismail Husseini, the man who had written to the American president complaining about the consul, said: "I don't believe in the evil eye, so send Rowada, my daughter, with the gift."[219] He then gave permission for his eight-year-old daughter to present the tapestry, and the Empress Augusta Victoria responded by giving Rowada a diamond pin in the form of the German eagle, and a bag of candy.

Late that afternoon, as darkness fell, a servant in the Husseini family home lighted all the lanterns, as he did every evening. Little Rowada was allowed to keep wearing her pretty white dress until it was time to go to bed. But suddenly the little girl came too close to one of the lanterns and her dress caught fire. Bertha and Rowada's mother were in the living room when they heard the screaming. They managed to throw the girl to the floor and roll her in a Persian rug. This put out the fire; but not in time. Rowada was burned badly, and the doctor who came could do nothing more than ease her pain. All night, Bertha and Rowada's mother stayed with her. At dawn, the girl died.

When Anna came to offer condolences, Ismail Husseini said: "Don't ever say again there is no evil eye. I know now that there is." The German empress sent her chief assistant to the Husseini family house to offer condolences to the parents. Rowada's mother did not appear, but Augusta Victoria's German aide was shocked when the girl's father said: "God has willed it; so one cannot do anything one way or other. It is probably the best thing that could have happened. It was great luck that it was not a son."[220]

In Jerusalem, meanwhile, rumours were rife. When Herzl heard that the kaiser wanted to cut short his visit and go back to Berlin because France had issued a declaration of war against England, he became worried that he would not get his official audience. He sent two of his colleagues to the kaiser's camp to find out more, and at 7.30pm on Monday evening he received word that Wilhelm II would receive him the next day.

I

219 Bertha Spafford Vester: *Our Jerusalem*, pp.196-97.
220 From *Das Deutsche Kaiserpaar im Heiligem Lande* (The German Imperial Couple in the Holy Land), cited in Olof Fahlén: *Nåsbonderna i Jerusalem* (Nås Farmers in Jerusalem), Höganäs 1988, p.153.

n the imperial camp, Herzl was received by an arrogant junior diplomat who returned the draft of his speech to him. Herzl, noticing that a number of sentences had been struck out, was ordered to come back with an amended document. Everything referring to Jewish national awareness, the Zionist congress, the Basel programme, even the expression 'German Protectorate' had been crossed out.

Herzl was not particularly troubled by these technical details. He was focused on the audience itself. The next day at noon Wilhelm received Herzl and the Jewish delegation. The kaiser was wearing a grey uniform, helmet and grey gloves. He greeted each one of the men then raised his right arm in a military salute. At a signal from one of the kaiser's aides, Herzl began to read from his revised speech. A German minister sat with a copy and followed each line with his finger. The speech was full of banalities, any possibly controversial sentences had been removed, and when Herzl was finished, the kaiser said merely: "I thank you for this communication which has interested me greatly. The matter, in any case, still requires thorough study and further discussions."[221]

It was clear the kaiser's flirtation with Zionism was over. He permitted only a brief conversation about Palestine and the need for water. "Water we can supply," said Herzl, "but it will cost billions, and it will yield billions."

"Well," answered the kaiser, hitting his boot with his riding crop, "money is what you have plenty of, more money than any of us."

"Yes, the money that gives us so much trouble is one commodity you possess in abundance," added Foreign Minister Bülow, who had been sitting in the background.[222]

With this comment about the financial power of international Judaism, the audience was over. It had lasted less time than the audience in Constantinople, and as a final humiliation, the Turkish guards refused to let them out of the compound. In the end a police spy lurking near the gate persuaded them to open it.

Herzl no longer felt safe in Jerusalem. When he returned to the house on Mamilla Street (*ma'man Allah* in Arabic), he became uneasy about the other guests staying there, and decided to leave. He accepted an invitation from a young Russian farmer who lived in a new Jewish colony in the hills west of Jerusalem. It was here, Herzl planted what everyone thought was a cedar tree – but which was later proved to have been a cypress. Only after

221 Patai (ed): *The Complete Diaries of Theodor Herzl, Vol II*, New York and London, 1960, pp.755-56.
222 Pawel: *The Labyrinth of Exile, a Life of Theodor Herzl*, New York, 1989, p.388.

it was dark did Herzl and his two friends return to Jerusalem. They rose at 2am to take the first train to Jaffa.

Herzl wanted to get out of Palestine as quickly as possible. He thought things were dangerous for him, and that if the Turks had possessed a little political foresight, they would have stopped him there and then. "When I came to Constantinople, they had a chance they may never have again," Herzl wrote in his diary. "All they needed to have done was to expel me." Instead, "they let me continue and complete my journey. And unless I am greatly mistaken, I am now already a political factor to be reckoned with."[223]

Kaiser Wilhelm left Palestine shortly afterwards. Just one week after he had assumed responsibility for the protection of German Christians in Palestine, he took on an even greater obligation. As he placed a wreath on the grave of Saladin, he made an oath that Sultan Abdul Hamid and his 300 million Muslims would forever have the German kaiser as their friend. Later, he wrote in a letter to the tsar: "If I had come here without any religion at all, I certainly would have turned Mohammedan."[224]

For the Muslims in the Ottoman Empire the kaiser was already one of them. He was presented as the Sultan's closest ally, honoured with the name, Haj Mohammed Ghalliun, the closest that Turks could come to the French form of Wilhelm. The German emperor did not know that the Christians considered him to be a crusader, or that he was seen by the Zionist leader as a means of achieving a Jewish homeland. He was also unaware of his role as the forerunner of a new activity which was to make the American Colony internationally famous.

223 Theodor Herzl's diary November 5, 1898, cited in Pawel: *The Labyrinth of Exile*, p.388.
224 N. Grant: *The Kaiser's letter to the Tsar, 1920*, pp.65–70, letter to Nicolas II, November 9, 1898, cited in Alan Palmer: *The Decline and Fall of the Ottoman Empire*, London 1992, p.192.

Chapter 18

The Prophet in Jerusalem

In the summer of 1897, Sophie Elkan and her close friend Selma Lagerlöf were on holiday on the Swedish island of Gotland. The couple were deeply in love, but had to keep their relationship secret. One day, Sophie showed Selma an article that had appeared recently in the publication *Gotland Allehanda* about the farmers of Nås who had emigrated to Palestine to join Anna's Colony. Selma spent a long time reading the story. She turned to Sophie and said: "This could be the subject of a novel."

"I was thinking that," answered Sophie, and they did not talk about it any more that day. But Selma continued to think. A few weeks later she said: "The two of us have to go to Jerusalem."

"Jerusalem?" Sophie had clearly forgotten the newspaper story.

"Of course. Don't you remember you suggested I should write about those farmers who emigrated to the Holy Land? To do that I would need to see their new home."

But it would be another two years before the women travelled to Jerusalem to celebrate the beginning of the 20th century. By that time, Selma had drafted the first part of a novel about the Dala farmers' departure.

Sophie and Selma arrived in Jerusalem at the beginning of March 1900. Although Sophie was Jewish and had been described as "a true Oriental with an Occidental upbringing", she did not think much of the Holy City. The two women stayed at the Grand New Hotel, virtually next door to the hotel where the Americans had stayed some 20 years earlier. From there, they took a horse-drawn cab to the American Colony. Selma was pleased to find that the boy who opened the door was Swedish and that she could speak to him in her native tongue. The two Swedish women were then escorted by Bertha to the large room on the first floor, known as the salon. The daily service had just ended. When Bertha asked the guests to be seated, she noticed that Selma Lagerlöf sat nervously on the edge of her chair. But when Mother Anna arrived, she was so friendly that Selma relaxed.

"You have many fellow countrymen here who will be happy to meet you," said Anna, before sending Bertha off to fetch a small group. When the Swedes heard that the visitors had come all the way from their homeland, they said: "God must have sent them." No other Swedes had visited the Colony in the four years since their arrival in Jerusalem. Selma showed Anna a letter of introduction from Nås. The two Swedish guests brought weaving patterns for their fellow countrywomen.[225]

They remained talking for two hours, and when Selma and Sophie finally got up to leave, they were invited to return the next day. Selma concluded she could tell people at home that the Nås farmers were doing just fine.

Back at the hotel, when Selma mentioned the Colony to some American women tourists, they told her that the American consul in Jerusalem had discouraged visitors from going there. The women reported his allegations that "it was not a place that ladies ought to visit", his regrets that the Colony bore the American name, and his determination to do "all in his power to break it up".[226]

Selma was upset to hear such things about her fellow Swedes. Could they be true? When, a few hours later, she herself met with the consul, he repeated his claims that the community was "a bad house", arguing that appearances could be deceptive and adding that Selma did not realize what went on there after dark.[227]

Selma was distressed, but Merrill continued with his accusations that Mrs Spafford was "a notorious free lover, and that after the meetings men and women went together into dark rooms to hide their love affairs... they broke up marriages between men and their wives and then threw young girls in the way of the men."

Selma could not know that the American consul had been at war with Anna Spafford for 18 years. Neither could she know that only a few days earlier a couple had come to the consul's office seeking his help to

225 Gunnar Hägglöf: *Jerusalem i taggtråd* (Jerusalem in Barbed Wire), Stockholm 1964, pp.77–78, Elin Wägner: *Selma Lagerlöf*, Stockholm 1958, pp.158–162.
226 Selma Lagerlöf's report to the Swedish-Norwegian consul in Constantinople. Copy in American Colony Collection, Folder: 1893 (sic).
227 Ibid. Also quoted in Alexander Hume Ford: "Our American Colony at Jerusalem", *Appleton's Magazine*, No. 6, December 1906, pp.652-53.

get away from the sect. The couple, 36-year-old American Constantin Antoszewski and his wife Jessie, were both from Chicago and had joined Anna's second group in 1896. According to the consul, Constantin told him that Anna Spafford had tried to break up his marriage by force and had selected an unmarried woman, who had been "chasing him for weeks", to be his 'assistant'. Constantin had resisted the temptation, so Anna had sent a new woman to him, who said bluntly: "God has appointed me for you."[228]

Consul Merrill had submitted a report to Washington based on Constantin Antoszewski's allegations. He added that Antoszewski had been shocked to learn there were several men in the Colony who had 'female assistants' and that Mrs Spafford's philosophy was that "a wife should be nothing more than any other woman, and that the husband had no more right to kiss his wife than to kiss any woman on the street". The consul also noted that Antoszewski and his wife no longer believed that "Mrs Spafford is blessed by God, and that every word she speaks comes from God".

Merrill's report went further, alleging that "Mrs Spafford has her own 'assistant', a man of about 36 who is not her husband". The consul repeated an account of how Jacob Elihau and Anna had stayed alone together in a room for two to three days and nights at a time. Food was brought to them and no one had dared ask why they were behaving as they did. He did not mention that Jacob Elihau was Anna's adoptive son.

According to Antoszewski, "living as a married couple in the Colony was forbidden because Mrs Spafford looked at it as a licence to sin. She says what she means every single day to everyone during the morning prayers in the salon above. Even the children get to hear it. It was also not true that there was harmony and unity in the Colony, as the visitors usually said." On the contrary, Antoszewski could vouch that "there were many others who felt as he did, but were afraid to leave".

Consul Merrill suggested that Antoszewski should call that evening at Selma's hotel. During the conversation there he spoke mostly about religious and economic conditions at the Colony. When Selma "pointedly asked him what he had to say as to the morality of the members", he replied that he "could say nothing against their morality and that they were all good people". [229]

By now, Selma was determined to discover whether any of the allegations were true. She set to work like a detective, but failed to find out

228 Dudman & Kark: *The American Colony*, Jerusalem 1998, p.142.
229 Selma Lagerlöf's report to the Swedish-Norwegian consul in Constantinople, April 22, 1900. Copy in Folder: 1893, American Colony Collection, Jerusalem.

evidence backing Merrill's accusations. In the course of her investigations, however, she obtained a number of colourful details for her future novel. Selma was not particularly troubled that the former leader of the Nås farmers, Olof Henrik Larsson, lived, as if exiled, in a shed at the back of the Colony's premises. She noted only that the man who would become the model for her novel's demonic preacher, Helgum, "seemed withdrawn and difficult to get in touch with".

In a letter to her mother, Selma wrote that Larsson had little to say, and that "now it is a Mrs Spafford, an American, who runs it all". The author also interviewed the baker, Jon Jonsson, and his great love, Karin. Even though Selma was full of admiration for Anna, the ban on marriage went strongly against her own view of love. Jon and Karin's tragic fate disturbed her.

Selma spent a lot of time with the colonists, observing their daily life. Following each visit she would scribble key words in her diary: "Mrs Sköldberg red hair... Jon Jonsson bread baker... Josef Larsson short with a goatee... the German who loved Mrs Spafford's daughter and may not marry."[230] Anna's beautiful daughter Bertha had seemed initially shy, but her reserve soon disappeared as she got to know Selma better.

The Swedish author noticed that the women seemed generally less quick and lively than the men. Anna was the exception. Selma was impressed with the story of her life. Anna also liked the visitor and her engaging stories. After Selma felt her relationship with Anna was firmly established, she said: "Mrs Spafford, you are the best looking woman I ever saw to be so wicked."[231]

But Anna did not respond, and Selma did not persist. It had not escaped Selma's attention that Anna was manipulative, that she censored all the colonists' mail and would not tolerate any form of opposition.[232]

Anna was not troubled by Selma Lagerlöf's assessment of her. She had heard such criticisms before. She asked Bertha to take special care of the Swedish guest, and although the two women sometimes went walking together, Selma never mentioned her plan for a novel with characters modelled on Bertha's mother and some of the Swedes.

The day before Selma and Sophie were to travel on to Damascus, they went to the American Colony to say goodbye. As they left, the Swedes joined in song to bid them farewell. Selma began to cry. She cried again

230 Sigvard Lindquist: *Kring Selma Lagerlöfs Jerusalem* (Around Selma Lagerlöf's Jerusalem), Dalarna Museum's series of short writings 55, 1990, pp.32–33.
231 Spafford Vester: *Our Jerusalem*, 2nd edition, p.201.
232 Eric Dinsmore Matsson: *The American Colony of Jerusalem, A Brief Historical Outline*, p.26.

the following day when several of them came to the Jaffa Gate with small gifts for their relatives at home. Even Sophie, who had little patience with missionaries and to whom religion was completely alien, was touched.

On their last evening in Jerusalem, something strange happened. The women's guide and interpreter, Jemil, knocked on the door of Selma's room to tell her that a guest was waiting for her at the reception.[233] Downstairs Selma found a large black man of unusual appearance. He had thick lips, long ape-like arms, bulging muscles and skin that resembled tree bark. It was as if he belonged to a race of men that existed only before the Flood. He was enveloped in long, dirty white sheets, wound around his body.

Some days earlier, Jemil had guided Selma and Sophie through the Noble Sanctuary. He had told them many intriguing stories and pointed to a dirty carpet lying in a window niche where, he said, a seer normally sat. Selma was sorry that he was not there. She would have liked to consult a real fortune teller, particularly one who was in a mosque on the same ground as Solomon's Temple. So Jemil had afterwards made a point of seeking out the seer and getting him to come to the hotel.

Selma was not quite as interested in hearing her fortune told in the reception area of her hotel as she would have been in the mosque, but she had no choice, so they sat down at a table in a corner. The seer had brought a container of sand full of small snail shells. He spread them across the top of the table, and spoke in Arabic to Jemil, who interpreted his words: "He asks that the lady should think about something she would like to know. The lady should not reveal what she is thinking, just keep it in her mind, and the seer will give her an answer."

During their entire Jerusalem visit Selma had been thinking only about one thing. She had come to visit the farmers from Nås to learn about their way of life, their faith and their sense of mission. Now, she burned with a desire to write their remarkable story. Yet, at the same time, she had begun to wonder whether her book would ever appear. It was not just that she doubted her own ability to handle the subject – but also, would anyone want to publish or even read it? Selma was sceptical about whether the primitive-seeming person before her had ever even seen a book. Did he know what a novel was? Nevertheless, she concentrated her thoughts on this central question: "Will I succeed in writing a book about the Swedish farmers in Jerusalem?"

The fortune teller placed his hand above the sand on the table. Then he straightened out his index finger, which had a long nail on it resembling

233 Selma Lagerlöf: *Höst*, Stockholm 1933, http://www.upnet.com/selma/hosta/ pp.9-11.

a claw, and wrote a few lines in the sand. He mumbled and appeared to be making calculations. There was a long period of silence before he turned toward Jemil and said something in Arabic, which the interpreter translated almost simultaneously: "He says that the lady is thinking about something she wants to write on paper. He is asking that the lady should not feel troubled. What she is thinking about she will achieve."

"Yes," Selma thought, "this black man can really read thoughts." The seer fell silent. Selma, who had been satisfied with his answer, paid him well.

After Damascus, Selma Lagerlöf and Sophie Elkan went to Constantinople, where they visited the Swedish-Norwegian consul-general. Selma had written a report for him that included an account of her first visit to Consul Merrill.[234] Selma wanted to put a stop to the American consul's rumours about Anna Spafford. She had learned, from gossip surrounding her own relationship with Sophie, just how malicious such allegations could be.

Yet, there was one thing which concerned Selma about the living conditions in the Jerusalem Colony: the ban on married life, particularly as it related to Jon Jonsson's and Karin Larsson's unhappy fate. When back in Sweden, Selma wrote a thank-you letter to Anna in which she said: "Now I am just waiting for the good news that the Colony is getting ready for a wonderful wedding."

234 Copy of Selma Lagerlöf's report to the Swedish-Norwegian consul, April 22, 1900, Folder marked:1893 American Colony Collection, Jerusalem. Lagerlöf's report can not be traced in the Royal Archives in Sweden.

Chapter 19

God's New Mission

Anna Spafford had realized that Doomsday prophets were not dependable. She was determined to stick to Jesus' word that no one could know the exact moment the Saviour would come.

After Kaiser Wilhelm's visit, several of the sect's members began working as guides and photographers. The American Colony received so many requests for their services that its name became known throughout Europe and the United States. One of the young Swedes, Hol Lars Larsson, had taught himself the art of photography before the kaiser came to Jerusalem. As a 17-year-old he had made his own camera and changed his Swedish first name to Lewis. He was now head of the photography department at the American Colony.[235]

Mother Anna believed that this work was a blessing for the Colony, and tolerated the fact that it sometimes prevented the young from attending the morning meetings. Occasionally, she would herself leave the meetings in the salon and go to the house in the Old City to sit in peace with her reminiscences. It was there that "the work had begun and all the battles... fought over self and sin. Each and every stone tells a story of victory and strength."[236]

One day in October 1901, Anna wrote to a relative in Chicago about life in the Colony: "This afternoon Bertha and the young are giving a roof party. About 30 women and men have been invited; they will have

235 Letter from Lewis Larsson in 1898 cited in Sigvard Lindquist: *Kring Selma Lagerlöfs Jerusalem* (Around Selma Lagerlöf's Jerusalem), Falun 1990, p.27, Dudman & Kark: *The American Colony*, Jerusalem 1998, pp.151–152.
236 Letter to George and Sarah Fredrickson, Chicago, October 5, 1902, Folder: 1902, American Colony Collection, Jerusalem.

music and entertainment. People like to come to our house. We have many different musical instruments, something which makes the evenings a joy."

But Mother Anna was not aware of the sexual frustration growing among the young people. Men and women worked side by side. They met at the breakfast table, for dinner, during prayers, at musical evenings and on outings, but were never allowed to show their emotions. One day, one of the young women could not stand it any longer. In the middle of the morning meeting in the salon she got up and cried: "What is a man without a woman?"[237]

At first, all was quiet, then the young woman's mother and an older sister seized her and took her outside. Later, she had her hair shorn and was confined to a small stone house opposite the mosque. People walking by could sometimes hear cries. It was said that the young woman was kept in a straight-jacket because she had gone crazy. After a while, she returned to the congregation but everyone could see she had been through an ordeal. Whenever she spoke to a man, her gaze went towards his feet instead of his face.

The Colony's 31-year-old baker, Jon Jonsson, was also deeply frustrated and unhappy. He had tried for a long time to convince his uneasy parents, perhaps also himself, that the sect's celibacy served a higher goal. But after five long years he realized that this could not be right. Jon also felt that his beloved Karin was becoming distant, and that she had transferred her love from him to Jesus. He wrote a letter to his parents in Nås in which he asked for 500 kronor. This was a call for help. "I have found the climate here to be unhealthy," he wrote, "I am tired and in a poor way, so am thinking, along with some others, of leaving the country."[238]

But by the time the travel money arrived, Jon had changed his mind. His love for Karin was too strong. Perhaps they could still get married after all? He had noticed that the relationship between Bertha Spafford and Frederick Vester had been permitted to develop. Perhaps Anna might eventually lift the celibacy requirement and the ban on marriage. At least it was a hope.

But before long, Jon's letter to his parents in Sweden became known to the whole of the Colony. Jon's mother and father, who had always felt that the conditions in the Jerusalem sect were intolerable, had allowed the letter to be published in a newspaper. It was followed by an article criticizing Anna's regime. A resident of Nås sent the article to Palestine.

237 Lind & Wallström: *Jerusalem Travelers*, Stockholm 1981, p.106.
238 Letter from Jon Jonsson to his parents, Mia Gröndahl's private archive, also cited in the documentary, *Drömmen om Jerusalem* (Dreams of Jerusalem), Swedish Television, Malmö, Production No. 30–96/0180.

After Anna had read it, all hell broke loose. No one was allowed to speak to Jon. Karin, who all this time had been helping him with the baking, was ordered to find something else to do.

However, the Colony's baker did not yield. He refused to ask Mother Anna's forgiveness. This made Anna so angry she decided that the Swedes should send a response to the Swedish paper. A letter was written accusing Jon of being "a person of the flesh" who had forced his way into the Colony in Jerusalem. To Jon's great sorrow, 18 members of the sect signed the letter, including his great love, Karin. Six years after their arrival in Jerusalem, almost to the day, she took her pen and passed the death sentence on their love. But the man who, at the time, had convinced Jon to leave Nås, the deposed sect leader, Olof Henrik Larsson, refused to sign the letter condemning him.

Jonsson decided to leave. Early one morning in August 1902, before the sun had risen, he went out of the gate for the last time. The only thing he had with him was a small bag of clothes and enough money to get to the United States. Karin, who knew that he was leaving, chose to remain in her room without saying farewell. Jon took the train to Jaffa where he found that a cholera epidemic was raging through the city. The streets were nearly empty. The bazaar was shut and Jon did not dare eat anything. The only thing he drank was boiled water while he waited for the ship that was to take him away from Palestine.

In Sweden, Selma Lagerlöf was finishing the second part of her novel *Jerusalem*. She had set the first volume, written back in 1901 in Nås. It opens as the hero, Ingemar Ingemarsson, prepares to go to a dance at the village hall to meet his true love, Gertrud. Ingemar's sister, Karin, goes with him. Suddenly there is a terrible thunderstorm and all the lights go out. A stranger, the preacher, Helgum, appears. He rails against sin and predicts the end of the world. He also cures Karin, who had become paralyzed during the thunderstorm.

Lagerlöf depicts the whole region as being possessed by religious fervour. Helgum leaves for America where he meets a group of Americans who share his messianic beliefs. He then writes to the congregation in Nås, asking them to sell their farms and property and emigrate to Jerusalem to await the apocalypse in the Holy City. But Ingemar does not want to sell the family farm, and decides instead to marry Gunhild, the daughter of a rich man. Rejected by her sweetheart, Gertrud decides to join the group sailing for Jerusalem. Later, Ingemar discovers that Gunhild has been cursed and that all her male children will become blind idiots. Their firstborn dies.

The second volume of the novel is equally tragic. Here, Anna Spafford is depicted as Mrs Gordon, and the ship on which she travels across the Atlantic is called *L'Univers*. The name is symbolic because Selma was a committed pacifist whose previous novels had reflected her anxieties about the future of mankind. Mrs Gordon's two small boys are drowned when the ship sinks. Lagerlöf felt that the loss of four little girls would be too unbelievable. But Mrs Gordon hears the same divine words as Anna Spafford: "Death is easy. To live is difficult."

Mrs Gordon's daughter, Miss Young, is easily recognizable as Bertha in real life. But in the novel the beautiful stone house near the Sheikh Jarrah Mosque was not bought from a rich Palestinian with four wives, but from a caring monogamous Muslim widower. Lagerlöf calls him Baram Pasha and explains that he built it for his wife "whom he loved above everything else in this world". But soon after the pasha's family moved in, his wife and two of his daughters died. Baram Pasha locked up the house and swore never to set foot in it again.

Lagerlöf also depicts the tensions that existed within Jerusalem's Christian community. In one chapter entitled 'The Jerusalem that Kills' she has Catholics speaking ill of Protestants, Methodists of Quakers, Lutherans of Reformists, and Russians of Armenians. The Jews do not exist in Lagerlöf's city, where there is no tolerance, only envy, and where everyone hates in God's name.

In the novel, as in reality, the colonists are accused of being immoral and not permitting marriage "as God has ordained". Some Americans, who "from the consul on down are the worst of the critics", visit Baram Pasha and tell him wild stories about Mrs Gordon and her flock. The old gentleman asks himself how he can permit such dubious people to live in a house he had built out of love for his wife? He decides to investigate. But instead of loose women and evil men who drink and throw dice, he finds an idyllic community, even down to the children, who all behave themselves in exemplary fashion.

Lagerlöf's character, Gertrud, was modelled on the real-life Karin. She is rescued from life in the Colony through marriage to Bo Ingemar Månsson, a figure based on the Colony's baker, Jon Jonsson. But, instead of the painful separation that happened in real life, Gertrud and Bo start a new life together in Sweden.[239]

239 Selma Lagerlöf was not satisfied with the second part of *Jerusalem* and wrote a new version in 1909. In this version of her novel, the farmers of Nås emigrate in response to a summons to save the new Palestine. Birgitte Rahbek og Mogens Bähnche: *Tro og Skæbne i Jerusalem* (Faith and Destiny in Jerusalem), København 1996, p.98.

Anna Spafford with Bertha (left) and Grace (right) in the American Colony garden

Despite overwhelmingly positive coverage of her work in the Swedish press, Lagerlöf did not have the courage to send the book to Anna Spafford. She was unsure whether Anna would appreciate seeing religious experiences represented in literature.[240] Lagerlöf was right. Anna did not like the way that she and her Colony had been depicted and decided to ban the book. She gave no reason for this – but then Mother Anna never explained her decisions to anyone.

After a while, accounts of Anna's authoritarian style began to surface in the outside world. One of them was written by Pastor Henrik Steen, a 29-year-old Jewish convert from Lithuania. In his youth, Steen had thought about becoming a rabbi but chose instead to study for the priesthood in Stockholm. After his studies he was sent to the Swedish Jerusalem Association in Palestine to start a children's school.

Steen first visited the American Colony shortly after a young man, a member of the group, had tried to shoot himself because the woman he was in love with was interested in another. The shot was not fatal. Anna had demanded immediately that the youth sign a statement saying he was not dissatisfied in any way with the Colony and that he was happy. "One does not go around shooting oneself because of happiness," thought the Swedish pastor as he began his investigation.[241]

The unhappy failed suicide was one of the Colony's most skillful photographers, 23-year-old Furman Olmstead Baldwin. He had tried to kill himself in the boys' dormitory, writing an explanation on the wall near his bed: "Having shot myself in a moment of frenzy and without provocation, I – now on the brink of eternity – look back and see that, if we have not overcome sin in thought, the end is failure. Take a warning from me and overcome thought by thought." Anna demanded that Baldwin write a letter in the presence of two witnesses in which he stated: "This house is in no way to blame and I declare with my dying lips that it is as pure as heaven. Your regretful son."[242]

240 Handwritten notes by Bertha Spafford Vester for a seminar at the University of Chicago, led by Enor Shelburg. On page 4, Bertha cites a letter from Selma Lagerlöf and comments that she "never excused herself to Mother for her free treatment of the facts". Folder marked: Shelburg, G. E. (Enor), American Colony Collection. See also Grace Whiting's explanation in Nås 1958, cited in Sigvard Lindquist: *Kring Selma Lagerlöfs Jerusalem* (Around Selma Lagerlöf's Jerusalem), Dalarna Museum's series of short writings 55, Grycksbo 1990, p.35.

241 Pastor H. Steen: *Sanningen om svensk-amerikanska kolonien i Jerusalem* (The Truths about the Swedish-American Colony in Jerusalem), Stockholm Dagblad January 26, 1903.

242 Copy of letters dated July 14, 1901, American Colony Collection, Jerusalem. Later Baldwin admitted that it was "during a fit of jealousy" that he had attempted to kill himself. Witness Examination of Furman Olmstead Baldwin, Circuit Court of The United States, Southern District of New York, Wallace, vs. Appleton & Co.

The Swedish pastor was suspicious about the suicide attempt, and when he dug deeper into the story he learned that Furman for years had been in love with Grace Spafford. They, like many other young men and women, met during meals and afternoons of music, but had been told that such contacts must not lead to feelings any warmer than as toward brothers and sisters.

Pastor Steen also found that there was a big class distinction within the congregation. The Swedes and the Americans lived in virtually separate worlds. The farmers from Nås bore the greatest burdens and did all the manual work. A few of the Colony's members felt as if they were living in a beehive. There was a lot of activity in the hive but no one could challenge the queen's sovereignty. The worker bees always had to be ready to do their duties and could be ordered from one job to another without ever earning a penny. At the same time, members of the inner American circle were exempt from hard physical work. None of the worker bees in the Colony could make any demands on them – they were immune.[243]

Pastor Steen believed that Anna Spafford was leading the Colony in a dangerous direction. He understood that, while on one level the sect's leader claimed to be striving for "social liberation, equality and brotherhood", Anna's brand of Christianity involved blind worship and obedience. Her power meant slavery for others.

The Swedish pastor was just as critical of the fact that the young were not able to marry or even be sweethearts. They were expected to experience sexual temptation and then overcome it, a difficult battle, which, even if won, would lead to great unhappiness. The pastor was not surprised that ugly rumours were circulating about the Swedes in Jerusalem.

After six months there, Henrik Steen returned to Sweden and submitted a long article to Stockholms Dagblad. It posed the question: "Are our Swedish brothers and sisters in the Dala Colony happy? Most would describe themselves as happy. But when I looked at their quiet, expressionless faces I saw that they did not reflect happiness, but rather resignation."[244]

The Colony presented its best face to visiting tourists, wrote Steen, adding that less favourable aspects emerged in the relationships between the members themselves as a result of the false teachings about 'overcoming'. He believed the colonists were being compelled to fight against nature and that their best and most noble emotions were choked.

243 Lind & Wallström: *Jerusalem Travelers*, Stockholm 1981, p.83.
244. Steen: *The Truths about the Swedish-American Colony in Jerusalem*, Stockholm *Dagblad* January 26, 1903.

The pastor also touched on Anna's resistance to medical intervention. This, he believed, explained the large number of deaths among the Swedes. The sick were turned over to God. This was a dangerous practice in Palestine where Europeans were vulnerable to fevers which, while not dangerous if treated, often ended in death if left unattended to.

The ban on medical intervention had particularly tragic consequences for the Lind family. Six members of the family (which had numbered 10 when they left Nås) died in the course of the first four years. When Mrs Lind had fallen ill in the autumn of 1898, Anna gave orders that she was to be moved to a house further away. Pastor Steen maintained that Anna hated Mrs Lind. It was only when the latter was on her death bed that word was sent to her husband, children and elderly mother. One month earlier the Linds' seven-year-old daughter had died. Six days after Mrs Lind's death, her mother suffered the same fate, and shortly after that their 11-year-old son died, followed by the youngest child. Finally, Mr Lind also died.

Steen remained unconvinced by Anna's insistence that no one was compelled to remain in the Colony and that "anyone who is dissatisfied with the Colony, can leave here whenever they want". He pointed out that members, on joining, were obliged to turn over all they owned. "Our money is given to the Lord and His bride. We have no right to use the money on those who are going to the devil," Anna had said.

"Woe on him," the pastor wrote, "who would be discovered writing home to ask for travel money." At such times Mother Anna and Brother Jacob became so angry they could not control themselves, he noted, adding: "With clenched fists and loud threats they shout at the unfortunate victim. If this is not enough the Colony members are ordered not to speak to the person. It is easy to understand how frightening it must be just showing any indication of dissatisfaction."

Nothing came of Pastor Steen's newspaper article. Some defended Anna and her policies. Most of the guests at the Colony did not notice the class separation that Steen referred to. When a 69-year-old Norwegian businessman, Thomas Møller Wiborg, came to Jerusalem in April 1904, he found that both Anna Spafford and Alvilde Strand were "honourable, good and kind people" for whom one "gains respect when one gets to know them". Alvilde's daughter and husband had died a number of years earlier.

Wiborg wrote to the newspaper *Vestmar*, pointing out that the Colony would welcome Norwegian men and women. But he had little appreciation of Jerusalem itself. He described the endless filth and a stench so awful he had been forced to walk long distances holding to his nose a handkerchief doused with eau de cologne.

"Burn down the old town," he wrote, "and save only the Church of the Holy Sepulchre and Omar's Mosque, so long as the Jews are not permitted to rebuild it, because then it will be just as it is now." Wiborg had stayed at Fast's Hotel, a handsome building owned by the Armenian patriarchate, close to the Old City. He was aware that the American Colony had opened its hostel two years previously, but preferred to stay at Fast's Hotel, which had baths and toilets in all rooms.[245] Wiborg was equally unimpressed by the surrounding villages, noting that in several of them female tourists were forced to hitch up their skirts and step aside to avoid people who were urinating in the street.

However, no amount of negative description could slow down the tourist traffic to Jerusalem. Many who travelled to Palestine after the millennium discovered it was difficult to find rooms in the towns at the height of the season. Baron Plato von Ustinow made an agreement with Anna to house his guests from Jaffa at the American Colony Hostel when they were in Jerusalem – an arrangement that suited them both well.

When spring came, many of the Colony's members were obliged to move to smaller houses in the neighbourhood so that rooms in the large house could be made available for guests. The Swedes and others outside Anna's inner circle had to eat their meals in a small wooden shed, while the guests got the best service in Jerusalem. Young Nordic girls made sure they were served freshly baked bread, home-made butter, jam, eggs, coffee and fresh cream for their breakfast. The young men were employed as tourist guides and travelled all around the region.

One morning in March 1903, as the congregation gathered under the vaulting of the salon, Anna announced a wonderful message from God. Marriage was now allowed within the Colony. There had been no children born, and no marriages, for 22 years, and Anna wrote: "When we came to Jerusalem, we gave up everything in order to put our faith in God to a test. Now the time has come for marriage, but it must happen in the right way. We may render unto Caesar what belongs to Caesar."[246] The Colony's first bride, Mother Anna announced, would be Bertha, her groom: Frederick Vester. They had been close for nine years, and Anna felt the time had come and that it was the Lord's will.

245 T. M. Wiborg: *Reisebreve* (Travel Letters), Kragerø 1904, pp.272–273, 293.
246 Larsson: *Dala Folk in The Holy Land*, Stockholm 1957, p.62.

Anna Spafford and family on the balcony at the American Colony

Frederick's father, former German missionary Ferdinand Vester, had become a businessman. But the business did not do well, and the company was nearly bankrupt when the American Colony took over the inventory and company name. The new name would be Vester & Co, American Colony Stores and the company rented premises in the Grand New Hotel.

The wedding would take place on March 1, 1904, and several hundred guests were invited. The children of the American Colony went out into the fields to pick flowers. Honeysuckle and clematis were in full bloom, as were the wild tulips and anemones. The flowers were arranged in small baskets, and an enormous bell made out of clematis was put up in the large dining room, with garlands of white flowers draped across the ceiling into each corner where they were linked to smaller bells. The house had never looked so magnificent.

For weeks, the seamstresses and tailors in the Colony had been busy making the bridal couple's clothing. Bertha's gown was made from soft white wool, decorated with small knots while a border of fine tulle edged the high collar and cuffs. The religious ceremony took place at the American Colony, which the German pastor in Jerusalem officiated. The sect now had its own orchestra, which played Mendelssohn's wedding march, and the huge wedding cake had been baked and decorated in the Colony's own bakery. The group's photographer, Lewis Larsson, immortalized the bridal couple as they cut the cake.

Bertha and Frederick moved immediately into their new home, in the old house, high above the Damascus Gate. It had been furnished with the help of the Colony's members, and was filled with so many presents it resembled a museum. Now the rubicon had been crossed, and in no time several of the Colony's young men dared to ask Mother Anna for permission to marry one of the other members, or to 'become one with her', as the engagement was referred to in Anna's house. None of the weddings that followed, however, was as magnificent as Bertha's.

The younger generation had not chosen to come to Jerusalem to live a holy life, they were there because their parents had brought them as children. They were more interested in this world than the next. In America, Jon Jonsson was still living as a bachelor. But he had not forgotten Karin. One day he received a letter from his friend, Erik Lind: "I believe you have heard that they are getting married here now. It seems so idiotic. When I see them, I laugh to myself since I cannot laugh with anyone else. That we now may marry is God's divine plan, which has been revealed only to Mrs Spafford... the speeches at the meetings are the same, day in and day out. I put a little 'French' book into the Bible so I can amuse myself. I think I will soon change my way of life. I have still not seen anything Godly here. And if I haven't found it by now, I will never find it."[247] But the letter made no difference to Jon. He chose to go back to Nås. Karin remained in the Jerusalem Colony, but never married.

247 Letter from Erik Lind to Jon Jonsson, May 1, 1904, Mia Gröndahl's collection. Quoted in the documentary: *Drömmen om Jerusalem* (Dreams of Jerusalem), Swedish Television, Malmö, Production 30–96/0180.

Chapter 20

"Take Uganda"

Hardly a month went by without the start of a new building project in Jerusalem. Many were the work of a new organisation founded by Baron Edmund de Rothschild for the purchase of land across Palestine. The sultan could no longer afford to restrict Jewish settlement: he was waiting for a loan from Europe that he hoped could save his empire from bankruptcy.[248] Abdul Hamid wanted a railway to run from Damascus to Medina. The project was not ideologically incompatible with the Jewish colonization of Palestine, and, like the Zionists, the sultan sought to strengthen his case with promises of material rewards and incitements to observe religious duty.

The Muslim world was asked to donate money so that travel to the sacred Islamic cities of Mecca and Medina could be made easier for pilgrims. But the proposed railway would also make it easier for the Turks to transport troops and weapons into the heart of Arabia. Telegraph lines along the tracks would facilitate greater control over the sultan's more distant provinces which, Abdul Hamid had long been aware, were slipping from his grasp.

The sultan understood only too well that economic progress threatened to undermine the foundations of feudal Ottoman society. But the need for funds was so great that he was prepared to do almost anything to secure them. So, in May, 1901, he granted Herzl an audience. He sought to enlist the Zionist leader's help so that Turkey's gigantic debt could be consolidated. The audience was to be combined with an interview, and the conversation was to be made public. There was one condition: Herzl could not discuss Zionism.

248 Derek Wilson: *Rothschild, A Story of Wealth and Power*, London 1988, pp.289–98. Alan Palmer: *The Decline and Fall of the Ottoman Empire*, London 1995, p.195.

When Herzl saw the sultan for the first time, he found the Ottoman emperor to be exactly as he had imagined. Abdul Hamid was a short, thin, man with a large hooked nose, a dyed beard and a weak shaky voice. Herzl noted the pitiful hands covered by oversized white gloves, the wide cuffs covered with diamonds, the cracking voice, the limited intelligence evident in every word, and the anxiety manifest in every glance.[249] After initial polite exchanges, Herzl asked in French: "May I speak completely freely?" The sultan nodded. Herzl continued: "The problem, as I see it, is the burden of the public debt. If this is wiped away, then Turkey will be in a position to begin afresh, something I have faith in."

The sultan sighed and answered that he had been trying to eradicate the debt ever since he came to power. Herzl eagerly offered his services in this area, but insisted on absolute secrecy. Otherwise, the great powers that wanted to exploit Turkey's weaknesses would do everything they could to torpedo his efforts. The sultan agreed, and Herzl proposed that with his majesty's agreement he would persuade his financial contacts to invest in the European stock exchanges on behalf of the sultan. In exchange, Herzl requested that when the time was ripe, the sultan would endorse publicly certain political actions, beneficial to the Jews, in a manner specified by Herzl.

Abdul Hamid was in full agreement. His court jeweller was a Jew, he told Herzl. Perhaps he could say something that was favourable about the Jews to him, or to the chief rabbi, and allow his comments to be leaked to the newspapers? Herzl answered that this was not exactly what he had in mind, adding that "he would send a suggestion for a suitable public statement at the appropriate time".

The Turk again agreed, and asked if Herzl could recommend a competent financier who might create new taxes that would not be too onerous, perhaps a tax on matches. Herzl promised to find the right man, and they remained sitting and talking for two hours. The words 'Zionism' and 'Palestine' were never mentioned, but Herzl was almost walking on air as he left the palace, believing he had convinced the sultan to swallow the bait and that he had entered a new phase – of realistic negotiations about the establishment of a Jewish corporation with special rights.

Nine months later, Herzl was again asked to come to Constantinople. It was a bad time for him to travel because his wife was sick, but worse

249 Herzl: Diary, May 19, 1901. *The Complete Diaries of Theodor Herzl* (ed. Patai); New York 1960, Vol III, p.1112. Only after Herzl was out of the country did he dare to commit his thoughts about Abdul Hamid to paper. He feared the sultan's agents might obtain copies of anything he wrote to use against him.

still he had not managed to find the promised funds. It is not generally known that Herzl had attempted to obtain millions of pounds in the form of crisis assistance for the sultan. But not a single Jewish financier was willing to place his wealth at the disposal of the sultan in order to gain his support for Jewish immigration into Palestine. Herzl was now physically exhausted and deeply depressed. Before he was given an audience he had to meet the sultan's closest advisers, and was confronted immediately with the question: "When is the money coming?" The advisers explained that Abdul Hamid II was willing to receive Jewish refugees, to give them Ottoman passports and let them settle wherever they wished in the Ottoman Empire – except in Palestine. Herzl declined, adding: "No Palestine, no agreement." After two days in the city, he left, without once having met the sultan. The Zionist leader decided to change focus. He now wanted to concentrate on Great Britain. First he visited the chief of the British branch of the Rothschild banking conglomerate, who later invited him to lunch.

Lord Nathaniel Mayer Rothschild, who was 20 years older than Herzl, was the son of England's first Jewish Member of Parliament. Rothschild was also enormously rich, a member of the board of the Bank of England and the first Jew to sit in the House of Lords. During lunch, Herzl explained his plan to ask the British government to establish a charter with special rights for Jewish colonization.

"Do not say charter. The word has bad associations at present," answered Rothschild.[250]

"We can call it whatever you like. I want to found a Jewish colony in a British possession."

"Take Uganda!"

"No. I can only take this." Herzl stopped. There were other people in the room, so he wrote down on a small piece of paper: "Sinai Penisula, Egyptian Palestine, and Cyprus." Then he added: "Are you for this?" Rothschild thought about it for a moment then said with a smile: "Very much so."

The words fell like gold coins into a poor man's hand. Herzl looked at the confirmation as a huge victory. He wrote further on the paper: "Prevent the sultan from getting money."

"I prevented Romania from getting money," replied Rothschild, "But this I can't do, because the powers support it, they want to have the

250 Herzl: Diary, July 5, 1902. *The Complete Diaries of Theodor Herzl* (ed. Patai); New York 1960, Vol. IV, p.1294.

railway built." Then he revealed that the powerful nations in Europe were hoping to negotiate an agreement with the sultan to consolidate his debt in exchange for being granted concessions on the railway project.

"The sultan has offered me Mesopotamia," countered Herzl.

"And you refused?" asked Lord Rothschild with surprise.

"I did." And with that, Herzl concluded the discussion. As a dramatist he knew the impact of a powerful ending to a scene.

Two days later Herzl was warmly introduced to the Royal Commission on Alien Immigration in London by Lord Rothschild. The financier proposed putting the suggestion of a 'Jewish Company' for Sinai, Egyptian Palestine and Cyprus before the secretary of state for the colonies. He felt, however, there should be a limit of 25,000 Jewish settlers. Herzl responded there had to be far more, or none at all, even if Sinai and Cyprus were to be only temporary colonies until the Jews could inhabit Palestine.

Herzl believed that if a Jewish Near Eastern Company with assets of up to five million pounds could be formed, both the Egyptians and the Cypriots would be eager for a share of its wealth, in exchange for providing land for the Zionists. In October 1902, Herzl was received by the Colonial Secretary, Joseph Chamberlain, but was told he could only discuss Cyprus, since Egypt was not a British colony, but came under the Foreign Office. Cyprus was populated by Greeks and Muslims, and Chamberlain pointed out that Britain could not simply drive them out for the sake of the Jewish immigrants. "We should be invited to come there," Herzl answered. "The Muslims will move away, the Greeks will gladly sell their properties at a good price and migrate to Athens or Crete."[251] Chamberlain remained unconvinced, but suggested that al-Arish in the Sinai Peninsula might be a suitable location for a Jewish settlement. The colonial secretary, however, was unsure where the area was located on the map. When he saw that it was part of Egypt he became more doubtful.

In December, Herzl received an historic document from the Foreign Office in London. The British were to send a commission to Sinai, and Herzl, at a stroke, became a serious partner in negotiations between the British government and the Zionist movement. But just two weeks later Herzl was disappointed yet again. The Sinai project had been put on ice. The official reason given was that the Nile would not be able to provide enough water for a Jewish colony in al-Arish and the British again put

---

251 Herzl: Diary October 23, 1902. Ibid. p.1362.

forward an offer of Jewish settlement in Uganda.[252] Herzl was at first unenthusiastic, but after a while, realizing he was unlikely to be able to negotiate a better arrangement, he went along with the offer. In 1903, the Zionist Congress in Basel also agreed. Of the delegates present, 295 were for the settlement in Uganda, 177 were against. Even Eliezer Ben-Yehuda, the indefatigable advocate of the Hebrew language, agreed that the Zionists would have to settle for Uganda or Brazil as the location of the Jewish state, since they would not be able to settle in Palestine. The result was a victory for Herzl, but it was a hollow one. The Zionist organization was on the brink of breaking up.

It was only after the brutal suppression of a coup attempt in Russia, in 1905 that the Zionist movement regained its momentum. Yet again, thousands of Jews fled tsarist oppression and headed to Palestine. With this, the so-called second *aliyah* or 'ascension' began. The wave of immigration grew so large that the Jewish population in Palestine rose to 60,000 in the course of a year. This was nearly double the number of Jews who had lived in the country in 1880.

But Herzl did not live to see this influx. He died of bronchitis in July, 1905, at just 44. A few months earlier, he had written down his thoughts about the Zionist movement which he had founded. Less than 50 years later, his movement would triumph in the establishment of a Jewish state in Palestine. Herzl's final observations on Zionism contain the following comment: "Don't do anything ill-advised when I am dead."[253] Emissaries from all over the world came to the funeral. Yet the man who was to take over Herzl's position was absent. Chaim Weizmann, the 30-year-old Russian, who would later become Israel's first president, chose to remain in Switzerland. He believed Herzl was a super-swindler and referred to his efforts at diplomatic Zionism as "charlatanism".[254]

In 1905, Bertha Spafford Vester gave birth to a girl – the first child to be born in the American Colony in 23 years. The birth took place in the couple's home, and for the first time since the Spafford family came to Jerusalem, a doctor was allowed to be present in the house. "Faith has met its test," Anna explained at the morning meeting in the salon and added: "A doctor may now be called as needed."[255]

252 The territory under discussion lay in what later became Kenya, and extended to the border with present day Uganda.
253 Amos Elon: "Israel and the End of Zionism", *The New York Review of Books*, December 19, 1996.
254 Moshe Leshem: *Israel Alone*, New York 1989, p.120.
255 Larsson: *Dala Folk in the Holy Land*, Stockholm 1957, p. 79. Birgitte Rahbek and Mogens

One of the Swedish women was appointed to care for mother and child, and Bertha and Frederick moved out of the house in the Old City into a rented property on the Nablus Road, closer to the American Colony. The little girl was not baptized, but was blessed at a morning meeting when she was a few weeks old. Brother Jessup prayed that she would grow up with the Lord's grace and announced to the congregation that the baby was to be called Anna Grace. At the end of the service all the community members went up, one by one, to look at the new arrival.

Mother Anna was busy with the business of running her Colony and did not concern herself with the power politics being played out between the Palestinians and the arriving Jews. She had made it a rule not to discuss politics with outsiders, and was unaware that some of the Jewish settlers were planning secretly to expel large parts of the Palestinian population.

One of the early advocates of Zionism, Menachem Ussishkin, believed that the Jews would need to gain control over the majority of the land before there could ever be a Jewish state. He was uncompromising in his vision of how this should be achieved: "By force – that is, by conquest, or in other words, by robbing land from its owner; by forceful acquisition, that is, by expropriation via governmental authority; and by purchase with owners' consent."[256] The prominent Zionist was not alone in his views. In April 1905, one of Ussishkin's colleagues said publicly: "There is, however, a difficulty [from] which the Zionist dares not to avert his eyes, though he rarely likes to face it. The pashlik of Jerusalem is already twice as thickly populated as the United States, having 52 souls to the square mile, and not 25 percent of them Jews, so we must be prepared either to drive out by the sword the tribes in possession as our forefathers did, or to grapple with the problem of a large alien population, mostly Mohammedan and accustomed to despise us."[257] Perhaps the greatest deception surrounding the establishment of the state of Israel was the now infamous statement: "Palestine is a country without people for a people without a country." British novelist Israel Zangwill adapted the phrase from its original form: "A country without a nation for a nation without a country", which has been attributed to Lord Shaftesbury. Zangwill said later he was "hypnotised by

Bähncke: *Tro og skæbne i Jerusalem* (Faith and Destiny in Jerusalem), Haslev 1997, p.122, Dudman & Kark: *The American Colony*, p.161.
256 Menachem Ussishkin: *Sefer Ussishkin* (Hebrew), Jerusalem 1964, p.105, cited in Gershon Shafir: *Land, Labour and the Origins of the Israeli-Palestinian Conflict, 1882-1914*, London 1992, p.42.
257 Izrael Zangwill in a speech delivered at Derby Hall, Manchester, April 1905, recounted in: Maurice Simon (ed): *Speeches, Articles and Letters of Israel Zangwill*, The Soncino Press, London 1937, p.210.

the legend that Palestine was empty and derelict".[258]

But Anna Spafford, for her part, had other worries. The war of attrition with the American consul in Jerusalem consumed a lot of her energy. There was always something to deal with, and in early July 1905, Anna learned that Consul Merrill had ordered the American flag to be removed from the American Colony Store inside the Jaffa Gate. At the same time, the diplomat forbade the Colony to celebrate, the 4th of July American Independence Day holiday.

Mother Anna ignored these latest prohibitions, but the consul persisted, visiting his German colleague to ask for help in getting the flag removed. Merrill argued that Frederick Vester was a German citizen and had married into the Colony. But the German consul, who had a good relationship with Anna, refused to take Merrill's threats seriously. Both the consul and the vice-consul were frequent guests at the Colony. The vice-consul and his wife (considered the best-dressed woman in Jerusalem) were particularly friendly and well liked. Their youngest son, however, was completely out of control, and whenever his parents visited the Colony Anna would appoint a 'guard' to watch over the little boy. The child would grow up to become the notorious Nazi, Rudolf Hess,[259] Hitler's private secretary, number three in the Nazi hierarchy, and, finally, the solitary prisoner of Spandau prison.

258 Izrael Zangwill: *Territoralism as Practical Politics, Address Delivered to the Union of Jewish Literary Societies*, March 1913, recounted in Simon (ed.): *Speeches, Articles and Letters of Israel Zangwill*, London 1937, p.314.
259 Spafford Vester: *Our Jerusalem*, 2nd edition, p.209.

Chapter 21

The Consul's Loss of Face

Just before Easter, 1906, an American journalist, Alexander Hume Ford, came to the houses near the Sheikh Jarrah Mosque and asked for Anna Spafford. Ford had heard about her in Chicago and wanted to visit Horatio Spafford's grave. He noticed a pained look come over Anna's face, and tried to change the subject, but Anna decided to tell her guest the story of the two American consuls. It did not take long for Ford to realize he was on the trail of a diplomatic scandal.

Ford and his friend, Dr C C Higgins, were staying at the Grand New Hotel. The American tourists had been able to complete the Damascus-to-Amman leg of their journey on the sultan's new railway, which would soon extend as far as Medina. On their first day in Jerusalem the two men paid a courtesy visit to the American consulate, just across the road from their hotel. But when Ford asked the consul about the American Colony, Selah Merrill rose abruptly from his chair. He demanded to know whether the journalist and his companion were friends of the Colony, adding that if they were, then he would not talk to them. At one point, Merrill denied that there was an American Colony in Jerusalem, adding that if it did exist there were certainly "no Americans there". In his next breath the consul condemned every single member of Anna's sect as immoral and said the stench of their "goings on" was the most putrid odour in the nostrils of Jerusalem.[260]

Ford tried to ask another question, but it was impossible to interrupt the storm of venom emanating from the consul's mouth. Merrill said he had not deigned to cross the threshold of the American Colony in the course of his many years in the city. The consul, nevertheless, claimed a

---

260 Alexander Ford: "Our American Colony." *Appleton's Magazine, No. 6* 1906, p.652.

full understanding of the inner life of the sect. The women, he claimed, were immoral, every one of them. They brought their children up to be immoral, and illiteracy and slovenliness flourished. Merrill added that the American Colony Store, whose premises were on the ground floor of the hotel where the tourists were staying, sold fake antiques. He told his two visitors that they would do better to buy from his friend, a local dealer.

When Ford asked if the consul had "any particular charge against the members from the Colony", the plump little diplomat exploded, accusing his guest of being "a friend of the Colony". The journalist persisted, asking why the consul refused to give the Colony the protection offered by the American flag. Merrill retorted that they were cranks and heretics. Ford then tried to enquire whether "cranks and heretics were barred by our constitution from the rights of citizenship", but "the flow of verbal lava was too strong to breast" and the reporter and his companion from Texas feared being "swept away", carried off in a "torrent of molten vituperation directed at the 'crimes' of the heretical Colony". They were both told that if they ever visited Anna Spafford they should never show themselves again at the American consulate.

When Ford emerged from the interview he commented: "I saw Vesuvius' biggest eruption in 34 years, but the memories of the volcano pale in comparison with this half hour with the American consul." The journalist was now so curious he could not resist committing the same 'terrible crime' as Selma Lagerlöf's six years earlier, and walking the few hundred yards to the American Colony.

Ford arrived later that afternoon to find that Anna had visitors. Some elderly American women on a cruise had travelled up to Jerusalem by train in order to see her. They were due to return to their ship in Jaffa the next morning. Ford and Higgins sat for some time amongst these white-haired women, whom the American consul had maintained 'loved freely' and even worse. Anna, the youngest among them, had just reached 64. Some of the guests became quite tearful when Anna related the shocking accusations that the consul had made.

The American journalist made detailed notes of his surroundings. Ford found the salon exotic, but at the same time felt there was an aura of purity in the air. On enquiring further about Anna's relationship with the consul, he was told the story of Pastor William Eddy, the man who had sold the American cemetery to German Jesuits without Anna's knowledge. The previous year, Eddy had returned secretly to Jerusalem to try to resolve the affair. Anna had been forewarned, and appealed to the

British and Swedish-Norwegian consuls in Jerusalem for help to protect what was left of the sect's remains.

Professor Gustav Dalman represented Sweden and Norway jointly. He was also the Director of the German Archaeological Institute in Jerusalem, and he remembered all too clearly what had happened when Eddy had assumed responsibility for the 'proper' removal of the remains of the American sect's members. When Consul Dalman had arrived at the British graveyard he had found a large open hole containing boxes. Some had been opened and he could see knuckles and skulls lying in a pile close by.[261] Pastor Eddy had maintained that he knew who the dead were, but as an experienced archaeologist, Dalman could see clearly that some of the remains had been mixed. For instance, he noticed two boxes with the same number, and two skulls in one box. The consul expressed surprise that Eddy was operating under the protection of Consul Merrill, and had failed to notify the families of the deceased about the proposed move. Eddy maintained that he alone had the right to move the remains, but had failed to provide Dalman with documents to support his assertion.[262]

One of the men from the American Colony who had gone with Dalman was able to take pictures of the boxes and of Pastor Eddy standing by the hole. Several times the pastor protested that it was forbidden to take pictures, and turned his back to the camera, but the photographer just carried on snapping. The next day, Dalman wrote a letter to the American consul, protesting over the desecration of the corpses. He argued that it was impossible for all of them to have decomposed completely and that some of them must therefore have been "torn apart" and shoved into the boxes by force.

Alexander Ford obtained copies of numerous letters and documents connected to the ongoing dispute with the consul, but unlike Selma Lagerlöf, the American did not give the world a great literary work. His article about the 'grave war' was printed in the Christmas 1906 edition of *Appleton's Magazine*. The feature was highly critical of Consuls Merrill and Wallace, and their treatment of both living and dead Americans in Jerusalem. Ford repeated in detail Merrill's salacious rumours about the 'free sexual life' practised by members of the sect, and his threats to crush the little community.

261 Witness statement of Gustav Dalman to the Circuit Court of The United States, Southern District of New York, Wallace vs. D. Appleton & Co. Folder 1908, American Colony Collection, Jerusalem.
262 Letter; November 27, 1905, Folder 1905, American Colony Collection, Jerusalem.

The editor of *Appleton's Magazine* realized that the article was controversial. But Ford had assured him that all available sources had been checked, adding that he had presented the disagreements between the parties in accordance with what the "documents from both sides show". The editor also asked the State Department to release the consul's reports, but it declined. Predictably, Merrill was enraged by Alexander Ford's article and demanded a full retraction and an apology, claiming that the article was "wrong from start to finish". He cited the fact that the story had referred to Mrs Whiting as being "quite old", even though she was only 54, as an example of its inaccuracies. *Appleton's* refused to retract, and Merrill, who by this time was on sick leave from Jerusalem, decided to sue. The State Department now became nervous. Its folder on the American Colony – already big before the magazine article appeared – had been swelled by letters of sympathy and support for Anna Spafford from many prominent Americans. Michigan Congressman George Loud said that everything in Ford's article was true, while the mayor of Philadelphia also voiced his support for Anna's house. Merrill ought to be replaced by a consul who was not tied to any specific religious institution, they argued.

The head of the State Department refused to allow Merrill to sue the magazine. He explained that while the article "without doubt feels misleading and incorrect… the department does not want to reopen any controversy". Finally, in March 1907, the department agreed that certain extracts from one of its internal reports could be revealed. Government officials asked only one question of Ford: "If celibacy in the Colony is a principle, how does one explain the bridal photograph?" His article had included a photograph taken at Bertha and Frederick's wedding, but had omitted to make any reference to the lifting of Anna's famous doctrine prohibiting marriage.

But if *Appleton's Magazine* avoided being taken to court because of the State Department's intervention, it was not so fortunate when it came to the other man targeted in Ford's story, the retired Consul, Edwin Wallace, who now worked as a minister in the Presbyterian Church. Wallace, too, felt he had been hung out to dry, and, untrammelled by the professional constraints that restricted Merrill, he filed a suit against the magazine.

In Sweden, Selma Lagerlöf had been following these developments attentively. In April 1907, she wrote to Anna: "I read your letter of this winter with the liveliest surprise and pleasure. Nothing has interested me as much during my life as to follow the way God manifests His ruling power... It was extraordinarily interesting to know the fate that overtook two of your chief opponents... From Mrs Elkan I can send you the warmest greetings. She is well, but she has had sorrow this year in losing her old mother...With the best of greetings to you, your wonderful daughter and my dear countrymen who belong to your Colony."[263]

The lawsuit was heard in August the following year, and the former diplomat lost on all counts. When the verdict was delivered, *The New York Times* observed that while Ford's article concentrated on Merrill, it was Wallace who had given the orders to remove the contents of the graves. Pastor Wallace had to resign from his work in the Presbyterian Church as a result of the furore.

Consul Merrill, who was by now 69, offered his resignation to the State Department after a career of nearly 30 years. This was not accepted, but after his posting in Jerusalem he was sent to Georgetown in British Guyana, a thinly veiled professional insult for the aging Bible researcher and archaeologist.

For Anna and the American Colony, the lawsuit brought to an end 25 years of diplomatic persecution. But Selah Merrill did not give up on Jerusalem entirely. Some years later, he returned to the city as a private citizen. By that stage, Anna Spafford's other son-in-law, 28-year-old John D Whiting, son of Mary Whiting, had been named American vice-consul in Jerusalem. The American Colony was no longer a dirty word in diplomatic circles. Everything seemed to be going in Mother Anna's favour, apart from the fact that the return of Jesus remained a delayed expectation.

In Sweden, Selma Lagerlöf decided to write a new version of *Jerusalem*. She wanted to depict the disillusionment felt by the Nås farmers after the promises of Jesus' return were not realized. Younger members of Anna's house found fulfillment through practical work, but the older ones remained stuck in their eschatological dreams – of death, judgement, eternal salvation and doom. The earliest members of the sect, the Overcomers, had arrived in Jerusalem with high expectations. They had focused initially on what the Holy City might do for their souls, rather than what they could do for the people of Palestine. Many older members, in particular, felt apprehensive, fearing that they might not be well enough prepared when Jesus came. Some wrote letters about their faith and their fear of being left behind on judgement day, anxieties that

263 Letter from Selma Lagerlöf to Mrs Spafford, April 24, 1907: Folder 1907, American Colony Collection.

arose from the New Testament references to the two women by the mill, one of whom was taken up to heaven, while the other was left behind.[264] It was only when opportunities for employment began to develop that waiting in Jerusalem took on a more permanent dimension. Despite the fact that Jesus did not come, Mother Anna exhibited no signs of doubt about her own teachings. She had taken on the task of caring for the soul, and remained convinced the path she had chosen was the correct one. Few dared to doubt her word.

While Selma Lagerlöf rewrote *Jerusalem*, a revolution was taking place in Constantinople that would have huge consequences for the future of Palestine. Throughout Turkey there was widespread dissatisfaction with the sultan's ineffectual, autocratic regime. Matters came to a head on July 2, 1908, when reformist army officers, who wanted to replace the existing despotic regime with a constitutional monarchy, raised the flag of rebellion in the mountains of Macedonia. The officers, known as Young Turks, believed discontent with the sultan's rule was so widespread that despite his notorious network of spies and informers there was now a chance that their coup attempt might succeed.

Abdul Hamid II failed to grasp how little support he had amongst his own people. Rebellions in Macedonia had been suppressed in the past and he believed that just one battalion would be enough to defeat the insurgents. When a force of some 800 Ottoman troops came to Macedonia, the soldiers refused to fire on their own comrades, but killed two of their own senior officers. The revolt began to spread. The rebels telegrammed an ultimatum to the sultan, demanding that the 32-year-old constitution be reinstated the next day. If not, then they would march on Istanbul.

At that point, the sultan summoned his council of ministers, which had not met for many years. After two days of intensive discussions the ministers took a vote. The majority sympathized with the army's calls for reform and feared civil war might follow if the rebels' demands were not met. Two rounds of voting produced a unanimous result, but none of the ministers had the courage to tell the sultan. Finally, the ministers found a solution. They approached the sultan's chief astrologer, who was known to be a brave, intelligent and widely respected man. The astrologer then told the sultan that higher celestial powers advised reconciliation with the Young Turks. Abdul Hamid listened carefully and that same evening he sent a telegram to Macedonia.

---

264 Olof Fahlén: *Nåsbönderna i Jerusalem* (Nås Farmers in Jerusalem), Höganäs 1988, p.167.

The next morning the newspapers of Istanbul reported the extraordinary news that the sultan had voluntarily reinstated the constitution of 1876, the year when a palace revolution had installed Abdul Hamid on the thrown in place of his mentally ill brother. At the mosque of Ayia Sofia, on the Galata Bridge and throughout the streets of the capital, Greeks, Bulgarians, Kurds and Armenians embraced each other as brothers. The Young Turks had declared that Jews, Christians and Muslims were now united in equality, regardless of religion, all working together for the honour of the Ottoman nation. The celebrations lasted for four days and culminated in a march by 70,000 people to a square near the sultan's residence, Yildiz Palace. The sultan had given his subjects a new vision of the future.

Only a very few of those celebrating would ever have seen Abdul Hamid in person. The Ottoman emperor now came out onto the balcony and waved to the masses. Even if he seemed rather pathetic as he stood there waving in the sunshine, his people considered him a liberator. They thought that his advisers were to blame for keeping him so poorly informed about the state of the empire.[265] In an ingenious way Abdul Hamid had stolen the rebels' thunder. The sultan was able to give the impression that it was he alone who had taken steps to reinstate the constitution. In practice, however, the Young Turks had taken over most of the power, and after 1908 the sultan became merely a constitutional monarch. A new parliament was elected and every adult male was given the right to vote, without regard to race or religion.

Under the new constitution, everyone enjoyed equal rights, and in the aftermath of the celebrations a Turk was jailed for having insulted an Armenian. Many Muslims took part in services at the Armenian Cemetery, in memory of those who had been killed in the massacres of the 1890s.[266] Two of the representatives elected to the newly convened parliament came from Jerusalem. They were both Muslims. One belonged to the powerful Husseini clan, the other from the influential Khalidi family. Both men had received their initial education at the American Colony School.[267] The following year, in November 1909, the two parliamentarians were interviewed by one of Palestine's Hebrew newspapers. One of them, Said Husseini, said there was no room for Jewish immigrants, and that the arrival of tens of thousands of newcomers would only harm the Jews

265 Joan Haslip: *The Sultan: The Life of Abdul Hamid*, London 1958, pp.266–267.
266 The Armenian revolutionary group, *Dashnak*, formed in Tiflis in 1890, cooperated with the Young Turks for some years.
267 Their names were Said Husseini and Ruhi Khalidi.

already in Palestine. His colleague emphasized that Jews from Europe had failed to understand or establish relations with the Palestinian Arabs.[268] For Anna this was nothing new. But she remained preoccupied with her own affairs.

268 Eliezer Be'eri: *The Beginning of the Israeli-Arab Conflict, 1882-1911*(Hebrew), Haifa 1985, p.146, cited in Benny Morris: *Righteous Victims, A History of the Zionist-Arab Conflict 1881–1999*, New York 1999, pp.56–59.

Chapter 22

The Russians are Coming

The Zionists opened an office in the port city of Jaffa, where most Jewish immigrants came ashore, to manage the influx of Jewish settlers. The establishment of 'the Palestine Office' marked the beginning of an organized campaign to take over as much of Palestine as possible and also represented a significant departure from Herzl's absolutist doctrine of 'all or nothing'. Now there would be coordination of the activities of the newly arrived colonists, the purchase of new land and weapons, public and philanthropic investments, and the establishment of a political and economic centre for the new Jewish immigrants. The office's director, a 31-year-old German lawyer, Arthur Ruppin, was a friend of the American Colony and a pragmatist who wanted the Jewish colonists to live in peace with their Arab neighbours "if this was possible".[269] It did not take long for Palestinian nationalists to become aware of the Zionist initiative to acquire more land. The Palestinians also understood that they could no longer depend on the Turks, their Muslim brothers and masters, to defend their land and faith.[270]

Angry, dispossessed Arab farmers, whose grazing land had been sold to Jewish settlers, often attacked the more isolated Jewish colonies. The Jews responded by hiring armed guards to defend themselves. These Jewish guards rode horses, wore *kaffiyehs* on their heads, spoke perfect Arabic and understood Bedouin culture. They were widely respected and in time became mythologized as the legendary Jewish cowboys

---

269 Yosef Gorny: *The Origins of Conscience in the Jewish-Arab National Conflict and the Reflections of the Hebrew Press 1900-18*, (Hebrew), Vol. 4. HaTziyonut, 1976, p.93.
270 Morris: *Righteous Victims*, New York 1999, pp.52–53, Baruch Kimmerling: *Telling it Like it Was*, Ha'aretz, December 17, 1999.

of 'the Wild East'. By 1909, the guards had organized themselves into a country-wide paramilitary organization known as *HaShomer* – the Guild of Watchmen.[271] The *HaShomer* modelled themselves on the Circassians who had a reputation for bravery. The Circassians were Muslims from the Caucasus who had come to Palestine at the beginning of the 19th century to escape persecution in their homeland by the Christian forces of the tsar. The *HaShomer* often convinced the newly arrived settlers of the need for their services by themselves attacking Jewish colonies to create an atmosphere of fear among the inhabitants. Despite the fact they were no more than 100 strong, mostly members of one large extended family, they managed to convince the settlers that they could defend their colonies against Arab attack.[272]

The Watchmen's leader was a black-bearded man who resembled Rasputin, the Russian priest who exerted a powerful influence over the Tsarina. According to those who knew both men, each had a predatory look. The Watchmen wanted to distance themselves from the image of cowardice that hung over many European Jewish communities. They were particularly contemptuous of the victims of the pogroms in the Ukrainian town of Kishinev, whom they referred to as 'yellow shits'. The Jews of Kishinev had done nothing when their wives were raped before their eyes. All they did was ask their rabbis later whether they could have sexual intercourse with them or whether they were 'unclean'.[273] *HaShomer* was a secretive organization, which only accepted new members after they had sworn an oath of allegiance to its leaders. When David Gruen, a short stocky Pole with dark curly hair, refused to swear the oath, he was denied acceptance.[274] The Pole later took a Hebrew name, that of the last Jewish defender of Jerusalem during Roman times. It was under his new name, David Ben-Gurion, that he would later become known internationally as the first prime minister of the Jewish state.[275]

271 Eliahu Golomb: *History of Jewish Self-Defense in Palestine,* cited in Arthur Koestler: *Promise and Fulfillment, Palestine 1917–1949,* MacMillan New York 1949, p.68.
272 Gershon Shafir: *Land, Labour and the Origin of the Israeli-Palestinian Conflict 1882-1914,* Cambridge 1989, p.139.
273 Martin van Creveld: *The Sword and the Olive, A Critical History of the Israeli Defense Force,* New York 1998, p.11, quotes Haim Bialak's poem about the pogrom, *Be-ir Ha-hariga* (In the City of Slaughter).
274 A. Pialkov & Y. Rabinovitch (ed.): *Yitzhak Tabenkin – Pirke Hayim,* Kibbutz Beeri 1982, p.54.
275 David Gruen – or Green, as he also called himself – was born in 1886 in Plonsk in Poland and came to Palestine in 1906, where he became one of the leaders of the Jewish Labor Movement. In 1922 he was elected General Secretary of the *Histadrut.* From 1935-1948 he was the chairman of the executive committee of the Jewish Agency.

At the American Colony, Anna was busy keeping her sect together, finding sources of income to support their charity work and securing the community's future. The Colony had invested in property and land inside and outside the Old City and its coffers now contained a substantial sum. Meanwhile, the American Colony Hostel was rapidly gaining a reputation as a good place for foreign visitors to stay. One such visitor was Klas Pontus Arnoldson, a 66-year-old Swedish peace activist. Arnoldson had received the Nobel Peace Prize two years earlier for founding the first Swedish peace organization.[276] On arrival in Jerusalem, he and his wife were met at the train station by Jacob Spafford and the two young Larsson boys. Anna had given orders that the prominent guests were to be taken especially good care of. The couple felt at home from the first moment they arrived, and Anna (who was by now 68) greeted them as if they were old friends. She led them upstairs to a bright and beautiful room on the second floor. It had two windows, and through one they could see the Mount of Olives. In the magical light of the night sky the Swede thought the mountain resembled arms in an outstretched embrace.

The next morning, after breakfast, the couple walked through fig and olive groves towards the Old City. When Arnoldson heard a faint tinkling sound he thought it must just be the wind. But he found that the noise came from small bells around the necks of horses, and when he saw a little girl carrying a sick lamb over her shoulders, he felt he had stepped back into the pages of the Bible. The couple arrived at the most attractive of Jerusalem's entrances, the Damascus Gate. From there, Brother Jacob offered to guide them around the Old City. He explained that an older gate, from the time of Jesus, lay under the existing one and that Jerusalem had been built on the ruins of earlier constructions, so that the oldest parts of the city now lay far beneath street level.

Jacob had been an enthusiastic amateur archaeologist from his time at missionary school. As a youngster he had made "one of the most important finds of biblical archaeology", an inscription cut into the wall of an underground aqueduct. The aqueduct brought water from what was known as the Spring of the Virgin Mary to Siloan (biblical name Siloam). It was only when young Jacob discovered six paleo-hebraic lines cut into the rock that historians understood properly the origins of the aqueduct. But in October 1890, the inscription was secretly hacked out of the wall and sold to a Greek in Jerusalem.[277]

276 Oscar J. Falnes: *Norway and the Nobel Prize*, New York 1938, p.103.
277 The inscription read: "This is the story of the excavation. While the diggers were still raising

More than 20 years later, Jacob Spafford led the Swedish couple down into a network of subterranean caves beneath the Old City. With candles in hand, the party walked slowly into the darkness as the flames cast a weak and fluttering light on the rocky walls. The Jews of Jerusalem knew the place as the cave of Zedekiah, the last king of the Judean kingdom. Zedekiah had fled there after the great Babylonian general, Nebuchadnezzar, had taken the city.[278] Brother Jacob explained that the grotto also went by the name of 'King Solomon's Stone Quarry', an empty space created when the king's engineers had quarried out blocks of stone for the temple. Many who had lost their way in the cave network had died there, their skeletal remains left behind in the darkness. It was said that the first man to find his way back to the entrance after exploring the underground labyrinth had brought with him a long ball of string, which unravelled as he went, enabling him to retrace his steps back to the entrance. But there was also another, frequently told story about the grotto, which connected it to the house on the ridge above. It was said that an Indian prince had built a house for himself on the Bethesda Heights. But after disparaging remarks were made whenever the prince and his entourage passed through the city on their way to Solomon's Temple, he built an underground passage from the cellar of his house to the grotto beneath the city, all the way to Temple Square. After the prince returned to India, Anna Spafford had been able to buy the house cheaply.[279] Of course, this story was not true, but, as was so often the case in Jerusalem, it was told and retold so often that people began eventually to believe it had really happened.

their picks, and while there were still three yards left to cut, a voice of a man was heard who was calling his neighbor, because there were side passages in the wall both to the right and the left. When on the final day the diggers met pick to pick, water ran from the spring to the dam over a length of 1200 yards. The height above the diggers' heads was about one yard." The theft of the stone was discovered when a missionary and a doctor visited the Greek to look at some other antiquities. The man was not at home, and his wife mistakenly showed them the slab bearing the inscription from Siloam, which had broken in two during its removal. After the British representative in Jerusalem informed the Turkish authorities, the stone was removed to a museum in Constantinople. Details of the theft were reported in a letter dated February 18, 1891, to the Foreign Office in London. See Mordechai Eliav: *Britain and the Holy Land, 1838–1914, Selected Documents from the British Consulate in Jerusalem,* Jerusalem 1997, pp.257–258.
278 Old Testament: Jeremiah 39:4–5.
279 The story was told in *Nordisk Tidende* by A.N. Rygg: "Below will be told the story of a Stavanger lady: Anna Tobine Larsen's strange fate." The series was printed the August 10, 17, and 24, 1950. Another Norwegian who visited the American Colony in 1904, claimed Anna Spafford no longer spoke Norwegian, T.M. Wiborg: *Reisebreve* (Travel Letters) Kragerø 1904, p. 291. Selma Lagerlöf chose to write her letters to Anna in Swedish, even though she knew English well.

For his part, Klas Pontus Arnoldson was just as interested in the daily life of the American Colony. He was familiar with some of the critical stories about Anna that had appeared in the Swedish newspapers, but did not mention them. The Arnoldsons were shown around the Colony's premises. It was explained to them that the congregation lived in four houses. In the main house there were 35 rooms; in the so-called Palm House across the dead-end street in front of the Nablus Road, there were nine bedrooms and seven work rooms. There was also a small stone house in front of the Palm House, where Anna's youngest daughter, Grace, lived with her husband John, and a large house a few paces further east with 10 family rooms, known as the East House. The Swede, who made copious notes, was particularly interested in the "photography business and its excellent laboratories", where 10 of the Colony's men now worked full-time taking pictures and processing them. The driving force in the photography department, Lewis Larsson, had fallen in love with Edith, the daughter of Olof Henrik Larsson, the deposed pastor, and Anna eventually gave consent for the couple to become engaged. Arnoldson was impressed by Lewis and his photography department, and was intrigued that the most famous travel book of its day, *Baedeker's Guide to Palestine and Syria*, contained pictures from his laboratory.

Late one evening, the Swedish tourists were brought into the Old City. Arnoldson was impressed by the fact that the city's creaky old gate, normally shut at sundown, was immediately opened up for visitors under the protection of the American Colony. The guard stood to attention as Brother Jacob led his group beneath the Damascus Gate and on through the deserted streets to a large house. There, the tourists were shown a wooden model of Jerusalem's old temple that had been assembled section by section. The visitors were impressed by the amount of patient work that must have gone into its construction. They walked home beneath a clear starry sky, as the Jewish convert, Brother Jacob, quoted a rabbinical saying: "The world is like an eye. The oceans of the world are like the white of the eye. The black of the eye is the land. The pupil is Jerusalem. But the reflection in the pupil is the Temple."[280]

The Swedish couple's stay in Jerusalem was nearly over. At their last religious service in the salon, they listened as Furman Baldwin, the photographer who had tried to kill himself in the summer of 1901, told the congregation in his powerful voice: "It is more blessed to give than to receive." As he spoke, everyone was aware of the bluish scar on his temple,

280 K. P. Arnoldson: *Jerusalems själ* (Jerusalem's Soul), Stockholm 1913, p.186.

where the bullet remained. Also listening on that day was a lonely Russian peasant woman. Although she did not understand what was being said, her eyes shone with love and admiration for the assembled company. Some days earlier, the woman had been found lying unconscious alongside her husband, on the road to Jericho. Brother William had helped them. The man had died soon after, but thanks to William's intervention the woman had now recovered. She would be driven to the Russian hostel nearby after the service was over.

Arnoldson decided to visit the Russian quarter northwest of the Old City, where the poor widow and her friends were staying. The walled Russian district covered the ridge which stretched between the Jaffa Road and St Paul's Road. The Palestinians called the quarter Moskobie – from Moscow.

Easter was approaching, the time when thousands of Christians made the pilgrimage to Jerusalem. Most were Russians, and during Holy Week, as many as 5,000-6,000 travellers might arrive in the city in the space of just a few weeks. They travelled under the protection of the tsar, and made the first part of their journey across the Black Sea in cargo ships. When the pilgrims arrived in Jerusalem, young and old would stand watching their procession. Everyone knew they were coming because their beautiful singing could be heard from far away. Some had deep, resonant tones that sounded like organ pipes. When their rich tones mingled with voices of several thousand other pilgrims, they created wonderful music as they walked in procession from the Mount of Olives, past Mount Scopus and Sheikh Jarrah, to the Russian quarter.

In the past, these pilgrims had walked all the way from their villages to Jerusalem, often accompanied by poor Armenian travellers. They would travel through the Caucasus and the Kars Gap into Turkey, then on to Syria and to Palestine. It was said that no more than half of those who set off on foot through Asia Minor ever came back to tell their stories. There is no way of knowing how many poor Russian Christians were robbed, tortured and killed by the Turks and Arabs. But the pilgrims were philosophical about these dangers. Travelling to the Holy Land was the last thing a Russian Christian was expected to do in this life, and, the pilgrims said, if you were killed on the way, your soul would at least arrive in Jerusalem sooner.

By the early 1900s, things had become much easier for the devout Russians. Ships from Odessa now brought the pilgrims to Jaffa. When they came ashore, they made the sign of the cross, fell to their knees and kissed the holy ground. Consular guards – *kavasses* – dressed in smart blue uniforms with gold stripes and holding curled-up whips, called out marching orders in Russian to the caravan, which moved slowly towards the train station, singing as it did so. The pilgrims were loaded into third-class carriages and as they approached Jerusalem their singing could even be heard above the noise of the locomotive. They were sometimes met with condescending laughter and insulting remarks, such as "the Russians are cattle", but others, perhaps the majority, made them welcome. Young boys would run alongside the procession calling out: "*Moskof khorsh, Moskof khorsh*" – "the Muscovites are good, the Muscovites are good".[281] Seen from the terrace above the dining room of the American Colony the long line of pilgrims resembled a huge army. They walked four and five abreast, dressed in heavy clothing with woollen head coverings. They carried large samovars and dry tea leaves, and when they rested, they brewed their favourite drink and ate dried bread crusts.

On arrival, the pilgrims were greeted by peddlers selling oranges and cakes, and money-changers rattling their boxes. The city's Russian monks spoke to each one in turn, asking them which province they had come from. The visitors swarmed into the monasteries, buying bundles of slender candles to light. They sang, prayed, gave thanks to God, and visited the Russian Orthodox priest to receive his blessing. But even after they had arrived in the Holy City, life remained difficult for the pilgrims. There were six Russian hostels in Jerusalem, with floor-to-ceiling cots rather than beds. As many as eight people would be stacked together like crated dates. The pilgrims had to adapt as best they could. They walked, slept and ate in the same clothes for several weeks.

Many wondered who these impoverished pilgrims were and why they had come. Had they been infected with a kind of Jerusalem fever, an epidemic over which they had no control? Were they village drunkards who had picked themselves up out of the muck and decided to go to the Holy City? Or had they seen the light one morning, given all their money away and begun to beg their way to a distant holy sanctuary? The pilgrims could not explain why they had come. They had not been persuaded by their priests, and since most left their villages alone, or in small groups of two or three, they could not have been part of any kind of mass religious hysteria which sometimes swept through whole communities at a time. What was clear was that once they were on board the ships bringing them to Palestine, their difficulties began in earnest. They were stowed like cattle, with as many as 700 passengers occupying vessels with a capacity

281 Stephen Graham: *With the Russian Pilgrims to Jerusalem*, MacMillan & Co. Ltd, London, 1914, p.76.

for only 100. Despite being out in the open on deck, the smell was terrible. Many were seasick; some died on the way.[282] One of those who managed to make his way to Jerusalem in 1911 was Grigori Rasputin. He complained that he and his fellow pilgrims had been treated like animals. "They should be given cheap transport," he wrote, pointing out that the Russian mission in Jerusalem "should not be demanding money for warm water, a room and one meal per day."

The British author, Stephen Graham, who travelled to Jerusalem with 560 Russian peasants, also observed how many people were ready to take advantage of the pious visitors. During his journey he encountered a pilgrim called Filip, who acted as an agent, convincing trusting pilgrims to pay the priests to say special prayers for them. One monastery contained a tariff for various types of prayers that could be said for the wellbeing of pilgrims who were about to make the journey back home. The monks charged five roubles to pray once a year and 10 roubles to pray once a day each week. A prayer 'each day forever' cost 30 roubles. And if the Russian pilgrim was happy to part with 100 roubles, he could even have a dedicated oil lamp burning in the monastery in perpetuity. But Graham also observed that Filip was pious and God-fearing in a childlike way, travelling as far as the Jordan River to fill 10 bottles with holy water to take back with him. There was no question of filling the bottles at a public tap in Jerusalem and then lying about the source of the water when he got home. Filip also took back gifts for his village. One day, his fellow pilgrims noticed him slicing up potatoes and hanging them up to dry on a line above his bed. He explained to Graham that the potatoes were for the peasant women at home, who broke them into small pieces and put them in their tea. Potatoes from the holy land apparently cured toothaches, headaches and stomach pains. Filip added: "Once I brought a pound back home with me and they liked it so much that each time I went to Jerusalem all the 'babas' now ask me to bring more."

Every year, after Easter, long queues of people began to form in front of the Russian consulate. The diplomats inside were besieged by peasants seeking to take out money they had deposited earlier for safekeeping and which was now needed to cover the costs of their trip home. In 1912, pilgrims returning home to Russia faced the added difficulty of getting through the Dardanelles before the sea route was closed because of the Turco-Italian war. Although this was a relatively minor conflict, it was to be a significant precursor to World War One, since it sparked nationalism

---

282 A. Goodrich-Freer: *Inner Jerusalem*, London 1904, p.80.

in the Balkan states. One of the Russian monks interpreted the conflict in millenarian terms. Doomsday was at hand; God's Judgement would occur near the Dead Sea by 1914.

Chapter 23

Mobilization

There was one Russian who longed more than all the others to go home. He was Baron von Ustinow. After 50 years in Palestine, von Ustinow realized finally that his real home was in Russia. As the crisis in Europe grew nearer the former officer felt pangs of loyalty towards his old regiment. The 80-year-old aristocrat presented himself at the Russian consulate in Jerusalem, stood to attention before the surprised consul-general and proclaimed: "My sword is at your disposal."[283] The diplomat declined politely the old aristocrat's offer. But when von Ustinow's funds also began to shrink he decided that the time was right for him to travel back to Russia. He sold his house in Jerusalem, packed up his belongings – including his enormous collection of antiques – and left Jaffa for good in September 1913. In London, von Ustinow approached the British Museum and offered to sell his collection of antiquities, but the museum declined, so the baron travelled to Norway. There, he succeeded in selling his collection to three prominent Norwegians. Having done so, he began the journey home to the place of his birth.[284]

Meanwhile, in Jerusalem, another man had grown profoundly dissatisfied with his life and had made the decision to move on. He was Eric Peterson, once one of the leaders of Pastor Larsson's congregation in Chicago. Since coming to Jerusalem his role had diminished considerably.

283 Ustinov: *Kjære meg* (Dear Me) Oslo 1978, p.19.
284 The buyers were the publisher, H. Ericksen, J. Sejerstad Bødtker and Dr Jur. Arnold Ræstad, who later became the Norwegian Prime Minister. After the University of Kristiania rejected the collection as too expensive it was put up for auction. Some items were bought by the Norwegian National Gallery, but most of the collection remained unsold. Approximately 1,800 pieces were put in the Ethnographic Museum, where they remained hidden for over two generations. Laszlo Berczelly: *Norway's Greatest Collection of Antiques from the Lands of the Middle East,* Nicolay, *Arkeologisk Tidsskrift* nr.72, 1997, p.36.

Now, this powerful, dignified man with a wife and two children could no longer see the sense in abiding by Anna's dictum that he should live a life of poverty in the Colony. Every day he toiled in the heat in a small hut, making horseshoes and iron bedsteads. The fact that his children loved watching their strong father work the glowing hot iron and making the sparks fly was not an adequate compensation. The blacksmith yearned to get away. One autumn evening he said to his wife: "I can't stand this life any longer. I work and slave from morning to night and don't earn a cent. I can never buy anything for you, not even toys for our children. I want to get away from here, and I want you and the children to come with me."[285] But Peterson's wife did not want to take the children from their home, since they would have no money and nowhere to go. The blacksmith decided, therefore, that he would leave alone. He managed to secure a loan from a friend to start a blacksmith shop in Jericho. Before he set off on the road towards the Dead Sea, he promised his wife: "I will come back and get you and the children when I have set myself up in business."

An epidemic of cholera broke out in Palestine in the last quarter of 1912. There was little medical help available and people died in great numbers. The Turkish authorities placed extra guards around Jerusalem to try to isolate the city and prevent the disease from spreading. Trains between Jerusalem and Jaffa were cancelled, and rumours spread through the American Colony that the epidemic had reached Gaza, Lydda – and Jericho.

Early in the morning of December 1, some of the Swedes who slept in a room near the entrance gate were woken by unfamiliar sounds coming from the yard outside. When they looked out they saw a donkey cart and two shadowy figures carrying something between them. "What are you doing here?" shouted one of the Swedes. The figures turned, but did not answer. Shortly afterwards Jacob Spafford and Frederick Vester arrived on the scene. It became clear that the two men were Jews, and that the burden they had been carrying was the body of the dead blacksmith. Peterson had contracted cholera as he accompanied the two Jews on the road to Jericho. He had died on the way. The Palestinians of Jericho had their work cut out dealing with their own dead, and had refused to take responsibility for the poor man's body. No one wanted to incur the expenses of a burial, or risk creating problems with the Turkish authorities.

285 Petri: *On Holy Paths*, Stockholm 1931, pp.137–138. Edith Larsson: *Dala Folk in the Holy Land*, Stockholm 1957, p.59.

By this stage, Bertha had also woken up. She made tea for the compassionate Jewish strangers, who had somehow managed to avoid the Turkish soldiers surrounding the city. She asked them to take the body to the American consulate, since Peterson was an American citizen. A little later, Jacob and Fredrick heard the carriage return stealthily. The two Jews told them that Consul Merrill (back in Jerusalem on his third posting, following another change of government in America) had advised them to dump the body outside the entrance of the Colony. Merrill further threatened to have the Colony quarantined, since the dead man had originally come from there. Mother Anna was summoned, but she did not want to take responsibility for the body either. She believed the blacksmith's fate proved that those who sinned against her house would be punished by death. A prolonged bureaucratic dispute with Consul Merrill followed, but finally, after the intervention of the Ottoman authorities, Eric Peterson was buried at the Colony's little cemetery.

Anna had other concerns. Her nearest friend, Amelia Gould, had suffered a stroke and was now paralyzed. Amelia and Anna were closer to each other than to any other members of the congregation. Late in the day on March 24, 1914, Anna, Bertha and a few others were sitting by Amelia's bed. Then, as the women began to sing Horatio's famous hymn 'It is well with my soul' Amelia sat up, smiled, and died.[286] Some months later, Anna arrived for the morning meeting in the salon looking tired and exhausted. Everyone wondered what had happened. "I have not slept all night," Anna told them. "I prayed to God that I would receive a message, and after many prayers one came."[287] The congregation sat as quietly as mice and listened as Anna spoke: "God's mighty wrath is moving from nation to nation. This was the Lord's message this night. And as I lay, wondering what this should mean, another message came: 'Nothing bad will happen to you as long as you love one another.' Something terrible will happen, but has not the Lord given us a divine promise?" A few days later Anna said the Lord had repeated the message in more detail: "'Everything will be fine with the American Colony, even if the world is facing terrible times.' Think what blessed comfort God has given us." She asked the congregation to sing the hymn 'It is my will that you love one another as I have loved you'.

Anna's most recent message was only a few days old when, on June 28, 1914, the successor to the Austrian throne, Archduke Franz Ferdinand,

---

286 Spafford Vester: Unpublished manuscript of *Our Jerusalem*, Chapter 29, p.3, American Colony Collection, Jerusalem.
287 Petri: *On Holy Paths*, Stockholm 1931, p.139.

was killed in the Bosnian capital, Sarajevo. His murderer belonged to a secret Serbian organization that wanted to unite all Serbs into one nation state. He had been protesting against Austria-Hungary's annexation of Bosnia and Herzegovina. Austria sent an ultimatum to Serbia with the demand that all southern Slavic organizations be dissolved and all enemy propaganda cease. It also insisted that the Austrian military should participate in the hunt for the guilty men. The Serbian government accepted all the Austrian demands except for one: it could not tolerate the participation of foreign troops in the investigation of the murder. The Austrians rejected their terms and declared war, exactly one month after the shots were fired in Sarajevo. Kaiser Wilhelm immediately sent German troops into France, and when the Russian tsar ordered full mobilization, he also declared war on Russia.

In Jerusalem, a group of German students who had come to the city to learn English, had been staying at the American Colony Hostel for several weeks. One of them was about to get married. Invitations had been sent, cakes baked, chickens prepared, and food for the breakfast assembled. The students met for supper as usual on the evening of August 2, but by the following morning they had all gone, including the bridegroom. The young people had travelled to Jaffa, where they had boarded a German ship. They had heard the previous day that Germany had declared war, but had managed to keep the news secret. Two days later, virtually all the French left Palestine. They did not want to stay in a country that might, at any moment, declare war on their homeland.[288]

Despite the fact that Turkey had declared itself to be neutral, Palestine was placed on a war footing and the Ottoman authorities requisitioned all horses and donkeys. The Turks had entered into a secret alliance with Germany, in which the Turkish minister for war promised to come to Germany's aid if Russia got involved in the Austro-Serbian conflict.[289] The mobilization orders resulted in the departure of all merchant shipping, which had previously transported oranges, Palestine's most important export, from Jaffa and Haifa. At the outset of the war, Britain controlled most of the Mediterranean, and Palestine became, for all practical purposes, cut off from substantial parts of Europe and from America.

288 George Hintlian: *The First War in Palestine and Msgr.Franz Fellinger, an Austrian Presence in the Holy Land in the 19th and early 20th Century*, (ed Marian Wrba), 1996, pp.179–193. Fr. M. Lagrange: *A Jerusalem Pendant La Guerre, La Correspondante*, 222, February 25, 1915, p.640.
289 It was Turkey's War Minister, Enver Pasha, who had secretly agreed on the treaty with Germany. Naval Minister, Djemal Pasha, had recommended that Turkey should delay becoming involved in the conflict since he believed the country was unprepared.

Anna decided the Colony should do as Joseph had done in biblical Egypt: build up stores of wheat in anticipation of seven lean years. Soon, local merchants and even Bedouin east of Jerusalem arrived with donkey and camel caravans laden with wheat for the American Colony.[290] All men between the ages of 19 and 45 were called up for military service – Christians, Arabs and Jews, something that had never happened before. But the Nås farmers were exempted because the consul in Jerusalem, Gustav Dalman, ensured they all had Swedish passports. Anna's oldest son-in-law, Frederick Vester, was a German citizen, but was not called up, because he had turned 45 on August 3, the first day of Germany's participation in the war. The German consul declared him to be too old however, only after checking with Frederick's mother what time of day he had been born.

Many Palestinians also tried to get out of military service. The rich bought themselves out, as they had done in previous conflicts, while the poor ate poisonous herbs or inflicted wounds on themselves so that they could remain at home. Some even blinded themselves in their right eye, or cut off their trigger fingers to make sure they would be unfit as riflemen. But few succeeded in escaping the Turkish recruiting service, which was determined that the youths of Palestine would become soldiers, even if they had to be horse whipped, or brought in half dead on the backs of camels. For the residents of the American Colony, the forced recruitment of young Palestinians into the Ottoman army was nothing new. In earlier wars, herds of Palestinian peasant boys had been driven over Mount Scopus and down into Jerusalem by armed Turkish troops. One of the earliest memories many Swedes had of the city was the penetrating shriek of women ululating as they passed the Sheikh Jarrah Mosque and followed their sons and husbands to the camps. The women feared they would never see their loved ones again, and if, by some miracle, a husband did come back, he was frequently just a shadow of the man who had marched away.[291]

Anna remembered well the time 30 years earlier, when one of the Colony's young workers, Maarouf Zaheikeh, had been forced to do military service. The 18-year-old was one of five Palestinian servants Anna had hired while the Overcomers were still living in the house over the Damascus Gate. No one had ever tried to convert any of the Muslim

290 Lars E. Lind & Tord Wallström: *Jerusalemsfararne*, (Jerusalem Travelers) Stockholm 1981, p.131.
291 Ibid. p.25.

servants, and so Anna was surprised when one spring day Maarouf announced he had become a Christian. Everyone in the sect was aware of the consequences. Maarouf would be persecuted and punished by his own people. But he had made up his own mind about his Christian faith, and Horatio had baptized him. As expected, the young convert's family rejected him – all apart from his mother. His stepfather was furious. He was the *muezzin* at the Noble Sanctuary and felt his step-son's conversion was an insult, not only towards Islam, but also towards him personally. For Maarouf's stepfather, the simplest solution was to ask the Turkish authorities to draft the boy into the Ottoman army for five years. In March 1884, Horatio Spafford received a letter from the United States consul stating that the governor of Palestine had ordered Maarouf, son of Abraham Zaheikeh, to be called up for military service.[292]

Everyone in the congregation felt helpless as the Palestinian teenager was picked up by the Turkish authorities. The Turks were assisted by the American consul's own armed guard, because Consul Merrill had suspected that the sect would refuse to hand the young man over. A few days later, Anna received a little note written in pencil: "Dear Brothers and Sisters. A man came and wrote down our names. There are three of us here, and the man said that we will go to Damascus early tomorrow. I am writing this letter so that you might visit me before I leave."[293] Maarouf was being held at a Turkish police station just inside the Jaffa Gate, and the following morning everyone from the Colony went to catch a glimpse of him before he disappeared. They saw him, bound, with his hands tied behind his back. He and several hundred other Palestinian youths were about to be force-marched to Damascus over 100 miles away, where the Turks had their military headquarters.

One night, several years later, there was a knock at the colonists' door. It was unusual for anyone to come at night, so everyone woke up. The door opened, to reveal a tired, dirty soldier in Turkish uniform. He said: "I am Maarouf." After he was fed, and had washed and slept a little he told them about his military service. He had been sent to fight in Yemen, but despite the fact that the Ottoman army had suffered huge losses against the warring Yemenis, he had not become sick or wounded, for which the Colony's members praised the Lord. But their joy did not last long. Six months after Maarouf returned to Jerusalem, his stepfather, whose

292 Letter to H. G. Spafford from Selah Merrill, March 17. Folder: 1884, American Colony Collection.
293 Letter from Maarouf to the American Colony, undated. Folder: 1884, American Colony Collection.

anger had not abated, arranged for him to be conscripted into the Turkish army again. This time he was sent to Crete, and his military identification papers said that he should never be decommissioned – because he was a *kafir* – a faithless one. For two years, Maarouf fought in the mountains alongside the sultan's troops as they attempted to suppress the rebellious Christian population of Crete. Yet again he was able to escape war's chaos alive. Eventually, he managed to reach Jaffa and then Jerusalem.

By this stage, his stepfather had given up. Together with Maarouf's mother, his sisters and brothers the ageing Palestinian came to the Colony and said humbly to his stepson: "You have not changed your religion; you have changed your heart. If I continue to fight against you, I will be fighting against God. It is written. I have become your friend; I respect you." Maarouf was no longer considered a servant, but remained in the Colony as a faithful member. By the time the First World War broke out Maarouf was 48 – too old for military service. But the Muslim convert was no longer in Jerusalem. He had managed to borrow enough money to travel to Chicago, where he married a Swedish woman.

In 1914, the Turkish recruiting sergeants in Palestine had more than enough young men to choose from. Since the constitutional revolution of 1909, Christians and Jews had become eligible for military service. Until then religious minorities had been exempt, but the reformist constitution stipulated that all Ottoman subjects were to be treated equally, regardless of religion. For the first time, many Jews were mobilized, among them a young man called Alexander Aaronsohn. Alexander's father came from Romania and had founded a Jewish colony in the fertile coastal region near Haifa. Alexander, his older brother, Aaron, and his sister, Sarah, later became highly valued British intelligence agents.[294] Initially, Alexander, like the other new recruits, was given no food, but was forced to forage and steal. At first, he and his fellow conscripts stole only small quantities – a chicken here, some vegetables there. Later they stole bigger animals, often from under the noses of their weeping owners. The Turkish officers, meanwhile, said nothing.[295]

On arrival at the barracks, the recruits were given khaki uniforms, similar to those being worn by the Germans. But only a few received new ones: most of the uniforms being distributed were second-hand. The thought that the clothes might have belonged to a soldier who

294 Anthon Verrier (ed): *Agents of the Empire, Anglo–Zionist Intelligence Operations 1915-1991*, London 1995.
295 Alexander Aaronsohn: *With the Turks in Palestine*, Constable & Company, London 1917, pp.20-23.

had perhaps died in one of the recent cholera outbreaks in Mecca or Yemen made Alexander Aaronsohn nauseous. He managed to bribe the distribution officer to give him a new uniform. Everyone received new boots and new headgear. The latter had been designed by Enver Pasha, and were modelled on the German helmet, with a turban wrapped around the outside, a combination, it was believed, that would satisfy the need to look Islamic, while remaining practical. Monotonous days and weeks of training followed, until one December morning the news came that Turkey was about to join forces with Germany. Copies of Arabic telegrams sent from Constantinople were circulated among the soldiers. They told of numerous German victories. The following Friday, prayers in the mosques ended with an invocation for the welfare of the sultan and 'Haji Wilhelm', the kaiser who had visited Jerusalem and Damascus, but had not reached Mecca.[296]

Anna Spafford was 72 when the First World War broke out. She was staying at the Augusta Victoria Stiftung, a spa hotel for German nurses, missionaries and pilgrims that had been opened in 1910 by the second son of the kaiser and kaiserin. Anna was exhausted and had been booked into the sanatorium on the Mount of Olives for a rest cure. The Wagnerian Palace, with its entrance lobby, was more expensive than other similar establishments, but was also much larger and far more splendid. Few believed that this luxurious palace had been built purely for the benefit of nurses and missionaries. It was rumoured that Kaiser Wilhelm II planned to occupy it, in anticipation of the Second Coming. The ceiling of the palace church, decorated in Byzantine style, depicted portraits of the kaiser and kaiserin in medieval imperial dress, offering the buildings to heaven. A sculpture in the courtyard also depicted a crusading figure, whom resembled the kaiser. But since 'the day' had not yet arrived the Augusta Victoria Stiftung was temporarily in the hands of Sister Theodora Barthausen and her staff.

Some months later, there was a water shortage in Jerusalem. There had been little rainfall and the influx of thousands of soldiers had put a strain on the water supply. Business was also at a standstill. Tourists no longer came to the Colony, and its store in the New Grand Hotel sold practically nothing. Banks closed, and no money was paid out against cheques or exchanges. John D Whiting – Grace's husband – wrote to friends in America asking for money for the Colony to continue its work helping the needy: "Just a few days ago, a well-dressed woman arrived at

296 Ibid. pp.31-36.

the store with her three children and said they had had nothing to eat for a few days. She got a large loaf of bread, and just at the sight of it, tears flowed from a mother trying to save her children. She did not return; she was no beggar. There are hundreds of similar cases." In a previous letter, sent from the Austrian post office close to the Colony store, Whiting asked that his correspondence should not be quoted publicly, since this might create problems: "We are under strict censorship and martial law."[297]

In October 1914, the Ottoman authorities in Jerusalem had closed the British, French and Russian post offices. No communication with the outside world was possible, except through neutral America. In November the British abandoned their traditional policy of supporting the integrity of the Ottoman Empire and along with France, declared war.

In Jerusalem, the police immediately attempted to seize the archives in the British Consulate. But they were too late. Everything had already been burned. The American consul assumed responsibility for British interests in the Holy City, and Bertha helped her brother-in-law to hide British silver and Persian rugs. She secretly took care of the silver cross, candelabra and linens belonging to the Anglican cathedral of St George near the Colony and hid important historic documents belonging to the École Biblique et Archéologique Française de Jérusalem. She did the same for the Sisters of St Joseph and the Catholics from Notre Dame de France. Many of these religious premises were commandeered by the Turkish army for use as barracks and offices.

A curfew was imposed in Jerusalem. But one night the bell rang at Bertha and Frederick Vester's spacious house on the Nablus Road. Their family had expanded and now comprised six children. After the oldest, Anna Grace, came Horatio, named after his grandfather. Anna sometimes chose to stay there so that she could be close to her grandchildren. Outside in the darkness stood a man whom Frederick Vester recognized, the son of an old Jewish patriarch from Bokhara, a family friend whom they referred to as 'Old Moses'. He had come to Palestine 10 years before, and had built a large house on the west of the city. Old Moses imported jewellery, which was sold by the American Colony Store. Now, the son explained, his father was on his deathbed and needed to speak to Mr Vester as quickly as possible. Bertha was afraid to let her husband travel about the city during curfew, but none of them felt they could say no to a dying

297 Letter from John Whiting to I. A. Ratshesky, Treasurer, US Trust Co., Boston, September 29, 1914, letter from John Whiting to Earl Rowe, Providence, August 17, 1914, American Colony Collection.

man. When Frederick arrived, Old Moses lay in bed supported by pillows, surrounded by his family. "I knew you would not refuse me, as you see, I am to be gathered to my fathers," [sic] said the dying Jew.[298] The others in the room were very quiet. Everyone wanted to hear what the patriarch had to say. "My children are good children. Their mother is like Sarah, a virtuous woman. She must be taken care of. But as soon as I am gone, my children will quarrel over my possessions. The property is arranged for, but there," he said, pointing to a dirty linen napkin which lay knotted on a table, "is all the jewellery that I have. It is worth many thousands of pounds. This I give you to keep. After the seven days of mourning are over, you will call my sons and daughters and divide it equally among them. They must abide by your division. It is final." Frederick could not deny the man his last wishes, but before he took the bag with him he wanted to write out a receipt. "Don't insult me," said Old Moses, "I trust you as I always have." Later that night, the sick man died, and Frederick did as he had promised and divided the jewels equally among the children.

298 Spafford Vester: *Our Jerusalem*, 2nd edition, p.255.

Chapter 24

The Locust War

In early November 1914, at Haidar Pasha railway station on the shore of the Bosphorous there stood a small, bearded, Turkish version of Napoleon. The platform was crowded with people and just before the stocky little Turk got on the train, he announced: "I shall not return to Constantinople until I have conquered Egypt."[299]

The First World War was barely four months old and Djemal Pasha, Turkey's 44-year-old navy minister, had recently been named commander-in-chief of the Turkish Fourth Army. It seems incongruous that the navy minister should be given control of a nation's land forces, but Djemal was the junior partner in the triumvirate which governed the Turkish Empire. The other two, Enver and Talat, wanted to keep him as far away from Istanbul, the centre of political power, as possible. As head of the armed forces he would be based at Turkish military headquarters in Damascus.

Djemal Pasha has been compared not only to Napoleon, but also to the Roman general, Mark Antony. Just like the Roman warrior, Djemal was part of a brutal troika, and, just as Antony had done nearly 2,000 years earlier, he too left his motherland to rule as a dictator in a foreign country. Like Mark Antony, Djemal was well known for his profligate private life, his insatiable appetite for gambling and his vanity. He too would play a key part in leading an empire to the verge of collapse.

When the new commander-in-chief of the Fourth Army came to Damascus he began to plan an attack on the Suez Canal, a vital military and economic objective. The British had occupied Egypt since 1882, and Djemal thought the Egyptians would be prepared to rise up against their colonial masters if they got a little help. London had just declared Egypt

299 Henry Morgenthau: *Ambassador Morgenthau's Story*, New York 1919, pp.171–173.

to be a protectorate and its deposed ruler, Abbas II, had assured the Turks that with the right encouragement his subjects would revolt.[300]

Djemal ordered that the French and British consulates in Damascus should be ransacked for documents. The Turks managed to retrieve only the French archive, since the British consul had burned all his correspondence as soon as Turkey had entered the war in support of Germany. But the French documents alone revealed that if war came, many Arabs would be ready to support the French against the Ottoman Empire. The Turks had never completely trusted the Arabs, particularly the Bedouin. It was said that the Bedouin's only religion was gold. They would steal horses and camels from the Turks and sell them to the British. But they would also steal from the British and sell to the Turks.[301]

To prevent the plans for an attack on the Suez Canal becoming known to the enemy, Djemal decided to expel all potential spies from Palestine. He gave orders for all members of Christian religious orders in Jerusalem to gather at a monastery for a medical examination. On Sunday, December 13, 1914, 150 French, Belgian and British priests and monks from Jerusalem, Bethlehem and Jaffa, reported as directed. Among them were monks from the Trappist Order in Latrun – men who had sworn to live out their lives in complete silence. Djemal considered these silent monks to be suspicious and dangerous.

The medical commission was made up of the police chief, three senior army officers, senior members of the secret police and a single doctor. The examination process lasted from 11am until 6pm. When the tests were completed, it was decided that just three of the oldest men and women who had appeared before the commission would be allowed to remain in the city. The rest had to leave. Fifty monks were told they would have to walk to Damascus, a journey of more than 100 miles. The others would be taken by car. The Spanish consul in Jerusalem, whose country had declared neutrality, intervened. He offered to pay for the entire transport costs on the understanding that everyone would be driven at least part of the way. The Turks agreed.[302]

300 Stanford J. Shaw & Ezel Kural Shaw: *History of the Ottoman Empire and Modern Turkey*, Cambridge 1977, p.319.

301 William R. Polk, David Stamler, Edmund Asfour: *Backdrop to Tragedy, The Struggle for Palestine*, Boston (no year), p.264.

302 Rapport Générale of College De Frères, Relations de la Fermature des Etablissements et L'expulsion des Frères, Octobre 1914 – Janvier 1915, p.8. (unpublished), cited in George Hintlian: *The First World War in Palestine and Msgr. Franz Fellinger*, Jerusalem 1996, p.184.

Most of the nuns were sent by train to Jaffa. After members of the Carmelite convent on the Mount of Olives were expelled, they were driven past the American Colony. The nuns, who belonged to an order known for its veneration of the Virgin Mary, had seldom been outside the walls of the convent. For some, this was the first time they had seen the outside world since they had taken their vows. Many of the younger members of Anna's House had never seen the Carmelite nuns and their white head coverings before.

Some days later, every adult in Palestine from 'enemy states', was deported. Around half of the Jewish population of Jaffa had to leave. In great haste, some 700 men, women and children were sent to Alexandria on an Italian ship. A little later, the Turks said that all Jews in agricultural colonies would be sent to northern Syria, to grow wheat for the Turkish army. But the Jews refused to leave their orange groves or be forced to farm alien wheat fields around the cities of Hama and Homs. Djemal called a meeting with the Zionist leaders. "You can choose," he said. "I am ready to deport you as we have done with the Armenians. But you will not have to walk; I will send you by train. I can agree that some of you may remain to guard your homes and plantations, and I will get police and soldiers as guards. If one Arab lays so much as a finger on a single orange, I will have him executed. If you will agree to this possibility you must ensure that the press in Vienna and Berlin does not write one word more about this situation. And this will be effective as of tomorrow." [303] The Zionists agreed and Djemal's private secretary noticed that, as they left, they headed straight for the telegraph office. With a two-line telegram they ensured the silence of the Jews of Vienna, Berlin, Paris and London.

The person who intervened to end the deportation of Jews to Syria was the American ambassador in Istanbul, Henry Morganthau. Thanks to him, Palestinian Jews were given the choice of becoming Ottoman citizens and remaining where they were, or retaining their existing passports and leaving the country. Those who chose to go were transported on the American warship, *Tennessee*, which shuttled between Jaffa and Alexandria. By 1915, 12,500 Jews had left Palestine.[304] Some of those who remained entered Turkish military service. One of them was Moshe

---

303 Falih Rifki: *Zeytindagt* (Mount of Olives), Istanbul 1932, pp.74–76, cited in Geoffrey Lewis: *An Ottoman Officer in Palestine, 1914–1918, Palestine in the Late Ottoman Period* (ed. David Kushner), Jerusalem 1984, pp.410–411.
304 As a result of pressure from the American press, the Turkish Governor of Jaffa, who had embezzled the assets of many deported foreigners, was removed from his post. Nathan Efrati: *From Crisis to Hope* (Hebrew), Jerusalem 1991, p.274. Morris: *Righteous Victims*, New York 1999, p.86.

Shertok, who, over 40 years later, became Israel's prime minister, known by his Hebrew name of Moshe Sharett. David Ben-Gurion also supported the Turkish war effort and encouraged the Jews of Palestine to become Turkish citizens. In Jaffa, the Zionists organized patriotic demonstrations and handed out propaganda in support of Turkey. But this did not prevent Ben-Gurion and others from being jailed. The Turks did not trust them. All Jewish settlers had to hand in their weapons and were forbidden to raise the white and blue Zionist flag.[305]

In Damascus, Djemal announced reforms, in the hope of ensuring Arab support in the battle against the British. But they had little effect in turning back the tide of rising Arab nationalism. The dictator's instinctive reaction was to act decisively to suppress this movement, but he knew that he had to avoid prompting an open revolt, or taking steps that might jeopardize his Suez campaign. Among the first to be affected by Djemal's new regime were the Lebanese. Lebanon had been a French province since Napoleon had marched into the country 100 years before. Now, for the first time, the Turks introduced trade restrictions between Lebanon and Syria. Syrian wheat was requisitioned for Turkish soldiers, along with quotas of grain, olive oil and dried fruit. In addition, Syria, Lebanon and Palestine were required to supply large quantities of water barrels for the army. Camels, horses and donkeys were also requisitioned, and all men between the ages of 45 and 60 were mobilized to supply drivers for the so-called donkey brigade.

Next, Djemal turned his attention to the region's infrastructure, demanding that a new road network be built around Damascus by the end of the year. The city's governor, a trained engineer, was co-opted to ensure the project was completed. But after a technical assessment, he concluded that such an ambitious project could not be completed within the proposed timeframe. He sent his deputy to explain why to Djemal.

When the engineer arrived at Djemal's headquarters at Augusta Victoria Stiftung on the Mount of Olives, he brought with him a pile of documents. Djemal began their meeting by saying: "Put all your papers on the table, and stand before me."[306] The unfortunate man stood up ramrod straight as Djemal continued: "Here are your orders: you are to tell my staff

305 Mordechai Eliav: *Israel's Land and Settlement in the 19th Century, 1777-1917* (Hebrew), Jerusalem 1978, p.443.
306 Rifki: *Zeytindagt*, Istanbul 1932, pp.94–96, cited in Lewis: *An Ottoman Officer in Palestine, Palestine in the Late Ottoman Period* (ed. Kushner), Jerusalem 1986, p.405.
Fr P. Medebielle, Bulletin Diocesain, M-J, 1976, p.91, cited in Hintlian: *The First World War in Palestine and Msgr. Franz Fellinger*, Jerusalem 1996, p.185.

how much money, how many men, how many picks and shovels you will need to have the road finished on the date you have been given. Then you are to go straight back to Damascus. If the road is not finished on time, then you will be executed on the spot where the last stone had been laid." The engineer knew that this was deadly serious. Djemal Pasha did not joke.

By the beginning of 1915, most Palestinians were experiencing hardship as a result of Turkey's involvement in the war. The Allied blockade of the Mediterranean meant that oranges, which would normally have been exported, were rotting on the trees. There were shortages of petrol, rice and matches. Sugar cost 25 times as much as it had before the war. But soldiers, too, had to learn to live with hunger. Officers and men got just a pound and a half of dry biscuit each day, along with a few dates and olives.

Despite Djemal's efforts to keep his plans secret, it was widely known that the Turks were preparing a major assault on Suez, since Turkish and Arab regiments had been seen on the march. But public interest was alerted particularly by the sudden appearance of two-humped Bactrian camels in mile-long caravans heading towards Sinai. Until now, most Arabs had seen only the single-humped dromedary.

The Turkish secret service was constantly on the lookout for spies who might betray details of the Suez campaign to the enemy. In an attempt to prevent information being leaked, the fishermen of Jaffa were sent to the Dead Sea with their families. Their boats were used to transport grain. It was forbidden to swim in the Mediterranean, and any Palestinians found on the beach were arrested and accused of espionage. In Nablus, a Catholic priest was arrested and accused of having spoken to soldiers on their way to the Suez Canal. He was released nine days later, thanks to the Austrian consul in Jerusalem, Don Juan.[307]

Djemal's headquarters on the Mount of Olives were protected by field cannon. It was from here that he demonstrated his total inability to carry out the detailed planning necessary for a properly organized campaign, or to think in anything more than the broadest strategic terms. Djemal's relationship with the German governor of Jerusalem was also breaking down, a reflection of the generally poor relations that existed between the two nations' armies in the Holy City.

---

307 Ibid.
Rifki: *Mount of Olives*, Istanbul 1932, pp.94–96, cited in Lewis: *An Ottoman Officer in Palestine, Palestine in the Late Ottoman Period* (ed. Kushner), Jerusalem 1986, p.405.
Fr P. Medebielle, Bulletin Diocesain, M-J, 1976, p.91, cited in Hintlian: *The First World War in Palestine and Msgr. Franz Fellinger*, Jerusalem 1996, p.185.

Jerusalem had gradually become a virtual German military encampment. The city was full of khaki-clad soldiers and the sound of their hobnailed boots echoed in the narrow alleys between synagogues, churches and mosques. The German officers had replaced their characteristic *Picklehaube*, or pointed helmet, with a sola topi covered in khaki. But this did little to protect their skin and their sunburned, peeling faces testified to the impact of the Mediterranean sun on pale northern European skin. Fast's Hotel in Jerusalem became the Germans' home away from home, a place where officers could enjoy drinks and cigars and let off steam, disparaging their superiors. It was rumoured that Palestine was a discrete dumping ground for the sons of wealthy families who had bought their way out of a posting on the Western Front. By this stage it was public knowledge that the organization of the Suez Campaign was in shambles. One evening a monocled officer stood up and shouted: "What we ought to do is to hand over the organization of this campaign to Thomas Cook and Sons."[308]

The remark was overheard by the British spy, Alexander Aaronsohn. He had managed to buy his way out of military service and had joined his brother Aaron's secret intelligence organization. Despite all the drinking that went on at the bar of Fast's Hotel, the young agent quickly realized that not all German officers were incompetent. Many did not believe that a major campaign in Egypt could succeed, favouring instead the more realistic objective of tying down the large British force around the Suez Canal. The top echelon of Turkish officers took an even bleaker view of their chances. They believed that British defences at Suez were so robust they would have little prospect of taking the canal, though they said nothing of this to their fellow officers. But the Turkish rank and file were filled with an unrealistic enthusiasm for the campaign. They believed they would soon march triumphantly into Cairo and prepared for the assault with great fervour. It was rumoured that the Suez Canal would be crossed by filling it in with sandbags, or by getting thousands of thirsty camels to drink it dry. Djemal's plan was to use up to 6,000 elite, battle-hardened Turkish troops to launch the attack and to follow up with the German-trained Arab regiments.

In all, the Turkish troops available to confront the British amounted to some 150,000. The Fourth Army's southernmost base before Sinai was Beersheba. Outside the town, a huge tented city had sprouted up before which tens of thousands of camels were assembled. It was said that as

308 Alexander Aaronsohn: *With the Turks in Palestine*, London 1917, pp.59–60.

many as 300,000 animals were being used in that part of the front. The campaign plan had required 20,000 soldiers to cross the Sinai Desert on the way to the Suez Canal over six days at the end of January 1915. But in the event, the soldiers had to carry much of their equipment themselves, after thousands of their pack animals died of thirst and malnutrition. Djemal's troops had been instructed to take, and hold, the town of Ismalia, in the hope that as news of the conquest spread, Egyptians elsewhere in the country would rebel against the British administration.

The British had been alerted to the Turkish advance by aerial reconnaissance. But the general leading the Turkish forces had no such prior warnings and was completely ignorant of the fact that as many as 70,000 Allied troops were waiting for him. The canal was to be crossed under cover of darkness, but the start of the assault was delayed. When it finally got underway, well into the night, the British, with the help first of spotlights and then the bright morning light, bombarded the attackers effortlessly. Three of the Turks' pontoon bridges were destroyed and the 600 or so elite troops who had actually managed to cross the canal were all taken prisoner.[309] The British pursued the Turks back across the canal, forcing them to retreat at a cost of up to 2,000 casualties. The Allies, by contrast, lost 32 men.[310]

Before the attack, the American Red Cross had sent a group of volunteers to Sinai, along with a field hospital of 200 beds. One of the members of the group was Anna's son-in-law, John D Whiting. In the desert around Auja al-Hafir, he found soldiers so thirsty that they were "willing to pay a dollar just for a little bit of water to drink".[311] Whiting flew back to Jerusalem and advised the consulate to prepare to evacuate the Red Cross contingent if it was abandoned by the Turks. To his surprise, he discovered that the Turks in Jerusalem were trying to create the impression that the Suez Canal had been successfully crossed. When it became known that the Germans had ordered a full retreat from the Canal Zone, the Turkish officers in Jerusalem became contemptuous of their German counterparts and their misplaced assumption of superiority over the British. After the disastrous attack on the Suez, three German officers were shot by their Turkish allies and a fourth committed suicide.

309 Djemal Pasha: *Memories of a Turkish Statesman,1913–1919*, Arno Press, New York 1973, pp.154-55.
310 Spencer C Tucker: *The Great War 1914 -18*, University College London, 1998, p.182.
311 Letter from John Whiting to William Coffin, Department of State, Washington, December 20, 1919, Folder: 1919, American Colony Collection.

The feelings of local Palestinians also began to change. Many now hoped that the British would win and the Germans disappear.

Djemal returned to Damascus, a failed, discredited leader, searching for someone on whom he could pin the blame for his own incompetence. When he was presented with evidence that a young Lebanese Maronite priest had initiated "a traitorous exchange of letters with the president of the French Chamber", he signed his death sentence without hesitation. Subsequent reports from his intelligence staff brought the 'proof' Djemal was looking for. They provided evidence of: the existence of an Arab underground movement; infiltration of the army by revolutionary elements; the presence of British and French agents stoking revolution; an imminent Allied landing on the Syrian coast, and promises made by Arab officers to help the invaders when they came ashore. Some of this was true, the rest was just speculation. Like other armies facing defeat, the intelligence unit of the Turkish Fourth Army was not able to separate fact from rumour. Djemal, by now, was feared by everyone.

The search began for collaborators among the Arab civilian population. A large number of men were arrested, tortured and put on trial. Thirteen were sentenced to death. Most of those hanged in Aley near Beirut at dawn on August 21, 1915, met their deaths courageously. They sang Arab fighting songs as they went to the gallows, an action which made a strong impression on Djemal's private secretary, who secretly referred to them as "patriots".[312]

One day earlier that same year, the residents of Jerusalem noticed that the skies had become dark. Clouds of locusts, not seen in Palestine for nearly 40 years, were blocking out the light. The Arabs referred to the swarm as 'God's soldiers' – *Jeish Allah* – but this invasion had advanced, not from heaven but from the deserts of Sudan, far to the south. The Colony's chief photographer, Lewis Larsson, witnessed the first swarm and was shocked to see how "locusts fell from the sky as thick as snowflakes in a Scandinavian storm".[313] Like most Christians, the colonists were familiar with the numerous biblical stories involving locusts. The Prophet Joel had described their destructive power and John the Baptist was said to have eaten locusts dipped in honey as a delicacy. In 1915, the Palestinians of Jerusalem followed his example. They plucked off the legs and wings of the insects, and then dipped them in olive oil. Certain individuals with healthy

312 Rifki: *Mount of Olives* Istanbul 1932, pp.57–58, cited in Lewis: *An Ottoman Officer in Palestine, Palestine in the Late Ottoman Period* (ed. Kushner), Jerusalem 1986, pp.405–406.
313 Gröndahl: *The Dream of Jerusalem*, Journal, Stockholm, 2005, p.213.

appetites managed to swallow as many as 100 locusts in the course of a meal.

At first, people tried to kill the insects by swatting them with domestic rugs and pans. But this was ineffective. The sky remained dark and the brownish-yellow horde covered everything that was green, even the cactus. This continued for several days. Then, when a desert wind began to blow from the south, the insects settled down and waited. The female locusts bored holes in the ground nearly two inches deep and placed pen-shaped sacks into them. Each one contained 100-200 eggs. The eggs would mature in two to three weeks, when the stony desert outside Jerusalem would be transformed into a sea of insects.

Lewis Larsson and the other photographers at the American Colony recorded all this with their cameras. They stood behind their tripods as the ground boiled with myriads of black larvae crawling out of their egg capsules. The insects were driven instinctively to sources of nourishment. Whole armies of larvae climbed over rocks and walls and ate everything they found that was green. The juvenile locusts left nothing behind except an ash-like soil and the skeletons of trees and bushes. They grew bigger as each day passed. Then, this insect army launched another attack on the Old City. The larvae crept up over the Citadel – the old fortress by the Jaffa Gate – scaling its 59-foot walls in minutes. They tumbled into David's Street despite the masses of people who had gathered to crush them in their thousands on the cobblestones. The streets of Jerusalem became slimy and the smell of dead larvae spread from quarter to quarter. Then the rumours began. It was said that the larvae army came crawling into houses and ate everything, even the eyes of the newborn.

Lewis found the study of this insect invasion both frightening and fascinating. Together with Lars Lind and John D Whiting, he was there at the moment when nature appeared to declare a truce. As if by a miracle, the entire locust swarm froze. The larvae stopped eating and sat as if nailed to the shrivelled branches, and stone walls, any place that offered protection. Each larva spun a protective thread around itself, which hardened into a crystal-like shell. The larvae had disappeared, all that remained were their pupae, blowing in the wind like branches and dried out leaves.

Then came a miraculous reincarnation: the skin of each pupa would crack and a new locust would appear from each one. First the heads appeared, followed by the front legs, which the insect used to drag itself out of the shell. The fragile wings spread out to dry in the sun and the metamorphosis was complete. By daybreak the next morning, the new generation of locusts had finished discarding their old pupae and gathered in thick clumps on trees and on walls. They were red, and looked like pieces of raw meat. Some time later, as if in response to a signal, they all noisily took to the skies together and flew off, like a flock of migrating birds.

The Colony's photographers had taken 58 unique pictures of the locust invasion. Whiting wrote a report, scientific in its detail and precision, which was published in the United States. When Djemal later heard about the photographs he bought several copies and sent them, together with Whiting's description, to Istanbul. There, members of parliament were shocked by the scale of the natural disaster and agreed immediately to release money for the affected area. At the request of the Germans, Djemal instructed Alexander Aaronsohn's brother, Aaron, to organize a campaign to eradicate the insects. Aaron was the head of a Jewish agricultural research centre near Atlit in northern Palestine and the Turkish leader put some 1,000 soldiers at his disposal. Aaron set them to work digging trenches, into which the hatching locusts were driven and destroyed. In addition, all adults and children were ordered to dig up a pound of locust eggs each.

Some months after the locust invasion, in the spring of 1915, the members of the American Colony experienced another drama, which, for those involved, made an impression that was even stronger than the locust plague. One day in early July, one of the congregation's younger men found a metal box buried in the yard. Inside, there were gold coins. Mother Anna called a meeting to tell the others about the miraculous treasure that had been found just when it was most needed. The next day, one of the Colony's oldest members, its treasurer, William Rudy, asked to speak to Anna. He confessed that he had hidden the money many years earlier. It consisted of the remaining balance from the sale of Pastor Larsson's church in Chicago and some funds from Amelia Gould's estate, over which Rudy had been granted temporary power of attorney when he was back in Chicago. Brother William had concealed them in an attempt to protect himself and the others, in case the Colony ran into economic difficulty. Just after the treasurer had told his story, he collapsed. Anna called for help, and when the others came they found Rudy resting on her shoulder. A doctor was sent for, but it was too late. Rudy had died after suffering a massive stroke. The stress had been too much for him.

Anna convened a meeting in the salon, to tell the others what had happened. She opened her Bible and read: "A man named Ananias and his wife Safira sold a property. But some of the money he put aside, and his wife knew about it; what he put before the apostles was just a part of the amount. Then Peter said: 'Ananias, why has Satan filled your heart, so that you can lie to the Holy Spirit and put aside some of what you got for your property? And when you had sold, did you yourself not decide what to do with the money? How could you do such a thing? You have not lied before man but before God.' When Ananias heard this, he collapsed and died." Many who heard this were gripped with fright. "Acknowledge your sins," Anna shouted out to the assembly. "Let this be a lesson for all of you who hold back parts of your lives and do not give yourselves completely to God."[314] William Rudy did not leave much behind – a penknife, a monocle, an old coin, some letters and fragments of biblical quotations.

His possessions were later handed over to the American consulate in the city, and from there, sent to the State Department in Washington. That is where they remained. Rudy had no heirs.[315]

The following year, 1916, the locusts returned to Palestine. Believing the locust plague to be a national emergency that threatened the army's food supplies,[316] Djemal again sent for the agriculturalist, Aaron Aaronsohn. In the course of his work to stamp out the locust, Aaronsohn had come into contact with the highest Turkish military and civilian authorities in the region and had been allowed to travel freely throughout the Levant. His work provided him with the perfect opportunity to continue spying for the British.[317] But despite these advantages and the professional support of Djemal Pasha, Aaronsohn gave up the battle against the locusts after just two months.

---

314 Petri: *On Holy Paths*, Stockholm 1931, pp.141–142. The description is taken from the Acts of the Apostles 5:1–11.
315 Dudman & Kark: *The American Colony*, Jerusalem 1998, p.199.
316 Anita Engle: *The Nili Spies*, The Hogarth Press, London 1959, p.60.
317 Aaron later left Palestine and joined the British HQ in Cairo, while Sarah Aaronsohn was arrested in September, 1917, and shot herself in October. Engle: *The Nili Spies*, London 1959, pp.202-02.

Chapter 25

Tea and Cakes with Djemal

One morning, members of the Colony found the bodies of a woman and three small children just outside the gate. They appeared to have died of starvation. Other women would come to the Colony offering to sell their babies in exchange for food for the rest of the family. But the worst of all, Mother Anna thought, was the number of young girls who had become prostitutes in order to survive.

A little later the mufti, the highest Islamic leader in Jerusalem, came to ask whether Anna's flock could take over the running of the city's soup kitchen. The provision of food for the poor had been a long standing Islamic tradition in the city. The kitchen, run by the local religious authority with the support of wealthy private individuals, operated from one of the old, dilapidated stone houses in the centre of the Old City. But the religious foundation in charge was no longer able to run the operation.

Anna replied that she would, even though everyone in her flock already had more than enough to do running its own soup kitchen, financed by donations from affluent Americans. Initially, they had served 400 hungry people. The most wretched were Jews from Yemen, Morocco and Syria. But Christians too – Latins, Greeks, Armenians and Lutherans – all joined the food queue. As the war grew closer and food supplies increasingly precarious, the line grew to several thousands.

When the funds from the US began to diminish, Anna was afraid that her kitchen would have to close. Then, several wealthy American Christians heard about the suffering in Jerusalem and the Colony's work, and the soup kitchen received new funds. Anna's staff went to the Armenian convent and borrowed enormous cooking pots suitable for mass catering. The Armenians had used them to feed the flood of pilgrims who arrived in Jerusalem every Easter. After a while, there were so many mouths to feed that food preparations had to begin at 5am and the large cooking pots were filled several times during the day. Relatively early in the war, most of the population of the coastal towns of Gaza, Jaffa and Haifa fled inland to escape the fighting. In Jerusalem, they placed themselves at the mercy of the city's numerous religious institutions. The American Colony alone fed around 2,000 people per day.[318]

After Mother Anna had agreed to assume responsibility for running the soup kitchen in the Old City, Bertha accompanied the mufti there to examine its working practices more closely and learn how the food was distributed. As the two of them approached the kitchen, which lay in a street parallel to the Via Dolorosa, they saw several hundred starving men, many of whom were starting to fight over their place in the queue. Only the whip of the Turkish police prevented a full-scale riot from breaking out. Bertha said that if the Colony were to take over the operation, her own staff must distribute the food. The mufti warned against this, arguing that the Americans would have problems keeping the peace. But Bertha, who was by now 40, stood her ground and, to prove she was serious, climbed onto a small wall, clapped her hands together and shouted as loudly as she could in Arabic. Bertha had a strong singing voice and she knew how to project. The hungry men looked up. Bertha recognized many of them as regulars at the Colony's feeding station. "The American Colony is going to take over the distribution of the food, but it has to be done in an orderly way," she shouted loudly in Arabic. "And I will get rid of the police if you will all work together. There will be soup for everyone – also for those of you at the back of the line." Unbelievably, the starving people quietened down, and, as Bertha had predicted, when the Colony took over, the Turkish police were not required to keep the crowds in order.[319]

One day, the head of the organization that supplied the soup kitchen came to ask if the Colony would take care of his seven-year-old daughter, Nimette. The girl's mother had died of tuberculosis and he had to spend most of his time at the Turkish military headquarters on the Mount of Olives. Once again, Anna agreed and asked Bertha to introduce Nimette to her oldest daughter, Anna Grace. Both women knew that the girl's father was a close friend of the Turkish commander-in-chief, Djemal.

When Djemal was at his regional headquarters in Damascus, Anna

318 Valentine Vester: *American Colony History*, Unpublished draft, Jerusalem 2006, p.25, American Colony Collection.
319 Spafford Vester: *Our Jerusalem*, New York 1950, pp.247-53.

Grace, would sometimes accompany her new friend to her father's office at the Turkish headquarters in the Augusta Victoria Stiftung complex on the Mount of Olives. Bertha was pleased to see that her daughter was enjoying herself. But her pleasure did not last long. One morning, British planes began bombing the city. Britain had full aerial control of the Near East and its Royal Flying Corps had gained considerable experience suppressing a rebellion in Sudan the year before. Bertha was awoken by an explosion, and looked out to see smoke rising from the Turkish headquarters. The entire complex appeared to be on fire and she feared the worst. In the course of a few minutes she got some of the Colony's men to fetch the horses and was driven, at great speed, up to the Mount of Olives to look for her daughter. But no one had been hurt. Only the church, which contained the portraits of Kaiser Wilhelm and his empress, had been hit, and the fire was quickly extinguished. Bertha was reluctant to allow the girls to visit Nimette's father's office on the Mount of Olives after this. But she continued to maintain friendly contact with the man who occupied such a powerful position in the city and might be useful to the Colony one day.

In Damascus, Djemal was staging a repeat performance of a gruesome public spectacle – the execution of suspected collaborators. The executions usually took place in the city's market place, early in the morning. June 1, 1916, was no exception. On a platform nearby sat a group of men, with Djemal in the middle. Alongside him were six Turkish officers, and an Arab named Feisal. The Arab had deep-set dark eyes, a long thin nose, and a beautifully formed mouth surrounded by a well-trimmed black beard. Even though he did not have a particularly impressive figure, his manner was regal. He was in fact a prince, the son of the protector of Mecca, Sharif Hussein ibn Ali. The title *Sharif* – the noble one – indicated that he was a descendant of the Prophet Mohammed.

As Feisal and the others sat there, a quivering shadow of a man was led out. The prisoner was marched over to a crudely erected gallows. A donkey cart was parked beneath. After the executioner had put the noose around the neck of the victim he whipped the donkey forwards. If death did not occur quickly enough, the executioner would pull at the dangling man's legs causing his neck to break. Prince Feisal's face gave no hint as to his feelings, or the fact that he was being subjected to the deepest of insults. He was well aware that Djemal's performances were staged as public demonstrations of Turkish power over the Arabs. Feisal was all too familiar with Turkish power politics. Half a generation earlier his father, along with his entire family, had been held in 'an honourable imprisonment' in Constantinople. Only after the Young Turks took power in 1908 was 60-year-old Sharif Hussein released and sent to his birthplace, Mecca, to be nominal emir and governor of the Hejaz Province. Sharif Hussein's three eldest sons went with him, dressed in European suits and with Turkish manners. These Western sophisticates were members of the noble Beni Hashem clan, descendents of the Prophet's own tribe, Quraish. Their father soon took steps to restore their Arab patrimony; they were ordered to wear only Arab clothing and to polish up their command of their mother tongue, before being sent out into the desert to be toughened up in the Camel Corps.

The Turks hoped the war would give them the chance to reclaim control of the regions of North Africa which they had lost to the British and French many years before. The ruling triumvirate invited Sharif Hussein to join them in Holy War, or *jihad*, to drive the heathens from Islamic soil. But Hussein, the great-great-grandfather of today's King Abdullah II of Jordan, was disinclined to join them. He disliked the fact that the Turks had allied themselves with the Germans. He knew that central Arabia, the lands of the Hejaz, over which he nominally ruled, would be vulnerable to British attack. The emir also had personal ambitions to become Arabia's king and felt it was the British, rather than the Turks or the Germans, who would grant the Arabs independence. For this reason, he secretly made contact with the British and offered to cooperate with them. So when, in 1915, the Turkish leadership approached Hussein requesting his support against the British, he played along and pretended to acquiesce. Feisal was sent to Damascus, ostensibly as his father's representative, but in reality, he was there to test the waters and see whether there was Syrian support for an Arab revolt. Feisal was welcomed publicly with open arms, but Djemal did not trust either him or his father, and he was politely detained as a virtual hostage in the city. As he sat on the stage that June morning, required to observe yet another execution, he was well aware of the danger he faced.

Only one Syrian was hanged that particular morning, but an entire group of Arabs had been condemned to death, accused of attempting a coup. One of them was Feisal's cousin, and all of them were his friends, men he had met secretly just weeks before their arrest. Djemal forced the prince to witness several executions in order to demonstrate to potential revolutionaries that the emir in Mecca and his family were loyal to the Turks. But Feisal's presence was required for another reason. Djemal hoped that one of the condemned men might reveal that, in reality, it was the Arab prince who was leading the nationalist movement in Syria. Or perhaps Feisal might reveal inadvertently his connection with the coupists. But no one betrayed him. The condemned men all went silently to the gallows.

In Jerusalem, too, people suspected of collaborating with the British were hanged. Photographers from the American Colony took pictures of Palestinians hanging from the gallows, and Anna Spafford referred to the executions in a letter to her childhood friend, Mary Miller, in Chicago: "We are not allowed to speak about these matters for good reason, because many will write untruths, each and every one based on their own prejudices, so it is better to be silent until there is peace among the warring nations."[320] The executions were terrifying enough, but for most people the scarcity of food was even more frightening. Long lines of sick and starving people came to the American Colony. Many collapsed outside the gate from exhaustion. The sick were placed under olive trees and tended to until they could be taken to hospital, while the hungry were given food. The Colony had managed to buy flour and beans from the Turkish authorities.

One day, Nimette's father arrived, asking whether Djemal might be invited to tea at the Colony. Mother Anna knew that the pasha had a difficult personality and that it would have been dangerous to refuse him. By the time he arrived, everyone at the Colony was excited. The head of the Turkish Fourth Army was served tea and honey cakes, the only sweets Anna could obtain. Djemal, for his part, was at his best. He explained that winds of change would soon be blowing fresh air through the Old City. He would tear down the ancient walls and modernise Jerusalem, building a boulevard from the Jaffa Gate to Temple Square. After tea, he took Bertha's two-year-old daughter, Louise, onto his knee. He played with the little girl, telling Anna: "Children are a piece of heaven, and God's greatest blessing for mankind is friendship."[321]

Djemal was also charmed by Bertha. She was an unusually beautiful woman with dark eyes, chestnut coloured hair and an excellent figure. Perhaps knowing that while he was in her house she had the pasha's ear, Bertha plucked up the courage to tell him the story of how her four-year-old son, John, had reprimanded a Turkish officer. The officer was head of the army's weapon's repair unit, near the Vester family house, in the

320 Letter from Anna Spafford to Mary Miller, June 7, 1916, Folder: 1923, American Colony Collection.
321 Spafford Vester: *Our Jerusalem*, 2nd edition, p.267.

shadow of St George's Cathedral. The building had previously been a British school. Now there were no longer any British children in the city, but from time to time Palestinian workers were compelled to line up in the schoolyard – usually to witness punishments. Usually, these took the form of beatings. The victim would be thrown to the ground with his feet tied to a pole. Two men would hold him up so that the soles of his feet were exposed and could be struck with wooden poles. The shrieks of those unfortunates could be heard throughout the neighbourhood, so Bertha gave the nursemaid orders to keep the children on the other side of the house during the afternoon, the time that the punishments took place. One day when Bertha came home from the soup kitchen, little John was not at home. After searching the neighbourhood, Bertha found him in the old schoolyard. He was pointing his index finger at the officer in charge, staring him in his face and saying gravely: "You will not get to Heaven." The officer, who spoke no English, merely smiled. When Bertha had finished her story, Djemal replied: "I shall not allow your children to witness such things."

Later, the Turkish guest made a speech to the effect that he admired the colonists more than any other Christian community he had ever seen, and that if there were others like them, he would wish nothing better than to join them.[322] Then, the third member of the ruling triumvirate, the head of Turkey's Fourth Army, took his leave from Anna and her family. Shortly afterwards, the punishments at the weapon repair unit stopped. Under the circumstances, the relationship between Djemal and the American Colony was as good as it could be.

322 Dame Millicent Fawcett : *Easter in Palestine, 1921-1922*, Frank-Maurice Inc, New York, p.82.

Chapter 26

Prisoners of War and Deserters

The situation in Jerusalem was growing increasingly desperate. The death toll rose daily, the result not just of a shortage of food and water, but also of poor hygiene practices and a lack of adequate sanitation. Like everyone in the city, Mother Anna's congregation struggled to get enough food. But thanks to the intervention of Sven Hedin, a Swedish aristocrat on good terms with Djemal Pasha, they were allowed to buy wheat directly from the Turkish military warehouses. In another concession, Anna's new treasurer, Frederick Vester, was able to use Turkish paper currency, which, due to wartime hyperinflation, was now barely worth the paper it was printed on. The precious wheat was stored in the main residential building for safekeeping.

By the early spring of 1917, it was clear the British had the capture of Gaza in their sights, so the civilian population of the city was evacuated. Shortly afterwards, the infantry brigades under the command of the British general, Archibald Murray, made unexpectedly rapid advances, penetrating Gaza's eastern perimeter and virtually encircling the town. But the cavalry, on the other side of the city, were unaware of the infantry's success and withdrew to water their horses. The Ottoman forces, under the command of the German general, Kress von Kressenstein, seized their chance, and forced the Allies to retreat. Seeking to protect himself from charges of incompetence, Murray exaggerated the enemy casualties and, as a result, the Imperial General Staff ordered him to launch a second attack on the city. The ensuing battle, which took place in the middle of April, was also a failure, and Murray was swiftly relieved of command. The capture of Gaza, however, remained a vital British objective, and in June, General Edmund Allenby, an experienced soldier, who had fought in the Boer War and on the Western Front, was appointed the new Allied commander in the region. Before he left for his posting, Allenby was told by Prime Minister Lloyd George that he wanted Jerusalem "as a Christmas present for the British people".[323]

In Jerusalem, the American consul advised Anna and her flock to leave: "You and the other members of the Colony ought to leave Palestine for safety. The Allies will sooner or later be victorious, but the Turkish army in retreat will not be pleasant."[324]

"Are you giving us orders to leave?" asked Anna.

"I can not give orders to anyone," answered the consul, "but I wish I could."

Anna considered this for a moment, and then said: "I left my country to help the people in Palestine. This is the ultimate hour of service. I do not want to leave."

The rest of the congregation shared her view, for it was obvious that the level of need in the city was growing with every day that passed.

Successive attempts to capture Gaza had taken their toll on the British military. Hundreds of prisoners of war were marched to Jerusalem where they were paraded through the streets. Large numbers of wounded were also brought into the city, and its medical facilities were soon overwhelmed. Dozens of soldiers were left on stretchers outside the former French Hospital where they lay for days at a time with their wounds untreated. Anna had little sympathy for the high-handed Turkish leadership, which always behaved so contemptuously towards the Palestinians. But the Turkish administration had been good to the Colony over the previous 30 years, and now it was time to repay the debt. It was decided that Bertha and Frederick would place a corps of 20 volunteer nurses at Djemal's disposal.

The Americans were made to wait a long time outside Djemal Pasha's offices in the Augusta Victoria complex. When the stout little Turk finally received them, he was not particularly friendly. The tea, cakes and friendly words of the salon had been forgotten. Djemal's piercing black eyes looked his visitors up and down searchingly. Like everyone in Jerusalem, Bertha was well aware that the minister had previously been head of the Istanbul police department, where his job had involved hunting down suspected dissidents, and jailing or killing them.

Bertha spoke first: "Your Excellency, we have come to offer our services and care for the wounded."

323 Spencer C. Tucker: *The Great War 1914-18*, University College, London, 1998, p.184.
324 Spafford Vester: Unpublished draft of *Our Jerusalem*, Chapter 32, p.1. American Colony Collection, Jerusalem.

Djemal seemed surprised. Normally, people only paid him official calls in order to ask for favours. But he quickly realized that this situation was slightly different, and answered: "Mrs Vester, unknown to you, today the United States has seen fit to break diplomatic relations with the Turkish Empire."[325] As he spoke, he stood up and from the look he gave her Bertha felt he would happily have skinned her alive. But then he changed his tone: "Are you still prepared to offer your service?" Bertha feared that a false move now might jeopardize the future of the entire Colony. She replied: "Your Excellency, we are not offering our services to Turkey or Germany or any other country. We are offering our service to humanity." The iron man's black eyes grew less angry and, for a brief moment, Bertha saw what she thought was almost an expression of gratitude as he thanked them for their offer and told them that the Grand New Hotel would be placed at their disposal as a hospital.

The hotel was neither new nor grand, but old, dirty and full of lice which spread typhoid. The volunteer nurses were unprepared for the appalling conditions they now faced. Many of the wounded had been transported through the desert by camel to Beersheba and then by slow train to Jerusalem. Some men had tried to dress their injuries themselves, and by the time they arrived their wounds were frequently infected. Some were unconscious, and most were so full of lice that they first had to be laid out on a stone slab, so that their uniforms could be cut from them. It was not long before five of the nurses also became infected. They all changed their uniforms several times a day, boiling their clothes to kill the insects. But even this was not enough.[326]

Bertha took responsibility for allocating beds to the wounded, whom she addressed usually in Arabic. One day she noticed that a lightly wounded man seemed to hesitate as she spoke to him. She realized immediately that the man did not understand, but was surprised when he said in English: "What did you say?" The wounded soldier had no uniform and no boots. He was a British prisoner of war, who had been sent to the hospital at the Grand New Hotel by mistake. That evening the Americans decided they would offer to run the main receiving station for the wounded. This was where the soldiers were washed, deloused and shaved before they were dispersed to the various hospitals in the city.

325 Bertha Spafford Vester: As recounted to Valentine Vester, May 1963, unpublished manuscript. American Colony Collection, Jerusalem. Spafford Vester: Unpublished draft of Our Jerusalem, Chapter 32, p.3.
326 Lars E. Lind & Tord Wallström: Jerusalemsfararne (Jerusalem Travelers), P.A. Norstedt & Sönner forlag, Stockholm 1981, pp.148–149.

The Americans were now able to identify British prisoners and provide appropriate help. The head of the city's medical services accepted their offer, which also involved taking responsibility for the correct burial of the dead. The Americans now had to ensure that Jews were not buried by Muslims, Catholics by Greek Orthodox or vice versa.

Initially the Americans had tried to persuade their Palestinian friends to volunteer at the hospital. Few did so. The usual reason cited was that they did not want to be mistaken for Turks when the British eventually captured the city. Others said they could not stand the sight of blood. One day Lars Lind met the Colony's butcher and asked him to volunteer; he, surely, could not claim to be made ill by the sight of blood. The butcher appeared reluctantly at the hospital, but promptly fainted as soon as he was asked to change a bandage. The man, who had butchered more than 50 sheep and goats a day for years, excused himself later by claiming that human blood was different.

Medicine and equipment were in short supply and Bertha's eldest son, 11-year-old Horatio, spent days on end rolling washed bandages ready for re-use.[327] The Turks were able to supplement the Colony's limited provisions for a while, but even they did not have unlimited resources, so the nurses resorted to tearing up curtains and even using soft paper as a substitute for cotton. After they had exhausted the oil supply, the Americans used olive wood and even candles, to heat the water. As fuel grew increasingly scarce, the staff was able to perform operations during daylight. There were hardly any surgeons capable of performing operations left at the hospital, and the pressure on those who remained was intense. The sole (one-eyed) Arab doctor still working was seen pointing to a wounded man's festering, limb and shouting despairingly: "Cut it off, cut it off, nurse." There was a second doctor at the hospital, but he had no surgical experience. More importantly, he was Armenian, so was hardly motivated to try to save Turkish lives. As a result, most of the treatments were undertaken by volunteers from the Colony. They removed grenade fragments, bullets and the remains of crushed bones. Meanwhile, in the courtyard, the pile of amputated limbs grew. Some even compared it to a wood pile.[328] This in itself soon became a health hazard, and a series of typhus epidemics led to large numbers of civilian deaths. The British military dead were buried in a simple ceremony on

327 Told to Valentine Vester by Horatio Vester. Interview: Valentine Vester, May 5, 2006.
328 Letter from John Whiting to William Coffin, July 17, 1919, p.7, American Colony Collection, Jerusalem.

Mount Zion. The Turks, by contrast, dumped their dead, naked, into a mass grave. But the Turkish authorities were impressed with the Colony's work – even Djemal expressed his satisfaction when he came to inspect the hospital. The Germans, on the other hand, remained aloof and refused to allow their wounded to be treated by Americans.

The Turks were constantly on the lookout for British spies. People were arrested on the smallest pretext. In Gaza, the mufti and his son were both accused of being pro-British. Despite the fact that they belonged to the powerful Husseini clan, they were condemned to death and executed just outside the Jaffa Gate. Others were hanged outside the Damascus Gate, a warning to those who might harbour pro-British feelings. Djemal was merciless, and one of Anna's friends compared him to the Babylonian King Nebuchadnezzar: "He butchers whom he wants to butcher, and lets live whom he wants to live."

While the wounded and dying were being cared for in Jerusalem, the British were using some unusual techniques in preparation for their planned attack on Gaza. At the Allies' forward-most field headquarters at Deir al-Balah, a British intelligence officer had decided that Gaza should be taken in the name of Zionism. Captain Richard Meinertzhagen, a gentile, with Danish and German ancestors, had adopted the Zionist cause.[329] On arrival at Deir al-Balah, Meinertzhagen had been shocked to learn that the frontline had no intelligence network. The British did not even have agents operating in the desert between the two armies. Meinertzhagen dispatched a desert patrol to capture some passing Bedouin, in the hope they could provide intelligence about conditions inside Gaza and Beersheba. After interrogating his captives, Meinertzhagen obtained the name of a Palestinian in Beersheba who ran a network of Bedouin agents for the Turkish authorities. He then wrote a letter to the Palestinian, thanking him for the information he had provided and enclosing a quantity of Turkish money as a mark of his appreciation. The Bedouin to whom he gave the letter, was, as expected, apprehended by the Turks, who promptly arrested and executed their 'double' agent. Meinertzhagen had used this ploy before, in the war against the Germans in East Africa. There, too, his actions had led to the execution of an enemy agent, and he had expressed doubts as to whether his tactics had been ethically defensible.[330]

329 Colonel R. Meinertzhagen: *Middle East Diary, 1917–1956*, London 1959, p.42. Lawrence James: *Imperial Warrior, The Life and Times of Field Marshall Viscount Allenby*, London 1993, p.126.
330 Peter Hathaway Capstick: *Warrior, The Legend of Colonel Richard Meinertzhagen*, New York 1998, p.240.

Allenby had 80,000 soldiers at his disposal, while his German counterpart, General Erich von Falkenhayn, had just over half that number. By this stage, relations between the Turks and the Germans had deteriorated to the point where their joint command was virtually paralyzed. It was not able to decide whether to launch an offensive against Baghdad, or to send reinforcements to southern Palestine. By the time von Falkenhayn secured agreement to bolster the Palestinian theatre, it was already too late.

Allenby resolved to attack both Gaza and the biblical town of Beersheba – Meinertzhagen was charged with misleading the Turks and the Germans as to where the main attack would take place. His plan was an elaborate one. First, he carried out aerial reconnaissance. Then, knowing that there was an acute shortage of cigarettes at the front, he began regular cigarette drops above the Turkish lines. The Turkish soldiers soon got to know when the cigarettes were coming and stood around expectantly, waiting for the plane. Meinertzhagen's plan involved dropping cigarettes filled with opium just before the planned attack. Before he could implement his scheme, Allenby ordered him to stop – perhaps he found the concept of doped cigarettes too reminiscent of the poison gas in use on the Western Front. But Meinertzhagen went through with his idiosyncratic plan anyway. For him, the end justified the means. He believed the conquest of Palestine was the first step towards the creation of a Jewish state and the fulfilment of God's promise.

When the date of the attack was set, Meinertzhagen began planning for what would be a far more effective deception. He created a detailed profile of a hypothetical staff officer at Allenby's headquarters. With considerable ingenuity, he filled an entire notebook with observations, biblical messages and, most importantly, an agenda for a meeting at Allenby's base. Many of the notes were in an easily breakable code. The notebook referred to a reconnaissance of Beersheba, and orders for an attack on Gaza. In order to lend greater authenticity to his creation, Meinertzhagen asked his sister in Britain to write a letter to a fictitious husband, mentioning the birth of their latest child. "Take care of yourself. The baby sends you a kiss," she wrote, and enclosed two 20-pound notes. On the morning of October 12, 1917, Meinertzhagen put letters and notebooks into a little bag, covered it with fresh blood, and rode out towards the Turkish lines near Beersheba. As expected, he was discovered by a Turkish patrol. But although the Turkish scouts pursued him for a little distance they soon gave up. To renew their interest, Meinertzhagen rode straight towards them and opened fire. The Turks chased him at a gallop, and, pretending to be hit, the intelligence officer allowed his rifle, field binoculars and bag to fall to the ground, before galloping off to safety. Initially, the Turks swallowed the bait, but von Kressenstein remained sceptical. Finally, he, too, became convinced that the British planned a major frontal attack on Gaza when German scouts found a second package just a few days later. It contained slices of bread that had been rolled up inside a military newspaper, printed by the British in Cairo. The paper contained a notice about a lost bag, requesting it should be returned to headquarters if found.[331] Von Kressenstein positioned his defence forces accordingly.

Allenby deliberately perpetuated the belief that he was about to launch a direct attack on Gaza and commenced a massive artillery bombardment designed to 'soften up' the city. The first shells were fired at the Turkish defences on the morning of October 27, while from the coast a fleet of British and French ships kept up a bombardment. His strategy had involved deceiving the Turks into thinking that his 'reconnaissance mission' of Bersheeba was just that and nothing more. But during the night, four cavalry and artillery brigades moved in and captured the town with ease. The Turks did not even have time to sabotage the wells. With Bersheeba taken, and several heavy brigades already stationed to the south of Gaza, Allenby was able to create a pincer movement, cutting off Turkish supply lines and their only route of retreat. On the night of November 4, von Kressenstein sought permission to give the order to retreat. Two days later the German-Turkish defensive lines collapsed.

It was the highly trained battalions from Anatolia who had borne the brunt of the British advance. They fought like lions, while their Arab counterparts deserted by the thousands. Hungry, and desperate to leave the front, so many ran away that Djemal became alarmed. He gave orders for the most severe punishments to be meted out to deserters who had been recaptured. The gruesome sight of the corpses of Arab deserters dangling from telegraph poles became a familiar one. But even this was not enough to halt the tide of deserters and Djemal resolved that even more spectacular deterrents needed to be employed. One day the Turkish authorities arrested a well respected, educated man, a mullah, who had deserted his post two years previously. Djemal ordered that he should be executed in front of the soldiers.

331 Spafford Vester: Unpublished draft of *Our Jerusalem,* chapter 33, p.2, American Colony Collection, Jerusalem.

The appointed day arrived and the condemned man's cortege was accompanied by the discordant sound of *cajas* (Ottoman drums) and of a military band, which played Chopin's 'Funeral March' scratchily and off key. Some 4,000 Arab soldiers had been assembled at the place of execution, along with several civilian and military officials. With great dignity, the condemned man walked before them, accompanied by another cleric who was to comfort him in his last moments. The men who would carry out the death sentence marched behind him, followed by practically the entire Jerusalem garrison.[332] The mullah, who wore a loose crimson caftan and a white turban, seemed completely oblivious to his fate. In one hand he held a thin cigar – a cheroot – which he moved to his lips with an elegant and relaxed motion. "Attention!" came the cry. Then the death sentence was read out and the man sat down cross-legged on a carpet facing the cleric who was to lead him in his final prayers. But instead of praying together, the two men began a heated theological discussion, which would probably have developed into a fistfight, had several members of the military band not dropped their instruments, rushed to the fray and separated the men.

When order was finally restored, the condemned man was moved to a post, bound and blindfolded. But he never stopped smoking his cheroot. When he heard the order "Attention!" he knew that the next word would be "Fire!" In a final display of courage and sang-froid, he lifted his cigar to his lips and took a last drag. Seconds later, he fell in a heap, with his hand nailed to his mouth by a bullet. His public execution did not deter the Arabs, who fled their Turkish and German masters as never before.

332 Rafael de Nogales: *Four Years Beneath the Crescent*, Charles Scriber's Sons, London 1926, pp. 273-74. General Rafael de Nogales: *Memoirs of a Soldier of Fortune*, Harrison Smith Inc., New York 1932, p.346.

Chapter 27

Five Pigs for the Germans

On the day that Gaza fell, November 7, 1917, Anna was part of a group that went for a picnic in the pine forest just north of the American Colony. The booming of artillery could be heard in the distance, and, as darkness fell, everyone could see the flashes of explosions in the sky. One of Djemal's close colleagues was with the party. He became increasingly depressed by what he heard and saw.

The following day the news reached Jerusalem that Gaza was now in British hands and that the Germans at the rear of the action had been among the first to flee. Yet again, the colonists struggled to attend to the thousands of wounded who came streaming into Jerusalem, as many as 50 of them were now working full-time as nurses. In addition to the Grand New Hotel, the neighbouring Hotel Ambursky had been converted to a hospital. All hospitals run previously by the British and the Italians were also by this stage under the Colony's administration. The hospital staff heard many stories from their Arab and British patients, and were able to piece together a picture of the progress of the war. Wounded British prisoners of war, for example, passed on the story of Captain Meinertzhagen's hoax plans, which had so successfully fooled the Germans and Turks with false information about British strategy.

By the autumn of 1917, Djemal was no longer commander-in-chief in Palestine. The latter came effectively under German command, leaving the Turks in control of the campaigns in Syria and Western Arabia. General Falkenhayn was now in charge of Jerusalem and his staff moved into the Augusta Victoria complex. The Germans, who had always been uneasy about seeing their wounded cared for by Americans, also began to scrutinize the Colony's management of the city's hospitals. One day the Germans' chief doctor, who held the rank of colonel, arrived on an inspection visit. He entered the clean and orderly Grand New Hotel just as John D Whiting had finished assisting in an operation on a German patient. The German doctor and his fellow officers complained that the patient, also an officer, had not had his hair cut short enough. The fact that the man had been brought in only the previous night, with a serious neck injury, seemed of less importance. Whiting pointed to the barber waiting to cut the patient's hair once the nurses had finished bandaging his wound. But the colonel turned instead to Bertha, who was also present for the inspection, and snarled:

"What is your nationality?"[333]

"I am American."

"But your husband is German."

"Yes, but I am American."

Then he turned towards Whiting and growled: "And who are you?" Once the colonel learnt that he, too, was an 'Amerikaner', and the director of all three hospitals run by the Colony, he made up his mind immediately. At 3pm that same afternoon, orders came that the hospitals were to close and that all patients should be moved elsewhere. At a stroke, the colonists had lost control over the fate of the wounded British prisoners of war they had quietly accommodated out of harm's way on the third floor. Bertha and John went immediately to the Turkish chief doctor, a Syrian from Damascus. He could offer no explanation for why the Germans had decided to close the hospitals, other than the fact that John and Bertha were Americans. They wondered aloud whether Frederick should take over administration of the hospitals, but the doctor said he failed to see how this could help. When Bertha explained that Frederick was in fact a German citizen, he exclaimed: "If Vester is German, why did Allah not create all Germans like him?" The admiration that the Turks felt for the Germans in 1914 had long since changed to hate.

Almost as soon as the hospitals had been emptied, and the American and Swedish nurses sent home, there came bad news. The entire American Colony was to be deported to the interior of Asia Minor – 90 men, women and children. When Anna heard of this decision, she began to sing a hymn to the Lord. The others followed. But Anna's two sons-in-law, along with her adopted son, Jacob, felt the Lord would also expect

333 Letter from John D Whiting to William Coffin, Dep. of State, Washington, dated July 17, 1919, pp. 3-9, Folder: 1919, American Colony Collection, Jerusalem.

them to help themselves. They went without delay to see Izzat Bey, the civilian governor of Jerusalem, to ask his advice.[334] The governor was friendly, but explained that now that the Germans had control of the city there was nothing he could do. They were insisting on deporting the American Colony, and could not be dissuaded.

"But we are not all Americans," said Frederick.

"No, I know that," answered the governor, "but the Germans believe you all sympathize with the Americans. I was even reprimanded for being too interested in the wellbeing of the enemy."

Then he told them that the German captain responsible for the deportation order had said: "They have pigs and cows and can have pork and cream while we, your allies, have nothing." Izzat Bey believed that the Germans were really after the Colony's pigs. He suggested a spontaneous gift to the Germans of maybe around five pigs might persuade them to review their decision.[335] Following his advice, Anna dispatched the pigs to the German mission and the matter was settled. Five pigs was what it cost for all 90 members of the Colony to avoid deportation. But the Germans did not want to lose face completely, so the initial order was amended rather than revoked: "Only the Americans must go." This was followed quickly by: "Only American males capable of combat have to leave Jerusalem." A little later, after the Germans had failed to track down the other Americans living in Jerusalem, most of whom were Jews, the seven American men in the Colony were permitted to remain until the others could be rounded up.

The Germans also had Frederick Vester in their sights. He was viewed as a deserter. So, despite the fact that he was over 45 and not in the best of health, Frederick was summoned for an army medical. Before this could take place, however, the head of Germany's diplomatic mission in Jerusalem gave orders to the chief doctor that whatever Frederick's medical condition, his papers were to be stamped: "Able to bear arms." As Frederick went to the consulate to meet the chief doctor, the entire Colony knelt together and prayed. Once again, their prayers were answered. When he returned, Bertha's husband was proudly brandishing a paper bearing the words: "Not able to bear arms." Just before the scheduled examination a senior German officer had been wounded and the chief doctor had

334 Lowell Thomas: "An American Heroine in Jerusalem", *This Week*, Magazine Section, November 27, 1938, p.15, statements of Frederick Vester, pp.3-4. Folder: 1922, American Colony Collection, Jerusalem.
335 Spafford Vester: Unpublished draft of *Our Jerusalem*, chapter 33, p.8, American Colony Collection, Jerusalem.

to leave suddenly. He had forgotten to explain to his assistant that Herr Vester was to go to Europe to fight, irrespective of any disabilities he may have. The junior doctor who examined Vester found him in poor health and did not want to take the responsibility of declaring him fit for war.

As the British forces approached, all Turkish civilians were ordered to flee the city. The American Colony was again placed in charge of the city's hospitals, which were once more filling up with wounded men. One evening General Fuad Pasha's chief doctor was invited to dine with Anna. The doctor was served the turkey that was to have provided a farewell meal for the Americans before they were deported. The doctor agreed to take Fuad Pasha on a tour of inspection of the 'American' hospitals. As the colonists had hoped, the general was so impressed with what he saw that he closed all the other hospitals in the city and transferred their patients to the 'American' hospitals, ignoring the German general's orders. Injured British prisoners of war could once again be brought under the protection of the Colony.

On November 2, 1917 – two days before the German defeat at Gaza – a letter was made public in London. It had been through several drafts before the Foreign Secretary, Arthur James Balfour, finally put his signature to the paper. It was then sent by messenger to Lord Rothschild. The letter would fundamentally change the face of the Middle East. It contained Balfour's promise that he would use his influence to ensure that a homeland for world Jewry was established in Palestine. The Jewish population in Palestine at this time numbered some 56,000, while there were around 600,000 Palestinians. Balfour had given the Zionists the foothold in Palestine that Theodor Herzl had sought for so long from Sultan Abdul Hamid. The Balfour Declaration, as it became known, ensured that the government in Westminster now became the Zionists' main pillar of support. One of the senior British officials involved in formulating British policy in the Middle East at this time, Sir Mark Sykes, supported strongly the principles enshrined in the declaration. In 1915 he had also been a key player in drawing up a secret Anglo-French agreement to divide up the post-Ottoman Middle East between Britain and France. The chief French negotiator was François Georges Picot. Having reached an agreement between themselves they travelled to Russia to consult with the tsar's advisers. In May the following year, the infamous Sykes-Picot agreement was signed. The accord meant that the British intended to break their promises to give the Arabs independence and self-governance if they rose up against the Turks. The British government was certain that no one would learn of this breach of promise until it was too late. They could never have anticipated that the Bolsheviks would seize power in Russia. It was only when a Russian Jew, Lev Davidovitch Trotsky, revealed the secret agreement in which the tsar had been complicit that the Arabs realized they had been betrayed, and that the Palestinians were about to become a British sacrificial lamb.[336]

When the leak became public knowledge, the Turks tried to make maximum political capital out of the news. But it was too late to turn it to any kind of military advantage. The battle for Jerusalem had been lost. Djemal Pasha was well aware of this as he walked to the podium to address a gathering in Beirut November 4, 1917. The Turkish commander-in-chief was about to be recalled to Istanbul, and his farewell speech was, predictably, a combination of propaganda and self-defence. Djemal insisted that Sharif Hussein had stepped into the British trap and that in doing so he had betrayed Islam, its unity and majesty. "That they are outside the gates of Jerusalem today is the direct outcome of Sharif's revolt in Mecca," the Turkish general and naval minister thundered.[337]

In the course of three short weeks the Allied expeditionary force of Britain, Australia, and New Zealand had advanced 80 miles. A British Zionist, Richard Meinertzhagen was part of the vanguard. Once Jaffa had been conquered, he went immediately to the Jewish colony, 'The First in Zion'. Meinertzhagen felt at home there and spent the evening discussing the Zionist movement with "tough-thinking and responsible Jews". The British intelligence officer believed they were an intelligent people, ready to do battle, who would manage to carve out a great future for themselves in Palestine. "They intend to follow their destiny out here until they reach the final goal, namely a living and well governed Palestine for Jews," he wrote in his diary.[338] Just before he visited the Zionists, Meinertzhagen had watched long lines of Turkish prisoners of war being marched through the Palestinian town of Ramleh. When the inhabitants saw the Turks, with no British soldiers leading them, they thought that the Turkish army had returned. People came out into the streets to shout their support, some even waved the Turkish flag. It was only when the British guards appeared that the Palestinians understood their mistake.

---

336 Bayan Nuwayhid al-Hut: al-Qiyadat wal-muʾassasat al-siyasiyya fi Falestin, 1917–1948 (Political Leadership and Institutions in Palestine, 1917-1948) Beirut 1981, pp.77–78. Rashid Khalidi: Palestinian Identity, Columbia 1997, p.159. Walter Laqueur: A History of Zionism, New York 1973, p.145.
337 George Antonius: The Arab Awakening, The History of the Arab National Movement, Capricorn Books, Fourth Impression, 1965, pp.255.
338 Colonel R. Meinertzhagen: Middle East Diary, 1917–1956, London 1959, pp.6–7.

Meinertzhagen had enjoyed seeing them lose face and return, humiliated, to their wretched homes.[339]

Meinertzhagen's superior, General Allenby, knew that the advance on Jerusalem would not be easy. His supplies had to be brought ashore in Jaffa in small boats, rowed by British naval conscripts from West Africa and from Roratonga in the southern Pacific, men who were unfamiliar with local waters. The roads in Palestine were in such poor condition they could barely support the continuous heavy military traffic. The weather had also changed; it was now cold and rainy, and the troops who advanced toward the Judean Hills wore only lightweight summer uniforms: no coats, only shirts and shorts.

Allenby, an intelligent, able general (known amongst his men as 'Bull Allenby') had studied the Bible, the stories of the Crusades, Herodotus' reports from Egypt and Phoenicia, and Strabo's *Geographica*. The Prime Minister, Lloyd George, had sent Allenby a copy of George Adam Smith's *Historical Atlas of the Holy Land* as a guidebook, so that he could assess the relative defensive strengths of the hills,[340] and the opportunities they presented for ambush and attack. Allenby did not give the Turks any breathing room. His troops pushed forward along the road from Jaffa to Jerusalem and spread out in a fan, at the start of what was to become the greatest cavalry assault in history.

The British government, aware of the international outcry that would result if the holy places in Jerusalem were destroyed, had issued firm instructions that Jerusalem was not to be bombarded with artillery from the air. The general's strategy, therefore, involved isolating the Holy City and forcing the Turks to retreat along the road to Nablus. Allenby's advance forces made contact with the new Turkish front on November 21. It extended from Bethlehem to the mountains north of Jerusalem, a distance of some 40 miles. The Turkish-German forces had deployed around 16,000 men. Even though increasing numbers of Arabs were deserting, the soldiers at the front were eager and brave. Each time the British and their allies moved forward, the Turks counter-attacked. Allenby was saved purely by superior numbers of men and equipment. Each time a crisis developed, the British general was able to send fresh troops to the front.

Some time earlier, Turkish nurses from the Red Crescent had arrived

339 Meinertzhagen was transferred shortly after to the War Office in London.
340 At least two distinguished persons, in addition to Lloyd George (see his *Memoirs*, vol. iv) have claimed the credit for introducing this book to Allenby. See also, General Sir Archibald Wavell: *Allenby a Study of Greatness*, New York, Oxford University Press, 1941, p.223.

in Jerusalem where they took charge of the former British hospital. But as the British advanced closer, they fled, along with the German staff. The single remaining doctor came to the American Colony for help. The Red Crescent workers had left 250 wounded patients behind and responsibility for their care now fell to Grace and others from the Colony. The Turks had moved most of their wounded to Nablus and Jericho. Many were taken straight from their beds and sent off, on crutches, to march northwards. Those who could not walk were thrown into trucks. The injured British prisoners of war were left behind. The hospital lay in West Jerusalem, close to a battery of artillery which was firing towards the British, so Bertha asked for permission to move the patients to the hospital inside the Jaffa Gate.[341]

The west balcony of the American Colony enjoyed a view of the highest ridge northwest of Jerusalem, Nebi Samuel, site of the Prophet Samuel's grave. After fierce fighting, the British forces captured the ridge. Members of the Colony were able to follow the course of the battle with the aid of binoculars, donated to them by the Dominican monks before they were deported. The Turkish forces made several successive attempts to retake the ridge. Each time posters were put up in Jerusalem reporting their success in retaking Nebi Samuel. The members of Anna's House knew differently, as they watched the Turkish soldiers firing on the hilltop from their positions in the trenches below. The Crusaders had, in their time, called the ridge Mons Gaudii – the Mountain of Joy – because it was from there that they had been able to see Jerusalem for the first time. Now, 700 years later, through the mist and the rain, the British could do the same.[342]

---

341 Letter from John Whiting to William Coffin. July 17, 1919, pp.2–5, Spafford Vester: Unpublished manuscript, chapter 33, p.18, American Colony Collection, Jerusalem.
342 Jan Morris: *Farewell to Trumpets, An Imperial Retreat*, London 1998, p.176.

Chapter 28

Breakthrough

The British were advancing on Jerusalem from several directions. For months, the troops had prayed for rain and a respite from the relentless, burning sun. But when the sky began eventually to cloud over on December 4, 1917, it became so black that day turned almost to night. The rain poured down and the narrow roads were transformed into swamps. The men's boots were virtually worn out after months on the march and by this stage in the campaign some were practically barefoot. A few had managed to improvise sandals from pieces of leather they scrounged along the way.

Among the three British infantry divisions marching from Jaffa to Jerusalem was the rifle company of Major Vivian Gilbert. In driving rain, Gilbert ordered his men to make camp near the village of Abu Ghosh. The soldiers dug themselves in, and, eventually, despite the appalling weather conditions, the cooks managed to raise the men's spirits with hot cups of tea.

Allenby's strategy for attacking Jerusalem involved advancing in a pincer movement from the Jaffa-Jerusalem road near the village of Lifta to the left, and from Deir Yassin to the right. Control of Deir Yassin, considered to be one of the gateways to Jerusalem, was strategically vital to the success of the operation, and Gilbert had barely the chance to drink his long awaited tea before he was assigned to a reconnaissance party to assess the best way of attacking the village.

As the major and his fellow officers climbed up towards Deir Yassin the rain eased and sunshine spread across the valley. Gilbert thought that, from a distance, the trenches below the village looked like a bandaged sore on the landscape. He reasoned that the almond groves on the terraced hillsides beneath would provide the men with a certain degree of protection, if only they could reach them before daylight. But from there onwards, the troops would have to force their way forward across bare ridges that offered no cover.

That night there was no moon and rain and gusts of wind came in waves. The previous afternoon, the troops had advanced in small groups to their positions further down the valley. Cannon and ammunition were brought up to the British forward base, where a mobile field hospital was set up.

At 1am, the first company advanced over the top and descended into the valley below Deir Yassin, followed by the pack animals, loaded with Gatling guns and ammunition. The rain had made the descent difficult, and both men and donkeys fell over. But the animals were loaded up again in the darkness and the advance continued. Gilbert was grateful for the rigorous training his company had undergone in the mountains of Macedonia earlier in the war. As a result, even the donkeys seemed to know what was expected of them. But the difficult terrain meant that as the sun came up the Allied force was still very far from its objective, and consequently exposed to Turkish fire. Gilbert ordered his troops to advance. Like ants they climbed from terrace to terrace, stopping only to shoot. Higher and higher they climbed with little cover to protect them from the Turks. In some places there was such a difference in elevation from one terrace to the next that the men were forced to climb on their comrades' shoulders in order to scale them. The donkeys had long been left behind and the soldiers were forced to carry their own ammunition, advancing over the last several hundred yards with fixed bayonets. The Turks fought hard, but were outmanned. Finally, at 7am, the great ridge was taken.

Early on the same morning of December 8, while it was still dark, Bertha's younger sister, Grace, was woken by machine gun fire. She turned to her husband and mumbled: "What does this mean?"[343]

"Our prayers have been heard," answered John D Whiting, imagining the battle was taking place just a few miles away.

Later that day, Frederick Vester received orders for all the wounded (including British prisoners of war) to be taken to Jericho by lorry. Frederick and Bertha decided to defy the order, sending only the Turkish patients. Almost as soon as the hospital had begun to empty, new wounded arrived, screaming and covered with blood. Many died as soon as they arrived, but there were not enough gravediggers available to dispose of the bodies and the mortuary was filled to overflowing.

343 Letter from John Whiting to William Coffin, July 17, 1919, pp.11–12, American Colony Collection, Jerusalem.

By this time, all Turkish civilian authorities in Jerusalem had fled, except for the city's governor. The Germans and the Austrians had already left, after sending the city's religious leaders to Damascus. Despite the obvious fact that the Turks were on the point of losing Jerusalem, posters appeared throughout the Holy City announcing that they would fight "street by street to the last man". The Germans, by contrast, had prepared the public in Europe for their defeat by claiming they were ceding Jerusalem "because the city was of no strategic interest".[344]

The nurses from the American Colony did their best to help the 200 wounded Turkish soldiers who remained. But the last Turkish doctors had also fled and the volunteers now had entire responsibility for running the hospitals. The British artillery sounded very close. Many volunteers, unaware of the British government's directive to Allenby not to fire on the city, grew anxious about their families' safety. It was agreed that married nurses would return to the house in Sheikh Jarrah at night, leaving six unmarried ones (three Swedes and three Americans) at the hospital. In the quiet of the night the cries of the wounded seemed louder. Men would call out for morphine, but the nurses could give them only occasional sips of water. The medicine store was long since empty.[345]

The three wounded British prisoners at the hospital were hidden in storerooms at the back of the building. Bertha told the men to be as quiet as mice. Two of them understood the seriousness of the situation and the danger they were in. The third had lost his mind as a result of the experiences he had been through, and could no longer understand anything. The two mentally cognisant patients protested that it was too dangerous for the Spafford-Vesters to take the risk of hiding them. They argued that while the Allied troops might arrive in the city the next day, it could equally take days or weeks before the Turks ceded victory.[346] But Bertha and the others decided to take the chance. They locked the doors of the storerooms and removed the three British men from the food list, sneaking in only when there were no outsiders present to observe them. The nurses feared that the third man might cry out and betray them. They prayed silently for help.

344 *Frankfurter Allgemeine Zeitung* wrote on November 28, 1917, that Jerusalem was of no strategic interest. Lawrence James: *Imperial Warrior, The Life and Times of Field Marshall Viscount Allenby*, London 1993, p.139.
345 Lind and Wallström: *Jerusalem Travelers*, Stockholm 1981, p.151.
346 Spafford Vester: Unpublished manuscript, chapter 33, pp.24–25, American Colony Collection, Jerusalem.

That afternoon the senior Turkish health officer, Tufik Bey, arrived at the hospital. He had never visited it before and Bertha was convinced he must know about the hidden British prisoners. Her heart pounded so hard she thought the Turk would hear it. Tufik Bey said: "Madam, I want to speak with you." Bertha tried to act as naturally as she could, but asked John D Whiting to attend the meeting for support. She was sure this was the end, and that she and Frederick were to be arrested. When the health official asked her to close the door, she became even more frightened. But she calmed down when he began to speak:

Tonight we are leaving *al-Quds al-Sharif* – the noble city. We will withdraw to Jericho… I am here on behalf of my commandant, and all of us, to thank you and the other members of the American Colony for all that you have done. We know once we have left the city that all the men we have placed in charge of caring for our sick will put on civilian clothes and save their own lives. As soon as the British are here, everything will be in order, but until then there will be a lot of confusion and our sick and wounded will suffer. For this reason we have decided not to take with us the six Americans who are of combat age whom we wanted to conscript. We are leaving 600 men behind us – those who are too injured to move – and we are placing them in your care. We can leave provisions for only one day; that is all we can spare. Here is an order which will let you requisition whatever you may find in the city's stores.

With that, Tufik Bey handed Bertha a piece of paper. Both of them knew it was worthless. There was nothing left in the city stores, or anywhere else in the city. Before he left, the Turkish medical officer extended his hand in thanks, saying: "I know that you have served neither Turks nor Germans, and that you will also not serve the British – you serve God and your fellow man." With shaky hands and a pounding heart, Bertha returned to work.

Shortly after this, Bertha learnt that the Turks had mined the city's grain mills, and, fearing that they must have placed mines elsewhere in the city, she hurried to the office of the civilian governor, Izzat Pasha. "Can you find out if the Church of the Holy Sepulchre is also full of explosives?" she begged. The governor went himself to investigate, and reported back to Bertha that the church was safe.

Orders were issued by the departing Turks that all civilians should sleep on the ground floor of their houses or in the cellar. Yet again it was said that the city would be fought over, street by street. But the Colony's nurses remained at their posts at the hospital in the Grand New Hotel. At 10.30pm, everyone in Jerusalem heard a thunderous barrage of artillery. It was outgoing fire and seemed to be coming from the outskirts of the city. The staff at the hospital wondered if this was the beginning of the street battle for the city.

Only then did Frederick and Bertha decide to go home. They wanted to be near the children and Mother Anna. As they walked through the city's streets they passed Turkish artillery being withdrawn from the city, their Gatling guns loaded onto donkeys. The Turkish infantry and cavalry were retreating in the same direction, but in a chaotic fashion. The Spafford-Vesters were struck by the quietness; the men barely spoke, and the only sound was the occasional deep cough from soldiers with colds. The soldiers were exhausted and hungry. Many were barefoot. It was raining, and the heavy traffic had turned the roads into mud.

As they watched, a horse that had been pulling a cannon collapsed from exhaustion in the middle of the road. A soldier cut off his reins, but the stream of traffic continued on over the half-dead animal. The horse barely managed to lift its head, pathetically seeking help that did not come. The fleeing army did not even bother to avoid trampling over its hooves. Bertha cried out in Arabic: "For Allah's sake, put a bullet through the horse's head and end his misery." From the darkness she heard only a tired voice: "Who thinks about a horse's pain now? Think of yourselves. The British will soon be here and send a bullet through your own head." Frederick tugged at his wife's arm and told her to keep walking; but Bertha refused to leave until one of the policemen put the animal out of its misery. Eventually someone stepped forward and obliged. Bertha, satisfied that the horse was no longer suffering, headed with her husband towards their house on the Nablus Road. There they found the children and Mother Anna asleep on mattresses that had been placed on the living room floor.

But before they could join them, Bertha and Frederick were alerted by the sound of German transport vehicles on the Nablus Road. They were carrying objects that looked like aeroplane parts, and they were heading in the opposite direction from the Turks. Were they about to start a counter offensive? That would make life in the city extremely dangerous. But a little later the German vehicles returned and Bertha tried at last to get some rest.

Around the same time, Lars Lind, one of the senior nurses at the Grand New Hotel, heard sounds of horses' hooves and the tramping of boots in the streets near the Jaffa Gate. From the balcony he could see an officer on horseback, followed by a company on foot. Suddenly there was a loud knocking at the door below, and someone called out in Turkish: "*Gitmeye mecburuz*" – "We are obliged to leave". This announcement was followed by the name of a badly wounded Turkish officer. Lars ran down the stairs and called out in Arabic: "Don't wake up the whole hospital." Before him was a Turkish colonel who greeted him, smiled and then said in French: "I have come to pick up my wounded man. He was brought here three days ago." Lind brought the Turk to the bedside of the wounded officer, who was too badly injured to be moved. But the colonel insisted the man should be dressed and given crutches to walk with. He added that the artillery bombardment they had heard just over an hour earlier was only an attempt to conceal the Turkish retreat. "By tomorrow morning there will not be a single soldier in the city when the British come to fight within the walls," he explained to Lind. "My company is the last to leave. The British will be able to march in without resistance." The last thing the Turk said was: "*Teşekkür ederim* – thank you." The officer wept as he spoke.

The Turk then mounted his horse and led the wounded officer, along with two other injured men, through the hospital gate and disappeared into the darkness. A little later, the sound of their horses' hooves was also gone. Lind was moved by this mournful departure. He knew that if the colonel had wanted to he could have plundered the city's holy treasures, or even burned and destroyed the sacred places. He tried to call Mother Anna to tell her the news, but the line had been cut.

That same night, the Turkish civilian governor, Izzat Pasha, had been pacing anxiously about his spacious office near to the American Colony. As he did so, he was watched by the Palestinian mayor of Jerusalem, Hussein Husseini. Izzat Pasha was about to sign a letter of capitulation, relinquishing the Holy City, which had been part of the Ottoman Empire for over 400 years. The pasha was anxious, but he conducted himself with the dignity appropriate to the occasion. The previous day the Turkish General, Ali Fuad Pasha, had given him a draft of the letter, stating that the Turks were withdrawing from Jerusalem to avoid damage to any of the holy places. But the governor, deeply ashamed by the disgrace of being forced to leave, had repeatedly postponed writing it out or signing it.

Finally, dawn began to break behind the Mount of Olives and the call to prayer was heard coming from the Sheikh Jarrah Mosque just down the road: "*La ilaha illa Allah, Mohammed rasoul Allah* – There is no other

God but Allah, Mohammed is God's Messenger". At last, Izzat Pasha sat back down, dipped his pen into his inkwell and, with a shaking hand, put his name to the letter of capitulation. Moments later he realized that the mufti of Jerusalem should also be informed. He wrote out a copy, signed it and gave both letters to Mayor Husseini. Then he left his office.

All night, one of the American Colony's carriages, pulled by two beautiful grey horses, had been waiting outside the pasha's office in the St George's Cathedral complex. Izzat Pasha had requisitioned the carriage to take him to safety in Jericho, but Anna had been more than happy to help the pasha, who had done so much during the war to help the Colony. The governor's family had already left, taking with them as much furniture as they could. Now, he himself had to make his farewell to *al-Quds*.

Mayor Husseini first went to his uncle, the mufti, Kamel Husseini. He took one look at the capitulation letter and said: "A Muslim regime leaves – a regime which has oppressed us – a regime that gave us neither freedom to speak, nor independence. A Christian regime is coming, one which will, *Inshallah* [if God wills it] bring freedom to the Arabs. *Allah Karim* [God is merciful]." Then the mufti threw the letter away.[347]

A few hours earlier, a British officer's cook, camped southeast of the city, was rudely woken and ordered to set off towards the nearby village of Lifta to find eggs for the major's breakfast. Lifta, about a mile distant, had been taken the evening before, and, on hearing the sound of a rooster crowing, the major had reasoned that a supply of eggs could not be far away. It was still dark when the cook trudged off in the direction of Lifta. But the deep Turkish trenches surrounding the village made it impossible to approach it directly, so he had to take a more circuitous route. As dawn broke, the cook looked about him for signs of a British encampment, but found nothing. The brief mile turned into two, then three. At last, the cook was able to reach a road leading to the village. Ahead of him were two horses and a small group of people, including women and children. They were waving white flags on long poles, some were even waving white handkerchiefs. "*Allahu Akbar, Allahu Akbar* – God is great, God is great," they cried as the lone British soldier approached. When he came close enough, one of the older Palestinians tried to embrace and kiss him, but the cook managed to avoid the kisses by pulling his arm free. The shouts quietened down and a short man, dressed in a black coat with a red fez, addressed him in a high falsetto voice from inside a horse-drawn carriage.

347 Spafford Vester: Unpublished manuscript, chapter 33, pp.29-30. Letter from Bertha Spafford Vester to Mr Clow, dated April 2, 1925, Folder: 1925, American Colony Collection, Jerusalem.

"You are British soldier, are you not?"[348]

"I should say so."

"Where is General Allah Nebi?" asked the man. That was the way the Palestinians pronounced Allenby.

"I'm 'anged if I know, mister."

"I want to hand over the city please. Here are the keys, it is yours," continued the Palestinian, presenting a ring of keys to the confused British cook. Believing Lifta was already in British hands, he began to think he must have stumbled across a party of lunatics.

"I don't want yer city. I want some eggs for my officers!" cried the cook in disgust.[349] This farcical encounter would mark the beginning of several attempts by the hapless mayor of Jerusalem to hand his city over to the British conquerors.

348 Major Vivian Gilbert: *The Romance of the Last Crusade*, London 1936, pp.165-66.
349 There are other versions of the first encounter with British troops on December 9, 1917. See, Cyril Falls: *History of The Great War, Military Operations in Egypt & Palestine, From June 1917 to the End of the War, Part I*, London 1930, p.252. In this version Privates H. E. Church and R. W. Andrews, mess cooks of the 2/20th London Regiment, lost their way during the night and wandered about in search of water until they reached the suburbs about 5 am. Here they met a crowd of civilians who informed them that the city desired to surrender. Not feeling themselves equal to the occasion, they returned to their battalion. The next soldiers to meet the Palestinians, were Sergeants F. G. Hurcomb and J. Sedgewick, of the 2/19th London Regiment.

Chapter 29

The March into Jerusalem

Lars Lind stood on one of the balconies of the Grand New Hotel. The only people he could see below him were Palestinians on their way to work, negotiating the worn cobblestones by the Jaffa Gate. He decided to return to the Colony to tell Mother Anna that the city was now free of Turks. On his way, he passed signs that the Turkish soldiers had not relinquished the Holy City entirely without causing damage. They had set fire to a walkway that led from the Christian quarter near the so-called New Gate, to the Vatican's Notre Dame de France Pilgrim Centre just outside the city walls. Also, the remains of telephone wires hung like broken spiders' webs above the muddy streets.

Lind passed through the Musrara quarter, just outside the Damascus Gate, and continued on to the Nablus road without seeing any sign of life. When he arrived at Bertha and Frederick's house and gave them the news, they praised the Lord and began to sing hymns of thanks.[350] As they did so, the mayor of Jerusalem, Hussein Husseini, arrived bearing a bunch of flowers. He was surrounded by a group of youths and accompanied by Palestinian policemen. "Where is Mother?" asked the mayor when Bertha came out. "I am on my way to deliver the letter of surrender to the English general, and I want her to be the first to know. I realize how relieved you all are, especially Mother, who has been looking forward to this day."[351]

When Anna came out and heard what Mayor Husseini had to say she began once again to sing a hymn of praise to the Lord. The others followed

350 Letter from John Whiting to William Coffin, July 17, 1919, File: 1919, p.12, American Colony Collection, Bertha Spafford Vester: memorandum, File: 1922, American Colony Collection.
351 Spafford Vester: *Our Jerusalem*, 2nd edition, p.273.

suit, including the mayor, who had been a frequent guest at the Colony and knew the Christian hymn by heart. Then Anna asked: "Where is your white flag? You cannot take a letter of capitulation without having a white flag. You will be shot." The mayor, who had not thought of this, was taken aback for a moment. He then went down to the Colony's stables to look for "a horse and wagon to go to the front by the Jaffa Road and hand the city over to the British". But the Colony's carriage had already been taken by Izzat Pasha for his flight to Jericho, so the mayor and his escort prepared to walk the few miles to the British front lines.

Photographer Lewis Larsson was sitting in the dining room with his wife, Edith, when the mayor arrived. Larsson asked whether it would be possible for him to come along and record the historic surrender of the Holy City. Husseini was happy for him to do so and a few minutes later Lewis and Lars Lind joined the mayor's delegation. The party went first to a nearby hospital that was also being run by American Colony staff. There, they found a white sheet, which they tore in two. After tying one half of the sheet to an old broom handle, they continued to the front.[352]

The accounts given by Larsson and Lind of subsequent attempts to surrender the keys to the Holy City differ only slightly in their absurdity from that involving the officer's cook. A little after 8.30am, when the delegation arrived at a crossroads on the heights above Lifta, they were startled by a sudden cry of "Halt!". Members of the party found themselves facing the rifle barrels of two British sergeants, who had been hiding in a ruin at the side of the road. The sergeants soon realized that the terrified Palestinians were unarmed. They allowed the mayor to explain his mission to hand over the letter of capitulation. But the sergeants pointed out that they did not have the authority to receive the letter, and had to wait for the arrival of a superior officer. Meanwhile, Larsson and Lind erected their large box camera on its tripod and took several pictures.[353]

352 Fannie Fern Andrews: *The Holy Land under the Mandate, Volume I*, Boston and New York 1931, p.68; Lind & Wallström: *Jerusalem Travelers*, Stockholm 1981, p.155; Theo Larsson: *Seven Passports for Palestine*. Longfield 1995, p.21; Larsson: *Dala Folk in the Holy Land*, Stockholm 1957, p.101.
353 W.T. Massey: *How Jerusalem was Won, Being the Record of Allenby's Campaign in Palestine*, New York 1920, p.189. Bertha Spafford Vester: Unpublished manuscript, chapter 33, p.30. The historic picture marking the occasion depicts: Mayor Hussein Salim Husseini, the mayor's nephew, Taufik Husseini, the police inspectors Abdul Khader Alami and Ahmad Sharfi, policemen Hussein Assali and Ibrahim Zanoukh. Hannah Iskander Laham was holding the broom handle with the white sheet. Jawad Ibrahim Husseini was also in the delegation. The two British sergeants with rifles and helmets are F. G. Hurcomb, and J. Sedgwick. Aref al-Aref: *Mufassal Tarich al Quds* (Jerusalem's History) Arabic, Jerusalem 1961, p.384.

Fifteen minutes later, two reconnaissance officers from the field artillery arrived and once again the mayor of Jerusalem explained his mission. The two officers promised to telephone headquarters, but before they could do so a lieutenant colonel appeared at the crossroads. His artillery brigade had been positioned near the village of Kastel a few miles away, and had advanced overnight. Husseini tried again: "I am the mayor of Jerusalem, and I intend to hand over the city to the British general." But the officer, Lieutenant Colonel Bailey, more interested in knowing in which direction the Turkish forces had retreated, replied that he, too, was not sufficiently senior to receive the capitulation letter. When the mayor told him that the Turks had gone north, the officer ordered his men to turn their cannon in the same direction and instructed his next-in-command to telegraph headquarters and say that Jerusalem had surrendered. Matters appeared to be degenerating into farce when Husseini, to his relief, saw a suitably senior British officer approaching. It was Brigadier General Watson, who had been at field headquarters when his breathless cook had run back from his egg-searching expedition with the momentous news that Jerusalem was prepared to hand itself over to the British. The brigadier general was intent on having the honour of receiving the surrender of the Holy City himself and listened while Husseini began translating the letter from Turkish to English. All of a sudden he asked, "Where can I get a cup of tea?"

Larsson said there was a Jewish hospital in the area, which would certainly be able to provide tea. He then took more pictures, before returning to the Colony to have them developed. He was pleased, and presumably amused, by what he saw. First, there was a picture of the delegation alongside the two British sergeants, then one of Husseini attempting to present the letter of capitulation to Colonel Bailey, and finally one of the mayor of Jerusalem standing next to Brigadier General Watson, who was on horseback.

Watson was not the only British officer to appreciate the tea provided by the staff of the Jewish Hospital. Another man, Lieutenant Colonel T B Layton, had arrived before him, and was now enjoying his first proper cup of tea, without chlorinated water, after 12 months. Layton, a doctor and commanding officer of the 2/4th London Field Ambulance, was looking for a place to treat the wounded. He was escorted around the hospital by a German doctor who spoke English. Layton was impressed. He thought it as good as any found in a small British or French town. The block floors shone. Everything was scrupulously clean. The air itself seemed impregnated with soap and polish. [354] Layton told the doctor that he wished to take over the hospital for the care of British wounded. There were a large number of casualties in the village of Ein Karem that would need to be brought into the city, and more were expected to arrive during the day. But the German hesitated, explaining that the building was small, with limited capacity, and that it was already full of civilian sick, among them women. After some thought, Layton decided to investigate other possibilities and set off towards the German Hospital marked on his map. This, too, was beautifully kept, but too small for Layton's needs. His next stop, the English Hospital, had been General Falkenayn's headquarters, and had been vacated only the previous night. Layton did not expect it would be useable, but he was unprepared for the chaos he found. The furniture had been thrown all over the place and the entire grounds were covered with waste paper.

There were no other hospitals marked on Layton's map. Then a man wearing a deep red *tarboosh* started addressing him animatedly in reasonable English, saying that he could help. The man, whom Layton took to be a Turk, led him to a hospital near an area known as the Russian Compound. On their way, they passed evidence of looting and even saw men hastily pulling down telephone wires in order to get their hands on the copper they contained. But the Russian hospital was also unsuitable for military use. Layton stood on the steps of the building, preparing to leave, when he was approached by Bertha Spafford-Vester, the woman whose name his local guide had been repeating like a mantra. At the time, Layton had barely registered her name, but Bertha now explained that the man whom he had taken to be a Turk was in fact a Christian Arab, a member of the American Colony.

Layton was the first British officer to enter Jerusalem, and Bertha now sought his help to stop the looting. She believed that merely the sight of his presence at the Jaffa Gate would be enough to calm the crowds in the Old City and prevent a riot. But Layton said this was impossible. He was not a combatant, merely a "medical officer looking for accommodation for our own wounded". Besides, British troops were under strict orders not to enter the city walls. Bertha persisted, saying that she could direct him to a hospital within the walls that could suit his needs, adding that there would be "serious consequences" if Layton failed to comply with her request. Again, the lieutenant colonel refused, and they parted company.

354 T B Layton: *Tales of a Field Ambulance, 1914-1918*, told by ambulance personnel, printed for private circulation, Southend-on-Sea, 1935, pp.211-17.

Layton recorded feeling annoyed that his "time had been wasted", but he also regretted that the American woman had probably "got a poor opinion of the first British officer she had met".

Meanwhile, in the hills above the city, Brigadier General Watson's adjutant had reported to division headquarters that his commanding officer was on his way to Jerusalem to accept formally the mayor's capitulation. This news was not well received by the brigadier's superior officer, Major General Shea, who seized the telephone and shouted: "Stop the brigadier; I will take the surrender of Jerusalem myself."[355]

But it was too late. Watson had already arrived in the Holy City. He had needed little encouragement, and when both the mayor and Thomas Cook's representative in Jerusalem had begged him to show himself on the streets in order to stop the looting, he had agreed. Shortly after, the cry went up from within the city walls: "*Ajou! Ajou!*" [They've come! They've come!"][356]

Following Bertha's unsuccessful encounter with Layton, she and Frederick returned to the Grand New Hotel, just inside the Jaffa Gate. From its balconies, she observed the brigadier's arrival, and, weeping with joy, she ran downstairs and kissed his stirrup. Frederick Vester and John D Whiting asked Watson to visit the three injured British prisoners of war, who had been hidden away at the back of the building. As the senior officer stood before them he was deeply moved, particularly when one of the men asked plaintively: "Why did we have to suffer so long?"

The brigadier then returned to his field headquarters, proud as a rooster. But when he was informed that Major General Shea wanted to receive the letter of capitulation himself and was on his way to the city by car, there was nothing for it but to make a u-turn and return to Jerusalem, find the mayor and return the letter to him. Bertha was standing outside the post office when she saw a car coming down the Jaffa Road from the west. There were no civilian cars in Jerusalem, so this had to mean the arrival of another British officer. She stood in the middle of the road and signalled to the car to stop. "We do not have any more food to give our patients," said Bertha, who only then noticed that the car was full of officers wearing medals and with a great deal of gold on their caps.[357] While Shea's adjutant was making a note of Bertha's needs, Mayor Husseini and his entourage appeared suddenly. Bertha introduced him to the major general,

355 Gilbert: *The Romance of the Last Crusade*, London 1936, p.168.
356 Spafford Vester: *Our Jerusalem*, 2nd edition, pp.274-75.
357 Ibid. pp.275-76.

and for the fourth time that day a British officer was handed the letter of capitulation, signed by the last Turkish civilian governor of Jerusalem.

The letter was then translated into English. As the general listened to the part describing how the Turks had withdrawn from Jerusalem in order to save the holy places from destruction by British artillery, he snarled: "That is a lie, it is a lie!" Bertha's knees shook. She wondered what had angered the general. But Shea, following orders that came directly from Lloyd George, had ensured his troops had not fired a single shell towards the Holy City.[358]

By this time it was 11am and sufficient numbers of people had gathered around Shea's vehicle for him to make a short speech on the steps of the post office. The major general then accompanied Bertha to the roof of the Grand New Hotel, which had an uninterrupted view of the entire city. From this vantage point they could both see clearly that shooting continued in the hills to the north around Mount Scopus, from where it was easy to fire down onto the Sheikh Jarrah district. Bertha, anxious about her family at the Colony, answered Shea's many questions about the city as quickly as she could before sending a note to Anna, asking if she and the children were safe. Anna replied that nine windows had been broken by shots fired by the retreating Turks, but no one in the Colony had been hurt.

Sometime later, Shea returned to field headquarters and sent a telegram to Allenby's office: "I have the honour to report that I have this day accepted the surrender of Jerusalem."[359] Immediately the reply came back: "General will himself accept the surrender of Jerusalem on the 11th inst. Make arrangements." Soon after that, Allenby sent more cryptic telegrams to his other divisions: "Look up Psalms: 122, verse 2." When his divisional commanders did so, they read: "Our feet shall stand within thy gates, O Jerusalem."[360] Later that evening, the British took Mount Scopus and the Turks finally stopped firing at the Sheikh Jarrah quarter.

Around 2pm that day the first prints of Hussein Husseini's initial encounters with the British emerged from the Colony's darkroom. General Watson, who was delighted, ordered several sets. Much later, he took Larsson aside and asked if he would be able to identify the white flag of surrender from the photographs.[361] Larsson replied that he would,

358 Ibid. p.276.
359 Vivian Gilbert: *The Romance of the Last Crusade*, London 1936, p.169.
360 Larsson: *Dala Folk in the Holy Land*, Stockholm 1957, pp.103–106.
361 H.P. Bower: *A Sapper in Palestine, True War Stories, Six Personal Narratives of the War*, London 1999, p.316.

particularly since "the broomstick had splinters on one side where it had been broken". The brigadier then produced the flag, which one of his officers had been carrying, rolled up under his arm. The photographs confirmed that this was indeed the flag that Husseini had been carrying at the time of surrender. "I went personally back to get it," Watson said. "I have to go to the north with my regiment now and I want to know that it will be in safe hands. If you can, ask the mayor to sign it, and take care of it until I return." For his part, Mayor Hussein Husseini was happy to see the flag again. "Where was it hidden?" he asked, adding that he had been searching for it for much of the previous day and had even offered a reward of a pound of gold to whoever found it. Then he wrote his name in Arabic and dated it. Larsson hid the signed flag behind the wardrobe in his bedroom.

One of the British officers who had seen the photographs advised Larrson that they would command a fair price in Fleet Street if they could be sent back to London in time for that week's papers. "Go to headquarters and ask General Shea to send the pictures to London with his courier mail," the officer told him.

Expecting that Shea would be impressed by the pictures, Larsson set off for the general's headquarters, which had been established at the English Mission Hospital. When he arrived, he found Shea sitting with a cup of hot chocolate in front of him. With a friendly gesture he invited the Swede to join him amongst the packing cases.

"It is terribly cold here," said the general. "What can I do for you?"

"I was hoping you could help me send these photographs that I took of the British conquest of Jerusalem."

"What kind of photographs? Did you take pictures of me reading the proclamation on the steps in front of David's Tower?"

"No, I mean the photographs I took of the first British division led by General Watson," said Lewis surprised. He was still unaware that the general had read a proclamation. Shea was furious. He grabbed the photographs, got up from the box he was sitting on and left the room. A little later he returned and said: "I will not send these pictures home, and you are not going to do it either. The pictures are to be destroyed together with the negatives."

"Why?" asked Lewis.

"None of these images show the moment of capitulation. That only took place when I read the letter out on the steps of the post office at 11 am."

"But why do you want to destroy the photographs?" asked Larsson. "I will not publish them without permission, but since they are of historic importance – the first time Jerusalem has capitulated without firing a shot – I think it would be a shame not to preserve them. At least the Imperial War Museum ought to have a set. If not, then I must be allowed to keep them."

"Out of the question! The pictures are to be destroyed," exploded General Shea, adding: "My decision is final." Larsson was obliged to leave without his pictures. Fortunately, the original prints remained at the Colony.

By December 11, all was ready for Allenby's triumphal march into the Holy City. The morning frost had disappeared and the sun shone from an azure blue sky as the general drove up towards the Jaffa Gate. To his right, a force of 50 British soldiers – English, Scots, Welsh and Irish – lined the route. On the right, allied soldiers from Australia and New Zealand stood to attention. Inside the gate, the street was lined with French and Italian troops. A mood of celebration filled the city, which was full of people. From the balconies and rooftops came shouts of "God bless the Englishmen!" Anna and her family watched his arrival from the balconies of the New Grand Hotel.

Early in the war, during the battles in the Dardanelles, Anna had feared the British might conquer Palestine from the north. According to the biblical prophecies, this was the direction from which judgement and evil came. But instead, the Christian invaders had arrived from the south, the direction of heavenly love. For her flock at the American Colony, the invasion represented a fulfilment of Mother Anna's prophecy.[362]

When Allenby's car stopped outside the Jaffa Gate, a blare of trumpets sounded, before a respectful silence settled over the arrival party. Instead of entering the Old City on horseback, like Kaiser Wilhelm, the general left his car and walked slowly through the gate, past the New Grand Hotel, before heading right towards the citadel. This small fortress dated back to the time of Herod, but no one knew exactly when it had been built. It lay on the site of an earlier fortification, believed to have been erected during the time of King David. As Allenby, dressed in his khaki uniform, flanked by his two adjutants, ascended the steps of the citadel, he caught sight of the minaret in the southwest corner of the fortress, known as David's Tower. Archaeologists and theologians believed this was where the Romans' palace in Jerusalem had been situated and that, therefore, it was possibly here that Pontius Pilate had condemned Jesus to death.

362 Petri: *On Holy Paths*, Stockholm 1931, pp.148–149.

When the Crusaders took Jerusalem in 1099, the fort was expanded in a westerly direction and became the residence of the Crusader kings. Barely 60 years later the great Muslim conqueror, Saladin, had stood there and watched as two long processions of defeated Christians left the city. One line consisted of men who had bought back their freedom, the other was made up of Christians who could not afford to do so. They would be sold as slaves.[363]

The ceremony to mark the arrival of these most recent Christian conquerors had been planned meticulously by the British government in London. It was to stand in stark contrast to Kaiser Wilhelm's self-aggrandizing entry, on horseback 19 years before. Roofs, windows and balconies lining Allenby's route through the city were packed. Priests and monks made the sign of the cross as he passed. Palestinian Christians cried out in welcome, along with their Armenian, Latin, Greek, Russian and Ethiopian brethren. The crowds included Copts, dressed in their white cloaks, Franciscans in brown, and the Orthodox who wore black. All Jerusalem, it seemed, had turned out to hail the first Christian conqueror since the Crusader kings. The Jewish rabbis, dressed in black, were also overcome by emotion. For them, although the city was in the hands of another occupying power, it was one which had promised that Palestine would be the Jew's national homeland. Tears ran down their cheeks. Bertha saw one Jew throw his arms around the neck of a Greek priest, who lost his hat during the embrace. But Allenby was also hailed by the Muslims, who clapped their hands and called out his name.

From the steps of the citadel, Allenby read a proclamation in English, which had been cabled to him from London three weeks earlier. It was then translated into French, Arabic, Hebrew, Greek, Russian and Italian. The city's notables were presented to the general, and the ceremony came to an end. Not a single British flag had been raised. Guards were posted to the holy places. The new British administration was careful to ensure that those assigned to the Islamic holy places of the Noble Sanctuary were all Muslims from one of the Indian brigades.

After the ceremony, Allenby returned to the Jaffa Gate. It was only after he had crossed out of the walled city that he mounted his horse. Larsson followed him, taking photographs all the while. But his pictures fell foul of the military censors, who were concerned that they might give the erroneous impression that Allenby had taken his horse into the city.

---

363 Jerome Murphy-O'Connor: *The Holy Land, An Archaeological Guide from Earliest Times to 1700*, Oxford and New York 1990, pp.23–24.

Only one picture was released eventually, showing Allenby on horseback, with the city wall in the background, clearly leaving, rather than arriving at the Holy City.

Jerusalem now had a Christian administration for the first time since the Crusaders had been driven out by Saladin. It was the Christmas present, that Lloyd George had longed for and he himself announced the news of the victory to a surprised British public.[364] For Anna Spafford, this was yet another heavenly sign that Christ's coming was imminent. Now the Jewish people could return to their homeland in greater numbers.

But not all Christians agreed, certainly not the Catholics. The day after the British took Jerusalem, the pope's representative, Cardinal Pietro Gasparri, confided to the French envoy to the Vatican his fears that a new war would now follow, since the British had given Palestine to the Zionists as a gift. He added that the Turks had been very respectful custodians of the holy places of Jerusalem and that it was "difficult to take back a part of our heart that we have given to the Turks in order to hand it over to the Zionists".[365] The message from the Vatican became clearer still after the pope ordered that the bells of St Peter should not be rung to celebrate the news of the British conquest of Jerusalem. As far as Pope Benedict XV was concerned, the Zionists were not believers; they were anti-religious Jews who could not possibly fulfil the biblical prophecies and had nothing to do with the return to the Promised Land. The Vatican feared that Jewish immigration would pose a threat to Christians living in the holy land.

This Catholic opposition came as no surprise to the Zionists. Nearly 14 years earlier, when Herzl had an audience with Pope Pius X, he had been told that the papacy could never support Zionism, since "the Jews did not recognize our Lord, and therefore we cannot recognize the Jewish people". The pope added that Jerusalem must never fall into Jewish hands.[366]

Anna Spafford, for her part, was already taking steps to charm the new British administration, inviting Allenby and four of his generals to Christmas dinner. The guests were provided with turkey, with all the trimmings, except cranberry sauce. It had not been possible to get cranberries. But there was plum pudding flambéed with brandy for dessert, followed by a

364 Lawrence James: *Imperial Warrior. The Life and Times of Field Marshall Viscount Allenby, 1861–1936*, London 1993, pp.140–141.
365 Charles Loiseau: *Ma mission auprès du Vatican (1913–1918), Revue d'histoire diplomatique (April-June 1960)*, cited in Sergiou I. Minerbi: *The Vatican and Zionism, Conflict in the Holy Land 1895-1925*, Oxford 1990, p.117.
366 Pawel: *The Labyrinth of Exile*, New York, 1989, p.518.

display of traditional dances put on by the Colony's Swedish girls. The party continued for several hours, and was broken up suddenly by the shattering noise of an artillery shell which shook the windows. Allenby and his staff left immediately. The cannon fire continued for two hours, while everyone at the Colony speculated whether the Turks were making a counter-attack to the north of Jerusalem. But from the roof terrace it became clear that the British were holding Mount Scopus and that the thundering explosions were coming from the Mount of Olives. Two Allied artillery batteries had been placed there and were now firing towards Jericho.

The following morning, word arrived from General Shea's staff that the Colony's photographic team would be permitted to take pictures of the battlefield. Larsson and Lind headed north along the Nablus Road to the village of Shu'fat. They were prevented from continuing any further, but from where they stood they could see clearly the medical corps bearing the bodies of Turkish soldiers on stretchers. The two men had never seen so many dead. Some still had German hand grenades grasped tightly in their hands. The British battalions with responsibility for burying the dead said they had counted more than 500, all members of the elite Turkish forces. The American Colony was now the unofficial photography agency of the British army, following its advance across Palestine.

Some weeks later, Larsson met General Shea again, and was asked whether he had destroyed his pictures of the capitulation of Jerusalem. When Larsson replied he had not, Shea insisted that the instruction came as a military order, one that had to be followed or there would be serious consequences. But the photographer had no intention of destroying the pictures. It was only when a British major arrived in his darkroom that he burnt both copies and negatives. The only picture from the series that Larsson was allowed to keep showed the two sergeants who had first accosted them at the crossroads outside Lifta, along with the mayor and his entourage, in front of the white flag. This was apparently acceptable, since it did not show any officers receiving the surrender. It was even sent to London in the military mail. Larsson did not say, however, that copies of the complete series of photographs had already been given to the two British sergeants and that, sooner or later, they would become available to the public. When Brigadier Watson returned to Jerusalem, he was furious that the pictures had been destroyed. "As soon as I am back in London, I will take up the matter," he said. However, he was pleased that the white flag had been protected. He later presented it to Lady Allenby, who subsequently donated it to the Imperial War Museum.

Chapter 30

The New Pontius Pilate

A few days after the British occupied Jerusalem, Anna's son-in-law, John D Whiting, was asked by the British consul to join British intelligence, assuming the rank of captain. Whiting was familiar with the area where the Turks now had their front lines, to the north and east of the city. He also owned detailed maps made during the 1870s by Lord Kitchener. As an American citizen, Whiting was not obliged to wear a uniform or swear allegiance to the king. His task as deputy chief of intelligence was to update maps of the eastern front to include information that was relevant to the military, stipulating quantities of water that would be available from certain springs or wells, assessing the load-bearing capacity of roads and bridges, and determining whether any of them had been blown up during the Turkish retreat.[367]

At the beginning of 1918, around the same time that Whiting left the hospital, its remaining inmates were dispatched to Egypt. At last, the American Colony could relinquish responsibility for the city's hospitals. Everyone thought they could relax now, but it did not take long before they received a request to organize welfare services in the city. Once again, Anna agreed to the request, and Jerusalem was divided into zones, similar to the way in which Chicago had been divided up following the Great Fire 47 years earlier.

Now that Anna was well into her 70s principal responsibility for the work fell to Bertha. She organized a workforce of 14 volunteers from the Colony. She also found Muslim, Christian and Jewish women to record the needs of the inhabitants of the city's various sectors. The women went from house to house interviewing the inhabitants and assessing their

367 Note written by John D Whiting, American Colony Collection, Jerusalem.

levels of need. Bertha had inherited her mother's talent for organization and had gained experience of working with the military from the war years, when she had been liaising regularly with German and Turkish officers. Now, though, she worked mostly with Englishmen and Scots. In her free time, Bertha and her husband played tennis with one of the British generals.

One day when Bertha and Frederick were on their way home from the Old City, a figure in Arab clothing emerged from Fast's Hotel, which, since the Fast family had left, had been run by Arabs. Frederick motioned to Bertha and said: "Do you see that Bedouin?"[368]

"Yes. Why?"

"He is not a Bedouin at all but an Englishman who has been among the Sharifian troops."

Bertha was surprised. She had never seen a European man wearing Arab clothing before. This unfamiliar sight had also made an impact on the American war correspondent, Lowell Thomas, who had previously noticed the distinctive northern European figure, with an Arab cloak over his shoulders. Thomas was familiar with the desert Arabs, whose "skin [was] burned by the sun to the colour of lava". But he was intrigued by this man who looked "like a Scandinavian with veins filled with Viking blood and the cold of the fjords", and believed he must have a good story to tell. The man who had aroused such interest was T E Lawrence, already a living legend in both England and the Arab world. Lawrence had managed successfully to bind the warriors of the fractious Bedouin tribes into a powerful guerrilla force, united against their common enemy: the Turks. It was Thomas who first gave Lawrence the name by which he was subsequently known: Lawrence of Arabia.

In his military uniform, Lawrence was invisible. Bertha had not noticed him in Allenby's entourage one month earlier. It had been only chance that had brought Lawrence to Jerusalem at the time the Turks surrendered. He had flown from Aqaba a few days before to report to Allenby on his activities in Syria. The two men had been sitting together in the general's tent, at his headquarters near Ramleh, when news arrived that the Turks had left Jerusalem without a fight.

Less than three weeks earlier, Lawrence had been captured as he gathered intelligence on an airfield between Damascus and Amman, He had been dressed as a Circassian, and when his captors brought him to

---

368 Spafford Vester: *Our Jerusalem*, 2nd edition, p.291, Bertha Spafford Vester: *Jerusalem, My Home*, National Geographic, Vol. 126, No. 6, December 1964, p.839.

Turkish headquarters in Deraa, they mistook him for a deserter. There has been much speculation about what exactly happened to Lawrence while he was in Turkish custody and many myths have subsequently grown up around him. Several accounts claim that his captors, believing him to have betrayed his own, whipped and raped him.[369] The following night, he managed to escape and was later flown to Allenby's headquarters.

After the arrival of the British, the American Colony kept what amounted to an open house. Guests came and went at all hours. When Lawrence arrived to pay a social call on the Colony, Bertha was thrilled to meet the man about whom she had heard so much. Bertha was an attractive and charming woman who was used to being noticed and admired. She began to talk to her guest about the Bedouin tribe of Adwan. But as soon as she mentioned the word 'Bedouin', Lawrence turned his back on her. Bertha was deeply offended and said nothing more. As soon as her mother arrived, she left the room. Lawrence enjoyed more success in his relationship with the boys of the Colony, agreeing to take up the unpopular position of goalie during their games of football.[370]

Lawrence of Arabia was close friends with the newly appointed military governor in Jerusalem, Ronald Storrs, and was one of just a handful of people who had known the governor before his appointment. Those who met Storrs for the first time in Jerusalem and recorded their impressions found him to be an intelligent, calculating, aloof, almost ascetic individual. Storrs was also an impressive linguist, who spoke French, Greek, Arabic and even some Hebrew. He appreciated classical music and was interested in architecture. The first military governor of Jerusalem in modern times was also a man with a sense of humour, who enjoyed introducing himself as "the successor to Pontius Pilate". But to Anna's six grandchildren, he remained first and foremost 'Uncle Ronald', who would sit for hours at a time on the floor, reading aloud from *Alice in Wonderland* and from other children's classics.[371]

Three days after Storrs assumed responsibility for the Holy City, he invited its Jewish, Christian, and Muslim leaders to a reception. The Zionists were ecstatic, believing that the British wanted to work towards a Jewish homeland in Palestine. Britain was one of the world's great

369 Flora Armitage: *The Desert and the Stars, A Biography of Lawrence of Arabia*, New York 1955, p.119.
370 Interview: Valentine Vester, Jerusalem, May 11, 2006, Spafford Vester: *Our Jerusalem*, 2nd edition, p.90.
371 Spafford Vester: Unpublished draft of *Our Jerusalem*, chapter 35, p.13. American Colony Collection, Jerusalem.

powers and they considered the letter from Foreign Secretary Balfour to Lord Rothschild (the 'Balfour Declaration') to be tantamount to a binding political agreement. Balfour's letter had referred only to a Jewish homeland in Palestine, not a state, but the Zionists concluded that the one was not possible without the other. Later, Lloyd George confirmed their assumptions when he said: "We meant a Jewish state." [372]

The Christian and Muslim leaders in Jerusalem could not have known what the implications of the letter would be, although they did know that Balfour had specified that the rights of "the existing non-Jewish population groups in Palestine" should be safeguarded. The Palestinians found it strange that the existing population of the country, both Christian and Muslim, had not been referred to in the letter by name. It seemed to be a way of denying their identity. It also seemed paradoxical that Balfour – the man who had put a halt to Jewish immigration to Britain 12 years earlier – was now supporting mass migration to Palestine.

In reality, Balfour's attitude toward the Jews was ambivalent. He thought that Jews were Jews and the British were British, and that it was best if the two remained separate. Generally speaking, he was suspicious of Jews who tried to integrate into British culture and society. But although he was anti-semitic in the context of his own country, he was quite prepared to support Jewish interests elsewhere in the world.[373]

Allenby had prohibited the publication of Balfour's infamous letter to Rothschild about a Jewish homeland. He did not want it to provoke public disturbances. Even so, anyone living in Jerusalem with an interest in politics was well aware of the Jewish triumph, the biggest feather in the cap of Zionist diplomacy to date.[374]

After her initial encounter with the legendary Lawrence of Arabia, Bertha was disinclined to be friendly towards him. She met him again several weeks later at a dinner party hosted by Ronald Storrs. The governor, unaware of their previous uncomfortable meeting, placed them next to each other at table. The place setting gave Bertha her opportunity for revenge. Turning her back on Lawrence, she addressed only the guest on her other side. Finally, as Bertha prepared to leave the table, along with the other ladies, Lawrence was at last able to make eye contact. As he did

372 Doreen Ingrams: *Palestine Papers 1917–1922, Seeds of Conflict*, New York 1973, p.146.
373 Blanche Dudgale: *Arthur James Balfour, Vol. 2*, London 1936, p.216, Connor Cruise O'Brien: *The Siege, The Saga of Israel and Zionism*, New York 1986, p.29.
374 J. M. N Jeffries: *Palestine, The Reality*, London 1939, pp.18–219, cited in John Marlowe: *The Seat of the Pilate, An Account of the Palestine Mandate*, London 1959, p.27.

so, he said with one of his most charming smiles: "We're quits."[375]

A little later, when the gentlemen rejoined the ladies in the large sitting room, Lawrence approached the window where Bertha was sitting. He was quite prepared now to talk about their common Bedouin friends. For her part, Bertha wanted to learn more about the war with the Turks. She knew that things had gone wrong for Lawrence and his fellow fighters when they had attempted to blow up a bridge in enemy territory several weeks previously.

Lawrence, who was in good humour, spoke willingly about the steep, narrow pass near the Yarmouk River where the Palestine railway ascended toward Damascus. The mountainous terrain had made construction of the railway technically very difficult, and the German engineers involved had been forced to run the line alongside the winding riverbed at the bottom of the valley. To make the line as straight as possible a series of bridges had been erected spanning the river.

Lawrence had planned to blow up one of these bridges. If successful, the sabotage would isolate the Turkish army from its headquarters in Damascus, for several weeks. As he spoke, Bertha discovered that, despite his shy nature, Lawrence was a skilled storyteller, who overcame his natural reserve and became lively and animated as he spoke. Bertha was able to picture for herself many of the places he described, having visited some of them before the war: "It was a dark night when we came onto an old pilgrim road with its deep wagon ruts. We followed the road and suddenly there were shots. It was an Arab goatherder who was shooting. He thought we were robbers and fled screaming as he shot haphazardly. Our nerves were on edge since we were far into enemy territory..."[376]

Bertha noticed that Lawrence described his exciting life and achievements in a natural way. He spoke as if it were nothing to lead a raid, or blow up Turkish bridges. She was impressed. Later the two saw each other often, but the shortsighted Lawrence remained shy with strangers and avoided large parties.[377]

The mayor of Jerusalem, Hussein Husseini, did not live long. Just a few weeks after handing over the Turkish letter of capitulation he contracted double pneumonia. Before he died, the mayor had sent for Bertha, but by the time she arrived it was too late. She later learnt that he had wanted to ensure that his wife and six children would be financially

---

375 Spafford Vester: *Our Jerusalem*, 2nd edition, p.290.
376 T E. Lawrence: *Visdommens syv søyler*, (The Seven Pillars of Wisdom) Oslo 1970, pp.347, 377.
377Spafford Vester: Unpublished manuscript, chapter 35, pp.6-7, American Colony Collection, Spafford Vester: *Our Jerusalem*, New York, 1950, p.271.

secure. Although he belonged to a rich and powerful family, Husseini had no great wealth himself. The mayor of Jerusalem was honoured with a military funeral. T E Lawrence attended, dressed in his Arab clothing, complete with curved sabre. Governor Storrs was also there. It now fell to him to appoint a successor to Hussein Husseini. [378]

John D Whiting's work with British intelligence, updating maps of the area east of the city towards the Jordan River, paid well. Whiting, who spoke several Arab dialects, was also invaluable as a translator, since the classical Arabic, taught by British intelligence in Cairo, was of little use when dealing with the Bedouin.

One day, Whiting noticed that a group of sheikhs from the Moab Mountains, who had come down to Jerusalem to meet Allenby, were particularly nervous. The Arabs did not know what the general looked like, and were concerned that they might make a mistake when they were presented to the officer corps. Whiting promised that he would point the general out for them. When they saw Allenby approaching at the head of his staff, the sheikhs were relieved. His presence and stature were they felt appropriate for a general, and they cried out: "*Wallah, general inglezi jaddaa*" [By God, the English general is an impressive man"]. After much discussion and the offer of generous rates of pay, the sheikhs were once again ready to help the British against the Turks.[379]

The first delegation of prominent British Zionists came to Palestine in March 1918. Its objective was the establishment of a liaison mechanism between the expanding Jewish population in the country and the British military administration. The head of the delegation was the Polish chemical engineer, Chaim Weizmann. Four years before the outbreak of World War One, Weizmann had successfully pioneered a process for the production of chemical substances through bacterial fermentation. His technique proved invaluable in the production of acetone, vital for the manufacture of cordite explosives. Some believed that Balfour's promise of a Jewish homeland in Palestine was a way for the British government to express its gratitude for his work.[380] Weizmann had also managed to

---

378 Anna Spafford ensured that the mayor's widow received immediate financial support, and later the Husseini family's properties were mortgaged through Barclay's Bank. When they were put up for sale, they became the subject of a bidding war between the Mufti of Jerusalem and the Zionist organization and eventually sold for a great sum. As a result, the widow had enough money to educate her four sons at the American University of Beirut. Spafford Vester: *Our Jerusalem*, 2nd edition, p.282.

379 Spafford Vester: Unpublished draft of *Our Jerusalem*, chapter 35, pp.20–26, American Colony Collection, Jerusalem.

380 Chaim Weizmann's contribution to the British war machine was the discovery of a method of

convince the British that a Zionist Palestine would be an asset for the British Empire.

Before his departure for Palestine, Weizmann's friends cautioned him that in negotiations with Arabs he must never confront an issue directly. He took their words to heart and said later that engaging the Palestinians in dialogue was like chasing a mirage in the desert.[381] Weizmann's delegation went first to Tel Aviv, the biggest Zionist colony. It comprised a few hundred houses on the coast, less than a mile north of Jaffa. Tel Aviv (Hill of the Spring) was given the biblical name used in the Hebrew translation of Herzl's novel, *Altneuland* (Old New Land), in which he depicted the future Jewish state as a socialist utopia.[382]

The British military field headquarters were still, at this stage, in Ramleh, and the following day Weizmann was invited to breakfast. Squeezed in between two generals, the honoured guest had to listen as they relived recent battles. Weizmann felt the atmosphere was tense, but he liked General Allenby, and in a letter to his wife he wrote: "There is no doubt that he [the general] expressed goodwill in trying to understand us and help us."[383] In Jerusalem, the Zionists paid a courtesy visit to the office of the military governor. There, they were introduced to the mufti of Jerusalem, Kamel Husseini, and his cousin, the city's new mayor, Moussa Kazim Husseini.[384]

But Weizmann's main concern during his weeks in the Holy City was to try to coax or threaten the city's Zionist and Orthodox Jewish communities to unite. But he failed to repair the rift between them. The Orthodox were strongly opposed to the concept of a separate Jewish state being established before the return of the Messiah, while the Zionists' whole raison d'être was to do everything in their power to bring about

producing large quantities of acetone through bacterial fermentation. Acetone, one of the most important components of TNT, was produced almost exclusively in Germany at the time. Phillip Knightley & Colin Simpson: *Lawrence of Arabia, Mannen og Myten* (The Man and the Myth), Oslo 1970, p.128.

381 Chaim Weizmann: *Et liv for Israel* (A Life for Israel), Oslo 1949, pp.141–145.

382 In fact, Herzl envisioned the northern town of Haifa as being the capital of the new Jewish state in Palestine. When he wrote his novel *Altneuland* in 1902, Tel Aviv was yet to be established.

383 Letter from Chaim Weizmann to his wife Vera, April 6, 1918, cited in: David Tutaev: *The Impossible Takes Longer: The Memoirs of Vera Weizmann:* Harper & Row, New York 1967, p.85.

384 Jerusalem's mayor was Muslim, but the British believed Moussa Kazim Husseini should represent all religions. The military governor, Storrs, therefore insisted that Husseini refrained from participating in demonstrations against Zionism. The mayor had earlier been an officer in the Turkish army in Yemen, and had been selected for the office because he happened to be in Jerusalem when his brother, Hussein Husseini caught pneumonia and died. Ronald Storrs: *Orientation*, Readers Union. Ltd., London 1939, p.345.

the creation of such a state as quickly as possible. "We do not care about religion or the holy places," they argued, "we want the country." [385]

Throughout the period of the British administration of Jerusalem, the American Colony was to be the focus of a great deal of social activity. When Mother Anna and Bertha invited a guest for dinner, he seldom refused. The British officers and civilian administrators were unaccompanied by their families, but their wives were provided with vivid descriptions of life in the city through letters.

"Life here is really amazingly interesting and picturesque. You've no idea of all the wonderful things that are going on," Storrs' municipal adviser, Charles R Ashbee, wrote to his wife. Ashbee was an architect by profession who was also a trained goldsmith. He continued:[386]

In the morning yesterday I was picking flowers in the Garden of Gethsemane after reading St Luke. In the afternoon, it being the Fourth of July, I was a guest of the American Colony, among generals, bishops and the 'best society' in Jerusalem. In the evening there was an official banquet... the governor in his chair, all the Arab chiefs and imams, and Greek Archimandrites in black flower-pot hats, and a Muslim aristocracy which goes back to the Prophet... I couldn't understand the speeches, but the music and the rhythms are more lovely than anything you could imagine.

Ashbee was the secretary of the so-called Pro-Jerusalem Committee – a small and exclusive group that aimed to protect the antiquities and heritage of Jerusalem. Ronald Storrs recruited Anna's adopted son, Jacob, to be a member. Along with the patriarchs, chief rabbis, leaders of the Muslim Higher Committee, and a representative of Palestine's Zionists, Eliezer Ben-Yehuda, Jacob Spafford would ensure that Jerusalem became even more beautiful.

385 Estelle Blyth: *When we lived in Jerusalem*, London 1926, p.335.
386 Charles R. Ashbee: *A Palestine Notebook, 1918–1923*, Garden City 1923, p.7.

Chapter 31

Revolt against the Jews

At the end of September 1918, General Allenby began a new offensive against the Turks and their German allies, succeeding in driving them out of Galilee in the course of a week. More than 4,000 Turkish troops were killed, and 30,000 taken prisoner. Syria also fell to the Allies – the Turks left their garrisons in Damascus on September 30 – and the following day Feisal's supporters raised the Arab flag in the city. Later, Sharif Hussein – the Protector of Mecca – was proclaimed the new King of Arabia.

The Arabs still believed that victory over Turkey would bring them independence; Sharif Hussein was nevertheless well aware of the secret agreement reached between Britain and France to divide up the Middle East between them, following the collapse of the Ottoman Empire. Britain insisted it was serious about its promise to the Arabs, renewing its pledges on November 7. But the British government had no intention of honouring this promise any more than the original one.

Meanwhile, in Istanbul, the end was near for the government of the three pashas: Djemal, Enver and Talaat. Under their rule, Turkey had endured four years of brutal war at the cost of 427,000 lives. Few Turks were prepared to tolerate their regime any longer. Thus, on the evening of November 2, the leaders of the once glorious Committee of Union and Progress met at the house of Enver's adjutant in Istanbul and prepared to flee to Germany. During the night, they were picked up by a German torpedo boat and taken to exile in Berlin.[387]

At 3pm on November 11, the news reached a rain-soaked Jerusalem that the war was over. Ronald Storrs was the first to hear, and immediately

---

387 Djemal Pasha was assassinated in the Georgian capital Tbilisi in 1922, apparently by an Armenian.

telephoned the military units stationed in the city with the good news. He then went to notify the various patriarchs, the mufti, and the American Colony. Everyone was informed that Germany had accepted a ceasefire at 6am that morning, and that Kaiser Wilhelm II and his family had fled to the Netherlands.[388]

The senior British officers based at the Augusta Victoria complex went to the chapel and sang three verses of 'God Save the King' in celebration, after which they toasted victory with large quantities of champagne. The Royal Flying Corps shot flares into the grey sky. All civilians whom Storrs encountered that day were overjoyed to hear the war was finally over. Most of the troops were as well, although some wondered what would become of them now.

However, some Palestinians believed that Germany and Austria-Hungary had been brought to their knees simply because of their initial refusal to countenance a separate Jewish homeland. It was felt that Imperial Russia had fallen for the same reason. The Palestinians concluded the British would therefore be extremely reluctant to deny the Jews their dream of Zion. [389]

The Balfour Declaration referred to a Jewish 'national homeland'. But Lloyd George had already made it clear that what this meant in practice was a Jewish state. Yet it still suited the British to maintain the ambiguity of the original phrasing. The key factor was timing. Only when conditions were favourable could the ultimate goal be talked about openly.

There were several reasons for this. The Zionist movement represented only a small minority of the Jewish people. Many Jews feared that the demand for a Jewish state could have negative consequences for Jews outside Palestine, and the Zionists, who were financially dependent on international Jewish support, could not ignore this concern.

Some Arabs thought that fate would intervene in any attempts to establish a new Jewish homeland in Palestine, believing that the little coastal town of Tel Aviv was 'built on sand' in more ways than one. In the past, Romans, Greeks and others had all attempted to colonize the region. But after tolerating them for a while, the desert always rose up in protest and pushed them back. No immigrant civilization had ever survived on the edge of the desert, and Zionism would be no exception.[390]

388 Storrs: *Orientations*, London 1939, p.333.
389 Martin Gilbert: *Jerusalem in the Twentieth Century*, Pimlico, London 1996, p.75.
390 Hector Bolitho: *The Angry Neighbours, A Diary of Palestine and Transjordan*, London 1957, pp.56-59.

But such political concerns still had relatively little impact on daily life in the city. Indeed, tourists were now starting to return to Jerusalem, keeping the American Colony busier than ever before. During the holiday season, the residents moved out of their rooms so that they could be rented as accommodation for visitors. They organized day trips to the Dead Sea, Jericho and Jordan while the souvenir shop in the Grand New Hotel also thrived. The British soldiers were keen on anything that had 'Jerusalem' written on it, snapping up photographs, rugs, jewellery and antiques to take home with them as souvenirs.

Swedish tourists staying at the house in Sheikh Jarrah were made especially welcome by their compatriots there, although Anna cautioned the Swedish members of her congregation not to show favouritism towards their countrymen. "This is what leads to war," she said time and again. When Swedish Colony members were asked if they were ever homesick for their relatives and friends, they always replied: "No, never. We are happy here." In fact, some did have other thoughts – but they were careful not to voice them.[391]

Olof Henrik Larsson, by contrast, who still lived in isolation, was not afraid to say he thought the sect had become too worldly. The young were allowed to dance, and alcohol was served in the salon, which Larsson felt should be kept for prayer meetings. But Anna refused to ban alcohol, telling him that if he felt unhappy attending meetings in the salon, he was free to absent himself.

Olof Henrik's wife, Mathilda, and his daughter, Edith, sympathised with his views, but said nothing. Anna had several times warned Mathilda about weakness of the flesh: "You must not be blinded by physical love for your husband," she said. Mathilda suffered in silence, furious at Anna's treatment of Olof Henrik, but at the same time believing that if she stayed away from the meetings it would only make matters worse for him. Thus the ageing pastor remained in his room while his wife went to morning prayers. He sang his favourite hymns each day and read from the Bible's ending his private service with a fiery prayer.

At the morning meetings, Anna set the order of the day. One constantly recurring subject was the importance of loving one's neighbour. Anna would ask Jacob to read from St Luke's Gospel: "If someone comes to me, he must put this before father or mother, wife or child, brother or sister, yes even before his own life. Otherwise he cannot be my disciple." Anna had not lost the ability to control her flock.

391 Larsson: *Dala Folk in the Holy Land*, Stockholm 1957, p.119.

One morning in April in 1919, when Mathilda brought her husband's breakfast up to his room, he appeared to be bent over in prayer, with his head resting on the table. In fact he was unconscious. He had suffered a stroke. Mathilda put down the breakfast tray and ran for help. A doctor was called, but he could do nothing and Olof Henrik died without regaining consciousness. On the table, at which he had been sitting, his Bible lay open at a chapter in Letters to the Corinthians. The old pastor had underlined one particular sentence, which read: "Love is patient and mild." And the psalm he had chosen for the day was: "To follow You through pain and sorrow, follow You wherever You lead me, from this moment on, O Saviour, I leave everything and follow You."[392] Mathilda and Edith were beside themselves with sorrow. Anna tried to comfort them in her own way: "When my husband died, I danced to show my joy at God's will," she said. "Death shortened his yearning for Jesus and Heaven."

For the two grieving women, the words had meaning. Both believed absolutely that Anna received God's words, and none of the colonists dared allow themselves be influenced by thoughts and feelings that ran counter to the community's creed. They believed that the sect's religion was unique and that they were all part of a plan, which would lead the world back to God. Three months earlier, Edith had lost her nine-month-old son, and Anna had reacted in a similar vein: "Do not grieve, Edith, but be joyful at God's will," she had said. She refused to deviate one inch from the religious course she had chosen after the catastrophe in the Atlantic 46 years earlier.

In November 1919, the British administration in Palestine decided to mark the anniversary of the surrender of Jerusalem with a review of troops and a public holiday. Major General Shea came to inspect the forces as the guest of Major General Louis Bols, who had succeeded General Watson as chief administrator of Palestine. Shea arrived on horseback, a monocle in his eye. William Denison McCrackan, the American editor of the newly established *Jerusalem News*, the city's first daily English language newspaper, was there to report on the event. He described Shea as "the typical smart British officer, a general favourite whose bonhomie was proverbial in army circles and who, when we got to know him, delighted in any new Americanisms with which we were able to furnish him."

Ronald Storrs joined the generals at the Russian Compound, and while the three men stood chatting together, awaiting the start of the inspection, the American journalist's thoughts turned to the historic

392 Ibid. pp.116–117.

significance of Jerusalem. It was not an ordinary city, but "the centre of the world's ecclesiasticisms, for good or for ill".[393]

Foreign and local observers were aware that conflict was brewing between the Jews and the Arabs, both Muslims and Christians. One point of contention surrounded the use of flags. The Jewish national flag was often raised in place of the official British Palestine one – a Union Flag with the word 'Palestine' in a circle in one corner. The Jewish flag was the same as that of modern-day Israel, with two blue horizontal parallel stripes and two triangles put together to form a star – the seal of Solomon. The Palestinians had their own flag that they wanted to fly – consisting of three horizontal parallel bars in red, white and green, a symbol of the Arab unity that would surely follow now that Sharif Hussein had freed Mecca from Turkish occupation. But use of this was forbidden. The Arabs did not see why this should be so when the Zionists were allowed to raise their flag. In fact, the flag controversy was merely a pretext for the much deeper issue of Zionist plans to make Palestine into a Jewish homeland, knowledge of which had now filtered down to the general Arab public. Many Palestinian Arabs vowed to resist this, by force if necessary.

One of the Zionist leaders who anticipated conflict was a German Jew, George Landauer. He said that unless the Jewish colonists in Palestine sought an immediate deal with the Palestinians there would be an all-out war, which, he feared, the Jews would lose. Other Zionists, though, had little faith in the Arabs' fighting abilities and were unconvinced. One of the most militant Zionists, Vladimir Jabotinsky, cited Britain's military successes overseas as an example to be followed. He asked ironically when, during the colonization of America or Australia, anyone had bothered to beg the natives for permission.[394]

Although the majority of Zionist leaders disregarded Landauer's warnings, the issue still provoked debate. During a conference in Paris on the future of Palestine, the American Secretary of State, Robert Lansing, asked what Chaim Weizmann meant by 'a Jewish national homeland'. Weizmann was quick to answer: "I think Palestine should become as Jewish as England is English, France is French, and America is American."[395] When the debate was over, Lord Balfour sent his secretary over to congratulate Weizmann, who responded warmly. But when one of his Jewish opponents, Professor Sylvian Levi, came with his outstretched

393 W. D. McCrackan: *The New Palestine*, The Page Company, Boston, 1922, p.82.
394 Amos Elon: *The Israelis, Fathers and Sons*, London 1972, p.227.
395 Tutaev: *The Impossible Takes Longer: The Memoirs of Vera Weizmann*, 1967, p.95.

hand to do the same, Weizmann refused to accept his congratulations, so bitter had the strife between the Zionists and their Jewish critics become.

In Jerusalem, John D Whiting decided to write a letter to the Atlas Shoe Company of Maine. Western-style shoes had always been hard to find in Palestine. The American Colony had once imported them, but since the outbreak of the war, it had not been able to receive goods from the United States. Whiting recounted in his letter how, during the war, the Colony had resorted to making its own shoes from the tanned hides of its slaughtered cattle. "During the recent fighting, our small tannery was in 'no man's land' for about three months," Whiting wrote. "The British shelled it as it was near a Turkish gun position, and the Turks robbed us of some 10 camel loads of finished leather. Turkish and German troops rifled the rest of the half-tanned raw hides to make sandals out of. In all we lost over 1,500 hides, but the blessing of having the British here overpays not only for this, but all losses and past troubles and anxieties. We trust the Peace Conference will decide that Britain will have complete control over this country; it will be the only suitable form of government."[396]

Some months later, at the beginning of 1920, the *Reuters* news bureau hired John Whiting as its correspondent in Jerusalem. He sent his reports to the bureau's Middle East office in Cairo. In March, just after Sharif Hussein's son, Feisal, was proclaimed king of Syria, Whiting covered a big anti-Zionist demonstration in Jerusalem. After he had filed his third despatch, *Reuters* received complaints from the Zionists. They alleged that Whiting's reporting was "not neutral". The bureau chief in Cairo sent a letter immediately to his correspondent: "You have to understand that you must use much discretion when you deal with events in Palestine." [397]

But there were no reporting restrictions when, that same winter, Jerusalem was enveloped by a huge snowstorm, the heaviest within living memory. The blizzard of 1920 was, for Jerusalem, what the blizzard of 1880 was for New York. On February 9, temperatures plummeted and frozen rain began to fall. During the evening, cold winds from Lebanon and Mount Hermon to the north turned the driving rain into snow. The snowfall continued for the whole night, covering the landscape. The weight of the snow in the trees caused many branches to snap. Indeed, whole trees were bent and broken, and roofs crushed. Two of Jerusalem's three cinemas collapsed, the sole remaining one adding to its line-up a

396 Valestine Vester: *American Colony History*, unpublished manuscript, Jerusalem 2006, pp.25–26, American Colony Collection.
397 Letter from *Reuters Limited*, Cairo, to John Whiting, American Colony, dated March 24, 1920. Folder: 1920, American Colony Collection, Jerusalem.

Main building viewed from the outer garden

locally-shot film entitled 'Jerusalem under the Snow'.[398]

By the following spring, the Zionists had become genuinely afraid of Arab violence, and began training themselves in the use of weapons. On Sundays, members of their 'Defence Committee' practiced throwing hand grenades on the outskirts of the city. Both the British authorities and Palestinian Arabs witnessed this, but took no action.[399]

There had not, thus far, been any serious clashes between the Palestinians and the Jews, but some feared that the annual Easter celebrations could develop into trouble, because that year, the Holy Days of all three religions coincided. The Jewish Passover and the Muslim Nebi Moussa festivities (a religious holiday in memory of the Prophet Moses) would both be celebrated on the same day as Christian Easter.

When the great day arrived, the sun shone from a clear spring sky. Chaim Weizmann, who was still in Palestine, was concerned about

398 McCrackan: *The New Palestine*, Boston, 1922, pp.204–5.
399 Robert Slater: *Rabin of Israel*, London 1977, p.23.

possible violence from the Arabs, but Major General Bols reassured him: "There can be no trouble. The city is stiff with troops."[400]

Weizmann disagreed. "I have some experience of the atmosphere which precedes pogroms," he said. "I'm afraid that troops usually prove useless at the last moment, because the whole paroxysm is liable to be over before they can be rushed to the field of action."

Vladimir Jabotinsky, the head of the Jewish quasi-military organization, Haganah, was also afraid of trouble. The group set up observation posts in the new districts of Jerusalem and sent its men into the Old City. However, the Orthodox Jews there did not welcome them – they had good relations with their Palestinian neighbours and did not want to be part of any defence force. They threatened to expel any armed members of the Haganah if they showed their faces again.[401]

For many Muslims, the Nebi Moussa festivities were one of the high points of the year. They dated from the time when Saladin captured Jerusalem from the Crusaders. According to Muslim tradition, Moses (whom the Muslims regard as a great prophet) had not been buried on the east side of the Jordan River, as the Old Testament claimed, but on the West Bank near Jericho.

Ronald Storrs had the job of marking the start of the religious festival. The army was ready to fire a salute, and a military band was on standby to lead the various processions. But anti-Zionist sentiment in Jerusalem had by now become so intense that at the last moment the mufti asked the British not to become involved.

A short while earlier, Major General Bols had issued an official proclamation stating that the British government would honour the Balfour Declaration. This provoked a swift Arab protest. Some 1,500 Palestinians took to the streets to demonstrate their opposition to the decision. During a similar protest a few days later, anti-Jewish slogans were shouted.[402] After this, Bols forbade all public demonstrations. But banning the Nebi Moussa festivities was out of the question. In fact, the British considered it an insult that the mufti did not want a British military band to lead the procession: this was the third such festival to have been held under the British administration, and the military governor insisted that the bandsmen should lead the way. Reluctantly, the mufti eventually agreed. He was reassured by being told that the

400 Chaim Weizmann: *Trial and Error*, Hamish Hamilton, London, 1949, p.318.
401 Letter from Vladimir Jabotinsky to *The Times*, May 15, 1921.
402 Gilbert: *Jerusalem in the Twentieth Century*, London 1996, p.82.

procession would be monitored by British military police, even though under normal circumstances the Nebi Moussa holiday was normally a peaceful occasion, with participants enjoying a week of festivities by the Dead Sea.

Storrs had placed all police units in Jerusalem under the command of a young lieutenant. Muslim pilgrims from outside the city were not expected to arrive at the Jaffa Gate before noon, and the military governor had accompanied his parents to an Easter service at St George's Cathedral. He had asked one of his staff officers to tell him when the Muslim procession was within half an hour of Jerusalem. But the staff officer forgot, and when Storrs and his family were en route to the governor's office after the service, his Palestinian security guard approached him and whispered in Arabic: "There have been clashes at the Jaffa Gate, and one man has been fatally wounded."

The disturbances began after the crowds from Hebron had arrived in Jerusalem. Outside the city wall, the Mayor Moussa Kazim Husseini, along with other prominent Muslims, addressed them from a balcony. The speeches were more political than religious, and after a while an anti-Zionist fervour took hold of the crowd. According to British intelligence reports, provocateurs also helped inflame emotions.[403]

The procession was behind schedule, and the British officer in charge decided to re-route it in order to make up time. Normally it followed the city wall to the Damascus Gate and then passed through the Muslim quarter down to the Noble Sanctuary. But this time the crowds from Hebron were directed towards the Jaffa Gate and then down through the Jewish quarter.

All of a sudden, someone in the crowd shouted out: "*Idhbah el-Yehud!*" ("Massacre the Jews!"), and "*el-Yehud klab!*" ("The Jews are dogs!"). The peaceful crowd turned into an angry mob, hurling stones and yelling abuse at all things Jewish. Shops were looted, and those Jews who happened to be out on the streets were attacked. The British military police were guarding only the city walls and were not stationed inside. The senior officer in charge had gone to Jericho, and only the young British lieutenant and his Arab police contingent were in the Old City when the disturbances began. Inexperienced and frightened, the lieutenant knew that his men could not be counted on either to stop the riot or protect the Jews.

---

403 Palin Commission Report: Report of the Court of Inquiry by order of H E The High Commissioner and Commander-In-Chief on the 12th day of April 1920, pp.62–65. Cited in A W Kayyali: *Palestine A Modern History*, London, p.76.

The crowd surged into the mixed residential areas where Jews lived peaceably with Arabs, beating and knifing any Jews they could find. Some Jews who had guns were able to open fire on the mob, allowing them time to escape. When Vladimir Jabotinsky tried to send his forces back into the Old City from the new district of Jerusalem to help the Jewish community, British troops blocked the entrances. No one was allowed in. Eventually, the British got the situation under control and managed to push the mob into the vicinity of the al-Aqsa Mosque, but by then six Jews had been killed, 211 injured and two Jewish women raped. Haganah had also attacked and killed four Arabs and wounded 21.

A few days later, Storrs went to the de facto head of the Palestine Zionist Commission, Menachem Ussishkin, to express his sorrow "for the catastrophe which hit us".[404]

"What catastrophe?" asked Ussishkin.

"I am referring to the unfortunate occurrences which took place here in the course of the past days," replied Storrs.

"Is Your Honour referring to the pogrom?"

Storrs became agitated: "There was no pogrom. It is impossible to call these disturbances a pogrom."

"Colonel, you are an expert in administrative matters and I am an expert in the laws of pogroms," responded Ussishkin. "I can assure you that there was no difference between the Jerusalem pogrom, and the Kishinev pogrom that took place several years ago. Those who organized the local pogrom showed no originality; they followed step by step in the footsteps of those who carried out the Russian pogroms."

But the massacre of men, women and children in the Moldavian capital of Kishinev in 1903 could not be compared with the clashes in Jerusalem. In Kishinev, 49 Jews had been killed, 500 were wounded, and the entire Jewish section of the city was destroyed.[405] Ussishkin, who was very emotional, ignored Storrs' objection to his choice of words, continuing: "Tsar Nicholas did not get involved in the pogroms either, he too oppressed us. Does Your Excellency know what has happened to the tsar? In his place you have Trotsky. Our enemies all over the world and in the Land of Israel will meet the same fate."

The chairman of the Zionist Commission, David Yellin, who was a good friend of Anna Spafford, wrote to the British prime minister, saying: "Wild pogroms, massacres, looting... have not happened since

404 Central Zionist Archives, Jerusalem: L/3/256; April 13, 1920.
405 Cecil Roth (ed.): *The Concise Jewish Encyclopedia*, New York 1989, p.311.

[the] Crusades." He demanded that, henceforth, at least half of Jerusalem's police force should be comprised of Jews. He also insisted on the dismissal of the mayor of Jerusalem, who had "always manifested public anti-Jewish feeling". In addition, Yellin demanded the most severe punishment of "Arab ringleaders, and the closure of the Arab Club and other 'propaganda centres".[406]

In the American Colony, Anna wrote about the civil unrest in letters to friends, among them Mary Miller in Chicago. Anna explained to Mary that in Palestine "a bitter hatred has arisen between those in possession – the Arabs – and those to whom it was promised – the Jews. The Jews claim they are the rightful heirs, and the fight for possession has begun and manifested itself in an attempt to massacre each other." Anna continued: "Where is the unity of the body of Christ in this city? Christians are at enmity with one another, the Catholics hating the Protestants and other Christians such as the Greek Orthodox, etc... The Christian Arabs as well as the Mohammedans hate the Jews and would wipe them off the earth, if they could. Thank God, the British stand between..."[407]

Accounts of the disturbances in Jerusalem spread quickly, and affected some people deeply. One member of the Jewish Legion, a Russian Jew, originally called Nehemia Robichov, had been so furious when the trouble first began that he went to the headquarters of the Jewish Defence Committee and reported for service. Vladimir Jabotinsky thanked him, but declined to accept him. "You cannot protect the Old City. I will not do it, and if you decide to go in yourself, I will resign from the committee." [408]

While the disturbances were at their height, Haganah had tried unsuccessfully to send hit squads into the Old City in defiance of the curfew. Only medical personnel were allowed to enter. Undeterred, Nehemia Robichov and his supporters broke into the Hadassah Hospital and stole hospital cleaners' uniforms, which they used to get past the British guard posts.[409] A 29-year-old Jewish woman, Rosa Cohen, also managed to get past the British sentries dressed as a nurse. She was a

406 FO 371/5117 E 3259, 15 April 1920. D Yellin to the Prime Minister, 12 April 1920, cited in Sahar Huneidi: *A Broken Trust, Herbert Samuel, Zionism and the Palestinians*, IB Tauris, London and New York, 2001, p.33.
407 Letter from Anna Spafford to Mary (Miller) dated April 28, 1920, p.7. Folder: Anna Spafford, American Colony Collection, Jerusalem.
408 Nehemia Rabin quoted in Haganah's Archive, Tzvi Nadav: *Days on Guard and Defense,* (Hebrew), p.238, cited in Uri Milstein: *The Rabin File*, Jerusalem and New York 1999, p.69.
409 Dan Kurzman: *The Life of Yitzhak Rabin*, New York 1998, pp. 49–50. Robert Slater: *Rabin of Israel*, London 1993, p.26.

Russian Jew, not a Zionist but a Marxist, who had been inspired by recent events in Russia and sought to help the proletariat in their struggle, wherever in the world they might be. Inside the Old City she saw Arabs armed with knives and clubs. The dead and wounded lay in the streets. Rosa stopped to help some of the injured. Close by, David Ben-Gurion and another man were carrying a victim on a stretcher.

As Rosa was crossing one of the streets in the Jewish quarter she was spotted by Nehemia, who shouted: "What are you doing here? Why are you not in hiding?" Rosa answered that it was none of his business. The two started to argue loudly in Yiddish and their confrontation became so intense that Rosa tried to grab Nehemia's pistol. At this point a passing British patrol intervened and tried to calm the situation down. The two then continued their separate ways looking for injured people who needed help.

Nehemia found one family of nine who had gone into hiding, and began escorting them to one of the city gates to safety. The Jewish group soon found themselves surrounded by Palestinians and Nehemia took out a grenade to throw at the mob. But before he could release it, a platoon of British soldiers arrived, shooting into the air and the Palestinians ran off.

The violent meeting between Rosa and Nehemia was to have remarkable consequences. Rosa, a passionate Marxist, had no plans to settle down and start a family. But when she bumped into her erstwhile opponent sometime later, she fell in love with him. Not long afterwards they decided to get married, and in the late spring of 1921 she became pregnant. Her husband no longer used his Russian surname of Robichov, having taken a new Hebrew name, Rabin, for the purposes of escaping the attentions of Jewish Legion recruiting officers.

On 1 March, 1922, Rosa's baby was born at the Jewish hospital, the same place where the first Englishman to arrive in Jerusalem in the aftermath of the Turkish defeat had gratefully consumed his longed-for cup of tea. The Rabins' baby was a boy. He was named Yitzha

Chapter 32

"Disgusting"

The mob attack on the Jews of Jerusalem in April 1920 took place only a few days after the League of Nations had formally requested that Britain should assume the mandate to govern Palestine. For the Palestinians, this was a day of mourning; all Arab shops in Jerusalem stayed shut, and people draped black flags over their doors. The same people who had first welcomed the British with open arms now accused them of being duplicitous. Had Lawrence of Arabia not promised the Arabs that they would be treated fairly? And now, their homeland was to be handed over to the Zionists. For their part, the Zionists accused the British authorities of being responsible for the 'massacres' in the Old City. They maintained "there had not been a single pogrom in Palestine during the entire 400-year-long Turkish rule. The Arabs would never have dared to attack the Jews if they had not been sure that the authorities would forgive their actions."[410]

This was unfair. Two Palestinians were convicted of rape and sentenced to 15 years in prison. The British also tried to arrest 25-year-old Amin Husseini, one of the most prominent Palestinian political activists, and a cousin of the mayor; but he fled to Damascus, together with another activist, Aref al-Aref, before he could be apprehended.

Vladimir Jabotinsky was given a 15-year sentence for having organized the Haganah counter attack on the Arab mob, although as a gentleman and former member of the Jewish Legion, he was given the right to surrender himself rather than be arrested forcibly. His trial was held in secret six days later. Even after sentencing, he was afforded privileges not normally granted to prisoners. Ronald Storrs went personally to Jabotinsky's home to collect some clothes for him. The military governor

410 Abraham Revusky: *Jews in Palestine*, New York 1945, p.261.

also let Jabotinsky's wife visit him in a specially equipped cell where they were served dinner, including wine.[411]

Jerusalem's Palestinian mayor, Moussa Kazim Husseini, was removed from office. Storrs had already secured a replacement for him – a man from the Husseini clan's great rivals, the Nashashibis. Ragheb Nashashibi agreed readily to become the new mayor of Jerusalem, mainly because he wanted to avoid an Englishman being appointed – the position of mayor was one of the most important that was still retained by Palestinians, and Ragheb was keen to ensure that this tradition continued. The 40-year-old Ragheb was already prematurely grey-haired when he took over the mayoralty, a position he was to keep for the next 14 years. He smoked 80 cigarettes a day through an amber holder, his suits came from the most expensive tailors in London and Paris, and he had a large collection of walking sticks, many with ivory handles and inlaid with gold, which were carefully chosen to complement his clothes. It was also said that Ragheb never took much money with him when he travelled; hidden in his watch pocket, however, he carried a diamond in a small box.

In July 1920, the British military authority in Palestine was replaced by a civilian regime. Herbert Samuel, a 50-year-old Liberal politician, who had recently lost his seat in parliament, was appointed high commissioner. Eleven years earlier, he had become the first practicing Jew to be made a member of the British government.[412]

Six years previously, on November 9, 1914, Samuel had submitted a draft cabinet memorandum to the prime minister of the day, Herbert Asquith, advocating the establishment of a Jewish state in Palestine under British protection.[413] Samuel was compared by his supporters to Simon Bar Kokhba, the last Jewish leader in Palestine under the Romans. Similarities were also drawn with King Hyrcanus II, the last king of the priestly clan of the Maccabeans; the tribe that in ancient times, had freed the Jews from Syrian domination.[414]

Samuel arrived at Jaffa on 30 June aboard the destroyer *HMS Centaur*, as the Union Flag flew proudly over a landing stage that had been decorated specially for the occasion. He wore his white diplomatic uniform, with full imperial regalia. Ronald Storrs was taken out by boat to escort the new

411 Lenni Brenner: *The Iron Wall, Zionist Revisionism from Jabotinsky to Shamir,* London 1984, pp.60–61.
412 Benjamin Disraeli, the British-born Jew who served twice as prime minister between 1868-1880 had previously converted to Christianity.
413 Wasserstein: *The British in Palestine,* p.74.
414 John Bowle: *Viscount Samuel, A Biography,* Victor Gollancz Ltd, London 1957, p.195.

commissioner ashore. Among the invited guests waiting on the quayside was John D Whiting from the American Colony, who was preparing to report the event for *Reuters*.[415] The editor of *Jerusalem News* was also there. The *Centaur* fired its guns in salute, and a battery of Royal Field Artillery stationed on the beach did the same. A guard of honour presented arms, while aircraft circled overhead like watchful eagles.

Once ashore, Sir Herbert was conducted into a marquee where the mayor of Jaffa delivered a short address in his honour, and then proceeded to an official limousine. The colonel appointed to act as Samuel's ADC "now stepped forward and performed one of those simple little acts which escape many people's attention, but which to the initiated are full of significance," noted one of the journalists there. The colonel produced from his pocket a small Union Flag and fastened it to the front of the car. It marked the first official display of the British flag in Palestine, despite the fact that the country had been under British control for more than two and a half years.

Escorted by four armoured cars, the motorcade swept off towards Lydda, from where the new high commissioner made the last stage of the journey to Jerusalem by special train, escorted by two aircraft. In Jerusalem, the Augusta Victoria Stiftung on the Mount of Olives had been adopted as Britain's new Government House, and the high commissioner was greeted with a 17-gun salute upon his arrival.[416]

General Bols, the departing military governor of Palestine, was waiting on the steps. As a joke, he asked for a receipt from the new high commissioner for having "received one complete Palestine". Samuel joined in the jest and signed, adding the letters 'E & O E' (errors and omissions excepted). Henceforth, the Occupied Enemy Territory Administration, known as OETA, officially ceased to exist.

Only a few women were invited to the inauguration of the new administration on 7 July, Bertha Spafford Vester was one of them. Soon afterwards, General Bols left Jerusalem, and the American Colony gave a farewell dinner in his honour. The American consul, Otis Glazebrook, was among the guests, and warmly complimented the British general's administration of the region over the previous few years. When he emphasized that "the military administration of the country would be missed", Bertha thought: "I could not agree more."[417]

415 McCrackan: *The New Palestine*, Boston, 1922, pp.359–62.
416 Storrs: *Orientations*, London 1939, p.348.
417 Handwritten annotation by Bertha Spafford Vester in a copy of McCrackan: *The New Palestine*, Boston, 1922, p.283, held in the American Colony Collection, Jerusalem.

The day after Samuel's arrival was the Jewish Sabbath, and thousands of people gathered in the streets to see the high commissioner walk from the Mount of Olives to the Hurva Synagogue in the Old City. He chose to dress in the traditional costume of an Orthodox Jew, in a long black coat and broad-brimmed hat.

The British government stood by its pledge to give the world's Jews a national homeland in Palestine. But at the same time, Prime Minister Lloyd George and Foreign Secretary Balfour wanted Sir Herbert to ensure that Palestinian rights were upheld and protected, to minimize the risk of further civil unrest. Above all, the new high commissioner was to guarantee Palestine's position as the British Empire's strategic buffer for the Suez Canal.

In making his first official appointments, Samuel made it clear that he wanted to try to satisfy everyone. The top position in the secretariat was awarded to a devoted Evangelical Christian, who believed that the return of the Jews to Palestine was a prelude to Christ's return. As head of his legal advisers, Sir Herbert named a pro-Zionist, who was married to his own niece. This appointment was welcomed by the Zionist lobby, but they remained unhappy that a number of high commission staff were opposed to the Balfour Declaration. The Zionists were also alarmed at Sir Herbert's declaration that he did not intend to preside over the creation of a full Jewish state, and that the nationality of all citizens in Palestine would be exclusively 'Palestinian'.[418]

The high commissioner decided that Hebrew would be introduced as an official language, alongside English and Arabic, and he endorsed plans for the new Hebrew University on Mount Scopus. He also made an effort to heal the wounds inflicted during the April riots, granting clemency to Aref al-Aref and Amin Husseini. They returned to Jerusalem, Aref taking up a job with the British authorities before going on to write several books about Palestinian history and culture. Amin Husseini was given a post in the administration. He later became mufti of Jerusalem and the most influential Muslim cleric in Palestine, playing a leading role in the battle for power in the country.

Before long, the high commissioner lifted the ban on Jewish immigration and renewed the right of Jews to buy land in Palestine. As part of a general political amnesty, he decided that Vladimir Jabotinsky and 19 of his supporters should be released, along with the two Palestinians convicted of rape. In response to being freed at the same time as the

418 Herbert Louis Samuel: *Memoirs by Viscount Samuel*, London 1945, p.170.

Palestinian rapists, Jabotinsky cabled Sir Herbert saying: "Don't make this mistake! Better to leave me here in Acre [prison] than to put me on the same level with a blackie!"[419]

On 7 August, 1920, Samuel sent a telegram to London requesting permission to place Transjordan (modern-day Jordan) directly under his administration. The response was negative. It was suggested instead that a compromise would be to despatch political officers to Salt and Kerak, without actually setting up a British administration in the area.[420] Nonetheless, plans had been mooted unofficially for the possible future use of Transjordan as a homeland for Palestinian Arabs, should any become displaced following the establishment of a future Jewish state. Alec Kirkbride, one of the Arabic-speaking British officers sent to Kerak noted:

> His Majesty's government were too busy setting up a civil administration in Palestine to be bothered about the remote and underdeveloped areas which lay to the east of the River Jordan, and which were being held in reserve for use in the resettlement of Arabs once the national home for Jews in Palestine became an accomplished fact. There was no intention at that stage of turning the territory east of the River Jordan into an independent Arab state.[421]

Sir Herbert's wife, along with his eldest son, Edwin, and two youngest children, arrived in Jerusalem in November. Edwin was engaged to a beautiful and charming Jewish girl called Hassada, and they were married just after arriving in Jerusalem. The bakery at the American Colony was asked to make the wedding cake, a confection produced under Bertha's watchful eye.[422]

The Zionists were forward thinking. To create a true Jewish state in Palestine, it was not enough merely to appropriate land from the natives; it was just as important to crush the Palestinians' hopes of independence. The Zionists had Britain and many other nations on their side. When the

419 Joseph Schechman: Rebel and Statesman, p.362, cited in Lenni Brenner: The Iron Wall, Zionist Revisionism from Jabotinsky to Shamir, London 1984, p.61.
420 Uriel Dann: Studies in the History of Transjordan, 1920-1949, pp.18-19.
421 Alec Kirkbride: A Crackle of Thorns, Experiences in the Middle East, John Murray, London (no date), p.19.
422 Edwin Samuel inherited his father's title of Lord. In 1948, he became the first head of the Israel's broadcasting company.

Palestinians suggested in December 1920 that majority voting should be introduced to the country, this was ignored, both by the British and the international community. The Palestinian Arabs constituted by far the majority of the population, so a democratic Palestine would have meant an end to the Zionist dream of a Jewish state. Turning the Palestinians into a minority became a Zionist goal. This could happen either by a massive influx of Zionist Jews, or by mass deportation of the Palestinians. Already by 1917, David Ben-Gurion was writing:

> The realization of Zionism is now on the agenda... History does not wait. Non-Jewish Palestine waited 1800 years without Jews... During the next 20 years we have to create a Jewish majority in the Land of Israel. This is the essence of the new historical situation.[423]

Many Jews had felt for some time that Herzl's *Der Judenstaat* was unrealistic, and for an entire generation after the book was written, furious arguments raged between moderate Jews who wanted to assimilate with the Arabs, and Zionists who wanted to have a purely Jewish state.[424]

One of Herzl's foremost critics was a Russian Jew who had come to Palestine in 1921 and wrote under a pseudonym. His real name was Asher Hirsch Ginzberg, although he wrote as 'Ahad Ha-am' ('one of the people'). Ginzberg came from an Orthodox family and had received a traditional Jewish education.[425] Both in speeches and in writing, 'Ahad Ha-am' argued that the Jewish people were not ready for Herzl's Zionism. The creation of a state should not be the first priority, he said. 'Ahad Ha-am' believed the Zionists were trying to settle the entire Jewish people into Palestine, a country which could never be a true Jewish state.

During the first Zionist Congress in Basel, 'Ahad Ha-am' sat "like a mourner at a wedding feast, because the Zionist bride had chosen to marry my philosophical rival". He wrote: "My head still aches, my nerves are on edge, and I will not allow myself to say what I think, because I

423 David Ben-Gurion: *Memoarer* (Memoirs), *Vol. I*, Tel Aviv 1971 (Hebrew), p.98, cited in Benjamin Beit-Hallahmi: *Original Sins, Reflections on the History of Zionism and Israel*, London 1992, p.75.
424 Geoffrey Wheatcroft: *The Controversy of Zionism*, New York 1996, pp.121-8.
425 Asher Ginzberg was born in Ukraine in 1856, and was an early supporter of Zionism.But after visiting Palestine in the 1890s, he became critical of Herzl's political vision, advocating instead what he described as cultural Zionism, in which Palestine became a spiritual centre for global Jewry. From 1896 to 1903, 'Ahad Ha-am' edited the periodical *Ha-Shiloah*. From 1908 to 1922 Ginzberg lived in London, and took part in some of the negotiations which led to the Balfour Declaration in 1917. He later moved to Tel Aviv, where he died in 1927.

cannot yet control my feelings. I hate to say it, but one could see how low we have fallen."[426]

Afterwards, Ginzberg continued to criticise the Zionist leadership under his familiar pen name. He repeated a question asked at the first Zionist Congress, as to whether the Jews were yet politically mature enough to establish their own nation state. He was doubtful, believing that although the Zionists might try to repair the conflicts between themselves and the Orthodox Jews, they would never succeed.

Ginzberg was not alone in fearing for the future. Arthur Ruppin, who headed the first Zionist office in Jaffa, predicted that the relationship between Western and Eastern European Jews would be just as hostile as it had been between the Sephardic and Ashkenazi Jews during the French Revolution. Back then, the Western Jewish lobby had been strongly opposed to giving the Eastern European Jews any kind of civil rights.[427] Among the Zionists in Palestine, few were bothered by this kind of criticism. Most ignored the fact that an internecine conflict had developed, amongst the Jews themselves. The zealous Jewish colonists were intent on creating a Jewish state in Palestine, whatever the cost in innocent lives.

For Vladimir Jabotinsky and for many others the idea of restraint was absurd. Jabotinsky believed it was naïve to hope for a voluntary agreement between the Jews and the Arabs – now or in the future. "Every nation, civilized or primitive, considers its land as its national home where that nation wants to be the sole owner," he declared. "Such a nation will never voluntarily agree to new owners, or even to a partnership."[428]

Jabotinsky's words represented a challenge to the Palestinians, but were even more provocative to the moderate Zionists, many of whom were good friends of Anna Spafford. Jabotinsky's peculiar logic gave them qualms of conscience: either Zionism was ethically responsible or it was not, and if it was, then Arab opposition had to be taken into account. According to Jabotinsky, Palestine had to achieve a Jewish majority as quickly as possible in order to guarantee the creation of a Jewish state, even by the use of force if needs be. These militant Jews appeared to have the tacit support of the British government, which slowly but surely seemed to be allowing Palestine to slide into chaos.

The Zionists had a strong ally in the new British Colonial Minister, Winston Churchill, who was soon to make a visit to Jerusalem. In March

426 Letter from Asher Ginzberg to J. H. Ravnitzki, cited in Leon Simon: *Ahad Ha-am, A Biography*, New York 1960, pp.171, 271.
427 Moshe Leshem: *Israel Alone*, New York 1989, pp.99–100.
428 Wheatcroft: *The Controversy of Zion*, New York 1996, p.207.

1921, before travelling from Cairo to Jerusalem with T E Lawrence to meet the new minister, Sir Herbert Samuel was told by the intelligence service that there was a plan "to blow him (Churchill) to bits by a mob, or shoot him somewhere on the route". Lawrence and Samuel had previously attended a conference in Cairo where Churchill had drawn up the borders of Britain's new territories in the Middle East, and were well aware of the anger this had caused amongst the Arabs.[429] The information was vague, but the high commissioner, nonetheless, warned Churchill of the suspected danger. Samuel had brought with him two police officers to provide extra protection, and Churchill's personal bodyguard was told they were about to enter "a climate of unclassifiable fanaticism", and that he was to shoot on sight if danger threatened.

On the way to Jerusalem the train stopped at Gaza, where Churchill was scheduled to receive an address of welcome to Palestine and to meet a number of dignitaries. The subsequent gathering of around 2,000 people became boisterous, but Lawrence viewed the crowd as friendly, and Churchill's personal bodyguard, Walter H Thomson, was not worried. He might have been had Lawrence told him that mingled with the cries of "Cheers for Great Britain" and "Cheers for the Minister" were others of "Down with the Jews" and "Cut their throats".[430]

"Is this demonstration for or against us?" Churchill asked. Lawrence was not worried. He held up his hand and said a few words to the crowd in Arabic before stepping behind Churchill. Instantly, the throng fell silent. Many prostrated towards Lawrence, and as Churchill saw this, he turned to his bodyguard and said: "They worship him."

There was, in the end, no assassination attempt on the colonial minister, who went on to enjoy a large dinner in his honour at Government House. Among the guests were Bertha and Frederick. During the course of the evening, the couple were unfortunately referred to as 'newcomers to Jerusalem' and 'members of a sect without a church', although Ronald Storrs tried to redress this indignity by speaking of "all the advice and assistance which we never failed to receive in the early days, when we knew nothing and they everything, from the great-hearted and charming leader" of the American Colony.[431]

429 Tom Hickman: *Churchill's Bodyguard, The Authorised Biography of Walter H Thomson Based on his Complete Memoirs*, London 2005, p.15, A W Lawrence: *T E Lawrence by his Friends*, London 1937, cited in Christopher Sykes: *Cross Roads to Israel, Palestine from Balfour to Bevin*, Collins, London 1956, p.64.
430 Hickman: *Churchill's Bodyguard*, London 2005, p.17.
431 Storrs: *Orientations*, London 1939, p.428.

But Anna Spafford's religious doctrine remained unclear to most, even to Storrs, who felt unable to enquire about the nature of the sect's teachings since they did not engage in mission work. For him, "the Colony represented a primitive churchless Christianity, whose exact tenets, a species of Latter Day Adventism, I never succeeded in discovering, but which at first caused them to regard the Anglican Cathedral as little better than the House of Rimmon, in which, however, an annual knee must be bowed on the King's Birthday." So great was the confusion that Storrs was not even sure if the majority of the American Colony's members were Swedish or Norwegian.[432]

Bertha's religiosity was of a completely different kind from that of her mother. Anna's oldest daughter was not filled with millenarian ideals from the time of the 'Great Awakening'. Hers was a more conventional Christianity, and she was quietly ambivalent about her mother's faith. Although she never denied that her mother was in direct contact with God, Bertha sometimes requested that more fanatical members of the Colony should tone down their behaviour, and even admonished them when their states of rapture became too great.[433]

When cynical commentators claimed that the Spafford sect had come to Jerusalem to "do good" for others and "stayed to do well" for themselves, Ronald Storrs replied: "The truth is that they did both." For Storrs, "the American Colony Store, besides producing infinitely the best photographic prints of Jerusalem and the Holy Land, catered also for the visitors, pilgrims and tourists with a thoughtfulness, and thoroughness, which defied the competition even of the Jews and Armenians. Their model camels, inkstands and Bible-binding in olive-wood descriptions, their Masonic gavels carved in the white limestone of King Solomon's Quarries, their sealed phials of guaranteed Jordan water, their copies of silver Jewel shown by the Franciscans as the Cross of Godfroi de Bouillon, their Bukhara silks, their Bethlehem Women's robes, were better, more knowledgably crafted and more attractive even than the antiques of the Protestant Armenian, Nasri Ohan." In addition, he said "a considerable portion of the Colony's income was ploughed back into the country in the form of charity for the Arab population, as much to Muslims as to Christians."[434]

Among those who came to Jerusalem to meet Churchill was the new ruler of Transjordan, Emir Abdullah, the second son of Sharif Hussein.

432 Ibid. p.427.
433 Olof Fahlén: *Nåsbönderna i Jerusalem* (The Nås Farmers in Jerusalem), Höganäs 1988, p.53.
434 Storrs: *Orientation*, London 1939, p.428.

On his arrival in the city, Abdullah was given a reception appropriate to a head of state. Following the subsequent official dinner, he and Churchill retired for cigarettes and cigars. When Churchill saw the emir take snuff from a beautiful golden box enamelled in green and red, he asked if he could try some, as he had never taken snuff before. He took some, sneezed, and laughed out loud.

At 9.30am the next morning, they met again, but this time the tone was more serious. During their meeting, Churchill warned Abdullah against challenging the French claim to Syria. As far as the Balfour Declaration was concerned, he said that the emir could discuss that with the high commissioner. "The people of Palestine have refused the Balfour Declaration and insist on the retention of the Arab character of Palestine," answered Abdullah. "We shall not agree to the annihilation of the Arabs for the sake of the Jews. The Arabs are not like trees, which grow again when they are cut."[435] The emir of Transjordan was all too aware of Arab public opinion. His earlier attempts to address a Palestinian crowd at the Noble Sanctuary, had been interrupted by shouts of: "Palestine is for the Arabs. Down with the Zionists." But Churchill did not like this answer and replied: "I'm afraid I have tired you. I shall look forward to your reply tomorrow morning."

Churchill also found time to visit the Old City while he was in Jerusalem. Thomson, the bodyguard, feared that he "would never get his boss back home alive", but the visit passed without incident and Thomson relaxed when they returned to Government House on the Mount of Olives. He was intrigued by the complex which Kaiser Wilhelm was to have claimed as his 'Eastern Palace' if the Great War had ended differently. He also examined closely the German eagle carved over the main gateway, as well as two rooms which had 'Kaiser's Bedroom' and 'Kaiserin's Bedroom' etched in gold above the doors.[436] But Churchill was more interested in the paintings of 'The Wilderness of Biblical Judea' and 'The Dead Sea' that hung in the corridors. The colonial minister was a keen artist, and during his week in Jerusalem he "painted furiously with great daubs of colour" his own more subdued sketches of the Sea of Galilee, Jordan and the Yarmuk Valley.[437]

Bertha and Frederick met Churchill several times while he was in Jerusalem, but they never discussed politics. Bertha understood well that

435 Ibid. p.204.
436 Hickman: *Churchill's Bodyguard*, London 2005, p.19.
437 Norman & Helen Bentwich: *Mandate Memories 1918-1948*, The Hogarth Press, London 1965, p.68.

he was on the Zionists' side, and whenever the colonial minister received a delegation of Palestinians, he seemed to show little understanding of the Arab perspective. One evening, Moussa Kazim Husseini, the former mayor of Jerusalem, presented a comprehensive memorandum to Churchill, stating that Palestine belonged to the Arabs and that the Balfour Declaration did them a great injustice. The memorandum's demands, made "in the name of justice and right," included the abolition of the principle of a national home for the Jews, along with all laws passed "after the British occupation"; the establishment of a national government which "shall be responsible to a Palestinian parliament elected by the Palestinian people who have lived here since long before the war"; an immediate stop to Jewish immigration "until such a time as a national government was formed" and finally, an undertaking not to separate Palestine from its "sister States".[438]

When Churchill had listened to the delegation, he answered: "You have asked me in the first place to repudiate the Balfour Declaration and veto immigration of Jews into Palestine. It is not in my power to do, nor, if it were in my power, would it be my wish. The British government has given its word, via Mr Balfour, that they will view with favour the establishment of a national home for Jews in Palestine, which will inevitably involve the immigration of Jews to the country. This declaration by Mr Balfour and the British government has been ratified by the Allied Powers, who have been victorious in the Great War; and it was a declaration made while the war was still in progress, while victory or defeat hung in the balance. It must therefore be regarded as a defining fact, established by the triumphant conclusion to the Great War."

Churchill continued that it had not been the Arabs in Palestine who had conquered the Turks, but "it has been the British army in Palestine which has liberated these regions. The position of Great Britain in Palestine is one of trust, but it is also one of right." In conclusion, Churchill told the Arab deputation: "If, instead of sharing miseries through quarrels you will share blessings through cooperation, a bright and tranquil future lies ahead before your country. The earth is a generous mother, and will produce in plentiful abundance for all her children if they will but cultivate her soil in justice and peace."

The Arab delegation withdrew, and a Zionist deputation entered with a memorandum signed by the newly established Jewish National Council. Thanks were given to the British for their help in rebuilding

438 Gilbert: *Jerusalem in the Twentieth Century*, London, 1996, pp.90-2.

a national home, and it was stated that genuine friendship should be established between Jews and Arabs. The Zionist leaders emphasized that the Jewish people, who were "returning after 2,000 years in exile and persecution to their own homeland, could not permit any suspicion that they wished to deny another nation its rights". The Jewish people had "full understanding of aspirations for an Arab-run Palestine, but we know that by our efforts to rebuild a Jewish national home in the country, which is but a small area in comparison with all the Arab land, we do not deprive them of their legitimate rights. On the contrary, we are convinced that a Jewish renaissance in this country can only have a strong and invigorating influence upon the Arab nation. Our kinship in language, race, character and history is assurance that we shall in due course come to a complete understanding with them."

"I am myself completely convinced that the cause of Zionism is one which carries with it much that is good for the whole world," answered Churchill, "not just for the Jewish people, but that it will also bring with it prosperity, contentment and advancement for the Arab population as well."

Churchill concluded his remarks to the Zionists with the following words: "I earnestly hope that your cause may be carried to success. I know how serious are the difficulties at every stage, but I also know of your great energy and determination, and you have my warmest sympathy in the efforts you are making to overcome them. If I did not believe that you were animated by the very highest spirit of justice and idealism, and that your work would in fact confer blessings upon the whole country, I should not have the high hopes which I have that eventually, your work will be accomplished." After the meeting Churchill posed on the staircase, where the American Colony's photographers were waiting with their cameras.

During the afternoon of March 29, 1921, Churchill stood on the Mount of Olives along with Sir Herbert Samuel and several other dignitaries, on the site of the planned Hebrew University. Three years had passed since Chaim Weizmann had laid one of 12 foundation stones for the building, and the land was now about to be officially rededicated as the site of the first Jewish University the world had seen since ancient times. The colonial minister was presented with a Scroll of the Law from the Old Testament, as read each Saturday in synagogues around the world. Churchill expressed his thanks and responded: "Personally, my heart is full of sympathy for Zionism. This sympathy has existed for a long time... I am now going to plant a tree and I hope that in its shadow, peace and goodwill may return once more to Palestine."

But when Churchill was handed the little tree to be planted, it snapped. The ceremony's organizers did not have another tree in reserve, and looked frantically for a replacement. When a man arrived finally with a miserable little palm, which no one thought would survive, Churchill looked annoyed, and the high commissioner snarled: "Disgusting!"[439]

439 Ibid.p.94.

Chapter 33

A Miracle

In March 1921, the mufti of Jerusalem, Kamel Husseini, died, and his half-brother Amin was named as his successor. The 27-year-old was slim, of delicate build, with a sandy-coloured beard. He wore a long robe and a turban, and, like many educated Arabs at that time, had a special admiration for America. His succession to the post of mufti was not straightforward. It was usual for the high commissioner to make his appointment from a shortlist of three candidates, who had been voted for democratically by the *Ulama* (committee of Muslim scholars).

Amin Husseini, known as 'Haj Amin', had come fourth in the contest. But Ernest T Richmond, a British architect who was both Storrs' assistant secretary and his chief adviser on Muslim affairs, lobbied Sir Herbert Samuel to appoint Amin, arguing that despite the vote, the majority of Muslims in Jerusalem actually wanted him as their new mufti. He added that the high commissioner was not obliged *by law* to abide by the decisions of the *Ulama*.[440]

Richmond, who specialised in Islamic architecture, was strongly anti-Zionist and opposed the leading candidate, Sheikh Jurallah. The latter was regarded as a pro-Zionist who intended to sell Muslim holy property to the Jews. Samuel accepted the advice, and Haj Amin became the mufti of Jerusalem, his prestige being further increased when this title was elevated to 'grand mufti'. The high commissioner subsequently established a new organisation, the Supreme Islamic Council, with Amin Husseini as its head. This was a major achievement for a young man who had studied for only a few years at the Islamic al-Azrar University

---

440 Foreign Office 371/5267 file E 9433/8343/44; FO 371/5268 files E 11720/8343/44, 11835/8343/44.

in Cairo, before going on to military college in Istanbul. Many people wondered why Samuels had chosen a partially-educated young man from the Husseini clan to lead the Muslims of Palestine. One reason was the fact that Ragheb Nashashibi had become the city's mayor. The Nashashibi and Husseini families had for centuries been great rivals, and the British sought to subdue Palestinian Arab sentiment through a policy of 'divide and rule'. Like several other influential Jerusalem families, the Husseinis were well disposed towards the British, and this was seen as a counter-balance to Mayor Nashashibi's more radical sentiments. [441]

Another consideration lay behind Sir Herbert's choice; it was better to have Haj Amin with him rather than against him. Jerusalem's new grand mufti was seen as knowledgeable, ambitious and incorruptible. His involvement in politics continued a long-held family tradition: not just his brother, but also his father and several other relatives had been muftis in Palestine. Haj Amin had the advantage of growing up at a time when Palestine was desperate for effective Arab leadership. The mufti may indeed have had some dictatorial characteristics, but at least he was dynamic and efficient.

Anna Spafford's relationship with Amin was strained. He was heir to the extensive property that the American Colony occupied, and was believed to be shrewd and avaricious. The congregation had already been able to purchase 22 of the 24 carats which made up the property, but the last two portions belonged to Amin Husseini and his brother, who were demanding $30,000 for their remaining shares. Despite his frequent claim that money was not everything, Amin insisted that unless they could pay, Anna's sect would have to set aside a part of the complex for him and his brother. The two men even suggested that they would commandeer the salon for their personal use.

Several prominent Zionists in Jerusalem had little sympathy for the American Colony, saying that it was an "anti-Zionist tourist undertaking", and that its members "influenced visitors who stayed with them".[442] These critics were partially right. Many in the Colony sympathised with Palestinian nationalism, and understood Palestinian bewilderment that while they were being denied independence, foreign Jews should be given the right to take over their land they had farmed for centuries. For many young Arabs in particular, it seemed wrong that a government some 2,000

441 Izzat Darawazah: *Concerning the Modern Arab Movement, Vol. 3* (Arabic), p.47, cited in Saïd Aburish: *A Brutal Friendship, The West and the Arab Elite,* London, 1997, p.115.
442 Bentwich: *Mandate Memories, 1918–1948,* London 1965, p.73.

miles away could decide to hand over Arab land to other people.

Jerusalem's Latin patriarch was also highly critical of the British. Luigi Barlassina was an ill-tempered, arrogant and ambitious Italian cardinal, who had little love either for the British government or for the Zionists. He wrote to the pope to complain about the falling moral standards in Jerusalem under the British administration, saying there were 500 prostitutes working in the city and adding that films were shown in public.

For their part, the British thought Barlassina was a narrow-minded bigot, and that he was encouraging Christian fanaticism to take root in Jerusalem. Barlassina's physical appearance was not particularly attractive either; according to British officials, he resembled the mediaeval Spanish Grand Inquisitor Niño de Guevara, as depicted by El Greco.[443] As a result of Barlassina's claims, Ronald Storrs travelled to Rome to meet the pope. He had been granted an audience with the pontiff once before in order to brief him on the situation in Jerusalem, and now he wanted to prevent the fanatical cardinal – who was conducting what amounted to his own personal war against Protestantism, Zionism, and the Freemasons – from influencing the pope. Storrs was given an audience the day after he arrived. Pope Benedict XV expressed his concerns about alarmist reports of the perfidious influence of Jews in Jerusalem and the lack of impartiality of the Palestine government.[444]

Storrs thought it best to focus upon the false claims, and to abandon any defence of Zionism for the time being. It was not the British who had introduced cinema in Jerusalem, he explained; films had been shown in the city many years before the British Mandate, and when he, as military governor, became aware of a particular film that might cause religious or moral offence, he had it removed immediately. Indeed, he added, the Latin patriarch had thanked him for doing this. As far as prostitution was concerned, these women had been there prior to British rule in Jerusalem. When the British occupied the city in December 1917, they found that an entire quarter was given over to brothels. Storrs said the British administration had prohibited this practice a full two years earlier, and all prostitutes had been deported to their places of origin. True, there were still a certain number of women of ill-repute in the city, but this was "in any case infinitesimal when compared with what we had originally found". Storrs pointed out that even "with the utmost vigilance it was difficult to ensure that any city had complete exemption from this particular form of abuse, however sacred".

443 Sir Harry Luke: *Cities and Men, An Autobiography, Volume II*, London 1953, p.208.
444 Storrs: *Orientations*, London 1937, pp.450-51.

Shaking his head regretfully, Benedict XV agreed that it was impossible to achieve such an ideal, and complimented the British administration on its efforts. The matter was thus settled as far as both the Vatican and Storrs were concerned, and the military governor was able to return to Palestine to continue his work of improving Jerusalem's infrastructure – although he never succeeded in ridding the city of all the prostitutes.

Storrs was prepared to enlist the help of anyone whom he thought might be useful in his mission to restore the Old City and one of his main supporters was Bertha Spafford Vester, who was very enthusiastic about his objectives. Although within the American Colony, Anna was still very much the sect's leader, outside its walls, her eldest daughter, Bertha, was its main representative, as well as one of the most prominent women in Jerusalem's social elite. The other women, aside from Bertha, who made up this cosmopolitan group consisted of: the high commissioner's wife, Lady Samuel, and the rector of the Evelina de Rothschild Jewish Girls' School, Annie Landau. Miss Landau, an Orthodox Jew from England, was described as more 'British than the British in Palestine, and more Jewish than the Zionists'. There was also the wife of the Muslim mayor, Laila Nashashibi, who had been born in Turkey to Roman Catholic parents and whose husband Ragheb had never sought to make her change her religion. Madame Nashashibi was very beautiful, and spoke French, Italian, and English, as well as Turkish and Arabic.

Parties at the American Colony were one of the highlights of the social calendar. Guests particularly enjoyed wandering around the beautiful gardens, and marvelling at the climbing shell plants, the heliotrope and hanging geraniums, which in May were in full bloom and produced the effect of a wall of pink flame. Flowering cactus were abundant, and in the centre of the courtyard the light sky-blue plumbago blossomed all summer. In early spring, violets and cyclamen bloomed, and at Easter time the lily, amaryllis, and lilacs joined in a profusion of fragrance and colour. Fan palms and acanthus added variety and beauty.[445]

One frequent visitor to the Colony was Charles Ashbee, the secretary of the Pro-Jerusalem Committee that was overseeing much of the city's architectural restoration. It was Ashbee who, in 1918, had arranged for three Armenian ceramicists to be brought to Jerusalem to make ceramic street signs and to repair the façade of the Dome of the Rock. The Dome, considered one of the world's most beautiful, with its glazed ceramic tiles

---

445 Fannie Fern Andrews: *The Holy Land under the Mandate*, Volume I, Houghton Mifflin Company, Cambridge, 1931, p.27.

from the time of Suleiman the Magnificent, had become weathered and partially damaged. The foreman of the Armenian restoration team had been born in Kutahya in Turkey, a town famous for its ceramic art. He brought his family with him and established himself in the city.

Charles Ashbee often wrote home to his family about his visits to the American Colony. Bertha and Frederick planned a trip to the United States at the end of April 1921, and a farewell dinner was given in their honour. Following this, Charles wrote: "We sat down, about a hundred of us, to the accompaniment of graceful music. There was the customary good food and fare, and sprite-like sisters to wait upon us, who flit through the great rooms like ministering angels. They offer fantastic service, and one always feels humble when one goes to the American Colony, a feeling that despite all, one's intellect doesn't count for everything."[446]

He continued: "I had the honour of sitting beside old Mrs Spafford – 'Momma' – mother of the Colony, who founded it all and has remained its guiding light ever since." The Englishman noted that some of the Swedes still retained words from their mother tongue, and had not entirely gone over to English. Ashbee thought Anna to be "a wonderful old lady, and I can't imagine what she must have gone through over the past years! She's quite old and feeble now, but I noted that she still has an awesome expression between her lip and chin, characteristic of all religious leaders. Selma Lagerlöf tells us all about her in her book *Jerusalem*. The Colony still keeps the book hushed up, but nonetheless, much of what it recounts is perfectly true."[447]

Meanwhile in Jaffa, Arab communists were distributing pamphlets amongst the population written in Hebrew, Yiddish and Arabic. These stated that there was soon to be "a great May Day Demonstration", and everyone was urged to participate. The Jews were characterized as "soldiers of the revolution" who had come to help their "Arab comrades and peasants to throw off the yoke of the oppressors". The leaflets were signed by 'The Executive Committee of the Communist Party in Occupied Palestine'.[448] Jaffa was the commercial and cultural centre of Palestine, with English, French, Italian and Arab language schools, three

446 Charles Robert Ashbee: *A Palestine Notebook, 1918–1923*, New York 1923, p.178.
447 But when the Swedish author, L. J. Saxon, visited Jerusalem later, he was told: "Selma Lagerlöf's description of the colony is anything but popular – to be quite frank, they despise the book." L. J. Saxon: *Det nye Palestina, Minnen och intryk från en färd genom bibelens land* (The New Palestine, Memories and Impressions from a Trip through the Land of the Bible), Stockholm 1921, p.157.
448 Al Ahram, May 2, 1992, Dr. Yunan Labib Rizk: *A Cause is Born*, Al Ahram Weekly, October 14–20, 1999, p.18.

newspapers and many printing houses. Many of the Palestinian political elite lived there and its cinemas showed films from Cairo and Hollywood.

The gap between the Zionists' intentions and Palestinian demands for freedom and independence for the Palestinians was widening, something which caused many moderate and left-wing Jews to despair. Thus on the evening before the 1 May demonstration, hundreds of Jewish communists gathered in Jaffa, where 26,000 Palestinians lived, alongside 16,000 Jews. They were determined that the voice of socialist Jews, who wished only to live in peace with their Arab friends and neighbours, should be heard.

At 7am the following morning, the demonstration started, with Jewish communists marching together with their fellow Arab party members under red banners to the centre of Jaffa. From another part of town came a Zionist counter-demonstration carrying the blue and white Zionist flag. It was not long before the two groups clashed. British police arrived and drove the communists back to the flat-sandy strip between Jaffa and Tel Aviv.

A number of neutral Palestinians had been stationed in the area as government agents, to report on the progress of the demonstrations to the British administration. As the communists were driven back, they cursed the agents, accusing them of cowardice and of failing to come to the assistance of their brother Arabs who were being abused and brutalized. This shamed them into joining the march. Hundreds of voices could be heard chanting in Arabic "*Alayhum, alayhum*" ("to them, to them!" – meaning the Jews).[449] The tumult reached a climax when the Zionists threatened the communists with guns. The Palestinians were armed only with clubs, and chaos ensued when Jewish immigrants from Poland threw hand grenades down from balconies. The enraged mob broke into Jewish stores and looted them, with a number of Palestinian policemen joining in. The most militant of the demonstrators went on to attack the Jewish immigration centre in Jaffa. Only later in the afternoon did the British army, supported by aircraft from the Royal Air Force, gain control over the situation. It was the first serious Arab-Jewish confrontation since the British had arrived in Palestine. When the smoke cleared, 27 Jews and three Arabs lay dead.[450]

News of the riot soon reached the American Colony, and the next morning at 6am its chief photographer, Lewis Larsson, set off for Jaffa in the Colony's new Dodge sedan, along with Eric Matsson and a visiting

449 Adam LeBor: *City of Oranges, Arabs and Jews in Jaffa*, Bloomsbury, London 2006, p.17.
450 *Palestine: Disturbances in May 1921, Reports of the Commission of Inquiry with Correspondence Relating Thereto* (Cmd.1540, London 1921) cited in Bernard Wasserstein: *British in Palestine, The Mandatory Government and the Arab-Jewish Conflict,1917-1929*, London 1991, p.101.

Swedish writer. On their way they stopped at the British field HQ in Ramleh and were told that peace had been restored. But when they arrived in the port city they found "the streets in great uproar".[451]

When they returned to Jerusalem, they were proclaimed as "the heroes of the day" for their coverage of the Jaffa riot. They recounted how "an Arab had pushed himself into a Jewish café and hurled a grenade left over from the war, killing himself and 10 Jews. In revenge, a Jew forced his way into an Arab family's home and shot dead six people."

The violence in Jaffa continued for five days. In all, 40 Jews and 18 Arabs lost their lives. According to a secret intelligence report by Captain C D Bruton "the condition of the dead and wounded proves that the Arabs were armed mainly with sticks, while the Zionists had revolvers".[452] Both the Zionists and the British authorities maintained that Jewish and Arab communists were to blame for the bloodbath. Fifteen communists were arrested and deported to the USSR, with scant regard for judicial or legal process. When they left Haifa, they sang the 'Internationale'.[453]

A British intelligence officer summed the situation up: "The Arab population has come to regard the Zionists with hatred, and the British with resentment. Mr Churchill's visit put the final touch to the picture. He upheld the Zionist cause and treated Arab demands as coming from a feeble opposition, to be put off by a few political phrases and treated like children."[454]

The clashes in Jaffa and in other parts of Palestine prompted the high commissioner to establish a commission of investigation into the violence. Its conclusion was clear: the fundamental reason for the trouble was Arab fears of Zionist plans. The high commissioner realized that drastic action was called for. Irrespective of how sympathetic he was towards the Zionist cause, as a British official he had to ensure peace and order in Palestine. Samuel knew that prison sentences would not solve the conflict. The disagreements were political, and he concluded that

451 Entry in Eric Matsson's diary and report by Johan Lindström Saxon, in *Det Nya Palestina* (The New Palestine), both cited in Gröndahl: *The Dream of Jerusalem*, pp.250-53.
452 CO 733/13, Secret Report by Captain Brunton of General Staff Intelligence to G H Q, Cairo, Jaffa, 13 May 1921, cited in Sahar Huneidi: *A Broken Trust, Herbert Samuel, Zionism and the Palestinians*, I B Tauris, London and New York, 2001, p.127.
453 Most of the deported Jewish communists subsequently disappeared during Stalinist purges. Société des Nations, Commission Permanente des Mandats. Procés Verbaux de la Cinquième Session (1924), Genève 1925, p.58, cited in Nathan Weinstock: *Zionism: False Messiah*, London 1979, p.194.
454 CO 733/13, Secret Report by Captain Brunton of General Staff Intelligence to G H Q, Cairo, Jaffa, 13 May 1921, cited in Sahar Huneidi: *A Broken Trust, Herbert Samuel, Zionism and the Palestinians*, I. B. Tauris Publishing, London and New York, 2001, p.128.

only a halt to further Jewish immigration into Palestine would calm Arab tempers. Immigration was suspended immediately after the riots, but was resumed on a stricter basis two months later, regulated according to the "economic absorptive capacity of the country".[455]

The Zionists were angry about the temporary suspension of immigration, and felt the high commissioner had been influenced by the leader of the powerful Husseini clan, Moussa Kazim Husseini. For the Zionists, British compliance with Arab demands could mean only more violence; Chaim Weizmann complained directly to Samuel that he was taking the Arabs' agitation too seriously and treating them too leniently. Sir Herbert tried without success to explain to Weizmann that he needed to acknowledge the strength of the Arab nationalist movement. Later, Samuel wrote to Churchill that "a new factor has entered into the political situation in this country, and that is an interest in public affairs in the minds of the population... They are now seen to be race-conscious in a more definite manner than before..."[456]

Zionist disappointment increased when the high commissioner issued a declaration limiting the terms of the Balfour Declaration. In a speech on June 3, 1921, Samuel spoke of the "unhappy misunderstanding that has existed" and that a "national home for the Jewish people does not mean the setting up of a Jewish government to rule over the Muslim and Christian majority". Weizmann was furious when he met the high commissioner, and became even angrier when Samuel asked him to assure the Arabs that the Zionist leadership did not intend to establish a Jewish state in Palestine. Weizmann flatly refused – for him, a Jewish state was a clear objective, and he was not prepared to accept Sir Herbert's statement. Weizmann had thought that the high commissioner was himself a solid Zionist, an impression that had been reinforced by Samuel's previous suggestion of reconstructing Jerusalem's Jewish temple.[457]

On November 2, many Jews decided to celebrate the fourth anniversary of the Balfour Declaration by closing their shops and businesses, and treating the day as a holiday. For their part, the Arabs had let it be known that they would not open any of their own businesses, making it a day of protest against the declaration. Only the American Colony Store inside

455 Order 1540 of 1921, cited in John Marlowe: *The Seat of Pilate*, London 1959, p.89.
456 Wasserstein: *British in Palestine, The Mandatory Government & The Arab-Jewish Conflict*, 1991, p110.
457 Yehuda Reinharz: *Chaim Weizmann: The Making of a Statesman*, New York 1993, p.22.

Jaffa Gate was open, as it was considered neutral ground.[458]

Six months later, on June 3, 1922, Churchill issued the so-called 'Churchill White Paper', which contained guidelines for the government of Palestine. The high commissioner presented its content at Government House, and Bertha was among those invited to the event. Every Zionist in the audience was disappointed by what they heard (one Jewish woman was so shocked that she fainted and had to be carried out)[459], but the Palestinian delegation was delighted. In essence, whilst the White Paper confirmed the British government's promise of a Jewish national home in Palestine, it also gave the Arabs an assurance that this promise would not be a threat to Palestinian wellbeing and independence. Herbert Samuel said no plans existed to make all of Palestine into a Jewish national home, adding that the British government would also put a ceiling on Jewish immigration.

At the end of June, the League of Nations finally ratified the terms under which the British government was to assume the mandate to govern Palestine. The ratification had been a slow process, largely because France and the United States had needed to agree on every aspect of its terms and the Vatican had insisted on having special assurances that Palestine's holy sites would be respected.

Some months earlier, Bertha and Frederick had returned to the US with their three oldest children, Anna Grace, Horatio and Tanetta. The children were to attend school in America, while their younger siblings would remain with their grandmother in Jerusalem, eventually joining their parents later in the charge of a Swedish nursemaid. Bertha and Frederick had vague plans of settling permanently in New York and opening a store in the big city, which could sell products from Jerusalem.

Another objective of the trip was to secure American citizenship for Frederick. He had received a number of letters of recommendation, including ones from the last American consul in Jerusalem and from General Allenby's chief of intelligence in Palestine, which recounted Frederick's efforts during the World War. Bertha and Frederick would also be seeking to secure a bank loan for the American Colony so that they could buy out the remaining shares held by Amin Husseini and his brother.[460]

458 McCrackan: *The New Palestine*, Boston, 1922, p.378.
459 Spafford Vester: Unpublished manuscript, chapter 36, *Historical Background Leading to the Civil Administration of Palestine under the British Mandate*. p.25, American Colony Collection, Jerusalem.
460 Eric Dinsmore Matsson: *The American Colony of Jerusalem, A Brief Historical Outline*, Men-

Mother Anna accompanied them to the train station. The Vesters were travelling first to Egypt and then to Naples where they would board a vessel that would take them to New York. A British regiment was departing Jerusalem the same day, and a military band was there to see the troops off with a rendition of 'A Perfect Day'. This was seen as a good omen.

A month after the family had left, Mother Anna asked the congregation to pray that the bank loan they needed to buy out Haj Amin and his brother would be approved. In the middle of the meeting John D Whiting was summoned to take receipt of a telegram. As he read it, he was overwhelmed. "Thirty thousand!" he breathed, "Thank God!" Then he collapsed. Brother Jacob picked up the telegram and read it out. When the congregation heard that the loan was assured, some began to weep with joy. They all believed in the power of prayer – but that it should work so quickly was, indeed, a miracle.

ton 1992, pp.36–37.

Chapter 34

Farewell Jerusalem

In the spring of 1922, Anna, who was by now 80, began to experience pains in her feet, but said nothing to the rest of the congregation. Her letters to Bertha in the US mentioned her discomfort only in passing, and focused mainly on the three grandchildren who had remained in Jerusalem. In fact, Anna told her eldest daughter little about developments at the American Colony, and it fell to Grace to keep Bertha updated on events there. Grace said the future of the Colony was looking grim. Several members had left the community, and now Lewis Larsson and his wife, Edith, were also beginning to drift away from it.

Lewis had been appointed Sweden's vice-consul the year before, and spent much of his time fulfilling the duties that came with this position. He had not taken the decision to accept the post alone, but had first asked permission from Mother Anna, who answered: "It is better for you to hold the office than another person, who perhaps would not consider our interests."[461]

Lewis had been recommended for the post by a senior Swedish diplomat in the Middle East, Baron Harold de Bildt. The baron, based in Cairo, believed the American Colony's chief photographer would make an excellent consular representative for his country in Palestine.

Lewis's main job involved the care of Swedish tourists and missionaries, but after a while he and his family became drawn into Jerusalem's diplomatic set. They moved into a rented house near the Colony, and began to live more comfortably than they had in the past. Not long afterwards, Edith became pregnant with another child.

461 Larsson: *Dala Folk in the Holy Land*, Stockholm 1957, p.118.

In the late spring, Anna suffered a small stroke. She became paralyzed on her right side and could no longer walk. Nevertheless, she was determined not to become isolated. Each morning she would be dressed and carried to the morning meetings in a chair. But she sometimes fell asleep in the middle of a sentence, and Grace felt that the most important thing for her elderly mother now was rest. She suggested to Anna that she go to stay at the Colony's summer house in the village of Ein Karem, half an hour away from Jerusalem by car. In this beautiful Christian village, built around an old convent, she would be in peace. Grace wanted to be certain that this was the best move for her mother, so she secretly consulted the family's doctor, who confirmed her decision.

At that time, the Colony was very busy, and Grace did not feel herself equal to assuming the roles both of her mother and Bertha. She had not inherited either Mother Anna's charisma or Bertha's talent for administration. She felt Lewis should be doing more to support her in her role of acting Colony leader.

One Monday in May, she walked over to the Larssons' house to discuss these matters. Lewis was in bed, and the heavily pregnant Edith explained that her husband was suffering from palpitations of the heart. He had been ordered to rest for at least three days. Grace could not help laughing to herself – it sounded so ridiculous to her, for as far as she could see, Lewis did scarcely any hard work at all. His job as vice-consul was far from arduous, and he enjoyed lunch at home each day, followed by a two-hour siesta.[462] More likely his exertions were a result of his relentless socializing; Grace knew that Lewis and Edith were constantly attending big receptions and private dance parties at the homes of various British officials. The following day, she wrote to Bertha, telling her that Lewis had not even felt well enough to attend to the needs of a visiting Swedish tourist. The Swede had arrived "a little after eight o'clock one Saturday evening, but His Excellency, the Swedish consul, had gone to bed! May God help us with that family and all the rest like them," wrote Grace.[463]

In a house not far from the American Colony, Eliezer Ben-Yehuda was on his deathbed. Anna had not had any contact with him recently, but her adopted son, Jacob, met with him occasionally at the Pro-Jerusalem Committee, of which he was a keen member.

Ben-Yehuda had returned to Jerusalem, having spent the war years

462 Letter from Grace Spafford Whiting to Bertha Spafford Vester, May 1922, Folder: 1922, American Colony Collection, Jerusalem.
463 Ibid.

in the United States completing his mission to create a comprehensive Hebrew alphabet. On his arrival, Ronald Storrs welcomed him with the words: "*Shalom alechem*" ("peace be with you").[464]

But the eccentric intellectual's labours would not be recognized during his lifetime. Neither the Orthodox Jews in Palestine nor the diaspora were keen on using Hebrew as their everyday language. Even Herzl preferred that German should be the official language of the state. But Ben-Yehuda carried on with his work regardless, and after a while noticed with pleasure that more and more Jewish immigrants were learning Hebrew.

The last thing Ben-Yehuda had been working on was a Hebrew word for 'soul'. He called it '*nefeh*', and fittingly, this was the last thing the father of modern Hebrew wrote before he died. Storrs declared three days of official mourning in his honour, and at the burial he quoted a line from *The Fifth Of May*, a poem written by the Italian poet Allesandro Manzoni for Napoleon's funeral: "And on the eternal pages fell the tired hand."

Back at the American Colony, nobody enquired after Mother Anna's health. No one asked whether she had sinned as she did when others became ill. To them, the idea that she might have sinned was impossible, and it was, therefore, inconceivable that she might be terminally ill. Only Edith Larsson dared to speak to Grace of the subject. When they met one Wednesday in May, she said: "I feel so troubled about Mother's sickness. I spoke with Lewis about it last night."[465]

But Anna's youngest daughter did not want to talk about her mother's illness, for she had other more important matters to raise with Edith. "Troubled you may be," she replied. "But let me tell you how very troubled we have been in the way that you and Lewis have drifted away from the assembly." Grace went on to mention the three other brothers from Nås brothers, who also appeared to have turned their backs on the congregation and were spending a lot of time with Lewis at the Swedish consulate. Nonetheless, she told Edith she was "so grateful to God" that she was engaging with the Colony again. Edith confessed to being worried about her husband's excesses and that it "frightened her that Lewis wanted to serve champagne" for the Swedish king's birthday as the other consulates did on special occasions. Lewis later maintained that he had only suggested serving champagne as a possibility. "That is so like Lewis," wrote Grace.

464 Robert St. John: *Tongue of the Prophets, The Life Story of Eliezer Ben-Yehuda*, New York 1952, p.319.
465 Undated letter from Grace Spafford Whiting and John Whiting to Bertha Spafford Vester, envelope marked: "Letters written to me by Grace & Jacob when I was in America 1922 relating to Mother's illness & home news." Folder: 1922, American Colony Collection.

"When he is reprimanded for his behaviour, he denies it from the outset!"

Despite her rest cure at Ein Karem, Mother Anna's health grew worse, and she was brought back to the Colony in Jerusalem. Olaf Lind arrived at her bedside and cried like a child; he hugged Anna and begged for her to forgive him all his sins. "I have been a terrible boy, forgive me," he said through his tears. "If you will forgive me, I will become a pillar of the Colony and work as hard as I can for us all."[466] Anna forgave him. But her health continued to deteriorate. The doctor discovered that she had suffered another stroke, but was no longer in danger. "Mrs Spafford is a very special person," he added. "I wouldn't normally dare put a patient of her age to bed, because as a rule they never get up again. But she has enormous willpower. Any other person would be dead by now, but Mrs Spafford is wonderful, she holds on to life for the sake of others, not for herself."

"Thank God," Grace wrote to Bertha. "This illness, though tragic, has had the effect of bringing the household closer together. It has brought us back to the centre."

Even though Anna was becoming weaker by the day, she announced that she wanted to make one last trip to the sea before she died.[467] Grace suggested she be driven to the Cliff Hotel in Jaffa, a Moorish-style building, situated on a cliff that offered beautiful views out over the Mediterranean.

Anna agreed to the suggestion, and lay in bed for three weeks in her sumptuous hotel room, often receiving visits from her congregation in Jerusalem. When the American Colony's choir came to sing for her one Sunday afternoon, she was deeply moved. When they sang the refrain 'No night, no pain, no death, no tears', the old woman was no longer able to control herself, and cried like a small child.[468]

After Anna had returned once again to Jerusalem, Grace wrote to Bertha saying that their mother was constantly asking for her and the three oldest grandchildren. Anna now had severe diabetes and was experiencing difficulty breathing. Grace felt it was important to gather the family together in Jerusalem, as her end might not be far away. Bertha gave up all her plans for Frederick to become an American citizen, and together they returned to Jerusalem in November 1922 after an absence of seven months.

Despite Anna's physical weakness, her mind remained sharp. "I am not going to die," she said one day when she felt somewhat better. One day,

466 Folder: 1922, American Colony Collection, Jerusalem.
467 Letter from Grace Spafford Whiting to Bertha Spafford Vester, Folder: 1922, American Colony Collection, Jerusalem.
468 Letter dated: Cliff Hotel; Jaffa 21. June 1922, Folder: 1922, American Colony Collection, Jerusalem.

Anna suddenly reverted to speaking to her two daughters in Norwegian. Bertha and Grace were mystified; Anna had never spoken her mother tongue even to the other Norwegian woman in the American Colony, and nobody realized that she could speak it so well.[469] Mother Anna's end was peaceful; she slipped away quietly. The congregation had gathered in the salon, and only her two daughters and adopted son, Jacob, were at her side when she died.[470]

Anna's flock had sung and prayed for a miracle. But early that morning, Bertha came in through the double wooden doors and said: "Mamma is with Jesus." Everything became very still. It was a time for private thoughts. Perhaps Mother would rise up again, like Jesus. The strong belief that nothing could go wrong for Mother Anna battled with the fear that she was gone for ever. No one had ever questioned her capabilities and her God-given mission, which had given the members of the Colony an even stronger faith. But now doubts began to grow.[471]

The funeral was magnificent. Bertha and Grace had decided that "the only music at the funeral would be a song of praise for a meaningful life, a life which had been a blessing for so many." No one was to mourn. There could be no mourning for such a life as Anna's. But as the Colony members filed past the open coffin, the atmosphere was filled with sorrow. They could not imagine carrying on without their Mother.

Telegrams and letters poured in. Lord and Lady Samuel each wrote a letter, the high commissioner stressing that "she left a deep impression upon the religious and social character of the Holy City." Mayor Ragheb Nashashibi emphasized how much help Anna had afforded the poor of Jerusalem. Many Jews mourned as well, and among the condolence letters came one from Professor David Yellin, who, as a boy, had learned English from Horatio Spafford and had later become a member of the Ottoman parliament. He was also one of the first public figures to announce that he was joining the Zionist movement. The American Colony had lost a mother, he wrote, but all Jerusalem felt the loss.[472]

Hundreds of people followed the bier up to the American Colony graveyard. The coffin was buried beneath two beautiful pine trees just under the summit of Mount Scopus. The inscription on the gravestone read: 'Anna T Spafford, born March 16, 1842, died April 17, 1923'. Below

---

469 Bertha Spafford Vester: Unpublished manuscript: *Trip to the United States*, p.13, American Colony Collection, Jerusalem.
470 Spafford Vester: *Our Jerusalem*, New York 1950, pp.288–289.
471 Larsson: *Dala Folk in the Holy Land*, Stockholm 1957, pp.121–122.
472 Letters in Folder: 1923, American Colony Collection, Jerusalem.

was a single word: 'Mother'.

Some months later, the Spafford family received a beautifully written letter from Selma Lagerlöf. No one could doubt Selma's fondness for Anna when they read: "To me she always stands as one of the most gifted, pious and religious women I ever met, and I am glad that I came to know her while she still was in full strength and power of mind."[473]

The converted Indian Jew, Elijah Meyers, recounted his first meeting with Anna to another Swedish author: "Never in my life have I had such a sense of holiness as when I, as a 37-year-old, stepped into the salon one evening in 1889. I cannot describe the sense of holy beauty which I experienced that evening. At the time, I was living at a Christian mission house for Israelites, and was forbidden by them to visit the Colony. One evening at supper I asked: 'I want to know why I may not visit the American Colony', and the director answered: 'Because they are bad people'. But, regardless of this, I visited the Colony thirteen days later. When I approached Mrs Spafford and said: 'I do not believe in God, but perhaps I will change my mind if I can stay here. May I live here with you?' She agreed. She was a wonderful person."[474]

Others who had grown up under Mother Anna and remained under her guardianship as adults found her a psychological mystery. She was a person with many faces, a person of power who knew how to use her spiritual resources. But she was also a friendly soul and a rock for the weak. Her magnetic influence came partly from her ability to manipulate the 'revelations' that she experienced, and to use them like a thread to bind her community together.[475]

Anna had not decided what would happen to the American Colony after her death. There were no written statutes, for while she was alive, her word had always been as final as that of the Bible. When she was gone, the leadership was shared between Brother Jacob, who became the spiritual guide, and Bertha, who took over the administration of the Colony with its 130 or so members.

Immigration to Jerusalem continued, and the city expanded accordingly. The Pro-Jerusalem Committee, headed by Storrs, established clear regulations for how houses should be built. Everything had to fit in with Jerusalem's traditional building style, and façades could be made only

---

473 Letter from Selma Lagerlöf to The Spafford family, dated Mårbacka, June 3, 1923. Folder: 1923, American Colony Collection, Jerusalem.
474 Petri: *On Holy Paths*, Stockholm 1931, p.15.
475 Olof Fahlén: *The Nås Farmers in Jerusalem - the Story of a Strange Migration*, Höganäs 1988, p.102.

from natural stone. The worn stone finials over the Damascus Gate were repaired, as was the Citadel with David's Tower, and the hated Turkish clock tower by the Jaffa Gate was razed. It had been built at the end of the 1800s as a tribute to Sultan Abdul Hamid II.

A 'green belt' was to be created around the city walls with more than 3,000 trees, and 130 streets received ceramic street signs in English, Arabic, and Hebrew. In the Old City, the Pro-Jerusalem Committee was inspired by history, poetry and folklore, with streets receiving such names as Feather Street, Watermelon Alley, Smiths Alley, Stork Street, and the Street of the Whirling Dervishes. Streets outside the walls received names such as Saladin Road, the Street of the Prophets, Herod's Road, Joseph Street and Josiah Street.

In many ways the British, the Palestinian Arabs and the Zionist pioneers lived in three different worlds. The British rulers spoke a different language and thought like colonial masters. Many had served elsewhere in the world. For the Zionists who came to Palestine and who thought in prophetic terms, the dream of a miraculous rebirth of Israel was an everyday part of life. While for the Palestinians, the land was part of their birthright – they knew the towns, villages and countryside inside out, and only a very few thought that the Palestine they knew was in danger of disappearing. In the mid-1920s, 50,000 Jews arrived in Palestine over the course of just two years, most of them from Europe. Many were young, aged on average not more than 27, and settled on the narrow coastal strip running from Jaffa in the south to Haifa in the north, while others went east to Galilee.

Some established *kibbutzim* (collective farms), which became the main symbol of rebirth in this period, whilst others became bricklayers, stonecutters and factory workers, organizing themselves into *Histadrut*, workers' organizations which took care of medical and social services for the Jews. The newcomers from Europe learned to read and write Hebrew, but only a minority bothered to learn Arabic. Their contact with the indigenous Palestinians was limited mostly to trade and the employment of badly paid seasonal workers.

For their part, the British authorities continued to exploit every opportunity to consolidate their influence in the Middle East. On May 15, 1923, King Abdullah of Transjordan proclaimed independence, although it would still take more than two decades for this to become a reality. Sir Herbert Samuel had considerable influence on the fate of Transjordan, believing that the land suited British interests in the region (primarily the protection of the Suez Canal) better than Palestine, since there was no Zionist problem there to complicate matters. Air routes to Iraq and India also overflew Transjordan, which made the country an important link in the chain of imperial communication. As a result, RAF bases were established there, and King Abdullah received all the subsidies he needed to stay solvent in exchange for cooperating with the British.[476]

Despite Britain's policy, in August 1923, the 13th Zionist Congress passed a resolution stating that "eastern and western Palestine are *de facto* a single unit, historically, geographically and economically", and that "the future of Transjordan shall be determined in accordance with the legitimate demands of the Jewish people."[477]

During the 1920s, the American Colony became increasingly famous in Palestine and abroad both because of its business activities and the congregation's religious and social involvement. One writer of the time commented: "No report on the religions in this country would be complete without a certain reference to the American Colony... Earlier they lived in Jerusalem as communists, but the only trace of communism remaining is that they live together in a large house equipped with a private chapel. Furthermore, they take on a self-satisfied bourgeois respectability, all the way to their fingertips."[478] This description of a more-worldly atmosphere in the Colony was accurate. Bertha was open-minded and would often arrange parties with dancing, where the guests smoked cigarettes and drank wine. Gone was any demand for an ascetic lifestyle in anticipation of the Lord's descent upon the Mount of Olives.

Nevertheless, writers continued to portray the Colony in idealistic and uncritical terms. For example, the American Colony Store at the Grand New Hotel was one of Jerusalem's most profitable businesses, but there was never any suggestion of giving open access to its accounts. Throughout the Colony's history thus far, the public were told, its members had been joined in an exalted brotherhood, practicing communism in a way that the Jewish Bolsheviks and their supporters could only dream of. Everyone participated in the creation of wealth, but no one retained either capital or inheritance for themselves. Everyone had turned over their money and property to the common cause. This was now being administered by Frederick Vester, and it was to him that the brethren

476 Martin Sicker: *Between Hashemites and Zionists, The Struggle for Palestine, 1908-1988*, Holmes & Meir New York/London 1989, p.88.
477 Aharon Cohen: *Israel and the Arab World*, p.190.
478 Horace B. Samuel: *Unholy Memories of the Holy Land*, London 1930, p.165.

turned whenever they had material needs.[479]

Brother Frederick was generally regarded as being kind and friendly. Everyone did his work as requested, and all work was considered equal. But this version of the Colony was mainly theoretical, as was the statement that nobody there was ever paid a salary. But most visiting authors did not mention this, preferring to see the community as a model for the Jewish socialists' kibbutz, where everyone was supposed to work according to his ability and receive according to his need.

Whenever members of the Colony complained about not receiving any pay, Mother Anna had always replied: "Does a husband get a wage from his wife, or a wife from her husband? Does a bride expect wages?"[480]

During the war years, all the Colony's property had been registered as German in order to avoid confiscation. But two years after the British arrived in Jerusalem, the American Colony was ordered to reveal the true ownership of its store in the Old City. If it was German property, it could be confiscated by law. Frederick Vester answered the letter, stating clearly that it belonged to the Colony and was run by those members who were most suited to the job. Those who managed the store were neither partners nor part owners; no one had shares, no one was paid, and all the profits went towards providing for the community's basic needs. If there was anything left, this went to the Colony's charitable work.

Three months after Anna's death, her daughters' husbands decided to register the store as a limited company. Now it would be called Vester & Company, American Colony Stores, and would be run officially as a partnership under the names of Frederick Vester and John D Whiting. They explained that the company had begun trading in 1903, with the purpose of selling oriental products to tourists, exporting local products and importing items such as cars, spare parts and accessories, electrical goods, and typewriters.

The other members of the Colony first heard of the partnership during a common meeting late in the summer of 1923, and it came as a shock to many that they had been excluded as partners. Theoretically, this meant that all income from the Colony's various businesses that had been built up over the years would go to Anna's heirs.

Olaf Lind, who had two sons, protested to Bertha: "We have all helped to build up the enterprise, and have just as much right to be part

479 Petri: *On Holy Paths,* Stockholm 1931, pp.153–157.
480 Letter: "*Antoszewski to Brother Elijah,*" Jerusalem, January 10, 1898, Folder: Ex members letters, A–I, American Colony Collection, Jerusalem.

of the company as your family."[481] Bertha became upset at the criticism. She replied: "It is precisely out of concern for you and your family that we have taken these measures. Can't you see? As a registered limited company we have greater control over our income. If you are not satisfied, you can leave us."

There was no full-scale confrontation at the meeting, but the festering resentment caused by this move did not heal and the Swedish members of the Colony began to talk openly about the resulting inequality. They still had to ask Frederick when they needed anything, no matter how small. By contrast, the Americans were able to travel first class to the US and could afford to pay for their children to study there.

Against this background, Bertha no longer participated in the daily prayer meetings, and adopted a tough line with dissenters. In this respect, she continued her mother's policy of cleansing the Colony of malcontents. If people complained about her decisions, she offered to pay for their tickets home. The first such person to be expelled was a Pole. Bertha insisted that he had a "Bolshevik nature and did not fit into the holy congregation". Several of the colonists disliked Bertha's methods. Edith Larsson reminded her that even if Mother Anna used to say "oil and water do not mix", she had never directly thrown anyone out. On the contrary, Anna had always allowed dissident members of the congregation to decide for themselves if they wished to remain.

481 Larsson: *Dala Folk in the Holy Land*, Stockholm 1957, p.126.

Chapter 35

"You may not come back"

There was a drought in Jerusalem during the winter of 1925. Not a single drop of rain fell after January, and the reservoirs (which were supposed to ensure a water supply until November) were nearly empty by April. At the hotels, guests were allowed to bath only once a week, and in hospitals, newborns were bathed every other day. Prayer meetings appealing for an end to the drought were held in the churches, mosques and synagogues, but to no avail. The British authorities tried to avert a full-scale crisis by bringing in several thousand tons of water by rail. Older people said that Jerusalem had not been this dry for 64 years.

Construction of new facilities for the city proceeded at full speed, however. New roads were built, along with factories and schools; but the 'crown jewel' of the construction programme was the Hebrew University. It was ready to be dedicated on April 1, with guests invited from as far afield as war-torn China in the east to America in the west. The *SS President Arthur* sailed over from the US flying the Zionist 'Star of David' flag – the first passenger vessel in history to do so.

From early morning on April 1, a steady stream of vehicles travelled from the Damascus Gate to the northern part of the Mount of Olives. The 500 most privileged guests had received white numbered invitations, and more than 1,000 people got red unnumbered ones. An additional 10,000 people, who had not received invitations, also came, and a big party of photographers was on hand to immortalize what many Zionists considered the greatest Jewish occasion of the decade.

High up on the eastern slope of Mount Scopus, facing the blue sky and the empty, rugged wasteland down towards the River Jordan and the Dead Sea, the guests were shown to their seats by members of Jerusalem's sports clubs, all dressed in white. A stage of some 30 square yards had been constructed out over the hill, and the stands were covered with carpets. In front of the most prominent guests stood uniformed *kavasses* – or ceremonial guards – with curved sabres and uniforms embroidered with silk.

By 3pm, people were wedged, shoulder-to-shoulder, beneath a sea of smart hats. There were silk top hats, red fezzes, blue turbans, brown monks' hoods, black berets and white tropical helmets, as well as ladies' hats of all shapes and colours. From a distance, the hillside looked like a living oriental carpet, just as colourful as the Persian ones which covered the stage.[482]

The main guest of honour was 77-year-old Lord Arthur Balfour, who was to preside over the formal opening of the university. He cut an impressive figure in his scarlet gown edged with lavender and his four-cornered mortar board atop his silver-grey hair, which gleamed around his head almost like a halo. At Balfour's side sat the Zionist leader, Chaim Weizmann, in a bright red gown with white edges, and a pointed hat atop his pale, egg-shaped head. Sir Herbert Samuel was also present, but he was so reserved as to be almost inconspicuous. Next to him sat the conqueror of Palestine himself, Field-Marshall Viscount Allenby.

Also prominent were two chief rabbis, one of whom served Palestine's Western Jews and wore a broad-brimmed beaver-fur hat and had a flowing grey beard. The other, the chief rabbi for the Eastern Jews, wore a brocaded caftan and a lavender and red turban. Other prominent guests included the great physicist, Albert Einstein, and the greatest of all living Jewish poets, Haim Nahman Bialik, who had settled in Palestine the previous year.

The Palestinian Arabs had called a general strike on the day of Balfour's arrival and the university opening. Christian and Muslim Arabs alike closed their shops, teachers did not turn up at school and taxis did not run. Only Jerusalem's mayor, three Palestinian officials and a few Bedouin sheikhs ignored the strike and attended the opening ceremonies.[483]

Despite her growing opposition to Zionism, Bertha Spafford Vester had accepted her invitation, and, from her seat near the stage, she could clearly see Lord Balfour's face as he rose and removed his cap, standing bareheaded with his back to the Nebo Mountains. At first, he seemed

482 John Frænkel: *Fra Nilen til Jordan* (From the Nile to Jordan), København 1926, pp.119–128.
483 Monthly Political Report, March 1925. Herbert Samuel to the Colonial Secretary. April 21, 1925, CO 733/92, p.2.

almost unable to speak; those who sat in the front row could see the tears running down his cheeks. But after a while he composed himself, and the two translators, one Hebrew and the other Arabic, relayed his speech to the non-English speaking guests, a paragraph at a time.

Balfour repeated what everyone knew – that the Arabs were deeply critical of recent developments in Palestine, and certainly could not imagine how a Hebrew university could be of any benefit to them. But the old statesman said that this was not so, and urged them to think twice about this: "There is no doubt that the language must be Hebrew," he said, "but I hope the Arabs will remember the darkest days of the Dark Ages, when Western civilization seemed almost to have disappeared... it was the Jews and the Arabs together, in cooperation, who brought forth the first shafts of light which later illuminated that gloomy period."[484]

But for all such idealistic hopes, Bertha was convinced there could not be cooperation between the Arabs and Jews of Palestine. The Zionists' plan was to create a Jewish state in a country where Arabs were in the majority, so how could they then expect Arab cooperation? She asked herself whether Balfour had any understanding at all of what the Palestinians were feeling. After the dedication ceremony, when Balfour was driven to Government House on the Mount of Olives, Bertha wondered if he would notice all the houses and shops bearing black banners and flags of mourning, and whether he could hear the women ululating, their tongues vibrating to make the characteristic Arab shrill.

Privately, Bertha thought it was absurd to hear talk of the Jews' 'return' to Palestine when most immigrants had no roots in the country. But even if they had, and if their claim to Palestine was indeed based upon Judaism's origins in the region, then by the same argument all Calvinists should be able to demand unlimited access to Switzerland, all Roman Catholics who wished should be able to move to Italy, and all Episcopalians, whether they were Americans, Chinese, or Eskimos, could insist on settling in England.[485] But although she held strong views on the subject, Bertha was careful whom she chose to share them with, making a point of maintaining friendly relations with the Zionists, even if she felt critical of their beliefs.[486] For most of the time, she concentrated on the Colony's charity work, as well as ensuring that the community continued to be highly thought of in Jerusalem.

484 Israel Cohen (ed.): *Speeches on Zionism by The Earl of Balfour*, London 1928, p.84.
485 Spafford Vester: *Our Jerusalem*, 2nd edition, p.361.
486 Bentwich: *Mandate Memories 1918–1948*, London 1965, p.65, Spafford Vester: *Our Jerusalem*, 2nd edition, pp.359–381.

Within the Colony, dissatisfaction with Bertha's style of leadership was growing. Even the ageing Alvilde Strand from Bergen began to think about leaving. She had joined Anna and Horatio's band of believers in Chicago in 1896, travelling to Jerusalem with her husband and an infant who died the following year. When her husband also died, Alvilde devoted much of her energy to caring for the sick and helping the poor in her personal capacity, rarely giving much time to assist in the running of the Colony. Initially she had incurred some disapproval with her desire to embrace a more militant, zealous form of Christianity, but she finally yielded to Anna's will and accepted that there should be no missionary work.[487]

When Anna died in 1923, Alvilde felt empty, and at one morning meeting said that she wanted to go back to Norway. The reason she gave was that she needed a change in order to develop spiritually, although in reality she was now disillusioned with life in the sect, and felt that Bertha lacked her mother's strength of faith. Alvilde wrote to the Norwegian consulate-general in Alexandria asking to have her Norwegian passport returned, since her citizenship had been revoked automatically after she emigrated to America. But changes in Norwegian immigration law meant that while Alvilde could be issued with a new temporary passport it would be necessary for her to return to Norway to reinstate her citizenship.[488] Thus on a summer day in 1925, Alvilde left Jerusalem. Three days after her arrival in Norway she wrote to Bertha to tell her that her family in Bergen was "happy to give me a home and a resting place". She enclosed some money for the Colony's work among the poor.[489]

One month later, something happened that neither Alvilde nor Bertha could have predicted. On August 26, Anna Spafford was the subject of a lecture given by Selma Lagerlöf to the Universal Christian Conference on Life and Work in Stockholm. The delegates gathered in Blasieholm Church, along with members of the Swedish Royal family, to hear the internationally renowned author speak about Anna's mission at the American Colony. Selma was introduced to the audience by the Swedish Archbishop, then walked in her slightly limping manner up to the lectern, around which most of the prominent delegates were seated in a semicircle. Every other seat in the church was taken.

487 Folder: Alvilde Strand, p.2, American Colony Collection, Jerusalem.
488 Letters from the Consulate-General in Alexandria to the Foreign Office, from 1923 to 1925, Riksarkivet, Box 6341, p.15, "Bibehold av norsk statsborgerskap" (Reinstatement of Norwegian Citizenship), Alvilde Strand.
489 Letter from Alvilde Strand to Bertha Spafford Vester, Bergen, July 25, 1925. Folder: Ex members' letters M–Y, American Colony Collection, Jerusalem.

The diminutive grey-haired woman remained standing for a brief moment in front of the microphone before beginning to narrate the story of Anna's life-changing experience in a melodic and beautiful voice: "It was a foggy night out on the Atlantic. Two great ships had collided..." When Lagerlöf recounted the moment when Anna "realized that her children had been torn away from her, and that they had been drowned", many of delegates wept. All were riveted by the narrative and by the moment when "she heard a mighty voice, a voice from another world that filled her ears: 'It is true that it is easy to die. That which is difficult is to live.'" [490] For one whole hour, Selma held the assembly in rapt attention as she told the story of the woman who, for nearly 40 years, had been one of Jerusalem's most prominent religious leaders and her work caring for Jewish refugees, for suffering pilgrims in danger of death, and of "the five hundred hungry war refugees who had daily been fed".

Selma knew little about Anna's origins; she certainly had no idea that the woman she spoke about had been baptized Anne Tobine Larsdatter Øglende. Indeed, no one present had any idea that she had been born Norwegian. For Selma and the others she was simply Anna Spafford. The Swedish author was aware that she had played a significant role in mythologizing Anna through the character of Mrs Gordon in her novel. She hoped that the ecumenical gathering would see the American Colony as an example of how peaceful communal existence could be achieved, and to learn too that sometimes that which seemed impossible was possible after all.

But inter-denominational relations amongst the conference-goers were not good. There was tension between the German and French delegations, as well as between Christian representatives from distant parts of the world. At the end of her lecture, therefore, Selma repeated that "harmony is possible, harmony can be achieved between people from many different nations... between Calvinists and Lutherans, between Protestants and Greeks, harmony between Greeks and Catholics, harmony between Christians and non-Christians..."

But Selma's words did not find fertile soil in Palestine. To the Arabs, Jewish plans for the country were all too obvious, and many were relieved in 1925 when the British government replaced High Commissioner Sir Herbert Samuel with Field-Marshall Herbert Plumer. After serving in Sudan and South Africa, Plumer had been commander of the Second

---

490 Copy of manuscript of Selma Lagerlöf's address to the Uiversal Christian Conference of Life and Work, Stockholm, August, 26, 1925. American Colony Collection, Jerusalem.

Army in Flanders during the Great War, an overwhelming victory over the Germans at the battle of Messines in 1917. Unlike Samuel, Plumer was not Jewish, which was taken by many Arabs as a good sign. The Arabs had been particularly indignant that Samuel had repeatedly turned a blind eye to the arming and training of Zionist paramilitaries in violation of the terms of the British mandate itself.[491]

For their part, the Zionist lobby were dissatisfied with the appointment of Plumer, and there was general apprehension that the choice of a Christian Englishman as high commissioner would be disadvantageous. Many Jews also opposed the appointment because the British government had chosen Plumer without first consulting Chaim Weizmann and the Zionists.[492]

Lagerlöf's call for "unity" would find little support within the American Colony either. Only four days after her homage to Anna at the Bergen conference, a public dispute erupted between Olaf Lind and his two younger brothers, Lars and Nils. The two contacted the Swedish consul, Lewis Larsson in response to inflammatory accusations Olaf had made against the Colony in the Swedish press. After Anna's death, Olaf had returned to Sweden where he had written a newspaper article denouncing Bertha's regime and accusing both Jacob Spafford and Pastor Olof Henrik Larsson of duping his parents into selling their farm and property in Nås. Now, he demanded that the money should be returned, or that he should be granted some kind of compensation payment from the American Colony's business activities. Olaf further accused Consul Larsson of having done nothing to help him. Olaf's brothers did not agree with his demands, and made their views plain in their letter to the Swedish consul.[493]

Bertha referred to a number of newspaper articles that had appeared recently in the Swedish press when she replied to Alvilde Strand. Alvilde, who had also read the articles in the public library in Bergen, replied that she thought the stories were "terrible".[494] In the same letter, she went on to say that her elderly mother, who had been ill for some time, had passed away. She also began to voice doubts about the wisdom of remaining in Norway and suggested that she missed the community in Jerusalem. One

491 Sahar Huneidi: *A Broken Trust, Herbert Samuel, Zionism and the Palestinians*, IB Tauris, London and New York, 2001, p.235.
492 Fern Andrews: *The Holy Land under the Mandate, Volume I*, Cambridge 1931, p.222.
493 *Dagens Nyheter* July 17, 1925. Copy of letter from Lars and Nils Lind to Consul H L Larsson, August 29, 1925, American Colony Collection, Jerusalem.
494 Letter from Alvilde Strand to Bertha Spafford Vester, dated Bergen November 18, 1925, Folder: Ex members' letters M–Y, American Colony Collection, Jerusalem.

letter ended poignantly "I pray to God daily to show me what to do, and how to live."

But Bertha had little sympathy for Alvilde's problems, and did not even answer the letter. Despite her devotion to Mother Anna, Bertha felt that her mother's friend had failed her badly at the time immediately following her mother's death, when she had most needed support. On the contrary, Bertha had been left alone to face the various disputes that had broken out in the Colony in the ensuing weeks. She now felt that holding the Colony together and administering its various charitable organizations was more important than tending to Alvilde's spiritual self-absorption. Christmas was approaching and Bertha had more than ever to organize. For the first time, a celebration had been arranged for the evening of Christmas Day in the fields outside Bethlehem. Bertha had been asked to sing at the event, since she had inherited her mother's beautiful voice and musical talent. Earlier that same afternoon, she had been helping with preparations for a Christmas party for the School of Domestic Science, of which she was head.

As Bertha walked back to the Colony that Christmas Day, she caught sight of a young woman in one of the city's alleyways. She was walking slowly, helped by a man and an old woman, and was carrying what appeared to be a bundle of dirty rags. Bertha realized that the woman was ill, and hurried to offer assistance. "Where are you going?" she asked. But the man only answered in weary tones: "God only knows." Bertha looked at the bundle and saw that it contained a newborn child, which could not have been more than a few days old. "Your wife is quite sick," she said to the man.

"I know," he answered. "She's been sitting on the back of a donkey for six hours in order to get to hospital, but we found it was closed to new patients today because it's Christmas, and many of the staff are on holiday." Bertha was struck by the biblical parallels of the situation. Here she was, standing beside an exhausted latter-day Madonna and child without shelter, while she herself was on her way to sing about baby Jesus – born in a stable and laid in a manger because there was no room at the inn.

By this stage, a number of people had gathered about them, and Bertha asked one woman if the sick mother could rest at her house with the baby while she went to the hospital to get a stretcher. She was also certain that she would be able to find the sick young mother a bed there. From the hospital she called Frederick and told him to take the children to the Bethlehem celebration anyway and explain that she would not be able to attend. But what the child's father had said was true; not only was the hospital not admitting any new patients, but most of the British nurses were absent, many of them being members of the choir about to sing at the Bethlehem fields. She did, however, manage to find two porters, who brought a stretcher and conveyed the new mother and her baby to a bed. Bertha stayed long enough to make sure that the woman was taken care of, and that the child was bathed and fed.

Boxing Day arrived with gorgeous weather. The birds were singing as if spring had come, and at the Spafford Vester's home the six children were full of excitement, playing with their new presents. Bertha had forgotten the sick woman and her infant completely when, suddenly, she looked out of the window and saw the husband standing outside the gate with the child bundled up in his arms. She went out and was told that the woman had died that night. "Could the American Colony take care of

Frederick and Bertha Vester with their six children

330

my poor child?" he said. "I love him, but I must put his welfare before my own, and if I take him back to the cave where we live, he will surely die."

Bertha knew this was very probably true. Frederick warned that the Colony did not have the resources to take on this extra burden, but Bertha could not refuse after what had happened the night before. They took the baby boy and baptized him Noel. A small room was set aside for the baby at the School of Domestic Science and Bertha found a nursemaid for him. Within two weeks two more motherless children were brought there, and Bertha realized that the Colony now had a new mission to fulfil. In time, the School of Domestic Science was relocated, and the American Colony founded a new charitable organisation: the Anna Spafford Infant Home.

From Bergen, Alvilde Strand continued to write to Bertha. "'If I forget thee O Jerusalem, let my right hand forget her cunning," she quoted from the Bible. "This my soul often sings. I feel like a pilgrim in a foreign land here in Norway, and I'll be so happy when I see there is a way open for me to return to my sweet home. May God show me the way how, and when… sometimes I feel frightened that I shall lose my judgment of what is right, and just grow to accept my strange life in Bergen. May God keep me, in his fear."[495]

Bertha did not answer this letter either, so Alvilde sent another, this time to Frederick, in which she enclosed her old passport. She asked for Frederick's help to get her an entry permit for Palestine, saying that she had been to the British consulate in Bergen and had been informed that the Palestinian immigration authorities now required all arrivals to have a valid entry permit.[496]

Alvilde was entirely unprepared for the reply she subsequently received from Bertha. "I took up the matter with the assembly," Anna's daughter wrote. "There was unanimity in their feelings that over the past ten years, you haven't spent so much as one in dedicating your work to the Colony's activities, and we feel that you are better off where you are. Nothing can prevent you from living a true Christian life wherever in the world you may be, so your separation from us should not make any difference. I am returning your letter and passport; you are now with your sister and her family, which is where we feel that you belong and where you can be of most support. Remember that your sister has been most kind to you, and needs you with her now. We say these things with the greatest respect, but speaking frankly, I feel it would be unwise for you to

495 Letter from Alvilde Strand to Bertha Spafford Vester, April 20, 1927. Folder: Ex-members' letters, M–Y, American Colony Collection, Jerusalem.
496 Letter from Alvilde Strand, to Frederick Vester, May 27, 1927. Folder: Ex-members letters, M–Y, Folder: Mrs Alvilde Strand. American Colony Collection, Jerusalem.

return to us... we all send our love to you, dear Mrs Strand. It must be a relief to know that your poor mother is at rest, it must have been deeply distressing to see her suffer and be so helpless."[497]

Bertha did not want Alvilde to return, and her forceful personality ensured that her decision was final. But some of the other colonists found this antipathy towards Alvilde hard to understand. The Norwegian woman had been well liked, and had always been one of the Colony's most helpful members, assisting both with the sick and with tourists who came to visit the Holy City. Many guests had remarked on Alvilde's friendliness,[498] and although she had withdrawn from much of the community's public life after the death of her husband, when Mother Anna was in her final illness it was mostly Sister Alvilde who had cared for her.

But none of this was of any consequence now. Bertha was unable to forgive what she felt was Alvilde's desertion following Anna's death. A month passed after Alvilde received Bertha's rejection before she found the strength to write a new letter: "It was such a shock for me, when I understood from your last letter that you all disowned me," she wrote. "True enough, for a long time I admit that I neglected both yourself and the Colony, and did not contribute to your work as I should have done. But nonetheless, I still hoped to God that He might allow me to return if I was prepared to learn from my mistakes, and get fully involved in the Colony's work in one way or another. Now this hope has come to an end, and as for me I feel quite homeless... forgive me for not having written earlier, but I have been so grieved at your decision that it's only now that I can find the strength. I learn from the newspapers that an earthquake has struck Palestine, and am thinking of you. How dreadful it must have been for you, please let me hear how everything is."[499]

Bertha answered, but remained unyielding – there was no question of Alvilde coming back.

497 Letter from Bertha Spafford Vester, June 13, 1927 to Alvilde Strand. Folder: Ex-members' letters, M–Y, Mrs. Alvilde Strand. American Colony Collection, Jerusalem.
498 M. E. Mogannem: "In the Matter of the American Colony and the Matter of the arbitration with [...] Mrs Alvilde Strand," May 28, 1931. Folder: Alvilde Strand. American Colony Collection, Jerusalem.
499 Letter from Alvilde Strand to Bertha Spafford Vester, Bergen July 13, 1927. Folder: Ex-members' letters M–Y, American Colony Collection.

Chapter 36

The Road to
Decisions and Divorce

Bertha's management style at the American Colony was only one of the issues that led to discontent within its ranks. Certain members were also critical of the elaborate parties she threw, and felt she lacked her mother's Christian qualities. By now, Bertha's sister, Grace, and her brother-in-law, John D Whiting, had moved to New York to run the American branch of the Colony Store, which was operating at a loss. John went reluctantly, wishing that he could remain in Jerusalem, his birthplace; but the move was necessary in order for their three children to maintain American citizenship.

In 1927, Nils Lind married Bertha's oldest daughter, Anna Grace, and became accepted as one of the Colony's 'inner circle'. Nils offered his help in trying to revive the fortunes of the store in New York, supervising the dispatch of a new consignment of goods worth $200,000. But its arrival did not change the shop's fortunes – trade remained poor, and not one cent was received back in Jerusalem.

Meanwhile, Nils' elder brother, Olaf, continued the battle to retrieve his share of the American Colony's wealth. He knew that the Colony had important assets that could, in theory, be realized: the property itself was worth a lot of money and the main Colony Store in Jerusalem also yielded large profits. Olaf Lind now had an influential job as director of the American Express travel bureau, and he was prepared to go to court if necessary to get money from the Vester and Whiting families, who had control over the major assets.

In June 1928, Olaf wrote to Lewis Larsson, seeking his support: Probably you have little understanding of my actions regarding the matter of Vester & Co, and may feel that I am persecuting the leaders of the Colony unnecessarily. Let me try to make my position clearer. As things currently stand, all the Colony's properties and business are now registered in the names of Vester and Whiting as a partnership with specified capital. They are listed as the only partners and owners, and there is no clause stating that they are holding it in trust for rest of the members. Not only is there no reason for them to object to such a clause, but I had a confidential meeting with Mrs Spafford shortly before her death, during which she informed me that Mrs Vester had recently signed an agreement binding her to a previous agreement that all the Colony's assets were the property of the entire congregation. But notwithstanding this, the establishment of Vester & Co as a limited company took place only three months after Anna Spafford's death. Thus, if you all agree to hand over all your rights to him now, Mrs Spafford's document will be annulled. I should warn you that in such an event, neither yourself nor any other members of the community would be left with any interests in the American Colony whatsoever. If Vester & Whiting died, their children could (if they so desire) sell the whole business without consultation with the rest of the congregation, and you could find yourself facing severe repercussions because as Swedish consul, you would be blamed for not attending to the rights of your fellow subjects. If the business activities of the Colony are to continue, let it be upon an honourable and respectable basis."[500]

Bertha had already realized it would not be possible for the Colony to continue on its current path. In the past, Mother Anna's word had been law, but Bertha knew that in order to retain any credibility within the community, she and the other leaders would have to become more accountable. In 1928, she sought legal advice, asking a New York lawyer, Arthur Townsend, to create a charter for the Jerusalem Colony.

Townsend's draft document was circulated among the members of the Colony for six months for discussion and approval. The lawyer's recommendation was that a separate company should own and operate the business activities, which, in turn, would finance the operation of the Colony and its work. Townsend had included a description of a company in New York that could act as a model.

A general meeting was called for on May 7, 1929 and it was agreed that Townsend's proposals were "the concrete expression of what had been the American Colony's unwritten laws from the beginning". The document was accepted and signed by all the members present, and later by those others who could not attend the meeting. Greatly relieved, Bertha and

500 Letter from Olaf Lind to Lewis Larsson, June 15, 1928. Folder: 1928 and Ex-Members' letters, A-I, American Colony Collection, Jerusalem.

Frederick then left for the US, to meet up with Grace and John.

Meanwhile, a number of Colony members, among them Lewis Larsson, began to have second thoughts about the new legal agreement. They feared that the Spaffords and Vesters wanted only whatever arrangements were in their own personal interests, and that the new statutes should be changed. By the summer of 1929, Lewis had decided that he would re-examine the new agreement to make sure that it was in the interests of the whole Colony. First, however, he felt that he needed a long holiday in Sweden.

Lewis required funding for his trip. In the absence of Frederick Vester and John D Whiting, Lars Lind was acting as head of the Colony's business, and transferred nearly £400 sterling to an account at Barclay's Bank for Lewis' use. This transfer was agreed to unanimously by the congregation, although several of the older members were sceptical of Lewis and felt that he had changed for the worse since becoming the Swedish consul.[501] They pointed out that he was no longer active as the Colony's official photographer, and that he sometimes refused to represent the American Colony when needed. Some said they doubted Lewis was interested in the Colony's spiritual life any longer, and questioned whether he would even participate in the Colony's work when he returned from Europe.

It was decided to call Lewis in to a meeting for him to explain what his agenda would be during his trip abroad, and Lars Lind was given the task of telling him that he was to be questioned. Lewis' response was to say he had no intention of explaining himself before the rest of the congregation. In taking this position, he had violated a fundamental tenet of the Colony: to present oneself for consultation when required. His refusal was duly interpreted by the community as a statement that he no longer cared whether he remained a member or not.

Lars Lind was told to go back to Lewis and Edith and inform them that they were no longer considered to be Colony members. Furious, Lewis threatened to withdraw Lars' Swedish citizenship. The congregation responded by appointing one of the assistants in their photographic laboratory, Mats Matsson, as the new head of the photography department; furthermore, Lewis was told he could no longer work at the Colony Store.[502]

---

501 Memoranda: "During the summer of 1929," pp.27–28. Folder: General Memoranda, American Colony Collection.
502 Undated memorandum to Sweden's Foreign Minister, Folder: Memorandum. Letter from Hol Lars Larsson to C H Perrotti, Esq Advocate, p r Fast's Hotel, March 1, 1931. Folder: Hol Lars Larsson (Lewis), Memoranda: The Occupation, p. 15, Folder: General Memoranda, American Colony Collection.

Despite these disagreements, everyone at the Colony remained very fond of the Larssons' youngest child, who was to remain in Jerusalem while his parents vacationed in Europe. Whatever they felt about his parents, the colonists were more than happy to look after the boy.

The emotional storms that were buffeting the American Colony in 1929 were nothing compared with what afflicted the rest of Palestine. In Jerusalem, many Muslims were afraid the Zionists would seek to lay claim to the Wailing Wall. The mufti asked the British authorities to confirm Islam's traditional rights to this wall, which marked the West side of the Muslims' holy area in the Old City. According to Islamic tradition, the wall was where the Prophet Mohammed had tethered *al-Buraq* [his horse with wings] that would take him up to heaven. Whilst it was true that the wall was holy for both religions, it was the Muslims who owned it, the land it stood on and the passage in front of it.

Jerusalem's grand mufti led an international campaign to prevent the Jews from getting greater rights to the wall than they already had. The issue became a symbol of the larger battle against Zionism; indeed, some Zionists were also demanding full Jewish control over the Muslim's Haram al-Sharif, with the aim of rebuilding the temple there. The tension came to a head in Tel Aviv on August 14, 1929, when a 6,000-strong crowd of Zionists gathered to protest against Muslim claims on the Wailing Wall. They chanted: "The Wall is ours." At the same time, thousands more Jews had gathered by the Wailing Wall in Jerusalem to pray. The following day, a group of Zionists armed with clubs arrived at the wall and raised the blue and white flag.

In the wake of such provocation, rumours spread throughout the Arab community. Muslims at prayer were told that the Jews were planning to destroy al-Aqsa and the Dome of the Rock, and reconstruct Solomon's Temple on its site. One group of Palestinian Arabs marched to the Wall, and clashes broke out. Palestinians came to Jerusalem from nearby towns and villages carrying clubs to protect the Islamic holy sites from Zionist attack.

The British were powerless. The high commissioner and many senior officials were on leave in England, and only 292 British policemen, supported by 100 soldiers with six armoured vehicles, were deployed throughout Palestine.

Furious Palestinians stormed up the Jaffa Road and attacked Jewish shops, and any Jew they saw. In mixed neighbourhoods, Christian Palestinians hid their Jewish neighbours to save them from being beaten to death. Nevertheless, 17 Jews were killed during the riots in Jerusalem. In Hebron, things were even worse, with about 70 Orthodox Jews living in the Muslim quarter of the town massacred by enraged Muslims. The mob had first broken into a Jewish religious school on August 23, killing the only student they could find there. The following day, they broke into Jewish homes, knifing or beating the occupants to death. Hundreds more Jews were rescued by their Muslim neighbours and by Arab policemen.

The British police chief in Hebron later recounted his experiences: "On hearing screams coming from a nearby house, I went up the entrance passage and saw an Arab in the act of cutting off a child's head with a sword. He had already struck him once and was preparing for another blow, but upon seeing me he tried to turn the weapon on me instead but missed. He was practically on the muzzle of my rifle, so I shot him low in the groin. Behind him was a Jewish woman smothered in blood, with a man standing over her with a dagger in his hand. I recognized him as a police constable named Issa Sherif from Jaffa; when he saw me he bolted into the next room and tried to bolt the door, shouting in Arabic: 'Your Honour, I am a policeman! I came here to help the lady, and I shot her attacker!'[503]

The same afternoon, British reinforcements arrived in Hebron, but they were too late to save the victims of the slaughter. The Jewish dead were buried in mass graves, which the British ordered the Palestinians to dig, and two days later the surviving Jews were evacuated from Hebron for their own safety. They left in a convoy of lorries and buses, with a British military escort; the Palestinians stood by the side of the road and watched in silence.

The wave of violence also spread to Safed, a Jewish holy town in the north of Palestine that was home to 10,000 Palestinians and 3,000 Jews. This time the British response was quicker, and the riot lasted only 20 minutes before the arrival of military police, who managed to shoot two of the perpetrators. Even so, the plundering and burning of Jewish homes continued for two more days.

In the meantime, Muslim gangs attacked southern districts of Tel Aviv, but this time the Zionists were ready for them. The mobs were met by Haganah riflemen, who counter-attacked and killed a number of Palestinians. In all, 133 Jews and 116 Palestinians were killed during the course of a week.

Yet again, the root of the trouble was deemed to be Jewish immigration and land purchases. In Britain, where the Labour Party had come to

[503] *Report by R Cafferata on events in Hebron on 24 Aug 1929* (1929 Palestine Commission, Minutes, Vol. II, p.983, exhibit no. 8). Cited in Wasserstein: *The British in Palestine, The Mandatory Government and the Arab-Jewish Conflict* Oxford 1991, p.237.

power under James Ramsay MacDonald, there was disagreement over the government's policy on Palestine. One Labour faction favoured the Jews because of the socialist policies of Histadrut, while another believed that the Palestinians were victims of Jewish imperialism. However, the governing party was united on one point – that a limit should be put on Jewish immigration to Palestine and a restriction placed on the purchase of land.

At the beginning of September 1929, Bertha and Frederick received a telegram urging them to return to Jerusalem. There had been a revolt amongst the younger members of the Colony. On their return, the couple contacted the American consul-general, Paul Knabenshue, to secure his support in seeking a settlement to the dispute. They brought with them a draft of the charter and by-laws for the future organization of the Colony. While they were in the US they had established two companies: American Colony of Jerusalem, Incorporated; and American Colony Stores, Incorporated. The registration documents for both had been issued in the United States.

Bertha explained that the charter and by-laws were to be presented to the entire community in the belief that this would help to end the revolt. Frederick said he favoured a system that would enable individual members to build up private assets from the accumulated common property. Consul Knabenshue assured Bertha and Frederick of his full assistance, and returned the draft copies within a week saying that he could see no objections to the contents.[504]

The Colony members were satisfied with the new charter and by-laws, and the crisis was soon defused. But Mathilda Larsson, the widow of Olof Henrik Larsson, remained unhappy about the expulsion of Lewis and Edith from the congregation. Mathilda still lived in the main house, but after Lewis and Edith had moved into the Swedish consul's residence nearby, she no longer took part in meetings. She also refused to join the rest of the Colony in signing the letter to the Larssons, informing them they were no longer members.[505]

504 Letter from Frederick Vester to Arthur Townsend, New York, April 3, 1930. Folder: Townsend letters, American Colony Collection.
505 The Resolution was adapted September 27, 1929: It stipulated that 'whereas Lewis and Edith Larsson separated themselves from the Colony and resigned from all committees of the American Colony Aid Association because they considered that they were not eligible, we therefore accept their resignation with regret, from membership in the Colony and from all committees pertaining thereto. Yours sincerely (signatures)'. Unpublished memoranda: Reconciliation with the Larssons, pp.29–30, Folder: General memoranda, American Colony Collection.

Bertha realized the expulsion of the Larssons had been too drastic a move, so at a communal meeting it was agreed that the letter expelling them should be rescinded. A committee was formed to liaise with Lewis and Edith when they arrived back in Jerusalem, agreeing that "if the Larssons wish to live in harmony with the remaining members and abide by the principles of the Colony, and if Lewis Larsson abandons his ornamental status and agrees to assume his part of the responsibility for upkeep and general welfare", then there would be a reconciliation. To aid this process, it was decided that the senior Swedish diplomat in Cairo, Baron Harold de Bildt, would act as intermediary, since he was a friend of both the American Colony and the Larssons. Lewis and Edith were in England, settling their son, Theo, into his new school, so a telegram was sent via the Swedish legation in London asking them to travel to Cairo because "we have asked Minister de Bildt to help us come to an understanding".

The answer from London was unequivocal. The Larssons would be returning directly to Jerusalem at the beginning of November. A meeting in Cairo was out of the question because, as far as Lewis and Edith were concerned, there was nothing to discuss. As a result of this response, a new general meeting was called. Since the previous one, attitudes towards the Larssons had hardened. Now, most of the congregation felt that Lewis had squandered his chance of making amends. A new committee was chosen to write a draft document of separation relating to the Larsson couple. In the meantime, the other members (except for Mathilda Larsson) approved officially the recommendations for the American Colony of Jerusalem, Incorporated, and for the American Colony Stores, Incorporated.

Lewis Larsson was not the only member of the community to clash with Bertha's powerful personality. Another was Elijah Meyers, the converted Indian Jew, who believed that the Colony and Mother Anna represented the fulfilment biblical prophecies that Christ would return. Elijah had written down all of Anna's 'messages' in a book, which he considered to be almost as sacred as the Bible. He often read from it to prove to Bertha that she had deviated from her mother's ideals and led the Colony into sin.

One day, Bertha could stand no more of Elijah's goading. She went over to the tall, thin Indian as he was reading aloud, snatched the book from his hands and tore it into little bits. Brother Elijah did not say a word, but looked as if he would faint: "Bertha!" he gasped. "You should

The American Colony's palm garden

never have done that. That book with your mother's messages in it was my whole life."[506]

"And you should not have it," replied Bertha, ripping up the remaining bits.

Elijah packed and left. He did not have much to take – his belongings barely filled a satchel. If Bertha felt badly, she did not show it. She told the others that Elijah was insane, and her family confirmed this by revealing that the 75-year-old man had recently married an 18-year-old prostitute, newly released from prison, in the belief that the marriage was the fulfilment of a prophecy.

Bertha did, however, provide Elijah with enough money to live on, even though he no longer lived at the Colony. When he died a year later he was buried at the American Colony's cemetery.[507]

When Lewis and Edith returned to Jerusalem, they refused to meet Bertha or any of the other Colony leaders. Lewis said that anyone wishing to see them would have to come to the Swedish consulate. Bertha was still hopeful that a reconciliation could be achieved, but she felt the consulate

506 Lind & Walström: *Jerusalem Travellers,* Stockholm 1981, p.43.
507 Letter from Horatio Vester to Arthur Townsend, Jerusalem, April 11, 1930, Folder: Townsend letters, American Colony Collection.

was not an appropriate venue for a meeting. Lewis agreed to another venue, on condition that the local director of Barclay's Bank, Stanley Clark, could be present as a witness. The Colony's members agreed. Approval was also given to send Bertha, Frederick and Lars Lind to the meeting.

During the meeting, Lewis repeated that he and Edith did not deserve the kind of treatment they had received from the Colony. He had done nothing wrong, and the expulsion letter had come as a total shock. Nevertheless, both wanted to reconcile with the Colony and accepted the newly ratified guidelines. But Lewis was not happy that the Colony's business activities had been registered formally in the United States without any of the rank-and-file members being informed. Bertha said there could be no question of making any changes now; everyone else had accepted the recommendations and, in any case, both corporations would also be registered in Palestine. The only thing remaining to do was to have it made public in the *Official Gazette*.

The recommendations were handed over to Lewis for his inspection, together with two pages of original signatures. He, Edith and Mathilda were asked to familiarize themselves with and sign the by-laws of the new organization, as the others in the Colony had done. Lewis answered that, as Swedish vice-consul, he first wanted to send the documents to the Swedish embassy in Cairo for their approval before signing them. Frederick agreed, and took them personally to Egypt.

Baron de Bildt suggested certain amendments. Frederick agreed to some of them and promised to put everything before the Colony members. But when he arrived back in Jerusalem, Lewis was still not satisfied: he wanted to speak directly with the Swedish diplomat in Cairo, rather than through an intermediary. He also insisted that the community should formally apologise to both him and Edith for the letter expelling them from the community As Swedish consul, he felt that he deserved a certain level of respect from the other members.[508]

It was agreed that there should be another meeting on December 20, and since Lewis had the certified documents, including the two pages of original signatures, he was asked to sign and return them. He replied that he had asked the American consul to study them "and be sure the rights of the Americans were also taken into consideration".

Frederick went to Consul Knabenshue to ask for the papers, but was told that under diplomatic rules they could be returned only to Lewis, as

508 Unpublished memoranda: Incorporation. Folder: General Memoranda, American Colony Collection, Jerusalem.

he was the person who had presented them in the first place. On December 20, Frederick finally received the documents back (still unsigned by the Larssons) just before the start of the meeting.

In the event, none of the Larssons attended. Instead, they sent a letter expressing displeasure at the formation of the two new companies: "We also protest that you have registered these in Palestine without our knowledge. Mr Larsson explained to you, Mr Vester, that the documents should have been sent to and approved by the Swedish ambassador in Cairo, but you did not bother to do this."[509] The letter was sent to Bertha and Frederick, with a copy to the American consul-general. Lewis seemed to think that he had an ally in Consul Knabenshue, and that together they could finally break the Whiting and Vester families' influence over the Colony once and for all.

509 Letter from Mathilda Larsson, H L Larsson and Edith Larsson to Mr and Mrs Frederick Vester, December 30, 1930, American Colony Collection, Jerusalem.

Chapter 37

Brother against Brother

During Anna's lifetime, the American Colony had been run through a system of general meetings at which her ideas and suggestions were approved via consultation with the rest of the congregation, an idea that Anna had taken from the Gospel of Matthew. She would sometimes quote this passage from the Colony's magnificent Bible with its olive-wood binding: "Moreover, if thy brother shall trespass against thee, go and tell him his fault between thee and him alone: If he shall hear thee, thou hast gained thy brother. But if he does not hear thee, then take in the mouth of two or three witnesses that every word may be established. If he shall neglect to hear them, tell it unto the church: but if he neglect to hear the church, let it be unto thee as a heathen man and a publican."[510]

At such meetings, any colonists who needed to be disciplined would be publicly admonished. The sinner would be permitted to defend him or her self, but had to accept criticism, which was not intended as a punishment, but as advice. If, however, the one being 'talked to' did not want to listen, another meeting would be convened and the individual was 'talked to' again.[511] Only as a last resort were they threatened with expulsion, for which a special session was needed, where the guilty party had to provide an explanation in front of the whole congregation. If they asked for forgiveness, or promised to reform, the matter was usually settled – but if they declined to do so, the special meeting had the ultimate power to expel the errant congregant. By the summer of 1929,

510 New Testament: Matthew, 18:15-18. The Red Letter New Testament, Authorised Version, showing our Lord's Words in red, Fr Vester & Co, American Colony Stores, Jerusalem, Palestine, 1922, p.24.
511 Bertha Spafford Vester: Memoranda re Origins and development of disputes within the American Colony Early Years. Folder: General Memoranda, American Colony.

the congregation had a membership of about 60 adults, together with 15 children and young people. Since its foundation, 19 adult members had left voluntarily, and six had been expelled. All of the latter group had been forced out for the same reason: their refusal to adapt to the will of the congregation following a final consultation.

In the conflict between Lewis Larsson and Bertha, Lewis also had his supporters, but they were few in number, and remained silent initially during the debates over the sect's religious leadership. The Swedish consul's sympathisers were mainly young fellow Swedes who sought an end to the sessions of criticism and punishment imposed on those breaking Mother Anna's rules, and demanded a new regime of 'love without the sword'. But the majority of the congregation was content to carry on living as they always had, with all colonists abiding by consultations and majority decisions. Bertha and her adoptive sibling, Brother Jacob, who now led the prayer sessions, were in the forefront of this group, supported by Frederick. Grace and John for their part, remained silent.[512]

The rebels directed their opposition at Bertha, but also at Brother Jacob, whom they felt was no longer suited to lead religious services. Jacob was deeply shocked at the behaviour of the younger generation, who smoked, danced, and drank cocktails in the manner of American society 'beaus'. He believed these practices to be inappropriate for a religious community. In this respect, however, Bertha disagreed with him; despite her autocratic style of leadership, she was socially very liberal, and believed that the younger colonists had to be allowed to have some fun and relax, to relieve what could be a monotonous and demanding life. Bertha would not yield to Jacob's indignation, so after a while he went to New York to take a break from the Colony's internal arguments.

After a few months, Jacob became homesick, and returned to find that increasing Arab hostility towards Zionism put the disagreements within the Colony very much in perspective. In a letter to a friend from around this time Bertha wrote: "There is a boycott on all things Jewish. People dealing with Jewish merchants are followed and insulted, and their purchase is taken away or spoiled by having ink thrown over it. The police seem helpless to cope with it."[513]

Palestinians (both Muslims and Christians) were also threatening to boycott British-made goods, for they realized that it was the British

512 Bertha Spafford Vester: Unpublished manuscript: Minority fight for control. Folder: General Memorandum, American Colony Collection.
513 Letter from Bertha Spafford Vester to Dr. Fosdick, dated November 2, 1929. Folder: 1929, American Colony Collection, Jerusalem.

government's acceptance of the Balfour Declaration that had encouraged the Zionist movement. Bertha believed that "in this they have sympathy and cooperation in Syria, Transjordan, Iraq, Egypt and India. It has become an Imperial question, not just a Muslim-Jewish problem confined to Palestine."

On October 26, 1929, the newly-founded Palestinian Women's Congress held its first meeting in Jerusalem. Several of the delegation requested a meeting with the new British High Commissioner, Sir John Chancellor. He received the women graciously, but for their part, the delegates let him understand that theirs was not a friendly visit. They had come to protest against the Balfour Declaration, against maltreatment of Arab prisoners and against the British Attorney-General, Mr Bentwich, whom they saw as an ardent Zionist.[514] Sir John promised to do all that he could for them and gave them coffee. Afterwards, 80 cars full of Palestinian women drove through the streets. Men standing along the route clapped and cheered, and even cried in their enthusiasm. "It made a great impression upon the Arabs, for they realized what it meant for women to depart from custom and assume a leading role in fighting for Palestinian rights," wrote Bertha.[515]

Until now, Lars Lind, the brother of Bertha's son-in-law, had publicly remained neutral in the power struggle within the American Colony, but one day in January 1930, Lind and a small delegation of congregants requested a meeting with Bertha. Lind felt that the old hierarchical system was no longer tenable, and that one group should not have the power to put restrictions on the others. He also emphasized that it was Bertha, and nobody else in the Colony, who had drafted the expulsion letter to Lewis and Edith.[516]

"But the Larssons were trying to undermine the very foundations of the community; they had to be expelled," answered Bertha.

"I don't believe that, and neither do several other members of our Colony," Lars replied. "But in any case, I think that they really do have a case here. I'm sorry, Bertha, but the *ancien regime* here is just too powerful. The majority of the congregation are being kept in subjugation by a small group of reactionary old fogies!"

But Bertha would not budge. "If the Larssons believe this, they are free to go and leave the rest of us in peace," she said.

514 Mrs Matiel E T Mogannam: *The Arab Woman and the Palestine Problem*, Herbert Joseph Limited, London 1939, p.75.

515 Letter from Bertha Spafford Vester to Dr Fosdick, dated November 2, 1929. Folder: 1929, American Colony Collection, Jerusalem.

516 Bertha Spafford Vester: Unpublished Manuscript: Minority fight for control. Folder: General Memorandum, American Colony Collection.

Lind and his delegation left eventually, but not before he had told Bertha that although he strongly disagreed with the way the Colony was being run his "overall loyalty to its basic mission overrides any arguments that I may have. I speak for this whole delegation when I say that if we had to choose between agreement and slavery, we would choose slavery."

After this, Lind decided to stay neutral, although he never stopped trying to convince Frederick to find a more egalitarian structure for the community. But Frederick answered that Bertha would "never give up her responsibility for her mother's ideals". This meant effectively that Bertha would never surrender financial control over the Colony's activities either.

"I would rather die than give up," she said one day, during one of Lars' subsequent visits.

"But is it worth dying for?" her husband asked.

Bertha did not answer immediately. She looked up at the wall where a portrait of her mother was hanging, showing Anna in later years with a shining gaze, straight posture and her hands in her lap. Bertha pointed to the picture and asked: "Can you look her in the eyes and say that we have done wrong?"

"Yes," answered Lars, "I can."

Bertha stared at the Swede with her hard, brown eyes and said: "You have to trust me."

"And you have to allow more freedom in the way the Colony is run," replied Lars.

Frederick sat silently. Bertha rose and left the room; Lars remained, leaving the house finally after midnight.

The following day, the young Swede went to Frederick's office and suggested that all property in the names of Vester, Whiting, and Lind should be re-registered in the name of 'the American Colony'. Although this would mean him forfeiting any personal claim he had to a house in Haifa, Lars felt that it might ease the tension amongst the Colony's rank-and-file members. Frederick agreed with the suggestion unreservedly. When the matter seemed settled, Lars went to the registration office and wrote out a declaration that his property in Haifa would, thereafter be in the name of the Colony. Several days later he asked Frederick if he had done the same.

"Not yet, but I will," was the answer.

A week later, Lars called at the American Colony Store in the Grand New Hotel to assure himself that Frederick had kept to the agreement. He was shocked to discover that Frederick had changed his tone completely:

"I am not such a fool," he told Lars dismissively. "I will never sign, and I do not wish to see you any more."

Feeling that he had been tricked and deceived, Lind immediately reported the matter to the American consul-general. Lind was one of the most influential and respected members of the community and could potentially play a decisive role in the dispute between the Colony's 'inner circle' and its rebel faction. Upon investigating the legal status of the Colony's assets, Knabenshue discovered that the Vester and Whiting families had covertly inserted new clauses into the charter, which ensured effectively that their respective families retained exclusive rights over most of the community's property. Knabenshue demanded that the Vester family provide written assurance that all the properties would be placed in the name of the entire Colony. He sent a copy of his letter to the Palestinian authorities.

Frederick was furious when he received the letter. He recognized that the American consul could become a dangerous enemy, but his anger overrode any sense of caution. He visited Knabenshue at the consulate. "This letter is unprecedented," he raged.[517] The consul explained that it was his responsibility to protect the rights of American citizens. As far as he was concerned, Bertha and Frederick were Germans and the American Colony was a religious autocracy. He felt that Anna Spafford had been a tyrant, and Bertha had become the same.

"And I'm afraid that you are complicit in the situation, Frederick," continued the consul. "The others, no doubt, will forgive you, but I'm sure that they would like to know how much they are being asked to forgive. And I would like to see the accounts for Vester & Co."

"These accusations of yours are groundless," replied Frederick. "And, what's more, your demands are beyond your mandate as American consul."

After returning home and discussing the matter with Bertha, Frederick calmed down and subsequently informed Knabenshue in writing that the American Colony would, thenceforth, be registered in Palestine rather than New York. "There are many members who want this, my self included," he explained. But whilst the company of American Colony, Inc would cease, Frederick reiterated that the firm of Vester & Company would continue to operate as before.[518]

Knabenshue was far from satisfied and decided, in January 1930, to

517 Letter from Frederick Vester to Arthur Townsend, New York, April 3, 1930, pp.5-6. Folder: Townsend Letters, American Colony Collection.
518 Letter from Frederick Vester to Paul Knabenshue, Jerusalem January 18, 1930. American Colony.

submit a report about the conflict to the American State Department. He explained his involvement by saying that the Vester couple had a "distasteful reputation" in Jerusalem, which had been reported to him by many people, "including the acting high commissioner last summer".[519] His blistering report continued:

> My investigation has convinced me that most members of the Colony, with a few exceptions, are honest, friendly, moral, compassionate, and law-abiding citizens, but there are indications that Mr and Mrs Frederick Vester and their family connections have used the Colony for personal advantage. Their management of the Colony gives the appearance of being a charitable monopoly – most of the members, mainly old men and women, are in their power. Some of those who have tried to discuss the issues, have been ejected without compensation. The Vester family is suspected, both by certain present and former members of the community, of having acquired property and funds from the Colony for their own personal benefit. It is easy for everyone to see in Jerusalem that the Vester family lives better, is better dressed, and educates their children better than do other members of the Colony. They have used large sums of Colony money for expensive trips to and from America.

Consul Knabenshue wrote further that Frederick Vester "is suspected of strange business activity in the running of the Colony's store, and at present the Palestinian authorities are evaluating whether to take action against him for having sold and exported valuable antiques without the authorities' knowledge. In short, the activities of the Vesters are looked upon as scandalous by many people in Jerusalem, particularly since it is said they are hiding their activities under the cover of Christendom and charity which seems to have fooled many influential American tourists. It also appears that Mr Vester has gradually worked to have all property belonging to the American Colony registered in his name."

A month after the consul wrote this report to the American secretary of state, Bertha and Frederick summoned their New York lawyer, Arthur

519 The consul was referring to Mark Aitchison Young, who was the acting High Commissioner when Sir John Chancellor returned home. In 1941, as British Governor of Hong Kong, Young had to hand the colony over to the invading Japanese forces. Letter from Consul General Paul Knabenshue to the Secretary of State, Washington, January 20, 1930, File no. 860,3 American Colony Collection.

Townsend, to Jerusalem. Townsend demanded an advance of $10,000, setting off for Jerusalem only once this had been agreed. When he arrived in the city at the beginning of March, his first action was to write a letter to every member of the Colony who supported Lars Lind and Lewis Larsson.

He soon received a prompt reply, not from the addressees, but from the British attorney-general in Palestine, Norman Bentwich. The Attorney-General informed Townsend that, as a US citizen, he could not practice as a lawyer in Palestine unless he had a licence, which he neither had, nor was able to obtain. He thus had no option but to return to the United States.[520]

With the Vesters' lawyer back in New York, Lewis Larsson began to believe that he could perhaps win the power struggle against Bertha after all. He had been the Swedish consul in Jerusalem for eight years, and as far as he could tell, his own position within the congregation was strong. He now lived just outside the village of Sheikh Jarrah with Edith and their children, but still remained in touch with his supporters in Jerusalem. He believed that the time had come for a direct assault upon the Colony's leadership.

Thus one day, he and Edith arrived in the salon during the morning meeting and took their seats along with everyone else. When one of Bertha's supporters, the American John Dinsmore – the little man with the big head who had taught botany to the Swedish children – saw them arrive, he stood up and began immediately to pray. Normally, prayers were said at the end of the meeting, but Brother John wanted to prevent Lewis from speaking. But Lewis would not be diverted. As soon as Brother John had said Amen, Lewis got up, folded his hands, closed his eyes and said:

I thank You, O God, that You are a true God. I thank You, O God, that You will lead us, for You stand for the right. And I thank You, O God, that You will punish the wicked.[521]

At this point a woman from Bertha's faction rose abruptly and marched over to Lewis. He was unperturbed and remained standing with closed eyes, continuing:

---

520 Letter from Attorney General Norman Bentwich to Arthur O Townsend, Jerusalem March 4, 1930. Folder: Townsend Letters, American Colony Collection.
521 Undated draft of Memorandum to His Exellency, The Minister for Foreign Affair, Stockholm, Sweden. Marked, American Colony Collection.

And I thank You, that in Jerusalem there is a true Pilate who will judge justly and not listen to the majority. I thank You, that You sent back the American lawyer; that he was not able to do anything, was foiled, and went back humiliated. I thank You, that You are my advocate – we are courageous, we are not afraid, for You are our Pilot. And God is going to cleanse this Colony, to get rid of the wicked ones who have led it onto the rocks.[522]

Bertha's supporter was Mary Louise Adams, a 75-year-old British-born American, who was ready to give Lewis what she called some "English pepper", but Bertha rescued the situation by beginning to sing 'Jesus Saviour show me the way'. Others joined in, and soon the hymn overwhelmed Lewis' provocative prayer. When the song was finished, most of the congregation left the room rather than engage any longer with Lewis, who remained behind with his wife. Edith had more or less remained silent during the debacle, saying only "yes,," when her husband needed to pause for breath during the prayer.[523]

The following morning, Lewis and Edith appeared again at the meeting. Most of the congregation were on their way out, and Lewis went over to the divan where John D Whiting and Fred Meyers were sitting. He seated himself facing the two, shaking his fist in the face of Meyers, and said: "I tell you, you have got to stop your behaviour. I know full well that you engage in indecent activities in the Colony's office here – fumbling women visitors and goodness knows what else. It has got to stop! We are going to cleanse the Colony."[524]

Bertha and Frederick's eldest son, 24-year-old Horatio, was also present. "Fumbling women?" he gasped. "Do you know what you are charging him with?! What on earth do you mean?"

"I mean that he puts beads around their neck, and tickles them under their chin and fumbles them in other places," replied Lewis. "You are only young, lad, and don't have full knowledge of everything that goes on here, so for your own sake, it's best if you stay out of all this." He then turned to Fred Meyers again: "The women you've molested don't even know who

---

522 Ibid. Also typed copy of the prayer (cited by Horatio Vester).Folder marked H L (Lewis) Larsson. American Colony Collection.
523 Letter from Horatio Vester to Arthur Townsend, April 1, 1930. Folder: Townsend letters. Typed copy of the prayer (cited by Horatio Vester) in Folder: H L (Lewis) Larsson, American Colony Collection, Jerusalem.
524 Note by Horatio Vester, marked "Larsson Incident of April 3, 1930". Folder: H L (Lewis) Larsson, American Colony Collection, Jerusalem.

you are, nor do they wish to know. But I tell you, I am going to cleanse this place. I will take a whip and drive you all out if needs be. And I shall again make this a house of worship."

"Yes, we are going to cleanse it, and make it a house of worship," repeated Edith. But the elderly teacher, John Dinsmore, interrupted her with an authoritative voice: "Let them talk all they like. We don't have to listen."

At this, Lewis shook his fist crying: "I don't care whether you listen or not! I am going to take a whip of small cords and drive you out! We are going to cleanse this house; it's become a madhouse of fornication, merchandising and I dare not imagine what else. But we are going to make it a house of prayer for all nations."

Eight colonists had been in the salon when Edith and Lewis came in, but they now swept out in disgust at Lewis' diatribe. Horatio immediately made notes of the vicious exchange, and later gave them to his family's new lawyer from Jerusalem, who advised Fred Meyers to sue Lewis for character defamation. Fred said he would do whatever the Vesters thought was best.

It was not long before Lewis and Edith again attended the morning service, and a new confrontation developed. Yet again, Lewis rose to pray, but before he could say a word, another of the Vester family supporters, the Palestinian, Elias Habib, started to sing. When the song was over, Lewis went up to Bertha and said loudly: "What God requires is a blood offering!"

"I agree," said Bertha and left the room. The others followed. Bertha's son, Horatio, was disappointed that Lewis' prayer had been stifled – he was training to be a lawyer and felt sure that the prayers would contain a "pearl string of metaphorical libel" that could have been used against Lewis in a legal action.

Meanwhile, Olaf Lind, who only a year earlier had started a private action against the American Colony, was demanding that it should be treated as a charitable institution. Together with five other former members, he wanted financial compensation from the Colony for the sale of his parent's farm in Norway. Olaf did not know exactly how much all the Colony's properties, the store and the houses were worth, but thought that it might be as much as one million dollars. But the highest court in Palestine rejected his case without even listening to the lawyers' arguments. On Wednesday, April 30, the *Palestine Bulletin* reported: "This Colony is one of the richest companies in Palestine, and is said to be valued at about 130,000 Palestinian pounds (about $800,000). The properties are mostly registered in the names of Vester and Whiting... Mr Olaf Lind had claimed that regardless of whether the property was in Vester's name or not, the court should decide that it belongs to the members of the American Colony, and that it was therefore a charitable institution. But yesterday, Lind's case, which has been going on for more than a year, was rejected."[525]

With the threat posed by Olaf Lind lifted, Bertha and Frederick were now free to focus upon the dispute with the Larssons. Lewis was a case unto himself, but they were seriously worried by the antipathy of Consul Knabenshue towards them, and could not understand his involvement or motive.

"What can he gain?" asked their son, Horatio. "And above all, why would he risk so much for a man such as Lewis?" Their former lawyer, Arthur Townsend, had previously thought that Zionists had been responsible for prejudicing the consul against them. But Horatio had assured him by letter that the Jews, "the better ones of them, are our best friends... English society here is, with very few exceptions, very second rate. They are mostly junior officials who, after years of strenuous effort, have at last raised themselves to a certain degree of seniority and are filled with pettiness, resentment and small-mindedness...many of them have been jealous of Father and Mother for years, and have been only too glad to humiliate them whenever the opportunity has arisen."[526]

Horatio feared there might be further lawsuits; because the organization of the American Colony was unique, and since there was no clear legal precedent which protected members' rights, either in Palestine or in England, any court case would be lengthy and burdensome. He also believed that Lewis had been wise not to sign the proposal to establish a corporation. It meant that if the majority of colonists tried to transfer certain properties to the corporation, Lewis could stop them with a temporary injunction, since he could argue that his rights would be affected by such a transaction.

The Attorney-General, Norman Bentwich, summoned Olaf Lind, Lewis Larsson and their supporters to a meeting at which he advised them "to accept separation, and at all costs to stop further litigation."[527]

525 *The Palestine Bulletin*, Jerusalem, May 1, 1930, p.1.
526 Letter from Horatio Vester to Arthur Townsend, dated Jerusalem, May 18, 1930, pp.1-2. Folder: Townsend letters, American Colony Collection, Jerusalem.
527 Letter from Horatio Vester to Arthur Townsend June 4, 1930. Folder: Townsend letters, American Colony, Jerusalem.

The lawyer who represented them declared that his clients were willing to "divorce", but when the parties met together it appeared that Lewis' faction did not want divorce after all. At that point a meeting was called in the Colony, to decide once again whether Lewis and his supporters should be expelled. Neither Lewis nor Edith attended the meeting, and the congregation decided the couple and their supporters should be expelled forthwith. It was ruled that they should be refunded for their shares in the Colony, but that this was to be paid out in cash only.

It seemed that an expensive and protracted legal battle would follow, when Bentwich suddenly informed the lawyer representing Lewis and his faction that both sides in the dispute had at last agreed to "divorce". The two parties agreed on arbitration, and elected a British judge based in Cairo, Charles Harold Perrott, to act as arbiter. He came to Jerusalem on June 14 and began attempting to assess the value of the Colony's assets. After many calculations, he arrived at a sum of 83,427 Palestinian pounds or about $500,000.

Lewis now revealed a new side to himself. Having previously based his arguments for the redistribution of the community's assets on concern for the welfare of the older colonists, he now suggested they should be divided on the basis of how long a person had left to live. He argued that some of the 12 oldest members would probably die within the next few years, and that their portion should be distributed amongst the remainder. He also believed that the needs of the older members were modest, and used this to support the idea that a percentage of the shares of the oldest members should therefore be awarded to him and other members of his faction.[528]

The older members, mostly Swedes, thought the suggestion was both unreasonable and distasteful, but they gave in to his pressure. Above all, they wanted an end to the fighting, and thought it worth the sacrificing of part of their shares, on condition that Lewis left the Colony for good. The Larssons accepted this, and both parties agreed to a preliminary arbitration agreement on July 25.

But before final arbitration could begin, Lewis' faction began to argue amongst themselves; new negotiations had to begin, and the final settlement was not reached until a year later. Eventually, the colonists were awarded the large building and the houses surrounding it, which later became the American Colony Hotel. The rebel group was awarded money and property elsewhere. To Bertha's great disgust, Lewis, Edith

528 Memorandum to His Excellency, The Minister for Foreign Affairs, Stockholm. Folder: Correspondence & memoranda re newspaper articles, American Colony Collection, Jerusalem.

and Mathilda received the 'Vester House' with its lovely garden on the Nablus Road, where Bertha and her family had lived since before the First World War.

In addition to their portion of the Colony's property, Lewis and his supporters were also to receive one-third of each of the shares of the older Swedes. The 47 younger Swedish colonists were full of anger at Lewis' inconsiderate greed, and decided to compensate the losses of the older members by sharing equally with them. The colonists now closed ranks around Bertha and her family; three of Lewis Larsson's sisters were among them, they did not want to have anything to do with their brother.

Lewis would not relent in his persecution of the older colonists, and, in his capacity as Swedish consul, wrote to the British Colonial Secretary, Lord Passfield, to suggest that the older members of the Colony should be "made no longer accountable or competent" under British law. He alleged that they were too infirm to make any decisions about what their best interests were, and needed help in protecting their material and financial assets.

The Swedes of the American Colony responded by writing their own memorandum to the Swedish foreign minister in Stockholm. It said that Mr Larsson "can no longer pose convincingly as a benefactor for the aged members of the Colony, and in view of his previous actions we are forced to question the motives behind his benevolent claims." Their letter also asked the Swedish minister to ensure that Consul Larsson no longer meddled in their private matters, and requested that he should investigate the matter via an impartial third party so that the Swedish citizens in Jerusalem could be protected from their own consul.[529]

Just before the properties of the American Colony were to be divided Alvilde Strand arrived unexpectedly, in Jerusalem. After having begged for several years for permission to return, she finally decided to ignore Bertha's rejection and to come back anyway. But she did not announce her presence by knocking on the door of the American Colony; instead she rented a house near the Sea of Galilee (Lake of Gennesaret) and sought legal help in securing her rights to the Colony's assets. Her attorney, M E Mogannem, maintained that Alvilde had still not given up her rights and interests in the Colony. Nor had she signed any declaration waiving those rights, and thus had a much stronger case than Olaf Lind, Lewis and their faction.

Everyone agreed that Mrs Strand had a right to her portion of the assets, and both the Colony and the rebel faction were willing to

529 *Dagens Nyheter* April 28, 1931. Memorandum to Minister for Foreign Affairs, Stockholm, undated, p.7. Folder: Memorandum, American Colony Collection, Jerusalem.

contribute. Alvilde received a sum of 70 Palestinian pounds, or about $400. In addition, she was granted an annual pension of 96 Palestinian pounds (or about $600), on condition that she give up her membership of the Colony and refrain from making further claims on its finances.[530] The arbitration judge, Charles Perrott, thought that the entire debacle had been most unpleasant, and said: "Never in my life have I handled a more distasteful settlement, and never have I had such impossible people to deal with."[531]

The split marked the end of the community as Anna Spafford had envisioned it. They were still a Christian group, but their lives were no longer focused on spiritual fulfilment of the world to come. Instead their energies were given over to charitable work, and for Bertha, personally, political activity.

530 Alvilde Strand went back to Bergen in March, 1932. Folder: Alvilde Strand. American Colony Collection.
531 Lind & Wallström: *Jerusalem Travellers*, Stockholm 1981, p.187.

Chapter 38

Palestinian Revolt

Major General Sir Arthur Wauchope arrived in Jerusalem in 1931 to be Palestine's fourth high commissioner. He had fought in the Boer War, and in India, France and Mesopotamia. He had also been wounded and had received a medal for bravery. However, despite his courage, Sir Arthur was not a polite person by nature, and the stout little Scottish bachelor soon became unpopular because of his unrefined behaviour. The new high commissioner soon discovered that diplomacy in Palestine could be tricky. For example, Palestinians who were invited to official dinners would not show up if they knew in advance that Zionists would be present. Wauchope was quick to grasp the complexities of operating in Palestine, however. He understood that the riots of 1929 had been prompted by the hastily conceived British immigration policy, and, unlike some of his subordinates, he believed Haj Amin to be a moderate, who attempted to prevent the spread of the violence. As far as the Zionists were concerned, Wauchope departed from the 'arm's length' policy of his predecessors and involved them much more in his plans for Palestine.[532]

The high commissioner liked to hear what ordinary Palestinians thought about their past and their Arab heritage. Many Arabs believed that they drew their character from the desert, and that the people from the West would never understand either the Arabs or the Middle East. They reminded him that the little Arab family along the coast has siblings living up in the hills behind. They also have relatives in the mountains, and those in turn have cousins in the interior deserts, forming a chain

---

532 Moshe Shertok and Sir Arthur Wauchope met May 27, 1936, Central Zionist Archive (CZA S25/30) Cited in Naomi Shepherd: *Ploughing Sand, British Rule in Palestine 1917–1948*, London 1999, pp.184 –185.

that stretches from the coast to the mystery of the sands.

Both the Jews and the Palestinians liked to pose philosophical questions about the differences between the Arabs and the Jews. The Arabs believed these went far deeper than disagreements over politics and that the Europeans ought to remember the great slumbering power that lay up in the hills, mountains and deserts behind Palestine. They concluded that the small strip of land, squeezed between the Mediterranean and the desert, that resonated with Arab tradition and heritage, could never change its character and become a land of Jews. This argument was put forcefully to the author, Hector Bolitho, by a well-educated Palestinian in the Old City whose family of teachers and judges had lived in Jerusalem for 800 years. The man had said: "You must also remember that no conqueror has ever changed our character, even with the force of armies behind him... the Romans were here for 600 years, but we emerged from their domination, unchanged and almost untouched. The Greeks came, and Greek became the language of our commerce, but the desert overcame them, so they stayed near the coast, and their artifacts are now turning to dust. The Crusaders came, and all that remains of them are a few churches. The Cretans and Egyptians were here, but both were dispersed and assimilated into the country. Before the British occupation the Turks were here for 400 years, and it is astounding to see how little impression they made on either the landscape or the people. Their very roads are overgrown and have been swallowed back into the earth from which they were cut. We have remained Arab, and even if it were our will I do not believe that we could change." [533]

The Palestinian was "willing to admit that the Jews had suffered terribly at the hands of both European and Eastern civilizations. But even the kindness of a British Mandate and the passion of the Zionists cannot establish a national home in Palestine without the will of the Arabs. It is impossible for the Jew to understand any nature but his own. Intellectually, he is completely selfish and self-centred." When the author left the Old City, the Palestinian's final words were ringing in his head: "You know, it will be a sad day for the Jews if they did get a national home, for their virility has been made through adversity, when the adversity ends for them decadence will begin."

Hector Bolitho stayed at the King David Hotel, where members of the American Colony often attended tea dances. He did not like the hotel, although it had been built of natural stone and had a view out

---

533 Hector Bolitho: *The Angry Neighbours*, London 1957, pp.39-43.

over the Jaffa Gate, the Citadel, and Mount Zion. Bolitho considered it a monstrosity. He was unaware that the first British High Commissioner, Ronald Storrs, and his Pro-Jerusalem Committee had decided that all new buildings must have stone façades, to prevent too great a contrast between the old and the new in Jerusalem. He was also unimpressed by the fact that the Greek Orthodox Church had sold the property for $150,000 to a group of Jewish investors, headed by Baron Edmund de Rothschild. The hotel, with the YMCA building across the street, indeed the whole new part of the city made Bolitho upset. He thought Zionist ambition, when blended with Christian entrepreneurship, was revolting. It was no wonder that Jesus left his crucified body behind and went off with his Holy Spirit. Never had he seen such worship of money and the flesh as in the New Jerusalem.

The author may have shared these feelings with the poorest Palestinians, but few wealthy Arabs would have agreed with him. Many of those who complained that Jewish immigration threatened their freedom and very existence had also sold large tracts of land to Jewish purchasers. Many of the biggest Arab landowners did not even live in Palestine, and most were quite willing to sell if offered the right price, even if this led to misery for the landless Palestinian population. Among the participants in a Palestinian delegation sent to London in March 1930 to demand restrictions on Jewish immigration, only one man, Jamal Husseini, had not sold large pieces of land to the immigrants. Even the mayors of Jerusalem and Jaffa had sold land secretly to the Zionists.[534] As the pace of land sales increased, the Jewish community came to own more in Palestine than the native Palestinians. The average Jewish family owned over 5 acres of arable land on which to make a living, while the Palestinian peasant had to be satisfied with a hand-to-mouth existence on less than two acres.[535]

The flood of Jewish immigrants now reached new levels, and the Palestinians became increasingly concerned. The Zionists, on the other hand, were satisfied with developments. Their leaders stated plainly: "If we can just keep up the tempo for five more years, we will have 500,000 Jews in the country, and then we do not have to live in fear any longer, as

534 The mayor of Jerusalem, Ragheb Nashashibi, the president of Jaffa's Muslim-Christian Association, Omar Baytar, and the mayor of Jaffa, Asim Bey Said, had sold 240 acres to the Jewish National Fund in the summer of 1924. A Palestinian real estate broker negotiated the transaction. *Bericht zum Mitglieder im Ausland* (Report to Members abroad), September 1, 1924, Central Zionist Archives, Jerusalem, KKL 5/file 1203. See also Kenneth W. Stein: *The Land Question in Palestine, 1917–1939*, Chapel Hill and London 1984, p.68.
535 Shai Lachman: *Arab Rebellion and Terrorism in Palestine, 1929–3*: "The Case of Sheikh Izz al-Din al-Qassam and His Movement," in Yehodaha Haim(ed.): *Zionism and Arabism*, p.60.

we now do, that the Arabs will destroy all our work."[536]

At the American Colony, the congregation remained busy with its charitable activities for the poor, but there was also now much more work generated by the increased numbers of tourists who came streaming into Jerusalem. The guest house was well visited, and, when he was not leading prayer meetings, Brother Jacob played a leading role in caring for the visitors.

One day in May 1932, a missionary who worked in Baghdad came to visit the city. Unusually, he had his own car, a Model T Ford, and Brother Jacob agreed with enthusiasm to go for a ride in it. But the missionary, not familiar with the hairpin bends around Jerusalem, lost control of the car on the road to the north of the city. Jacob Spafford was thrown from his seat and fell against a rock. He died instantly, but neither the driver nor the car suffered any damage.

The funeral took place the following day, but just before the coffin was to be taken from the American Colony to the graveyard below Mount Scopus, a Dominican priest, Father Vincent, asked if he might be alone with the deceased. It was then revealed that for several years Brother Jacob had been going secretly to services at St Stephen's Church. He had converted to Catholicism. This did not prevent Brother Jacob from being buried in the Colony's cemetery, where he was placed at the side of his adoptive mother, Anna Spafford.

The following year, 1933, Adolf Hitler came to power in Germany. Few in Palestine could have had any idea of the consequences this would have for the Holy Land. But before many months had passed the people of the Middle East had realized that he was going to force the Jews out of Germany.

The start of the Third Reich triggered the Fifth *Aliyah*. By 1933, more than 30,000 new Jews had arrived in Palestine, three times as many as the year before. Most of them came from Poland, but a fair number were also from Germany. The German Jews – known as *yekkes* – were well educated and wealthy. Often dressed in three-piece suits, they sat sweating in Tel Aviv's cafés, pining for their countries of birth. They were now residents of a swelling township – the de facto capital of the *Yishuv*.

The Palestinian Arabs responded to this influx of Jews by organizing a general strike and demonstrations. A British official in Jerusalem

536 Naval Intelligence Division: *Geographical Handbook Series, Palestine and Transjordan*, Oxford and Cambridge 1943, p. 177. The number of Jews who immigrated to Palestine in 1931 is estimated to be around 4,000, in 1932, 9,550, in 1933. The number grew to 30,330, in 1934 to 42,360 and nearly 62,000 the following year. By 1935 Tel Aviv's population had reached 120,000.

observed with foreboding that the city was almost too quiet: "The absence of traffic and the closure of shops, partly due to the strike and partly out of fear, is unnatural in this town of so many people… the attacks have been anti-government, not anti-Jew: Not that the Arabs are any more amicably disposed towards the Jews, but they hate the government more."[537] In the end the strike was a failure, it did not result in anything more than greater unhappiness.

A new mayor was elected in Jerusalem in 1914, replacing Ragheb Nashashibi, who had held the post for 14 years. Hussein Fakhri Khalidi, had been supported by the Nashashibi family's traditional rivals, the Husseini clan, and also by the Zionists, who regarded him as more progressive than his predecessor.[538] The Palestinians wanted a more democratic government, and the leaders of the country's five Arab political parties submitted a letter to the high commissioner demanding an end to the purchase of land in Palestine by Jews, and also an immediate halt to Jewish immigration.

For the Palestinians it was no longer a question of whether Zionism was acceptable or not. The half million Jews in Palestine were now a political reality, and all the while, the British government's policy of 1917, which the Arabs regarded as treasonable, continued to be pursued. The Palestinian leaders recognized that only a united Arab opposition would have any chance of convincing the British government to revoke its policy. For their part, the British suggested that a legislative council should be established in Palestine, but this was not well received by the Arabs who said it fell too far short of the independence they longed for. The British government felt that the Palestinians lacked the political maturity necessary for self-government. The British proposal for a legislative council was also opposed by the Palestinian Zionists: in their view, there were not yet enough Jews in the country.

The British government had another suggestion. Any talk of stopping or reducing Jewish immigration was out of the question, but the sale of Arab land to Jews was to be restricted. The migration would continue according to "the economic capacity the country had to absorb newcomers, a principle which had been implemented when Great Britain

537 H E Bowman, Diary, 29, October 1933, cited in A J Sherman: *Mandate Days, British Lives in Palestine 1918–1948*, Thames and Hudson 1997, p.92.
538 Philip Gillon: *Israelis and Palestinians: Co-Existence or The Credo of Eli Eliachar*, Tel Aviv 1977, p.68. Benny Morris: *Righteous Victims, A History of the Zionist-Arab Conflict 1881–1999*, New York 1999, p.124.

received the mandate to govern Palestine."[539] But few Palestinians found this argument convincing, and Bertha certainly did not, writing in a letter to a friend: "The Arabs, the old inhabitants of this land, see themselves being outnumbered and outwitted by the rapid increase of Jews through immigration. Although one's sympathy goes out to the Jews who are persecuted and left homeless, it does not remedy that evil by inflicting the same unjust situation in another part of the globe."[540] In another letter, in August 1936, she said: "Not since the World War have we been through such dangerous and trying times as we are going through now. We are beginning the Fifth month of the Arab strike, which is more devastating than any of their many protests against Jewish Immigration."[541]

Despite the strike the stores, restaurants and cafés remained open. The port of Haifa functioned, and the trains still ran, although there was not much traffic on the roads between the large cities. Then, in the middle of the strike, in the spring of 1936, the British decided to negotiate. The Palestinian leaders agreed to come to London, but before they could leave, clashes broke out in the neighbouring cities of Jaffa and Tel Aviv, which left 16 Jews and six Arabs dead. A curfew was imposed on both and a state of emergency declared in the rest of Palestine.

Attitudes on both sides grew even more entrenched as a result. Arthur Ruppin, the man at the forefront of the organization responsible for buying large tracts of land, noted in his diary April 25, 1936: "Under the circumstances it is natural that the antagonism of the Arabs to Jewish immigration should find release in periodic outbreaks... we are living in a sort of latent state of war with the Arabs which makes loss of life inevitable. This may be unacceptable, but it is a fact; and if we want to continue our work in Palestine despite the Arabs, we will have to expect such losses."[542]

The Palestinian leadership responded by forming a committee to represent all Palestinian interests–the Arab Higher Committee. The grand mufti in Jerusalem was elected chairman, and sent out a declaration that the strike would continue until all Arab demands were met. The Palestinians would refuse to pay taxes until Jewish immigration was stopped. In this tense and difficult climate, a group calling themselves

539 H J Simson: *British Rule, and Rebellion*, London 1937, pp.183–185.
540 Letter from Bertha Spafford Vester to Miss Hargear, May 20, 1936. Folder: 1936, American Colony Collection, Jerusalem.
541 Letter for Bertha Spafford Vester to Mr Russell, August 23, 1936. Folder: 1936, American Colony, Jerusalem.
542 Arthur Ruppin: *Memoirs, Diaries, Letters*, New York 1971, p.277.

the *mujahedin*, or holy warriors, established themselves in the northern part of Palestine, in the area between Safed, Acre, and Nazareth. The holy warriors used to say: "Zionism is an extension of British colonialism. Cut the tree down and the branch will wither and die."[543] Many guerrillas took this slogan literally, and destroyed Jewish orchards and crops in northern Palestine, but they also attacked military units and police stations and placed mines in the roads. These operations were conducted with the support of volunteers from neighboring countries.

One of the best known of these volunteers was Fawzi Kawukji, a Lebanese in his thirties who had fought for the Ottoman Empire during World War I. He had led a revolt against the French in Syria in 1925, and when that failed, he fled to Saudi Arabia where he became an instructor in Ibn Saud's army. Later he taught at the Iraqi military academy in Baghdad, where he was promoted to the general staff. Kawukji travelled to Jerusalem in secret, to finalize his plans for a revolt against the British.

Sheikh Izz al-Din al-Qassam was a completely different type of revolutionary leader. A deeply religious Palestinian, he appealed to the ordinary man, who no longer felt he could remain a passive bystander to the Jews' creeping annexation of Jerusalem. By this stage, most Palestinians had grown tired of the prominent Palestinian families, such as the Husseinis or the Nashashibis. None of them had been able to get rid of British rule, none of them had brought the dream of an independent Palestine any closer. So when Sheikh Izz al-Din al-Qassam, the Imam of Haifa and Lower Galilee, started to talk about political freedom, he gained eager supporters.

Sheikh Qassam declared that, from this point on, all Palestinians who sold land to the Jews would be treated as infidels and denied an Islamic funeral. The imam believed that Palestine could become Arab again only through an organized, armed struggle to drive the British and the Jews out, and, in justification, Qassam quoted verses from the Quran, which referred to *jihad* – holy war. The uncompromising Sheikh Qassam had already proposed starting a revolt in 1933, suggesting that Haj Amin should lead an armed insurrection in the south, while he himself would take the lead in northern Palestine. However Haj Amin declined, saying that he wanted to look for a political solution first.[544]

543 Thomas A Idinopulos: *Weathered by Miracles. A History of Palestine from Bonaparte and Mohammed Ali to Ben-Gurion and the Mufti*, Chicago 1998, p.203.
544 But the Muslim guerrilla chief would not wait, and secretly established 'The Black Hand', a guerrilla group, primarily composed of people from the countryside. Cells were established in most of the Arab villages in the area around Nazareth, Nablus, Jenin and Tulkarem. They directed

Sheikh Qassam was the first Palestinian leader with sufficient insight to see that Palestine's Arab elite were not capable of leading a full-scale revolt against the British, or serve at the forefront of a revolution. When guerrilla soldiers began to emerge from the grassroots of Palestinian society, the prestige of the old urbane Palestinian elite began to decline. More and more people believed that Haj Amin in Jerusalem was fundamentally just a British errand boy, and the mufti's arch-rival, the former mayor of Jerusalem, Ragheb Nashashibi, just a puppy dog, panting for foreign recognition and money.

The Arab political parties, which in theory worked toward democratic ideals and objectives, failed to unite the Palestinians. They organized themselves around the powerful pro-British claims and achieved little beyond agreeing on anti-Zionist manifestos. Beyond the war of words against the Zionists, the Husseinis, Nashashibis, Alamis and all the other important families were actually interested in acquiring power and in scheming against one another.

In November 1935, Sheikh Qassam was killed by British soldiers outside Jenin. Overnight, the dead imam of Haifa became a cult figure, his grave the destination for pilgrims. The mufti in Jerusalem seemed relieved to be rid of a dangerous rival, and it was said that his condolence telegram to the Qassam family was so lukewarm as to be insulting. The condolences from the Husseini family's competitor, the Nashashibis, were not much better.[545]

Bertha Spafford Vester believed that many poor Arabs could not afford to be on strike, and barely knew what it was about. Many women "only know they are hungry and that their husbands cannot work, but as the strike continued, the situation got more serious." The Palestinian revolt also created difficulties for the American Colony, and for the Anna Spafford Infant Home. One day, when Bertha was about to send home a fully recovered patient, in order to give the bed to a new arrival, she discovered that the parents of the healthy child had been unable to come to Jerusalem. They had no travel documents, and even if they had, they would probably not have been able to use them. Bertha and a nurse took

their anger at Palestinians, who had sold land to Jews or did business with them. Members of the Highest Muslim Council, and Palestinians who worked for the British were also targeted. Joseph Nevo: *Palestinian Arab Violence During the 1930s* cited in Michael J. Cohen & Martin Kolinisky (ed.): *Britain and the Middle East in the 1930's*, London 1992, p.175.

545 Saïd K Aburish: *A Brutal Friendship: The West and the Arab Elite*, London 1997, p.156. In the 1990s, some 60 years later, the militant Islamic Palestinians tried to honour their hero by naming the military wing of Hamas as the Izzedine al-Qassam's Brigade.

the child in the Colony's Ford to the village of Taibeh, where its parents lived. Northeast of Be'erot – where the infant Jesus had wandered away from his parents during a caravan journey from Jerusalem to Nazareth – the car was prevented from going any further by a khaki-clad Palestinian insurgent, carrying a rifle. He asked brusquely who they were and where they were going. Bertha explained in Arabic about the child, but the guerrilla said he did not have the authority to let them continue. He disappeared and shortly returned with several men. Bertha recognized one of the khaki-clad men as Fawzi Kawukji, the man they called the 'Lion of Damascus'.[546]

At first, the guerrilla leader accused Bertha of being a spy. She argued forcefully that she knew better ways to disguise herself, if that had been her object. When he heard she belonged to the American Colony, his tone became milder. Both Kawukji and the Palestinians with him knew of the Colony's charity work. But, to be on the safe side, Kawukji sent one of his lieutenants along in the car to check the story of the infant who was to be reunited with its parents.

In the village, the family was overjoyed to have the baby back. They also confirmed Bertha's story that she was in charge of the American Colony's charitable activities. On her way back she met the guerrilla again. Kawukji said: "Go in peace and continue to work and God will help you. But do not change the colour of your car." The guerrilla leader told her that he had noted both the make and registration number of the car, as well as the one on the engine. Bertha thanked him and drove on. She never saw him again.

546 Spafford Vester: Unpublished manuscript, chapter 39, p.10, American Colony Collection, Jerusalem.

Chapter 39

"A Jewish State without Jews?"

Lewis Larsson wrote a letter to his relatives in Nås regretting that his three sisters at the American Colony no longer wanted to have anything to do with him, despite the fact that they lived just a few hundred yards away. [547] Lewis felt they had been tricked by Bertha and the rest of the leadership to keep as far away as possible. Lewis' private correspondence charted the breakdown of the American Colony in detail. At the same time, the reports he submitted to the foreign ministry in Stockholm, in his public capacity as the Swedish consul, record the destruction of a traditional way of life in Palestine. Larsson's reports recorded the scale of Jewish immigration and land purchase, which, in many cases, led to entire Palestinian villages being emptied. [548]

Palestinian men and women demonstrated against Britain's Zionist-friendly policy. The Palestinians were demanding a boycott of Jewish and European goods and wanted an end to all foreign influence, in all walks of life. For instance, the activists also did not want Arab men to wear the Turkish *fez*. They considered the red cylindrical hat to be symbolic of a foreign domination in Palestine. The demonstrators wanted men to wear the Arab head covering – *kaffiyeh* – and women to use veils and traditional Palestinian clothing. Those who did not follow these demands were threatened with acid attacks. But this pressure to dress in a politically correct manner had little effect. The Palestinian community was controllable only to a limited degree. [549]

547 Letter from Lewis Larsson in 1936, cited in Birgitte Rahbek & Mogens Bähncke: *Tro og Skæbne i Jerusalem*. (Faith and Destiny in Jerusalem) København 1997, p.171.
548 Kenneth W. Stein: *The Land Question in Palestine, 1917–1939*, Chapel Hill and London 1984, p.216.
549 Selma Ibrahim Ismain Husseini: *The Revolution 1936–39* (Arabic), unpublished note, Sep-

The Zionist organizations functioned better, acting collectively as an independent administration in Palestine. The Jews had built important industries in many parts of the country. Nearly all electric power was produced by a Jewish company. The *Yishuv* – the Jewish community in Israel – was spread over large parts of Palestine. The *Yishuv* had its own elected representative assembly, organized education and health systems, and banks and trades unions (headed by the mighty labour organization, *Histadrut*).

The intermittent waves of protest that swept across the Palestinian community posed no serious threat to the Zionists, neither did the sporadic armed attacks on their collective farms, or *kibbutzim*. Every one of the Jewish agricultural colonies needed only a handful of armed men to defend themselves. The Arab guerrillas were so ineffectual they could not manage to seize control of a single Jewish settlement, even though they were often situated far apart from each other. The Jewish pioneers could continue their expansion unchallenged and new colonies were established across large areas, all the way up to the border with Syria in the north-east.

The Palestinian revolutionaries had no comprehensive strategy beyond blowing up oil pipelines, bridges and railway lines. Granted, there were occasional battles between Arab groups and British forces, but they just drove the British into alliance with the Zionists. Britain had no large military units in Palestine at this time and relied on the local police to maintain order. Members of the Jewish paramilitary organization, Haganah, were recruited into the police force, and given the task of defending the Jewish colonies. This gave them legal status, even though the Haganah, in theory, was illegal.[550]

The mufti's nephew, 45-year-old Jamal Husseini, was the leader of the non-violent Palestinian nationalists. He was also a close friend of Bertha's and lived in a house on St George Street, between the American Colony and the Damascus Gate. In May, 1936, Willy Falkman, a journalist with Oslo's leading newspaper, *Aftenposten*, came to interview Husseini, who did not wait to be asked questions. "It is common knowledge," he said, "that Colonel [T E] Lawrence gave up a promising political career when he refused to accept the honours the British authorities wanted to give him. The reason he did so, was because he knew that the British government would not live up to the promises that he and other British officers had given the Arabs on Great Britain's behalf."[551] Willy Falkman made notes while his subject

tember 7, 1999.
550 H J Simson: *British Rule and Rebellion,* London 1937, p.261.
551 Willy Falkman: *Kampen mellom jøder og arabere i Palestina* (The Fight between Jews and Arabs in Palestine), *Aftenposten,* May 26, 1936.

continued to pose rhetorical questions, which he also answered:

> How has England kept to these promises? Why, by subjugating
> Palestine, Iraq, and TransJordan, by letting France occupy Syria
> and finally by opening up Palestine to an unending swarm of
> foreigners, who threaten to displace the country's own people. This
> is the way England treats its old allies… We are not fighting against
> any race, but against anything which forces itself into our homes
> and steals our land. In 1922, the British government promised that
> immigration into Palestine would never be so great as to threaten
> the country's economy. That same year 6,341 Jewish immigrants
> arrived. Now, 14 years later, 50,000 Jews stream into Palestine each
> year, and the Jews, who before were a small declining minority,
> represent 25 percent.

Husseini paused for a moment, took a new cup of coffee from a black
manservant and lit a cigarette. *Aftenposten*'s correspondent grabbed the
chance to ask his own question about the future of Pan-Arabism. "England
has promised us its help to create a Greater Arabia, which will encompass
the entire Arabian Peninsula, and this is our goal," Husseini began, but
before he could launch into another monologue, he was interrupted by
loud shouts coming from the direction of the Damascus Gate, followed
by gun shots. This was followed by more shouts and screams, then silence.
Falkman thought it was probably time to leave, and thanked Husseini for
his time.

The interview appeared in *Aftenposten* on May 26, 1936. The previous
day, the newspaper had written that the Arabs were "running wild" in
Palestine, and that the intermittent violence which had been going on
between Arabs and Jews for the previous six weeks had now escalated,
causing "a complete reign of terror".

British efforts to find an exit strategy once again took the form of
an independent commission of inquiry, this time under the leadership
of Lord Peel. Peel visited Palestine in October 1936, but the Arab Higher
Committee decided it would have nothing to do with him unless Britain
agreed to the immediate suspension of all Jewish immigration. London
again suggested a cap on the number of immigrants, but Haj Amin, the
grand mufti of Jerusalem, rejected the proposal. The British believed the
Palestinians were shooting themselves in the foot, some even maintained
that the boycott of the Peel Commission was so stupid it must surely have

been the work of Jewish agents within the Palestinian leadership. [552]

The Jews played their cards well, and finally Haj Amin realized that it was in the Arab interest to begin discussions with Peel. The following year, Lord Peel's commission issued its 404-page report. It was based upon two premises: that the conflict was unsolvable and that the British Mandate to govern Palestine could not function in its current form. It concluded that the country had to be divided. The Arabs would get four-fifths, the Jews the rest, among other things, most of Galilee, and a coastal strip down towards Gaza. An international zone was to be established around Jerusalem with a corridor out to the sea at Jaffa. This area would be administered by the British.

The report was met with protests from both sides. The Palestinians did not want to partition their land, while, for their part, the Zionists felt the proposed Jewish state was too small. Ever since Herzl's time there had been discussions about the possible 'transferal' of Arabs, a phrase which sounded undeniably better than deportation or forced removal. In 1930, Menachem Ussishkin, one of the earliest proponents of Zionism, said that the Arabs "had to be transferred to other places. We have to take over the country. We have a greater and nobler idea than to maintain several hundred thousand Arab peasants."[553] At last the idea had gained legitimacy thanks to the Peel Commission's proposal for forced removal.

Jewish groups, meanwhile, had adopted a new, much more aggressive strategy. In November 1937, a new paramilitary organization known as Irgun began a wave of bombings against Palestinian civilians – placing bombs in market places and on buses.[554] These indiscriminate attacks brought a new dimension to the Jewish-Palestinian conflict and shocked the more moderate Jewish Agency and left-wing Zionists who refused to believe that Jews could be responsible for them.[555] Haganah also changed its tactics, adopting an offensive approach. The man responsible was Orde

552 Michael Cohen: *Palestine, Retreat from the Mandate*, London 1978, p.30.
553 Nur Masalha: *Expulsion of the Palestinians, The Concept of "Transfer" in Zionist Political Thought, 1882–1948*, Washington 1992, p.50.
554 Irgun Tzvai Leumi (The National Military Organization) was formed in 1931 by a number of ex-Haganah commanders. They attacked Arabs, but later also the British. At the outbreak of the Second World War, the leadership declared a ceasefire and one of its senior members, David Raziel, was killed in Iraq while working for the Allies. Under the leadership of Menachem Begin, Irgun resumed its armed struggle against the British in 1944. Many members were arrested and sent into exile. The relationship between Haganah and Irgun fluctuated between close cooperation and extreme tension. After the establishment of the state of Israel, Irgun was disbanded, following a conflict between Ben-Gurion and Begin.
555 David Niv: *Irgun's Battles* (Hebrew) Vol. 2, Jerusalem 1965–80, pp.80–94, cited in Morris: *Righteous Victims*, New York 1999, p.147.

Wingate, an idiosyncratic Christian Zionist and British intelligence officer who arrived in Palestine in 1937. Wingate recruited Haganah members into an elite combat division whose mission was to put an end to Arab guerilla activities, in particular the sabotage of British assets. Wingate's priority was the protection of the British-owned oil pipeline that stretched from Iraq to the Mediterranean and ran over parts of Palestine.[556]

But despite Wingate's efforts, the Arab revolutionaries still managed to gain control of large parts of Palestine, and in September the British reported that civil administration did not, in practice, extend to the countryside. In the cities, things were different. There was a curfew from 5pm until 5am and any Arab who broke it, or was found to be carrying an offensive weapon could be shot on sight. The Arabs complained bitterly of double standards, arguing that these restrictions did not affect the Jews.

The British army mobilized 30,000 soldiers and launched a military offensive against the Arab insurrection. But with no support from neighbouring Arab countries, the fractured Palestinian opposition quickly crumbled. More were killed by their own people than by the Jews or the British. The remaining members of the fractious Arab Higher Committee had been deported to the Seychelles, while the mufti had fled to Lebanon.[557] By the end of the year militant Arab opposition to Zionism had been effectively extinguished and the Palestinian political leadership dissipated.

The Jews now felt sufficiently secure not to need British protection against the Arabs. Although they remained a minority, they controlled all the key economic positions and were militarily superior. They had no plans for an offensive war, as long as Jewish immigration and colonization of Palestine could continue unabated. But the situation remained tense. The Peel Commission's recommendation for partition of Palestine had, in the meantime, been put aside and a new commission formed in an attempt to devise a viable British policy for the country.

---

556 The blended units were dissolved after the Arabs stopped their sabotage of the oil pipeline owned by the British Iraq Petroleum Company, Yehuda Bauer: *From Cooperation to Resistance: The Haganah 1938–46*, Middle Eastern Studies, Vol. II, No. August 3, 1966, p.195.
557 The Mufti settled into a small village outside Beirut, and the Zionists resumed contact with the Christian Lebanese Maronites. Their leaders had long been known to sympathise with Zionism, largely out of fear of the Muslim majority. In the last half of 1937, the Lebanese president, Emil Edde, a Maronite, met Chaim Weizmann secretly in Paris. During the meeting Edde said: "It is my privilege to greet the first president in the future Jewish state." Eliahu Elath: *Zionism at the UN*, Philadelphia 1976, p.240.

Chapter 40

War and Peace

In January 1939, Britain's Colonial Minister, Malcolm MacDonald, invited delegations of Jews and Arabs to London for talks. The Jews were represented by the Jewish Agency, but the British rejected any Palestinian delegates who had been involved in acts of violence. This meant that the Mufti, Haj Amin Husseini, could not attend. But members of the Arab Higher Committee, now freed from exile in the Seychelles, were allowed to consult with him from London.

The British were optimistic when the delegates arrived at St James' Palace in London – even though they expected tough discussions. But when the Arabs refused to sit at the same table as the Jewish representatives, the opening was postponed. The Arabs maintained that face-to-face meetings with Zionists at an official conference implied recognition of the Jewish Agency, and that was out of the question. As a result, the conference took the form of proximity talks, with each side presenting its case to the British intermediaries.

None of the parties was ready to compromise. The Zionist leader, Chaim Weizmann, insisted that the Balfour Declaration should be the foundation for Palestine's future, while the chief Arab spokesman, Jamal Husseini, was just as rigid in citing the promise of Arab independence, given to Sharif Hussein of Mecca in 1915 and 1916. Arab delegates made the point that there would never have been any Palestinian revolt, and no blood spilt if the British had kept their promise. In the end, the conference failed to achieve any agreement, but this did not prevent Britain from drafting guidelines for a new Palestine policy, presented in a White Paper on May 17, 1939. The document stated that the ambiguous term "a national home for the Jewish people" was the fundamental reason for the enmity between Arabs and Jews. It added that Palestine would not become a Jewish state because this contravened Britain's obligations to the League of Nations and went against Britain's promises to the Arab people.

The Jews in Palestine were angered by the White Paper. Jerusalem's chief rabbi tore it to shreds before the eyes of his congregation, and militant Zionists launched attacks against the British police. The British reacted strongly. Up until this point, only Arabs carrying firearms had been imprisoned. Now Jews were given the same treatment. But just when it looked as if Palestine was descending into another, possibly more deadly, round of violence, events in the region were overtaken by cataclysmic developments in Europe.

On Sunday, September 3, 1939, Bertha and Frederick Vester went to church as usual. After lunch at home, Bertha turned on the radio and listened to the Prime Minister, Neville Chamberlain, announce that Britain was at war with Germany. Bertha and Frederick stood to attention as the national anthem played. Bertha began to cry, unaware that three British soldiers, rifles at the ready, had already come into the house, claiming to have orders to arrest Frederick Vester. Bertha protested, but to no avail. Putting on her hat and gloves, she told the soldiers they would have to arrest her as well. One of the soldiers said: "We only have orders to arrest Mr Vester."[558] "I am complicit in everything my husband has done," answered Bertha.

Frederick began to laugh at his wife's demand to be arrested, and said Bertha would be of greater use if she stayed in the house. The soldiers marched Frederick out to a waiting car. Bertha grabbed the telephone, called Government House and told the high commissioner's adjutant what had happened. After a few minutes waiting, the adjutant came back on the phone and said it was all a misunderstanding.

Within an hour, Frederick had been released and was back in the house. The chief of police had given him a letter saying that, despite being a German citizen, Frederick was being accorded special treatment, just as had been the case during the Great War.

Even though Tel Aviv was bombed nine days after the outbreak of World War II, Palestine did not get involved in the conflict in any great degree. Only later, in the spring of 1941, did it appear the British-controlled areas in the Middle East might be threatened by a pincer movement from the south and the north. In the meantime, the British in Palestine were

558 Bertha Spafford Vester: Unpublished draft of *Our Jerusalem*, chapter 39: *Second World War*, pp.13–14, American Colony Collection.

View across Jerusalem's Old City from the roof of the Spafford Children's Center

mostly busy trying to stem the influx of Jews to the country, and restrict Jewish purchase of Arab land, in order not to anger their Arab allies in the fight against the Germans.[559]

People in Palestine, in general, found life easier than they had during the First World War. Food rationing was introduced, but despite this, life at the American Colony was largely unaffected. Because the Colony had sufficient funds, it could buy what it needed on the black market. One day, Bertha heard an English lady ask a policeman: "Where is the road to the black market?"[560]

"When you have found it, let me know. I'd like to go there myself," answered the policeman – apparently more interested in buying or selling goods himself than seeking to uncover illicit trade.

Bertha was encouraged that, during the war years, Arab and Jewish women got together again to sew, knit and chat. For the moment the controversies were buried. It also became much safer to move about the country, now that British troops were stationed all over Palestine.

559 Palestine was divided into three zones. In the largest zone, which encompassed Gaza, Beer-sheba, and the hills in Palestine, it was forbidden for Arabs to sell land to Jews. In the second largest zone, on the Esdraelon Plain, in eastern Galilee and along certain coastal areas, every sale had to be approved by the High Commissioner in person. The smallest zone, which comprised the cities of Palestine, allowed for unrestricted land purchase by Jews.
560 Spafford Vester: *Our Jerusalem*, 2nd edition, p.348.

In September 1941, Bertha threw a party to celebrate the 60th anniversary of the American Colony. On the guest list were Jews, Christians and Muslims. Bertha gave a speech in which she referred to her father's involvement in Jewish agriculture in Palestine. A few days before the jubilee, she and her husband had visited Mikveh Israel, the agricultural school near Jaffa, to which Horatio had donated eucalyptus seeds. Together with Arthur Ruppin, the Jewish property purchaser, and his wife, they walked beneath the tall trees that lined the road. The trees formed a cathedral-like arbor, and Ruppin suggested the place should be called the Spafford Forest. Bertha thought this was a marvelous idea. No memorial to her father could be more visible than a forest near Jaffa.[561]

Five months later, Bertha's husband died suddenly on January 3, 1942. Frederick collapsed in the middle of a reception being held at the Colony. While he greeted the guests Bertha had been in the kitchen giving instructions to the cook. When she returned to the living room, she found her husband on the floor and her daughter, Frieda, an experienced nurse, massaging his heart. But she could not save his life. Bertha later described their marriage as "thirty-eight perfect years".

After the Germans had been defeated, and the threat that the Arab states might join forces with Germany had disappeared, British policy on Palestine changed again. An earlier British promise that May 31, 1944, would mark the end of Jewish immigration into Palestine was ignored. On the contrary, as of February 1, the number of Jews permitted to come legally to Palestine was set at 1,500 per month.

But the most extreme Zionists were still not satisfied. It meant nothing to them that Churchill had promised the Jews a "fair" share of Palestine as soon as the war was over. They wanted the British gone as quickly as possible. The militant underground group Lehi, which took its name from a Hebrew acronym for 'Fighters for the Freedom of Israel' and was also known as the Stern Gang, plotted to kill the British Minister for the Middle East, Lord Moyne. And in April 1944, he was shot and killed in Cairo by two young Jews. The murder of Churchill's close friend dampened the prime minister's enthusiasm for Zionism. Addressing parliament he said: "If our dreams of Zionism are to end in the smoke of assassins' pistols, and our labours for its future to produce only a new set of gangsters worthy of Nazi Germany, many like myself will have to

---

561 Bertha Spafford Vester: *Founding and Work of the American Colony*, p.4. Unpublished note. Folder: 1941, American Colony Collection.

reconsider the position we have maintained so consistently in the past."[562] The two perpetrators were caught, condemned to death and executed.

The Second World War ended formally on May 8, 1945 – almost immediately the old hatreds erupted again in Palestine. "Explosions, murder, kidnapping were nearly daily events," wrote Bertha. She thought life had become a nightmare; but carried on working with the few remaining members of the community to provide help to as many of the needy as they could.

---

562 Churchill in the Lower House, November 17, 1944. Moshe Sneh: *Haganah's History, Vol III:From Resistance to War* (Hebrew), Tel Aviv 1973, pp.531–43, cited in Eric Silver: *Begin, A Biography,* London 1984.

Chapter 41

The Twelve Apostles

In the autumn of 1945, the American president, Harry S Truman, became interested in the Palestinian question. He had been affected deeply by the fate of the Jews, and wanted to help as many of the survivors of Nazi extermination as possible. But he, like most Americans, did not feel they should be given a home in the United States. Instead, he felt that Britain should allow European Jews to emigrate to Palestine.

British Foreign Secretary Ernest Bevin welcomed Truman's engagement in the Palestine problem and suggested the creation of a joint Anglo-American commission to study the question of Jewish immigration in Palestine and the Jewish refugee situation in Europe. The commission convened in Washington in November 1945. It consisted of six British and six American members, who were quickly dubbed 'The Twelve Apostles'. It was required to issue its recommendation within 120 days.

The American representatives were virtual unknowns. The Zionists, frustrated that their ranks did not include more eminent individuals, dubbed them 'pygmies'. Their British counterparts, by contrast, included more prominent people. Among the British delegation were a high court judge, an army major (representing the Conservative Party), a member of the House of Lords and the newspaper editor and Labour member of parliament, Richard Crossman. During the war Crossman had worked for the BBC, and subsequently edited the left-leaning publication, *The New Statesman*.

He was disconcerted initially to learn that his selection had been based not on his intellectual abilities and razor-sharp mind, but rather on the fact that he had never made any public statements about either

Palestine or Zionism. He knew relatively little about either, beyond what he could remember from his school days about the geography of the region and various Bible texts from church. When he joined the commission, Crossman leant instinctively towards the Arab cause, writing on his way to the United States:

> We start with a blankness towards the philosophy of Zionism which is virtually anti-Zionist. We have the feeling the whole idea of a Jewish national home is a dead-end out of which Britain must be extricated; that, whereas it is obvious that Arab independence in the end must be granted, we have not a similar obligation to permit the Jews in Palestine to fulfillment of Zionism. So the tendency is to define the problem as one of finding homes somewhere for the surplus Jews in Europe in order to cut away the Zionist case for an impossible immigration into Palestine.[563]

But after the hearings in the State Department conference room began, Crossman's views gradually changed and he became more convinced of the moral and practical virtues of the Zionist cause. The Zionists had prepared well for the commission's hearing. They brought with them 1,000 pages of documents, which supported their case that Arab society was primitive, while they themselves were the flag-bearers of progress and modernism. Several members of the commission became convinced that Polish Jewry, in particular, should be allowed to emigrate to Palestine, having been taken to the former Nazi extermination camp in Dachau.[564] Others argued that moving Jews from Europe to Palestine would be tantamount to a victory for Nazi anti-semitism. They thought the Jews ought to be integrated into Europe.

From Poland, the commission traveled to Palestine, and it was during encounters with Chaim Weizmann and David Ben-Gurion, that Crossman's growing sympathy for the Zionist movement changed to active support. The commission's work in Jerusalem began in earnest on March 8, 1946. One of the first people to appear before it was 73-year-old Chaim Weizmann, who, despite his age and frailty, spoke for two hours. Weizmann maintained the issue was not between right and wrong

563 Richard Crossman, M.P.: *Palestine Mission, A Personal Record*, Hamish Hamilton, London 1946, p.25.
564 Amikam Nachmani: *Great Power Discord in Palestine, The Anglo-American Committee of Inquiry into the Problems of European Jewry and Palestine, 1945–1946*, London 1987, pp.143–146, pp.121–122.

but between the greater and lesser injustice. "Injustice is unavoidable," he told the commission. "We have to decide whether it is better to be unjust to the Arabs in Palestine or to the Jews." The words were to stick in Crossman's mind. The next day he visited Weizmann at his elegant home in the little Jewish colony of Rehoboth and spent two hours alone with him discussing the nature of Zionism and European Jewry.

One expert witness, from whom the commission did not hear, was Bertha Spafford. She had been asked to attend by the British Chief Secretary in Palestine, Sir John Shan, but she had declined. She was sceptical about the commission, believing its recommendations would share the same fate as the results of the 16 reports that had preceded it.[565]

Two days later it was the turn of Palestine's foremost representatives to appear before the commission, including Jamal Husseini. But his case was fatally undermined when the commission produced photographs showing Haj Amin Husseini, the former grand mufti of Jerusalem, shaking hands with Hitler and reviewing Bosnian Muslim troops of the *Nazi SS*. The pictures merely reinforced the prevailing conviction amongst the majority of the commission that the Arabs could not be trusted and would ally themselves with anyone in order to get rid of the British. The British historian, Albert Hourani, who worked at Britain's Arab Office in Jerusalem, attempted a defence of Arab interests, adding that the merits of the Arab case had been almost entirely overshadowed by the horrors of the Holocaust. This had been caused, not by the Muslim Arabs but by the Christian Europeans, he said, adding: "Despite this, it was the Arabs not the Europeans who were asked to provide the help."[566]

A few days later, Crossman met Jamal Husseini again, at the elegant villa of society hostess Katy Antonius, where he was also introduced to other members of the Arab intelligentsia. Crossman may have been convinced of the value of the Zionist cause, but he was perceptive enough to understand why the majority of British administrators working in Jerusalem felt more comfortable in the company of upper class Arabs, rather than the Jews. They had a cosmopolitan, European air, were amusing and cultivated, theatrical and vivacious. The Jews by contrast, seemed like intense petty-bourgeois Eastern Europeans. As Crossman and the other commission members returned to their hotel after their first visit to the Antonius villa, one of the British civil servants said to

565 Spafford Vester: Unpublished draft of *Our Jerusalem*, Chapter 39, "Second World War," p.16, American Colony Collection.
566 Christopher Sykes: *Crossroads to Israel, 1917–1948*, New York 1965, p.292.

Crossman: "There are two societies in Jerusalem, not three. One is Anglo-Arab and the other is Jewish. The two can't mix."[567]

After a tour of some *kibbutzim*, Crossman became even more enthusiastic in his support for Zionism. A future Jewish state could become a beacon of the left, an example of what was possible when the common good was put before individual gain. Before leaving, he and others, met the head of the Jewish Agency, David Ben-Gurion, for dinner. Crossman found the stocky man with white hair to be stimulating company and they spoke for half an hour about Greek literature. As he was on the point of leaving, Ben-Gurion told him: "Imagine that we're Englishmen fighting for our national existence, and calculate that we shall behave as you would behave if you were in our situation... make up your minds one way or the other, and remember that either way we shall fight our Dunkirk."[568]

The commission's report stipulated that Palestine's doors must be opened for the 100,000 Jews who were living in refugee camps in Europe. It also left the door open for further immigration when the economic conditions improved and said that sanctions against Jewish purchase of land in Palestine must be lifted.[569]

In the end, the British government rejected the proposals, which would have meant abandoning existing British policy in Palestine. When Prime Minister Clement Attlee received the report, he expressed disappointment, and told Crossman he thought it was unfair. Crossman, surprised, replied: "Unfair toward the Jews or the Arabs?"

"No, unfair to Great Britain, of course. You have turned your back on us and given in to the Jews and the Americans."[570]

567 Crossman: *Palestine Mission*, pp.132-33.
568 Ibid. p.172.
569 Order 6808, cited in John Marlowe: *Seat of the Pilate, An Account of the Palestine Mandate*, London 1959, pp.207–208.
570 Richard Crossman: *A Nation Reborn*, London 1960, p.69.

Chapter 42

The Birth of Israel

Early in April 1948, Fred Meyers, one of the American Colony's oldest members, died aged 81. The funeral ceremony was to be held amongst the bougainvillea and oleander of the courtyard, beneath Baron von Ustinow's palm trees, now grown tall, which had been his wedding gift to Bertha and Frederick. Bertha had ordered a hearse and three cars for the funeral procession to the American Colony's graveyard on the western slopes of Mount Scopus. More importantly, she had obtained an agreement from the Haganah forces stationed just above the graveyard that they would hold their fire for the duration of the service.

At the last minute, however, the funeral company announced that none of its drivers was willing to risk his life by making the dangerous journey within range of the Jewish snipers. A little later, two British tradesmen from Haifa arrived in their van, asking for a room at the American Colony Hostel, and Bertha convinced them to help. In the end, Fred Meyers' body was taken to its final resting place in a delivery van, escorted by a single police car. John D Whiting was the only other representative of the American Colony at the burial. But all went well – not a single shot was fired – and after the burial the delivery van returned safely to the Colony.

By this stage, West Jerusalem was under siege, cut off from the coast as the main road into the city was controlled by Arab forces. The Haganah began an offensive aimed at gaining control of the arterial route into Jerusalem. Haganah's elite Palmach force took the strategically vital village of Kastel, three miles from Jerusalem on April 7. Less than a mile away, the inhabitants of the neighbouring village of Deir Yassin witnessed the fighting with growing apprehension. Despite the fact that their mayor had already secured a promise from the Haganah that they would be left in peace, they feared that they might be attacked next. No one in the village could know that a decision had been made at the highest level of the Haganah to dispatch the extremist paramilitaries of Irgun and Lehi to storm Deir Yassin.

That evening, the wife of a villager called Mahmoud Yassini, went into labour. All through the night, the couple's oldest daughter, 16-year-old Ratiba, tried to comfort her brothers and sisters who were disturbed by the sound of their mother's screams. Early the next morning, as dawn broke, the family heard the sound of rifle fire and villagers shouting "*el-Yehud jayeen A'laina!*" ("The Jews are coming!").[571]

The sound of shooting grew closer, and Ratiba hid her siblings as best she could, in cupboards and behind sacks of cement. From his hiding place, eight-year-old Mustafa could see his mother curled up on the mattress on the floor. Four men burst into the room and shot the figure on the mattress. Mustafa held his breath. He saw that two of the men had guns and the other two carried a small, green, square package that they placed on the floor. One of the gunmen uncurled a long fuse and attached it to the package. But it failed to light properly, and after all the attackers had left the house, Ratiba tore the fuse out and flung the bomb out of the door. Sure their mother was dead, all four children then ran towards the ruins of a nearby house which they thought would be a safe hiding place. Later that day, Musfata crept back to their home to retrieve some food. He found a trail of blood leading down to the cellar where the family kept chicken. There, amongst the chicken coops, he found his mother, alive.

By pure chance, little Mustafa's entire family survived the massacre of Deir Yassin and were eventually reunited in the neighbouring village of Ein Karem. The Yassinis were lucky. The Jewish paramilitaries had advanced systematically through the entire village, house by house, throwing grenades through the doorways and shooting those inside as they tried to flee. Other children who had crawled under beds or concealed themselves in cupboards had been forced to listen to the screams of their parents as they were shot down, or watch as their bodies were dragged outside and mutilated.

In all, 107 people were killed in Deir Yassin, the vast majority of them shot inside their own homes.[572] Neither Arab nor British forces intervened

571 Daniel McGowan: *Remembering Deir Yassin*, New York 1998, p.35, Larry Collins & Dominique Lapierre: *O Jerusalem*, London 1972, pp.267-71.
572 Irgun's commander in Jerusalem, Mordechai Ra'nan, said at a press conference in Givat Shaul that 240 were killed. That figure was reported in the BBC and Hebrew news media. On April

to help the villagers and the massacre did not stop until Jews from the neighbouring village of Givat Shaul, with whom the villagers had agreed a mutual assistance pact, arrived to see what was going on. Irgun's leader, Menachem Begin, sent a message of congratulations to his commandants and soldiers: "We are all proud of the outstanding leadership and willingness to fight in this great attack… tell the soldiers that they have made history in Israel with their attack and conquest. Continue forward to victory. As in Deir Yassin, so everywhere…"[573]

Twenty-five years after the massacre in Deir Yassin, Israeli historian Arie Yitzhaqi wrote that the attack on Deir Yassin was part of a recognized pattern in 1948. During the 'war of liberation', both the Haganah and the organization's elite troops, Palmach, carried out dozens of similar operations. Ben-Gurion even sent an apology to King Abdullah. But this horrific act served the future state of Israel well. As Begin wrote in *The Revolt*:

> Arabs, throughout the country, induced to believe wild tales
> of 'Irgun butchery', were seized with panic, and started to flee
> for their lives. This mass flight soon developed into a maddened,
> uncontrollable stampede. The political and economic significance of
> this development can hardly be over estimated.

Fifty-five children from the village, whose parents had been killed, were taken to the Jaffa Gate in Jerusalem's Old City, and left there. The next day, Hind Husseini of the Arab Women's Union found several blood-covered children leaning against the walls in a state of shock. They were sitting, staring into space, unable to say what they had experienced.

When Bertha heard about the massacre, it reminded her of the biblical story of Joshua's conquest of Jericho. She brought all the children under two years of age to the Anna Spafford Infant Home, where she also found space for some of the slightly older orphans. The children remained very fearful. Catching sight of Bertha for the first time, one six-year-old boy screamed: "Is she one of them?" He thought that the fair-skinned, grey-haired woman resembled the European Jewish women who had taken

13, 1948, the *New York Times* reported that 254 Arab men, women, and children had been killed at Deir Yassin. Finally, the correct figure was presented in 1998. The survivors of Deir Yassin compiled a list of 93 names, after the names of those who had been visiting the village from the surrounding area were also added, the total figure came to 107 dead. This was announced by Dr Sharif Kanaana, University of Bir Zeit in a lecture on the 50th anniversary of the massacre.
573 Menachem Begin: *The Revolt, The Story of Irgun*, Tel Aviv, 1983, pp.162–65.

part in the massacre, and he collapsed in terror. Bertha ran to fetch some water for the lifeless boy. But when she returned, he was dead.[574]

Seeking their revenge, the Palestinians attacked Jewish civilians. They laid ambushes on the road that led to the Hebrew University and the Hadassah Hospital on Mount Scopus. The road went past the American Colony. Three days after Deir Yassin, Bertha discovered as many as 150 armed Arab guerillas lying in wait in a cactus grove a hundred yards away from the building. Furious, she told them to leave the Colony's land, arguing that to shoot from the grounds of the religious community was tantamount to "shooting from a mosque or a church".[575] But the Palestinians refused to move and, in desperation, Bertha went to the offices of the chairman of the Arab Higher Committee. Many years before, the man had been one of her students. Now, Bertha insisted that she would not leave his office until he had promised to do everything in his power to ensure the American Colony stayed neutral territory.

But Bertha soon discovered that the promise she had been given was worthless. The attack had already begun by the time she arrived back at the Colony. Palestinian guerillas, their eyes filled with hatred, screamed "Deir Yassin! Deir Yassin!" as they fired on a convoy of buses making its way towards Mount Scopus.[576] Terrified passengers tried to crawl from the buses to a British guard post further along the road. Most were killed as they did so. The firing continued all morning and into the afternoon. Finally, nearly six hours after the attack began, the British intervened and brought the situation under control. Seventy-five Jews had been killed in retaliation for the massacre at Deir Yassin.

By April 1947, Britain had abandoned hope of finding a solution that was acceptable to both communities in Palestine and brought the matter before the UN General Assembly. A special committee set up to make recommendations for the future status of Palestine proposed its partition into an Arab state and a Jewish state, with an international regime for Jerusalem. The partition plan was adopted by the Assembly in November. The Jewish leadership accepted the plan, but the Arabs argued that it was unfair: the Jews, comprising about 32 percent of the population would get 56 percent of the territory.

As the political and diplomatic impasse continued, fighting intensified. For the British administrators and security forces, the ordeal of trying to

---

574 Spafford Vester: *Our Jerusalem*, 2nd edition, p.375.
575 Ibid. p.353.
576 Larry Collins & Dominique Lapierre: *O Jerusalem*, London 1972, pp.281–288.

maintain peace and order in Palestine would soon be coming to an end. For their part, the inhabitants of Jerusalem had been counting the days to the time when the British would leave their city for good. Bertha found it hard to imagine a time after the British Mandate, even though she knew it was coming. When the day arrived for Sir Alan Cunningham's farewell dinner, Bertha and the other guests were picked up in bulletproof cars. The high commissioner was on good form, receiving his guests hospitably, as if the event was a normal dinner party. Sudanese waiters, still wearing their winter uniforms of dark blue cloaks with red shoulder scarves, drifted soundlessly about with trays of glasses.[577] Other servants brought canapés on silver trays, salted almonds, stuffed olives as big as pigeon eggs, pickles, pretzels and caviar. Two cocker spaniels and a Great Dane lay before a blazing fire, completing the picture of relaxed British gentility. The high commissioner spent time with each of the guests. He did not talk about the impending British departure, but several guests believed they could detect a sense of 'après moi le déluge' in his eyes.

Shortly after the farewell dinner, Bertha approached the head of the Red Cross in Jerusalem to offer the use of the Colony's large dining room as a first aid station, in the battles that would surely follow. Soon, the Red Cross flag flew over the large house by the Sheikh Jarrah Mosque.

The shooting continued night after night. On April 24, Haganah forces, led by a young Yitzhak Rabin, captured the Sheikh Jarrah district,[578] giving them control of the main road to the airport. But it was quickly recaptured by the British, who needed free access to the airport for the withdrawal that was to follow.[579]

At 9pm on May 13, 1948, Bertha, like virtually everyone else in Palestine, sat listening to the radio, as Cunningham announced the precise details of the British departure. Bertha knew the high commissioner so well she could detect a shake in his voice as he announced: "Tomorrow, at midnight, the last page will be turned in the history of Palestine and the British Mandate. The day after will open a new chapter and Palestine's history will continue."[580] When he had finished the chief of the radio station asked if Cunningham wanted him to add any words in Arabic. "No, just play 'God Save the King' please," he answered quietly. "It's perhaps the

577 Malkah Raymist: *The Stiff-Necked City, A Journalist's Personal Account of the Siege of Jerusalem, 1948,* Jerusalem 1989, p.119.
578 Itiel Amihai: *The Palmach Book, The Occupation of Sheikh Jarrah* (Hebrew), p.238.
579 Uri Milstein: *The Rabin File,* Jerusalem & New York 1999, p.289.
580 Zeev Sharef: *Three Days,* London 1962, p.258.

last occasion you'll have to play it."[581] The anthem's sombre tones fitted the occasion perfectly. Great Britain's time in Palestine had started so well, but ended disastrously. A world of ruined hopes lay between Allenby's memorable entry on foot through the Jaffa Gate and Britain's ignominious departure from the Holy City.

The Haganah moved in to take control of strategically important buildings in the centre of West Jerusalem almost as soon as the British closed the doors behind them. They occupied the building of the Palestinian Broadcasting Service, and the central Post Office, which gave them control of telecommunications throughout the city. From the post office building they telephoned Arab-occupied buildings nearby and tried to intimidate the occupants into fleeing.

At Jerusalem's hospitals, there was a shortage of doctors and nurses. Bertha offered her services at the American Mission Hospital, which lay just outside the city walls and was now in the middle of the battle zone.

Meanwhile, even as the fighting continued, the Zionist leaders were preparing for their most important historical event since King David brought the Ark of the Covenant to Jerusalem. In front of a museum building in Tel Aviv, David Ben-Gurion stood beneath a large picture of Theodor Herzl that had been placed there for the occasion. At exactly 4pm on May 14, 1948 (the mandate expired on 15 May, but this was the Sabbath), the small, white-haired man began to read aloud from a typewritten piece of paper, which was attached to a roll of white parchment:

In Israel's land the Jewish people came forth. In this land their spiritual, religious and national character was born. Driven into exile from Israel's land, the Jewish people remained faithful to all the countries they came to, without stopping their prayers, and with the hope of coming back to regain their national freedom. I hereby proclaim that the Jewish state in Palestine will be called Medinat Jisrael... and it will be known under the name, Israel.[582]

581 Collins & Lapierre: *O Jerusalem*, London 1972, p.376.
582 Walter Laqueur and Barry Rubin (ed.): *The Israel-Arab Reader*, London 1995, pp.107–109.

Chapter 43

The Aftermath

Precisely at midnight on May 14, 1948, when the British Mandate over Palestine expired, King Abdullah of Transjordan pulled out his revolver and fired symbolically up into the night sky. "Forward!" he shouted. The long line of military vehicles, which had been standing with their engines idling, began to move. In all, some 4,500 soldiers from the Arab Legion, the army of Transjordan commanded by General John Glubb, advanced westwards towards the area of Palestine that had been assigned to the Arabs under the UN partition plan.

Soon the first column was in Jericho. A little later, Arab League troops were in place in Ramallah. Not far behind came volunteer forces from Iraq. In the Sinai, the Egyptian columns with air support moved northwards into the newly established Jewish state. The first Arab-Israeli war was under way.

The total number of Arabs who fought in Palestine in May 1948 was fewer than 25,000, including local Palestinian guerrilla soldiers.[583] They were poorly equipped and trained. General Glubb (Glubb Pasha), a former British army major who had served the Hashemite Royal Family since 1920, knew of the Jews' preparations; he also knew that the Arabs had neither coordination, nor strategy. They had not even received new supplies of ammunition. Yet most people believed that the Arab Legion would capture Tel Aviv in the course of two or three days. The general fell on his knees by his bed and prayed to God for help.

At midnight on 14 May, Jewish forces were also on the move around Jerusalem. Bertha Vester was enraged when she heard that Jews had attacked the Dormition Abbey Monastery on Mount Zion where,

583 John Bagot Glubb: *A Soldier with the Arabs,* Hodder and Stoughton, London 1957, p. 94.

according to legend, Jesus had held the Last Supper and which overlooked a great part of the Old City from the south. The head monk tried, but failed, to block the Jewish forces. "This is a monastery," he said. But the Israeli forces would not stop. High in the belfry of the abbey, Jewish snipers could look down on the lanes and open spaces within the city walls, and later took a heavy toll of civilians who were careless enough to come into view.[584]

The Jewish forces continued on around the Old City walls to the Jaffa Gate, where they forced their way into Government House. They also entered the Sheikh Jarrah area, not far from the American Colony, which was on the Arabs' front line. Bertha Spafford Vester decided to have her own private protest against the Zionist aggression. Ever since the British came to Jerusalem, she had worn a ring that Frederick had designed. It was decorated with a Crusader Cross, and on the inside was engraved '9th December 1917', the date of the British capture of Jerusalem. For Bertha, this date marked the beginning of what she thought would become a democratic Palestinian state. "Thirty-one years ago Jews and Arabs alike were tearful in their gratitude for their deliverance from the Ottoman yoke," Bertha said. "What a tragic end to a glorious beginning!" Now that hope was gone, and on the first day of the existence of the state of Israel, she removed the ring, never to wear it again.[585]

Late in the afternoon of May 15, the Haganah tried to persuade Palestinians living in Sheikh Jarrah to flee before daybreak. A loudspeaker blared out in Arabic: "Take pity on your wives and children, and get out of this bloodbath... Surrender to us with your arms. No harm will come to you. Or get out by the Jericho Road, which is still open to you. If you stay, you invite disaster."[586] But only a few residents fled. Just before dawn on May 19, around 300 men from the Arab Legion pushed southward along the Ramallah-Jerusalem road, retaking the Sheikh Jarrah.

The Jewish forces also kept up their attacks around the old walled city. Arab Legion forces repelled a number of attempts to enter the centre of Jerusalem. But eventually, a unit of Haganah's elite forces, the Palmach, managed to blow its way in through the Zion Gate to the south, gaining control over the isolated Jewish quarter with its 1,700 inhabitants. But under an increasingly tight siege, a truce was arranged on May 28 to allow the Jewish citizens to leave the Old City.

584 Ibid. pp.127-30.
585 Spafford Vester: unpublished draft of *Our Jerusalem, Chapter III, The Last year, 1947–1948 in Palestine*, p.21, American Colony Collection, Jerusalem.
586 Harry Levin: *Jerusalem Embattled, A Diary of the City under Siege*, London 1950, pp.160–161.

The eruption of war in Israel/Palestine was a matter of major concern at the United Nations in New York. UN Secretary-General Trygve Lie needed the support of the United States for any plan that might be acceptable to the warring parties and felt he could no longer tolerate American vacillation on the Palestine question. At first, the Americans had supported partition, then later suggested the country be split into Jewish and Arab cantons, before, finally, proposing that the whole of Palestine should be put under United Nations administration. But the UN had acted as midwife to the state of Israel and could not change course now. It would be a setback, not just for the UN, but also for Lie himself, whose socialist background gave him an instinctive sympathy for the left-wing Jewish leadership.

The secretary-general thought the way out of the dilemma was to find a strong negotiator to act on the UN's behalf. He believed he had found the right man in Count Folke Bernadotte, head of the Swedish Red Cross. He contacted him on May 13, 1948. Bernadotte's wartime record of rescuing thousands of Jews from Nazi death camps meant that he was initially viewed favourably by the Jewish leadership.[587]

Bernadotte was appointed, despite the US reservation that he was "too deeply tied to the Jews", and went to Paris to meet the UN Secretariat's representative to the Truce Commission, Ralph Bunche. But before he left Stockholm, Bernadotte contacted Lewis Larsson in Jerusalem to ask his advice on several questions concerning Palestine's borders, and the attitudes and feelings of the people. He was told that the Palestinian Arabs had lost confidence in the UN and did not trust anyone.[588]

The physical differences between the two UN representatives was striking. Silver-haired Count Folke Bernadotte, tall and elegant, wore his Swedish military uniform with medals and the emblem of the Red Cross. In contrast, the short, 44-year-old black man from Detroit wore a crumpled suit and smoked constantly.[589] But Bunche soon learnt to respect the straightforward Swede who was not above taking advice from others. Initially amused by the size of Bernadotte's entourage, Bunche subsequently learnt that the Swede's physician had to be in constant attendance, since the envoy suffered from haemophilia and, in a war situation, could be at serious risk.

587 Ibid.
588 Larsson: *Dala Folk in the Holy Land*, Stockholm, 1957, p.200.
589 Kati Marton: *A Death in Jerusalem*, Pantheon Books, New York 1994, pp.119–20.

Courtyard of the American Colony Hotel

On June 3, Bernadotte flew to Amman for a meeting with King Abdullah. While there, he also met Edith and Lewis Larsson's two sons, John and Theo. They joined his staff and, as they drove to Jerusalem in convoy, were amused to see other recent recruits frantically reading their way through a publication entitled *Palestine in 10 Minutes*.[590]

Despite the fact that the Red Cross flag flew over the American Colony building, bullets and grenades still landed there. When Bertha's brother-in-law, John D Whiting, was hit, none of the few remaining doctors in East Jerusalem would come to Sheikh Jarrah. But one of the Colony's faithful retainers risked his life to get the penicillin needed from the Arab Hospital in the Old City.

Once again, daily life in Jerusalem had become difficult. The electricity power lines had been shot down and there were fears that an epidemic of typhoid was about to sweep through the city. Fortunately, the main building of the Colony had a large water cistern in the middle of its central courtyard and Bertha placed the penicillin and some anti-typhus serum into a bucket and lowered it into the drinking water to keep it cool.

One night, the fighting seemed particularly heavy and mortars and bullets crashed all around. Bertha and the others listened as bullets ricocheted off the stone walls. Suddenly they heard a powerful explosion in the Colony's main building, but as she opened the door to investigate a bullet whizzed past Bertha's face, striking the wall beside her. "I will have to wait until it gets light and the shooting dies down," she thought, and sat down to read.[591] But she found it difficult to concentrate and managed to ease her nerves only by playing a solitary game of Chinese checkers. Then, when the first rays of sun began to cast their pale shadows on the large house, the shooting abated and she went into the courtyard to investigate. A mortar shell had landed just by the cistern, one of the palms in the corner of the courtyard had been damaged and the inner garden looked a sorry sight. But Bertha was just relieved that the shell had not hit the roof. A direct hit there might have destroyed the beautifully painted ceiling and vaulting of the salon for all time.

At the beginning of June 1948, with the blessing of several prominent Palestinians and church leaders, Bertha went to America to present the Arabs' case. She had obtained letters of recommendation from the head of the Arab Legion in Jerusalem, Major Abdullah Tell, and the Greek

---

590 Theo Larsson: *Seven Passports for Palestine, Sixty Years in the Levant*, Lonfield, London, 1997, p.82.
591 Spafford Vester: *Our Jerusalem*, 2nd edition p.354.

Orthodox and Armenian Patriarchs. Ahmad Hilmi Pasha, a member of the Arab Higher Committee had also written to King Abdullah inAmman, supporting her mission:

> Since she saw with her own eyes the barbarous Jewish atrocities, and since she felt the American policy supported Zionism, she is moved to go to the United States in order to meet responsible officials and tell them the truth. Moreover, what makes Mrs Vester's mission of importance is the fact that a great number of her friends in America are men of wide influence.[592]

In the United States, Bertha aimed high and requested a meeting with President Harry Truman. She had brought along a personal letter from King Abdullah that she sent to the State Department. But despite personal contacts there, she was told that the president was unable to see her and that "therefore the letter cannot be delivered". The message accompanying it continued: "I am returning it herewith; and hope that these developments will not be embarrassing to you in any way." Bertha was also snubbed by the American delegation at the UN Headquarters in New York.[593]

By the summer of 1948, the Jewish leadership had lost confidence in the UN mediator. During a truce that lasted from June 11 to July 8, Count Bernadotte presented a new partition plan that envisaged a Palestinian Arab state alongside Israel, with a 'union' between Israel and Jordan (incorporating the West Bank); that the Negev be included in the Arab state and that Western Galilee be included in Israel; that the whole of Jerusalem be part of the Arab state, but with Jews in the city locally self-governed; and that Haifa should become a free port and Lydda a free airport for common use. Israel refused to accept any proposal that included the loss of its control over Jerusalem and rejected the plan. The

592 Letters dated June 2, 1948, American Colony Collection, Jerusalem
593 Letter from Department of State to Mrs Vester, dated July 26, 1948, American Colony Collection, Jerusalem. Just before she travelled back to Jerusalem Bertha received a second letter from the State Department which read: "I understand that you are on the point of returning to the Palestinian area. I am therefore writing to tell you that the letter from King Abdullah, which you brought with you from Amman, is now in the possession of the Department. I regret that due to the pressure of business it was not possible for the President to see you when you were in Washington. If you see the King when you are in Amman, you may wish to tell him that the information on the Palestinian question which you made available to me and to other officers in the Department and to officers of the United States Delegation to the United Nations was very much appreciated by this Government." Signed J.C. Satterthwaite, Director for Near Eastern and African Affairs, dated April 15, 1949.

Arabs, too, rejected it, insisting on an independent Palestinian state.

As far as Israeli leaders were concerned, Bernadotte no longer served their cause; they wanted to get rid of him as soon as possible. Secretary-General Lie sympathized with them, but advised Abba Eban, Israel's observer to the UN in New York, to work discretely. "The conditions here are fruitful," wrote Eban to Foreign Minister Moshe Shertok. He planned to undermine fatally Bernadotte's position by submitting a highly critical report to the Security Council, which would force him to abandon his mission.[594]

But the underground Zionist terror group Lehi had already made its own plans for disposing of Bernadotte. That evening, its radio station broadcast a message of warning to the peace mediator: "If he tries to put his claws into Jerusalem, we will take care of him."

At the beginning of September, 1948, Ralph Bunche and his staff finished a revised plan for the partition of Palestine. Secretary-General Trygve Lie had asked for their report to be ready no later than September 13, so Bunche's team worked for six days and nights to complete it. Under the plan, Jordan would annex Arab areas, including the Negev, Lydda and Ramleh, and the whole of Galilee would become part of Israel. Jerusalem would be internationalized.

It was important for the US and Britain that their support for the new model, which linked the Arab part of Palestine to Transjordan, should remain secret. The idea was to let the Anglo-American suggestions appear to come from Bernadotte himself. The Americans were unhappy with parts of the proposal – that the Israelis would get valuable agricultural land in Galilee, while the Arabs would receive most of the deserts of the Negev. They tried to persuade Bernadotte to amend his proposals. But the Swede stuck to his guns, maintaining that his solution was fair to both parties and that it was now or never. The General Assembly must take advantage of this opportunity.[595]

Bernadotte signed the report September 16 and left the same day for the Middle East. He landed at Qalandia airport outside Jerusalem and was driven to Ramallah in an armoured car. From there, Bernadotte and the head of the UN Truce Supervision Organization – UNTSO, General Åge Lundström, prepared to go to Jerusalem. The situation, as usual, was

---

594 Documents on the Foreign Policy of Israel, Volume I. May 14 – September 30, 1948, No 309, p.312.
595 The Foreign Relations of the United States (FRUS), vol. 5 (1948) pp.1399–1400, Brian Urquhart: Ralph Bunche, An American Life, W.W. Norton & Company, New York and London, 1993, p.176.

tense, and Lundström accepted the offer of an Arab Legion escort as far as the Mandelbaum Gate – the only crossing point between Arab-controlled East Jerusalem and the Israeli-controlled west of the city. The gate was close to the American Colony, and the Orthodox Jewish Mea Shearim quarter. Despite its armoured escort, Bernadotte's car, which had been provided by Theo Larsson, was shot at on its way to Jerusalem. But the Arab sniper only managed to strike a hubcap and the Swedish aristocrat took it all in his stride.

During lunch in Jerusalem, Bernadotte decided to make an impromptu inspection of the former Government House, south of Jerusalem, now in no man's land between the Jewish and the Arab lines, from where it operated as a Red Cross clinic. Next, Bernadotte was driven to an agricultural school in the demilitarized zone where, it was reported, a group of Israeli students had kept their weapons. The UN mediator said he would raise the issue with UNTSO and the Red Cross. Then, they set off for West Jerusalem in a three-car convoy. Travelling with Bernadotte were a French UN Observer and an Israeli liaison officer who would ensure smooth passage through Israeli checkpoints. As usual, his car was flying a white flag on one side of the bonnet, and a blue UN flag on the other. The convoy left the demilitarized zone at full speed, in case of sniper fire, passed an Israeli checkpoint and headed for one of the new districts of Jerusalem.

Their route was to take them through the Katamon quarter. Waiting for them there was a stolen UN jeep containing members of Lehi, who had planned, in meticulous detail, how they would assassinate Count Bernadotte. The Lehi member charged with masterminding the operation was Yitzhak Shamir, who later served as prime minister of Israel. Shamir viewed the murder as an extension of the war against British imperialism. He believed that Bernadotte's latest proposal for the partition of Palestine was unacceptable.[596] But, like other Lehi members, he feared that the Israeli government might come under international pressure to sign. The best way to scupper the plan, they thought, would be to assassinate its author. The chosen assassin was 24-year-old Yehoshua Cohen. Despite his youth, he had already trained the four killers who took the life of Lord Walter Moyne, the British High Commissioner in Egypt four years earlier.

The three men in the Jeep in the Katamon district had to wait for an hour before they saw Bernadotte's car approaching. To those inside the diplomatic convoy it seemed that the driver of the jeep was trying to turn around. But as they grew closer, the jeep stopped, completely blocking

596 Interview: Yitzhak Shamir, Tel Aviv, March 11, and July 2, 1996.

the road. General Lundström saw uniformed men in shorts and caps, carrying automatic weapons approach them. The Israeli liaison officer assumed, as the others did, that this was merely a routine weapons search and called out in Hebrew that everything was in order. But within seconds, Cohen had stuck his weapon in through the window of Bernadotte's car and fired. The UN mediator and the French observer were hit. The other two gunmen shot the tyres of the car, then jumped into their Jeep and sped off. Yehoshua Cohen ran into the woods nearby.

Lundström had realized that the Frenchman was dead. He was riddled with bullets. Folke Bernadotte was bent forward. "Are you wounded, Folke?" asked Lundström. He thought the count nodded and mumbled something, but perhaps it was only his imagination, for seconds later Bernadotte raised his upper body then sank backward into the seat.[597] He was pronounced dead on arrival at hospital.

Ralph Bunche was named as the diplomat's successor, but when he arrived in Paris on October 8, 1948 for a UN General Assembly meeting he realized that any debate on the Bernadotte report would be delayed. The focus of the Assembly was now on the growing Berlin crisis. This had knocked the Palestinian conflict off the top of the list. Bernadotte's peace plan died with him.

The Arabs had wanted the debate on Palestine to be postponed until after the presidential elections in the US in November, and preferred an extended armistice arrangement, rather than seeking a final settlement. Ambassador Eban noted that whereas the US and Britain were anxious to use the shockwave of the Bernadotte murder to push through his plan quickly, the Arabs, as usual, had unwittingly come to Israel's aid by insisting on a postponement, in the hope that this would prevent the General Assembly from coming to grips with the problem at all.[598]

Bertha Spafford Vester was still in the US on her unsuccessful mission to see President Truman, when the mediator was killed. The day after, she wrote three words in her diary: "Count Bernadotte assassinated." Bertha was upset by the actions of the Israelis. But the fact that the US president had recognized the Jewish state "almost before it was born" made her furious. "How can we, as Americans living in Palestine, vindicate such an action? We are ashamed to acknowledge that American statesmen can be moved either way to acquire votes," she wrote later.

---

597 Åge Lundström: *Minnen* (Memories) Landskrona, 1970, pp.18-20.
598 Report, September 30, 1948, Documents on Foreign Policy of Israel, Vol. II., Urquhart: *Ralph Bunche*, New York & London, 1993, pp.186-87.

On October 16, 1948, the Israelis started a new offensive in the southern part of Palestine, not yet in Jewish hands. They wanted to create 'facts on the ground' in the Negev, before the next UN General Assembly session later in the month. The government's aim was to connect the Jewish enclaves in the Negev with the state of Israel. The day before the offensive, the UN Security Council met in Paris to hear a report from Ralph Bunche in which he accused the Israeli government of being guilty of the murder of Count Bernadotte.[599]

The murder of the UN mediator caused mixed reaction in Israel. Those who heard Ben-Gurion's speech in the Knesset after the killing noticed that his voice shook as he said "the crime was even more gruesome because it was directed against the most humanitarian institution in our time." But beyond the official condemnation, the Israeli prime minister did little to find and punish the murderers, and Yitzhak Shamir felt it was safe enough to emerge from his hiding place. Shamir wanted to enter the political arena. After being promised safe conduct, the Lehi leader asked first for a meeting with one of Ben-Gurion's closest associates, Deputy Defence Minister Shaul Avigur.[600] "I want to know the names of Bernadotte's assassins," the minister said. "Nothing will happen to them. I want the names only to have them on record." But Shamir refused. A few days later, the issue was consigned to history when Ben-Gurion granted an amnesty to all members of the underground organizations.

At the end of October, Israel accepted a truce in the Negev, having taken control of much of the central section. Just before Christmas, Egypt again complained to the UN that Israel had started a large-scale attack in the southern Negev triangle. Ralph Bunche who was in New York, wrote detailed reports about the battles, and criticized the Israelis for having ejected UN observers from the area of operations.

Bunche worked hard to get Bernadotte's recommendations regarding the partition of Palestine through to the General Assembly. He knew better than anyone else that neither the Israelis nor the Arabs liked the plan. And soon the UN's new mediator understood that the battle was lost. The alternative was to establish a truce followed by an extended ceasefire.

On January 6, 1949, Bunche informed the Security Council that Egypt and Israel had accepted an unconditional truce, and that the ceasefire would be followed by negotiations for a line of demarcation under UN

599 Report, October 15, 1948. *Ministry of Foreign Affairs*, Oslo. Dossier 30.5/10.3 Palestine, Vol. I.
600 Interview: Yitzhak Shamir, Tel Aviv March 11, 1996. Yitzhak Shamir: *Summing Up, An Auto-biography*, Weinfeld and Nicolson, London 1994, pp.75-76.

auspices. The negotiations would take place in Rhodes. The general truce between Israel and Egypt was signed on February 24, 1949, and allowed Beersheba and the Negev to remain in Israeli hands. The demarcation line between Egypt and Israel was identical to the border between Palestine and Egypt, except for the Gaza Strip which stayed in Egyptian hands. One zone around Auja, inside the former Palestine, became demilitarized, and the Egyptians, who were holding the enclave, were evacuated.

Bunche did not have much time to rest, since Israel-Transjordan talks were imminent. On March 11, both sides signed a ceasefire agreement, and three weeks later they agreed on the armistice lines. The modifications of the line in the north favoured Israel, and around Hebron, Transjordan. But the Israelis had achieved a significant enlargement of their coastal strip. Bunche commented: "Another deal, and as usual the Palestine Arabs lose."[601]

But the Jewish state had not yet achieved Ben-Gurion's dream – to secure control over the West Bank, including the cities of Hebron, Nablus, Jericho and East Jerusalem. That part of Palestine was still in Jordanian hands. When Ben-Gurion was asked why he had not "liberated the entire country" the Israeli leader answered: "There is a danger of being burdened with a hostile Arab majority." Ben-Gurion did not want to get into a "compromising relationship with the UN and the Great Powers." He also did not want the treasury to be emptied. The Jewish state was confronting big challenges, the main one being the absorption of the stream of Jewish immigrants.

Then he added: "We have nevertheless liberated quite a large area, much more than we had thought possible. Now we must work for two or three generations. What is left we will have to come back for later."[602]

601 Urquhart: *Ralph Bunche*, New York, and London, 1993, p.217.
602 Michael Bar-Zohar: *Facing the Cruel Mirror*, Charles Scribner's Sons, New York 1990, p.17.

Epilogue

For Bertha Spafford Vester, the establishment of the Jewish state was the end of a dream. She had long hoped the British march into Jerusalem would represent the Final Crusade, and that Palestine would be an independent democratic state. But this was not to be. For the Palestinians, the creation of the Jewish state was more than a disappointment: it was the catastrophe–*al-Nakbah*. For the Zionists, the state was the gift they had all been waiting for since colonization had begun in earnest.

When Anna and Horatio Spafford came to Palestine in 1881, they spoke of the Second Coming of Jesus. Their daughter, Bertha, had long since stopped believing that the mass immigration of Jews was a sign of the Thousand Year Kingdom. She was also sceptical of Zionism. Bertha was alarmed by the way that nationalist Jews had exercised their might – so soon after they themselves had been subjected to horrific persecution. The civilian Palestinian population, living in the homeland of their forefathers, had not committed any crime against the Jews.

After Jerusalem was split into Israeli and Jordanian halves in 1948, big changes occurred in the American Colony. No more did cattle graze in the fields, for this area had become the front line. There was no contact between the two sides of the city. No one other than priests, diplomats and other privileged people were allowed to pass from one half to the other through the Mandelbaum Gate. Once a week, a convoy of vehicles passed the Colony, escorted by United Nations observers, carrying supplies for the small Jewish enclave on Mount Scopus. Along the Nablus Road on the west side, a wall was built, marking the borderline. From the salon one was able to see over into a wide stretch of no man's land and into Israel.

The atmosphere in Jordanian Jerusalem was very different from the way it had been in the city during the days of Britain's Mandate. Then, "there had been a large British community and a distinct flavour of the British Raj, with tennis parties and picnics, dinner and dancing at the King David Hotel."[603] Jerusalem had been a city facing both east and west. Now, the Arab part faced only east.

Changes took place also in the American Colony. The affairs of the diminished community were run by Bertha's brother-in-law, John D Whiting. On his death in 1952, Bertha, finding herself bearing all the re-

---

603 Anna Grace Lind & Valentine Vester: Epilogue to *Our Jerusalem*, New edition 1988, p.359.

sponsibilities, asked her daughter, Anna Grace Lind, who lived in New York, to come back to help.

When Anna Grace returned the following year, she began modernizing the American Colony Hostel. Bathrooms had been scarce, and bath water, on request, was heated by an olive-wood fire lit under a large water container. Heating for the buildings was provided by a wood-burning stove in the middle of each room. Now, many of the rooms were equipped with baths and toilets, and central heating was installed in the main building. A significant feature of the hostel was its bar where alcohol was served – unlike in the rest of Jordan. At the end of the 1950s, the standards of the establishment had risen to such an extent that it was upgraded to become a hotel.

In 1963, Horatio Vester, Bertha's oldest son, gave up his legal career in London and returned to Jerusalem with his wife, Valentine. She had visited Jerusalem 28 years earlier and stayed at the American Colony with her father, Admiral Herbert Richmond. At that time her uncle, architect Ernest Richmond, was serving in Palestine as an adviser to the British high commissioner. Valentine Vester was also connected to the Middle East through her mother's sister, Gertrude Bell. The British writer, traveller and political analyst played a major part in the creation of the modern state of Iraq, and was an unrecognized force behind the Arab revolt in World War I.

As the Arab-Israeli conflict continued to attract international attention, journalists and camera crews discovered the secret appeal of the American Colony Hotel. Every year, too, television teams came to make religious features in connection with Easter and Christmas. In one of them, "Georgette, a Christian maid from the hotel, was cast as the Virgin Mary. But it really went to her head," recalled Valentine Vester. "She got delusions of grandeur and could not accept that the Virgin Mary was working as a chambermaid."[604]

After repairs and expansion work had been completed, the hotel boasted 100 bed. Even if Anna's House itself was much the same as its former inhabitants had known it, the ambience would have been unrecognisable. As tourists and journalists rushed in and out, and taxi drivers and guides touted for business at the entrance, the sacrifices that the followers of Anna made, and the joys and sorrows, and the headaches and disappointments that they experienced over the decades were largely forgotten.

On the morning of Monday June 5, 1967, just 20 years after the Jewish state had been established, the Israelis went to war against Egypt. In East

604 Interview: Valentine Vester, April 28, 2006, American Colony, Jerusalem

Jerusalem, several consuls telephoned their nationals and advised them to head without delay for Amman. The following day, Jordan was pulled into the conflict, and the only two journalists staying at the American Colony watched Jordanian soldiers at their outpost just across the road begin shooting. Yet again, the American Colony was in the line of fire.

Since the Colony was situated on the direct route to the Jewish enclave on Mount Scopus, which the Israelis were determined to hold onto and the Jordanians equally determined to capture, the hotel was hit from both sides. Shrapnel caused considerable damage.

On the second day of the war, Israeli troops crossed the demilitarized zone at the Mandelbaum Gate and entered the district around the hotel. The soldiers broke in through the front door and went from room to room, firing at the locks to force the doors open. From that Tuesday, the American Colony came under Israeli authority.

Despite the upheaval caused by the war, guests started returning to the hotel after a surprisingly short time, and when, the following year, Bertha celebrated her 90th birthday, the large reception given for her in the American Colony was attended by both Jews and Arabs. Asked how it felt to live under Israeli rule, Bertha answered: "I have lived under the Turks, the British and the Jordanians, and we have got along well with everyone. We shall do the same with the Israelis."[605] That same year, in June 1968, Anna Spafford's oldest daughter died peacefully in her sleep.

As the years passed, much more reconstruction work was carried out at the hotel, but the little cluster of houses near the Sheikh Jarrah Mosque has never lost its character. In the courtyard there are still the worn red paving stones, which were there when the magisterial house was built in the 1860s. On the walls hang pictures from the turn of the century, and in the salon, renamed the Pasha's Room after being renovated, guests can admire the original painted ceiling with its heavenly vaulting in blue and gold under which Anna's followers used to meet and pray.

Anna Spafford never lived to experience Israel or the millions of Jews from all over the world who came to live in the Jewish state. In her lifetime, Jesus did not return to the Mount of Olives. The dream of Judgement Day ended instead with Anna's House becoming a luxury hotel, a world famous haven for journalists and a neutral meeting place for Israeli, Palestinian and international peace negotiators. Anna Grace Lind died in December 1994 and Valentine Vester in June 2008, the last of the generation that had personal ties to the extraordinary saga of Anna's House.

605 Anna Grace Lind & Valentine Vester, Epilogue to *Our Jerusalem*, New edition 1988, p.364.

Index